A People and a Land

VOLUME 2

The Road to Kingship

1–2 Samuel

Johanna W. H. van Wijk-Bos

William B. Eerdmans Publishing Company
Grand Rapids, Michigan

Wm. B. Eerdmans Publishing Co.
4035 Park East Court SE, Grand Rapids, Michigan 49546
www.eerdmans.com

Published 2020
Printed in the United States of America

26 25 24 23 22 21 20 1 2 3 4 5 6 7

ISBN 978-0-8028-7744-4

Library of Congress Cataloging-in-Publication Data

A catalog record for this book is available from the Library of Congress.

"A wonderfully practical guide through the most exciting story in the Bible. Johanna van Wijk-Bos exposes the complexity, subtle suspense, and immense charm throughout Samuel. Her down-to-earth approach will enhance every reader's understanding and appreciation of one of the most mature historical and biographical works the ancient world ever produced."

— Baruch Halpern
University of Georgia

"Johanna van Wijk-Bos's compelling reading of the Samuel narrative combines attention to women's voices and perspectives in the narrative; erudite discussion of historical, social, and religious contexts; and sensitivity to the unresolvable complexities of story and character. The result is a lively and elegant accompaniment to some of the Hebrew Bible's richest narrative."

— Rachelle Gilmour
Trinity College, University of Divinity

"The books of Samuel are a rich theological blend, exploring a complex and multifaceted period in Israel's life. With careful attention to the contours of the text and awareness of what it means to read this text, Johanna van Wijk-Bos guides us to a deeper awareness of how these elements function within the text and their implications for reading it today."

— David G. Firth
Trinity College Bristol

For my students
Louisville Presbyterian Theological Seminary
1977–2017

Contents

Preface

The Former Prophets of the Hebrew Bible are a part of the great arc of biblical narrative that begins with the creation of the world and ends with the Babylonian exile. The framework of entry and exile encloses the four books of Joshua, Judges, Samuel, and Kings, texts that include some of the most familiar and some of the least known material in the Bible. In Christian circles, where there is a certain amount of acquaintance with the Bible, the outlines of the David and Goliath story will be remembered, as well as the story of Solomon and the two prostitutes. Few, however, will recall the tricky Gibeonites or the prophet killed by a lion on his way home after dining at the house of one of his colleagues. The names of the prophets Elijah and Isaiah we recognize, but Deborah and Huldah are unlikely to have importance in the collective memory even of those who attend church or synagogue.

One purpose of this writing is to offer a close reading of the Hebrew text in translation to reacquaint us with the path taken by the people called Israel as they cross the Jordan into the land of the promise, live there—first under loosely organized tribal leadership but eventually embracing a form of monarchy—and finally lose the land and go into exile. In studying these books, we traverse more than six hundred years of history, much of it periods of great turbulence for the people of the Bible as well as the surrounding nations. The land the Israelites believed to be granted to them as a gift from God is a reality into which they cross, where they learn to live together, become divided from one another, and which they eventually lose. This land is not only the place where they live but it betokens for them the presence of God, a utopian ideal concentrated in the city of God, Jerusalem/Zion, and most of all in the temple. In the end, ironically, it is not land or city or temple, even less kingship, that guarantees for this people their ongoing identity, orientation, and self-definition. Rather, the words spoken, written, and read—deposited in documents—became the lodestar for the community out of which Rabbinic Judaism and Christianity were born.

Some of the stories we find here may move us; some may appall; all will speak to the imagination if we let them. The histories were written for education, edification, and also entertainment. This is the way the people went; this is the way God went with them as they saw it and described it. It is a remarkable collection describing an ancient people in an ancient world—far removed from ours, that at the same time invokes contemporary situations and questions. In considering these accounts, we also look in a mirror. We engage in our own quandaries regarding our communities and the God of our faith. The people who wrote the narratives, the ones who collected and edited them, believed that God was involved in their story—in the way they went, with all its ups and downs. By getting closer to their story, we may find a guiding hand in our own lives as individuals and communities. There is no boilerplate here, no script to copy, but in it and through our reading, we too may encounter the presence of the Holy One and derive a moral compass for our lives.

As always, I have written as a scholar of the Bible with deep commitments to feminism and issues of gender and to analysis of patriarchal structures and ideologies. Women's voices and the roles they play in the various accounts have received special attention. I also write as a child of World War II who absorbed in mind and heart the sights and sounds of atrocious violence and inhumanity that infested communities and individuals when entire groups were defined as outsiders, deprived of the basic claim to have a share in the human race. My awareness as a writer and interpreter of Scripture is attentive to the historical Christian dishonoring and victimization of the Jewish people, and it has been my aim to be respectful toward a part of Scripture that describes a history of which Jews are the direct descendants. The history we find here may not be history as it would be written today in the modern world. It is nevertheless history in the sense of a people writing about its past. The name in the Jewish community for what Christians call the Old Testament is "Tanakh," or "Miqra." Because Christian communities are unfamiliar with these terms, I have for the most part chosen "Hebrew Bible" to refer to the first part of Christian Scripture. The sacred Name of God, called the Tetragrammaton for its four consonants, is often presented as "Lord" in translations but is here rendered "Adonai," which is how it is read in Reform Jewish congregations.[1]

All translations of biblical texts are my own, based on the accepted Hebrew text of the Bible. For biblical quotations, set on the page as inserts, I use short, so-called colo-metric lines, giving the appearance of poetry.[2] Setting the biblical text on the page in short lines was advocated by Martin Buber and Franz Rosenzweig in their translation of the Hebrew Bible into German.[3] Their method was adopted and explained in the United States by Everett Fox in his translation of the Torah and the Former Prophets.[4] More recently, Susan Niditch has advocated the method and discussed it in her commentary on Judges.[5] The short lines emphasize the structure of a

1. For an extensive discussion of responsible Christian references to the sacred Name, see Johanna W. H. van Wijk-Bos, "Writing on the Water: The Ineffable Name of God," in *Jews, Christians, and the Theology of the Hebrew Scriptures*, ed. Alice Ogden Bellis and Joel S. Kaminsky (Atlanta: Society of Biblical Literature, 2000), 45–59.

2. Hebrew poetry distinguishes itself from prose mainly by a sequence of clauses in which the second one corresponds to the first, a phenomenon usually called parallelism, although the dividing line between prose and poetry in the Bible is to my understanding often not sharp. For insight into issues of poetry and prose, see Robert Alter, *The Art of Biblical Poetry* (New York: Basic Books, 1985); Robert Alter, *The Book of Psalms* (New York: Norton, 2007), xx–xxviii; and James L. Kugel, *The Idea of Biblical Poetry: Parallelism and Its History* (New Haven: Yale University Press, 1981).

3. Martin Buber and Franz Rosenzweig, *Scripture and Translation*, trans. Lawrence Rosenwald with Everett Fox (Bloomington, IN: Indiana University Press, 1994); trans. of *Die Schrift und ihre Verdeutschung* (Berlin: Schocken, 1936).

4. Everett Fox, *The Five Books of Moses* (New York: Schocken, 1995); Everett Fox, *The Early Prophets: Joshua, Judges, Samuel and Kings: A New Translation with Introductions, Commentary, and Notes* (New York: Schocken, 2014).

5. Susan Niditch, *Judges*, OTL (Louisville: Westminster John Knox, 2008),

unit, reveal the parts that create the whole and emphasize key words that serve the interpretation of a passage. Translators who follow in Buber's footsteps also focus more on being as faithful as possible to the word order and word choice of the Hebrew original and less on the accessibility of the translation in the receiving language. The purpose of my translations and of this book is to draw the reader/listener "into the world of the Hebrew Bible." To paraphrase the German scholar Franz Rosenzweig, we "need to hear its alien tone in all its alienness . . . its cast of mind, its heartbeat." For Rosenzweig, the translator becomes "a mouthpiece for the alien voice that transmits it across the chasm of space and time."[6]

In the books of the Former Prophets, this alien world unfolds itself before us in all its variety, its different sights and sounds, its foreign nature and texture, and especially its multiple voices. The multivoiced character of the text is on full display in these books of the Bible. In the books of Samuel the hesitancy with which charismatic leaders embrace the notion of kingship is palpable and the road to a hereditary monarchy is a rocky one. The crucial question facing Israel is whether acceptance of a royal leader signifies a rejection of the kingship of Adonai. Samuel therefore issues stern warnings about the consequences of royal rule for the people. The first king, Saul, explicitly chosen by God, anointed by Samuel and elected by the people, turns out to be unable to establish his throne in perpetuity, and the upstart David, lurking in the wilderness of Judah or collaborating with the Philistine enemy, challenges his authority at every turn. David, also appointed by God and anointed by Samuel, succeeds in establishing his own hold on the throne. But at the end of 2 Samuel it remains to be seen if his achievement will result in hereditary kingship. The flourishing of Israel in its own land and its

19–26. See Phyllis Trible, *God and the Rhetoric of Sexuality* (Philadelphia: Fortress, 1978); Phyllis Trible, *Rhetorical Criticism: Context, Method and the Book of Jonah* (Philadelphia: Fortress, 1994); J. P. Fokkelman, *King David,* vol. 1 of *Narrative Art and Poetry in the Books of Samuel* (Assen: Van Gorcum, 1981), 1–20.

6. Franz Rosenzweig, "On the Scriptures and Their Language," in *Franz Rosenzweig: His Life and Thought,* ed. Nahum L. Glatzer, 2nd ed. (New York: Schocken, 1961), 253.

own royal house still hangs in the balance. The voice that is critical of kingship and holds it accountable for the dissolution of bonds of kinship and the eventual loss of the land is certainly present in this material, to be picked up more strongly in the book of Kings.

The writing and shaping of the book took place in the absence of my primary conversation partner of more than forty years, my beloved husband, A. David Bos, of blessed memory. Our son, Martin, is an example of one who had the courage to traverse his own boundaries, stepping forward into unknown territory to embrace life while daily confronting giants in this new land.

Other important conversation partners were present. They patiently listened to my enthusiastic ramblings and responded with interest and insight. I acknowledge with gratitude my assistant Christiaan Faul, who checked the manuscript for accuracy of biblical citations and who eased my transition from full-time professor to full-time writer in many ways. I am indebted to my former student Elana Keppel Levy for her generosity in allowing me to incorporate material from her sermon. My special thanks go to my friend Aaron Guldenschuh Gatten, whose presence supported me through the grievous loss of my beloved only sister, who made my garden a place not only of beauty but also of rest and tranquility, and who was always ready to exchange thoughts about the latest Scriptural adventure. My friends at Saturday morning Torah study not only gave me a place for weekly intense concentration on Scripture but made this stranger in the house of Israel feel welcome and loved. Rabbi David Ariel Joel of Temple Adath Israel Brith Sholom in Louisville, Kentucky, has a special place in this list. I am deeply indebted to his outstanding teaching and his meticulous, unfailing attention to the biblical text and the rabbis and sages who comment on it. I am profoundly appreciative of his patience and readiness to respond to my inquiries.

I am grateful to Louisville Presbyterian Theological Seminary, its board of trustees, and its faculty for allowing me to articulate the first outlines of this book and begin my work during a sabbatical leave. To my first editor at Eerdmans, Allen Myers, and my present editor, Andrew Knapp, go my thanks for their patience with this "slow professor" and their meticulous oversight of the project. The copyeditor, Samuel Kelly, also has my gratitude for his judicious work cleaning up this book. I dedicate the book to my students at Louisville Seminary, who provided the stimulus and the sounding board for all my writing during my forty years of teaching.

The texts under consideration in this book do not have a happy ending; the adventure that begins in great expectation and hope with the crossing of the Jordan River ends in loss and exile. Yet out of ruin and destruction, a new way was found toward life as a community that discerned guidance and divine presence in the words it preserved and guarded. The Teaching enjoined upon Joshua at the beginning of the Former Prophets, authorized by the prophet Huldah in a document at the end, endured in time.

When Torah entered the world, freedom entered it.
The whole Torah exists only to establish peace.
. . .
Let us learn then in order to teach.
Let us learn in order to do![7]

7. *Mishkan T'filah: A Reform Siddur* (New York: Central Conference of American Rabbis, 5767/2007), 257.

Introduction

Visions of the Past

It was never said of history that it shouldn't be talked about; on the contrary, in terms of history silence was forgetting, and it was the thing people feared most of all, when it was their own history that was at risk of being forgotten.[1]

Midway through the first millennium BCE, there could hardly be a community whose history was under greater threat of being forgotten than the remnant of the people who once inhabited the strip of land located between the Mediterranean Sea and the desert in southwest Asia. They called themselves Israelites and at the end of the second millennium conquered the land called Canaan, partly through peaceful infiltration and partly by great violence. Their organization consisted of tribal groups, led locally and intermittently by charismatic military leaders, and they made alliances with indigenous inhabitants they could not displace or annihilate. The leadership was incapable of preventing intertribal rivalries and antagonisms, which in the end broke out into open warfare. The stories of these early beginnings were eventually collected in the biblical books Joshua and Judges.

Toward the end of the eleventh century BCE the need for more centralized leadership became evident and a successful attempt was made to establish a monarchy. Voices of resistance to this move were not absent, but they were in the minority and Israel elected

1. Rachel Cusk, *Outline* (New York: Farrar, Straus and Giroux, 2014), 245.

its first king. The road to kingship was, however, not a smooth one. Following the first anointed king, Saul, a contender for the throne appeared on the scene who in time established a new house and a hereditary kingship. These radical changes in the political and religious landscape of ancient Israel are told in the books of Samuel with their detailed narratives of King Saul and especially the legendary King David.

Kingship was not to be the saving grace of the Israelites, however, existing as they did at the crossroads of vast and aggressive empires. In the end they succumbed to the hungry maw of Assyria and subsequently Babylonia to lead lives under foreign overlords, first as exiles, then as a small province with a limited degree of self-determination. They had very little going for them and could easily have disappeared into the melting pot of nations of the period, were it not for their desire to maintain and strengthen their identity through the stories and theological ethos preserved in their teachings. They knew that silence was forgetting and that their ongoing existence was to a great extent dependent on the preservation of their history in text.

Recognition of the importance of memories and their safeguarding in the written word was not new—it had accompanied the Israelite community very likely from its beginning. The impetus for the collecting and editing of the material was, however, provided by the Babylonian exile in the sixth century BCE. At that juncture the risk to the continued existence of the people became abundantly clear. To be sure, their efforts to maintain a distinct identity as a people with their own culture and religion while existing as a province of a large empire included the establishment of a sanctuary and the rebuilding of the town of Jerusalem. The centrality and importance of the written text, however, are evident from the record preserved in Nehemiah 8 and 9. While uncertainty exists about the exact period in which the collecting of the texts that now make up the Torah and other books took place, we assign it generally to the era of the restoration of Judah following the Babylonian exile, the second half of the sixth through the first quarter of the third century BCE. The Torah was and is the great collection of the Teaching, the laws and narratives to instruct the life of the community, in its social and religious relations. The Historical Books that include Samuel are also intended to instruct, in the way that remembering and reciting communal memories aids a community to move forward in the present by regarding itself in the mirror of past events.

In some ways the ancient Israelites who survived the Babylonian exile were not so different from cultures and religions that existed in the rest of the ancient world. There too peoples wrote their stories; their myths tell of the creation, their annals of conquest recite triumphs achieved with the aid of divine assistance. More primary documents originating in Mesopotamia and Egypt from the biblical period and earlier have survived until modern times than from the land of the Bible. Yet these texts were not instrumental in sustaining a people's identity, their beliefs and ethos into the modern era. What then made the texts of the exiles, both in Judah and those who remained in the diaspora, so different that they survived not only continued political dependence but ongoing catastrophes and destruction to eventually produce and foster two major world religions?

There is not just one factor that set the biblical texts apart from the literary output of other peoples and cultures. One aspect that stands out is that the texts, especially those incorporated in the Torah, contained not only myths of world creation and ancestral narratives but also, and especially, detailed religious and ethical demands for the life of the community. Three chapters in the book of Nehemiah elaborately describe the features of the public recitation and interpretation of the "scroll of the Teaching of Moses, which Adonai gave to Israel" (Neh 8:1). Precise information about the time and the exact place of the reading marks the occasion, down to the wooden platform facing the Water Gate on which Ezra stands to recite. The names of all the participants are there, including the Levites with the task of helping people to understand what they hear. The reading is by request of the people, who are central to the proceedings, made clear by repeated references to the community as "the people" or "all the people," or "men and women and those who could understand" (Neh 8:1, 2, 3, 5, 6, 7, 8, 9, 11, 12). The reading and the explanation will help them not only to understand where they came from, and how God went with them in their history, but to know in the present day how they should conduct their common life.

How important this event was in postexilic Judah becomes clear from the reaction of the people who listen and receive interpretation. Their first response shows the profound impact of the recital on the listeners: “For all the people were weeping when they heard the words of the Teaching” (Neh 8:9). The reading may have been a part or all of Deuteronomy, the scroll of the “second law,” the rules and regulations stipulated by Adonai through Moses to the people before they entered the land. The Torah contains more than law, however. There are also the stories. There are the stories of the creation of the world, of individual ancestors and of their descendants, of the escape from a land of bondage and oppression, and of the trek through the wilderness. A great part of the story of the past concerns the subject of how community and individuals failed to live up to their obligations before they entered the land God had promised them.

A second factor that distinguishes the written material produced by ancient Israel is thus the full humanity of the characters and their adventures. Not only is the community displayed with all is flaws and failures, individual characters receive the same treatment. Beginning with the stories of the first creatures in the Edenic garden through the patriarchs and matriarchs who founded the ancestral lineage, continuing through bondage, liberation, and beyond, the biblical page reveals no superheroes. All are portrayed warts and all. In fact, from beginning to end, it is abundantly clear from the Bible that human beings have a talent for mayhem. In view of this propensity it is the divine project to deliver humanity and the creation from the consequences of human inclinations and resulting actions. In this process the covenant community of ancient Israel had a special task. The fact of its chosenness laid on it the special burden of becoming a showcase for God’s righteousness, to be holy as Adonai is holy, mirroring the passion of God for the outcast and the lowly.

Heroes and Villains

On a recent trip to my mother country I find myself in the city of Delft, staring at a statue of Prince William I of Orange. William, in national memory revered as the father of the fatherland, became one of the leaders of the Dutch revolution in the sixteenth century and I am standing in the garden of a former convent, adapted to be a residence for the prince. He stayed there frequently and it was the site of his assassination in 1584. The statue is clearly modern and one I have not seen before.[2] Rather than wearing military garb, the prince is depicted in a cloak that falls to his feet. A close-fitting cap adorns his head. I am well aware of the way the historical figure has been idealized in subsequent centuries; I know something of his flaws and that later generations created the glamorous picture which came to dominate the memory. I have long fostered great admiration, perhaps even hero worship, for this person who lived in such tumultuous times and died such a dramatic death at the hands of an assassin. I know that he could not possibly have uttered the poetic phrase "my God, my God, have pity on me and my poor people" before he expired, since experts have deduced that the bullets killed him instantly. And yet, I know the phrase by heart, in French, the native tongue of the prince. None of this bothers me at the moment when I stand staring up at the statue placed in the garden of his residence not so very long ago. Surely, the giants of our imagination stand tall. How is it then that this "father of the fatherland" stands here before me at just a bit over five feet, slightly shorter than my own height? In fact, were he not placed on a pedestal I would not be looking up but slightly down.

It should not have mattered that the hero of my youth had a stature that was most likely typical for the period. But, when recreating the past in story most cultures are tempted to portray the heroes who were a part of the shaping of their national identity in ways that are larger than life. Great deeds of valor and courage from our heroes, surely accompanied by a splendid physique, are a staple of national foundational mythology. Ancient Israel was no stranger to this mode of presenting the tale. King Saul reportedly stood head and shoulders above his people (1 Sam 10:23), and even in a record with predominantly negative elements, notes of approval could not be entirely suppressed (1 Sam 14:47–52). Stories with heroes must also have villains as their foil. Certainly, King Saul engages in vil-

2. The statue was created by the Dutch sculptor Auke Hettema and unveiled by Queen Beatrix in 2003.

lainous actions. Yet he is not a villain only and the narratives elicit compassion for his predicament. King David, who comes on the scene as a valiant eloquent hero and deliverer, descends to depths of human depravity once he has gained the throne. Even the most perfect hero partakes of flawed human nature.

Just as was the case with my shock at the representation of one of my national heroes at the height he must actually have been during his life, we may not be ready to face biblical heroes in a nuanced way. We may want our heroes to be taller and grander and may be in for a surprise when they do not quite turn out the way we had envisioned. The realistic contours of character description in the ancient stories lend them an almost modern feel. Even when the spirit of God drives central characters, they can appear impulsive, violent, even treacherous. Once we consent to embrace biblical heroes in all their humanity, the story becomes more interesting. In addition, there is a particular solace in this feature of the literature for those who attempt to learn from it. This world, these people, with whom the God of Israel chose to engage in a particular way, are not so far removed from the listener/reader when they recognize themselves in the events. In any case, I believe the realistic manner of portraying communal and individual character, setting biblical literature apart from the rest of the ancient world, is another important factor in safeguarding the continued existence of not only the community that created it, but also of the communities that inherited it and hold it as sacred.

The texts were collected under the impulse of great trauma. I have described this wounding of the spirit and the need to address it in stories in the introduction to the first volume in this series (*The End of the Beginning: Joshua and Judges,* A People and a Land volume 1).[3] There may be no greater trauma for a community than that created by the devastation of war. We view the stories that speak of the establishment of ancient Israel's kingship against the backdrop of this trauma. They had a need to speak of the heroic deeds of their kings, Saul's campaign against Ammon, David's defeat of the Philistines and Goliath. But they also had to speak of their failures,

3. Johanna W. H. van Wijk-Bos, *The End of the Beginning: Joshua and Judges,* A People and a Land 1 (Grand Rapids: Eerdmans, 2019).

Saul's jealousy and rage, David's soldier spirit turned to aggression, his disregard for human life that finally led him to murder and other faults besides. Although I take the historical context and the setting of the events seriously, as well as the context of its transmission, it is not my purpose to dig beneath the stories and unearth the historical truth of any of the characters.[4] The stories themselves in the way they are told, the questions they raise and reactions they provoke, are the focus of this undertaking.

Content and Historical Setting

For any scholar aspiring to write on the book of Samuel at the outset of the 21st century, the flurry of scholarship is overwhelming.[5]

The tumultuous episodes concluding the attempts at leadership in Judges left the question open as to what or who would guide the community of ancient Israel into a life in which everyone would cease doing what was wrong in the eyes of Adonai and instead follow religious and ethical codes as a guarantee of their existence in the land of the promise. One possible solution to the conundrum created by a context in which "everyone did what was right in their eyes" was a central administration represented by a monarchy—clearly hinted at the two times the statement "everyone did what was right in their eyes" was augmented by the phrase "in those days there was no king in Israel" (Judg 17:6; 18:1; 19:1; 21:25). While this solution had been explored in Judges, ending in failure, it had not been put to rest for good. In Samuel, kingship comes to the fore again, demanded by the people to ward off the chaos threatening to engulf them both from outside and inside.

4. Joel Baden makes such an attempt in his book *The Historical David: The Real Life of an Invented Hero* (New York: HarperCollins, 2013). I refer those who would like know more about my approach to Scripture as history to *The End of the Beginning* (1–6).

5. Mark Leuchter, *Samuel and the Shaping of Tradition* (Oxford: Oxford University Press, 2013), 1.

1 Samuel 1–8 describes the period directly before the monarchy, followed by the first attempt at establishing a hereditary monarchy (1 Sam 9–15) and, once David arrives on the scene and becomes a threat to the reign of Saul, the subsequent entangled history of the rivalry between Saul and David (1 Sam 16–31). The strife between the two protagonists ends with the death of Saul and his sons in his last and losing battle against the Philistines. Second Samuel is entirely devoted to the rule of David, first in a partial and contested reign, competing with one of Saul's surviving sons for the throne (2 Sam 1–4), subsequently as military and administrative monarch of the entire people (2 Sam 5–24). The story of David does not end until the second chapter of 1 Kings.

Both Saul and David are presented in the text as leaders divinely appointed through the agency of Samuel, the prophet/judge/priest who functions as a bridge-figure between the period of the judges and the monarchy. Saul eventually loses divine favor, while David is the one whose house is established as a royal house in perpetuity by Adonai (2 Sam 7:8–11). One section of the David narratives, set apart by its distinctive style and perspectives, is often entitled "The Court History of David" and runs from 2 Samuel 9 to the succession of David's son Solomon in 1 Kings 2, interrupted by 2 Samuel 21–24.[6] The Court History only occasionally makes mention of divine engagement with the human scene and is marked by increasing turbulence in both royal family and nation, beginning with David's adultery with Bathsheba, followed by the arranged murder of her husband Uriah, continuing with the rape of his daughter Tamar by one of her brothers, through two rebellions against David's reign—the most serious led by his son Absalom—and into his old age up to the first blood-soaked days of the reign of Solomon (1 Kgs 2:23–46). It shows in close-up how the fate of the

6. It is possible that the ending of the Court History was added to Kings because of the length of the scroll devoted to 1 and 2 Samuel. On the other hand, chapters 21–24 interrupt the continuous narrative in interesting ways, adding two stories that exhibit the power of the king limited by divine interference, as well as poetic material that forms a framework around the narration together with 1 Sam 2:1–10.

king and his family is intertwined with that of the people. Crimes committed in the family circle are like stones thrown in a pond creating ever-widening circles, and rebellion at home expands into rebellion in the nation.

The period in question concerns roughly the last two decades of the eleventh century BCE and the first three of the tenth.[7] More like Joshua than Judges, the text covers a limited amount of time and for the most part follows a distinct timeline, beginning with Samuel embodying the final days of judgeship, moving through the first efforts at kingship with Saul, and ending with David in old age. Samuel, Saul, and David are the towering figures, with a large cast of characters revolving around them as planets around stars. The beginnings of the monarchy are clearly shown as troubled by both human and divine displeasure (1 Sam 8), by continuing hostile engagement with the Philistines, and by the bitter contest between the two major protagonists, Saul and David. Even when the Davidic house appears to have established a more secure kingship than Saul was able to achieve, the throne does not rest on secure foundations. Witness David's struggles with crimes within his family and threats to his rule before finally succumbing to old age and indecision about the succession. Whether kingship was indeed the solution to the problems facing the people, procuring their ongoing existence in their own land remains at least ambiguous in Samuel; both positive and negative evaluations of kingship and individual kings may be drawn from the text.

Positions about the period in which the texts originated include the late tenth or ninth century BCE, the period following the Babylonian exile, and everything in-between. My predilection for its origins runs toward an earlier rather than a later era, allowing for redactions of the material in subsequent periods with a final editing process during the restoration of Judah.[8] The theological voice

7. Dating of this period, and thus of Saul and David, is notoriously unstable and contested, but the biblical account places Saul in the period 1025–1005 and David in 1005–965.

8. Baruch Halpern's (*David's Secret Demons: Messiah, Murderer, Traitor, King* [Grand Rapids: Eerdmans, 2001]) arguments for early sources of the material in this regard carry a great deal of weight. For an overview of the theories and my own position, see Johanna W. H. van Wijk-Bos, *Reading*

in Samuel is limited to specific sections rather than exhibited in a frame around the narratives.

There is no doubt that this recounting of ancient Israel's history is woven into a magnificent whole with fascinating insights not only into social and religious contexts but also into character and family relationships, creating one of the jewels of storytelling in the Hebrew Bible. In what follows, we will give a great deal of attention to *how* the stories are told, with the aim of engaging the reader/listener in this old world of intrigue and both the fortunes and misfortunes of flawed humans in their dealings with one another, with the world around them, and with the presence of the Divine. We remind ourselves of the importance of reading with "patience, attention and openness" before letting our questions interact meaningfully with those of the writers and their perspectives.[9]

Approach to the Text

After all, a text can speak only when, and to the extent to which, a reader devotes competent attention to it.[10]

The content divides itself quite naturally, and we will for the most part follow the cycles in which different protagonists play a major role. Cycle I, "The Last Judge" (1 Sam 1–12), highlights the person and role of Samuel through the moment the people choose their first king. In this first cycle the initial chapters (1–3) feature Samuel's mother Hannah in a prominent role. They include Samuel's birth and his service in the Shiloh sanctuary as a young boy. The three episodes that follow focus on the Ark of the Covenant, first captured by the Philistines and finally sent back to Israel because

Samuel: A Literary and Theological Commentary (Macon, GA: Smyth and Helwys, 2011), 3–5; and Christophe Nihan and Dany Noquet, "1–2 Samuel," in *Introduction à l'Ancien Testament*, ed. Thomas Römer, Jean-Daniel Macchi, and Christophe Nihan (Geneva: Labor et Fides, 2009), 358–83.

9. Van Wijk-Bos, *Reading Samuel*, 15.

10. J. P. Fokkelman, *The Crossing Fates*, vol. 2 of *Narrative Art and Poetry in the Books of Samuel* (Assen: Van Gorcum, 1986), 8.

of the havoc it creates in Philistine cities (1 Sam 4–6). The next two chapters return to Samuel, who issues warnings to the people and voices dissent to their demand for a king (1 Sam 7–8). Saul's rise to kingship takes place in three chapters (1 Sam 9–11), and the cycle concludes with Samuel issuing a final warning to the people in regard to kingship (1 Sam 12).

Cycle II, "A King on His Throne" (1 Sam 13–31), begins with three episodes during Saul's kingship, two of which focus on his fall from favor (1 Sam 13 and 15). The rejection announcements frame a campaign against the Philistines (1 Sam 14), which introduces Saul's son Jonathan in a detailed episode of military engagement, putting on the scene a character who will play a significant role in relation to David. From chapter 16 on, with the introduction and anointing of David, Saul remains on the throne, with David first by his side but soon his arch rival (1 Sam 17–18). Eventually fleeing Saul's presence because of attempts on his life, David lives as a guerilla fighter, first in the Judean wilderness with Saul in pursuit (1 Sam 19–26) and then as hired sword for the Philistines (1 Sam 27–30). The end of the struggle between the two comes on Mount Gilboa when Saul, whose sons, including Jonathan, have already fallen in battle, dies by his own hand (1 Sam 31:4).

Cycle III, "Ascent to Kingship" (2 Sam 1–8), describes David's rise to the throne following Saul's death (2 Sam 1). First, he is crowned in Hebron to reign over Judah (2 Sam 2:1–7). This is followed by a period when two kings rule in the land (2 Sam 2:8–4:2), and finally, after the demise of Saul's son Ishboshet, David rules all Israel from Jerusalem, which he establishes as his capital (2 Sam 5:1–9). The last three chapters in this cycle (2 Sam 6–8) relate various episodes of David's rule, including his desire, thwarted by God through the agency of the prophet Nathan, to build a temple, and David's prayer in response. The cycle ends with a series of David's wars of aggression against neighboring peoples.

Cycle IV, "A King and His People" (2 Sam 9–20), is marked by closeup views of David's intimate relations both inside and outside his family, and his fragile hold on the reins of the kingdom in fending off several rebellions.

Cycle V, "Hazards, Heroes, and Poetry" (2 Sam 21–24), rounds off the Samuel text with various accounts during David's reign, two lists, and two poems ascribed to David. All in all, there is not a single person in the Hebrew Bible to whom as much material is devoted as David, in all his complexity: ideal king supported by the Deity and flawed human being who experiences the consequences of displeasing Adonai and ineptitude in dealing with his family.

Each cycle is marked by the presence of women. With the exception of Hannah in 1 Samuel 1–2, most of these characters are not foregrounded in the narratives; they are nevertheless present in significant ways, exerting influence over the course of events.[11] While it is a common assumption that women served as items of exchange in the ancient culture of Israel, women in Samuel may also be seen as escaping enforced passivity to carve out their own sharply delineated presence in the story. Some, like Michal and Bathsheba, initially function only as passive tools in the hands of powerful men around them, but develop into characters portraying autonomous resistance to dominating male presence. Others, like Hannah, escape their triangulated position in the family to speak and act in ways that crucially advance the course of events.

Although a few individuals have profiles that are more negative than positive, almost all, and certainly all the most interesting characters, exhibit the weaknesses and flaws common to all human beings across time and space as well as admirable traits of loyalty and devotion, courage and wisdom. These are not flat depictions of idealized women and men or larger-than-life heroes. These are ordinary individuals with all that entails. Generally, inner disposition and the life of thought is revealed through speech or action, although there are exceptions when mood and emotions are mentioned and underlined—for example, in the opening scenes of the first cycle.

11. In the context of Judges 21:14, Susan Niditch (*War in the Hebrew Bible: A Study in the Ethics of Violence* [Oxford: Oxford University Press, 1993], 135) observes, "Women thus serve in a typical role assigned them by biblical writers and Israelite culture as transition-makers, connectors, and items of exchange between opposing groups." In the Samuel texts, women may, in addition, be viewed as agents of change with a prophetic presence.

Cycle I: The Last Judge (1 Samuel 1–12)

And Samuel judged Israel all the days of his life. (1 Sam 7:15)

In his role as judge, Samuel bridges the period between the charismatic military and administrative leaders that preceded him and the royal house that will follow him. His role in the community is not confined to that of judge alone, since he also acts as priest and prophet. After him, separate functionaries will fulfill these tasks.[1]

I divide the cycle into four acts. Act I, "Where Is the Glory?" (1 Sam 1–4), takes place in or near Shiloh, with one excursion to a battle scene on the plain to the west in the first half of chapter 4. The first two chapters introduce Samuel's parents, Elkanah and Hannah, as well as the location of the sanctuary and the Ark with their priestly personnel, Eli and his sons, Hofni and Pinhas. Chapter 3 portrays young Samuel ostensibly as priest-in-training in service to Eli, and gradually evolves into a depiction of his prophetic role as he performs his first task as mouthpiece of God. Chapter 4 rounds off the career of Eli in a tragic manner when he dies upon hearing the news that the Ark of the Covenant has been captured by the Philistines.

1. Mark Leuchter (*Samuel and the Shaping of Tradition* [Oxford: Oxford University Press, 2013], 8), in his review of the figure of Samuel, considers him typical of the liminal characterization of such figures and argues that Samuel was understood as "one of Israel's sacred liminal figures whose qualities reaffirmed the forces that brought the nation into existence." In this conception, Leuchter considers Samuel's priestly role to be the one that formed the basis for the others.

In Act II, "Who Can Stand before This Holy God?" (1 Sam 5–6), the Ark goes on a journey in Philistia before coming under the care of Israelites again at the end of chapter 6. Almost the entire narrative takes place inside the cities of the Philistines, where the Ark is wreaking havoc among the population; this inside look into enemy territory, shot through with humorous overtones, is unique in Samuel.

Act III, "Samuel's Word Was to All Israel" (1 Sam 7–8), returns to the career of Samuel and highlights his activity as judge in chapter 7 with emphatic notations of his judgeship in the final three verses. In chapter 8, the wheel of political leadership turns to an explicit demand for kingship on the part of the people; it consists for the most part of dialogue, between the community and Samuel on the one hand and Samuel and God on the other, ending with God's command to Samuel to find a king.

Act IV, "Everybody's Looking for Something" (1 Sam 9–12), introduces Saul and the start of his initial kingship and closes the career of Samuel as Israel's sole leader.

Taken as a whole, the tempo of the narratives is relatively fast, with Samuel yet to be born at the outset and an old man in chapter eight. Within this span of time, many episodes slow down to linger in detail on specifics, such as Hannah's moment of prayer in the sanctuary at Shiloh, Samuel's experience of the presence of God near the Ark of the Covenant, the reactions on the battlefield and at home during the fight with the Philistines, and the discussions of the Philistines about the predicament they face while the Ark is in their midst. Overall, the chapters move forward from the moment that only hints at kingship in the opening scenes to the demand of the people to establish central leadership on the model of the people around them: "Now, set up a king over us,/ to judge us like all the peoples" (1 Sam 8:5). At the end of the cycle, leadership that arises spontaneously is a thing of the past, and hereditary kingship has been potentially established, although it will not quite turn out that way with Israel's first king. Leadership and the proper exercise of authority and power are central to understanding these chapters. The exercise of power, in Hannah´s prayer ascribed to the Most High and thenceforth reflected in human leadership, will guide the people in their national affairs.

Act I: Where Is the Glory? (1 Samuel 1–4)

Four chapters center on Shiloh and its environs. Only the battle scene in 4:1–11 moves us outside the narrow region between Ramah and Shiloh to the coastal plain where the Philistines and Israelites meet one another for the first military encounter of the book. Continuing the themes of Judges, large national questions concerning leadership and the exercise of power are embedded in a narrow focus on family and family ties. There are first Elkanah and the two women, Hannah and Peninnah, who exist in an adversarial relationship. The childless woman, Hannah, comes to the fore as a central character and the mother of Samuel, the first male protagonist of the text. The second family, whose fate is linked to the first through the service of Samuel at the Shiloh sanctuary, is the house of Eli. Prophetic voices make themselves heard already in the second chapter when the collapse of Eli's house is announced, an event that receives a double notation, as it is repeated in chapter 3 by the word of God to Samuel and then to Eli.

Chapter 4 begins the deportation of the Ark, heretofore residing in Shiloh, first to the battlefield and then to Philistine territory. The downfall of Eli's house begins at this point with the death of his sons and his own demise at hearing the news about the fate of the Ark. As the episodes began with the birth of a child whose stature among the people appeared to open a way forward, they end similarly, albeit in contrast, with the birth of one who is named after the Ark in exile. The presence of God exhibits itself in the lives of individuals—Hannah, Eli, Samuel—and the issue of appropriate and inappropriate ways of responding to God is woven into the fabric of the narratives that make up these initial chapters.

Act 1, Scene 1: A Family in Shiloh (1 Samuel 1:1–8)

The story of Hannah's request for a son is intended to introduce, foreshadow, and ideologically comment upon the story of Israel's request for a king.[2]

The story begins with a standard introduction of a man and his ancestry, town, and family. The first three verses (1–3) provide all the necessary information to arrive at a detailed picture of the man, Elkanah, and his habits.[3] He travels from his residence, which is in the "hill country of Ephraim," to Shiloh to make the annual sacrifice "year after year." He is quite well-to-do; not only is he able to provide this substantial contribution to the sanctuary, but his family includes two wives, Hannah and Peninnah, a notation made in the central verse of the unit. While we read frequently about a man having more than one wife in the Bible, the practice of polygyny in this hard-scrabble, self-sustaining agricultural society would have been an option open mostly to those with the means to sustain a larger nuclear household, not one within the reach of ordinary people. Elkanah, then, is clearly a man of substance who regularly fulfills his religious obligations.[4]

The opening lines establish a number of links with other episodes in the Historical Books, both backward and forward. The hill country of Ephraim plays a central role in the final chapters of Judges, and it

2. Robert Polzin, *Samuel and the Deuteronomist*, vol. 2 of *A Literary Study of the Deuteronomic History* (Bloomington: Indiana University Press, 1993), 25.

3. Verbal references to activity in both vv. 3 and 7 indicate that the actions were habitual. This is also indicated by the expression "year after year" in v. 3 and "year in, year out" in v. 7. On the iterative nature of the verb forms, see J. P. Fokkelman, *Vow and Desire*, vol. 4 of *Narrative Art and Poetry in the Books of Samuel* (Assen: Van Gorcum, 1993), 9.

4. In addition, the narrative records Hannah bringing a bull, flour, and wine to the sanctuary in v. 24, another sign that this is not a poor family. Also, to make the yearly trek of perhaps 15–20 miles to Shiloh in the hill country, they were probably in possession of donkeys to transport the children, goods, and perhaps the women.

echoes with the serious disturbances that took place there, which were already anticipated in Joshua 17:15. It will also be the origin of Sheba, the instigator of the last rebellion against David in 2 Samuel 20 (see v. 21). Ramah, which in 1 Samuel is always used in reference to Samuel, is mentioned as a possible lodging for the Levite and his entourage in Judges 19:13.[5] The territory of Zuf will reappear in the initial episodes about Saul, and, together with other hints in the opening scenes, signals the impending kingship of Saul (1 Sam 9:5). Shiloh, here the place for annual sacrifice, we find in the Historical Books in Joshua as a place for the Tent of Meeting and the location where the lot is cast for the remaining land division. The Levites approach Joshua there to request their assigned towns, and the "entire congregation of Israelites" prepares in Shiloh for battle against the Trans-Jordanian tribes (Josh 18:1; 21:2; 22:12). Most notably, it is the site in Judges from which the Benjaminites steal the young women needed to replenish their tribe (Judg 21:23; see van Wijk-Bos, *The End of the Beginning*, 310–12). Shiloh, then, is a place for sacrifice with a sanctuary, with priests, and, as we find out later, with the Ark of God (3:3). It is a place with an ambiguous legacy, where the memories of abducted family members may still linger. This is where the Elkanah family treks year after year to fulfill its religious obligations.[6]

Three verses introduce four men by name (eight if we count the ancestors)—all of them important for one reason or another—surrounding the names of the two women, both without antecedents, one of whom carries almost no importance because of her lack of children. While the mention of Eli with his sons Hofni and Pinhas seems out of place, it underlines the cultic significance of Shiloh through the priestly presence and at the same time rings an early bell for subse-

5. With Fokkelman (*Vow and Desire*, 8), I take the indication *ramatayim* (1:1), literally "Two Heights," to be a figurative reference to Ramah, "cocooned" as it is in a network of the numbers one and two. It is clear from 1:19 that Elkanah's family residence was in Ramah, as it was later for Samuel.

6. In Judges, the Ark is mentioned only once, placed "in those days" in Bethel, where the assembly congregated to seek counsel from Adonai during their struggle with Benjamin (20:27). The Ark was portable, of course, and may well have moved from one place to another, Bethel being at a distance of approximately ten miles from Shiloh.

quent events surrounding these three. We note also that only the sons receive the priestly designation, which raises questions about who is actually in charge. Eli will eventually receive his title (1:9), but here, in Fokkelman's words, Eli appears to be "pottering along behind."[7]

The next four verses (4–7) continue to describe habitual actions, with additional information increasing interest in what goes on in this family. First, Elkanah is in charge both of sacrificing and doling out portions to his wives, only one of whom he is said to "love." Also, we find out that Peninnah has both sons and daughters. Now we see her surrounded by a flock of children next to Hannah, who has none and who receives either a *double* or a *special* portion of the sacrifice (5).[8] Finally, the situation between the two women, already unequal in view of Hannah's lack of children, is adversarial because Peninnah has made it her business every year to burden Hannah's life by taunting her with her lack of offspring.

1 Samuel 1:6–7

6 And her adversary would torment her sorely
for the sake of humiliating her
with the fact that Adonai had shut her womb.
7 And so it went, year in, year out,
as often as she went up to the house of Adonai,
so she tormented her,
and she wept and ate not.

7. Fokkelman, *Vow and Desire*, 19. Fokkelman, who pays more attention to sound in the text than most commentators, also notes that the sounds of the names Hofni and Pinhas in Hebrew echo those of the names of Hannah and Peninnah.

8. Literally, the Hebrew reads that "to Hannah he gave one portion of the face," a phrase in which the word *appayyim* is notoriously difficult to translate. Most English translations vary between "one" or "one portion only" and "a double portion," while Buber (Martin Buber and Franz Rosenzweig, *Bücher der Geschichte* [Cologne: Jakob Hegner, 1965], 151) renders, "Hanna he could give only one portion, with woeful look, for Hanna he loved, but . . ." The Hebrew has the qualifying conjunction *ki*, "because" or "for," following the phrase about the giving of the portion.

The wording identifies Peninnah as her (i.e., Hannah's) *adversary*, a strong root that puts the two women at odds with one another. It adds to *adversary* the verb *torment* (*ka'as*), used only here in Samuel and elsewhere in the Historical Books reserved exclusively for the Israelites' tormenting Adonai with their idolatry, especially in Kings.[9] It appears three times in these two verses, with a doubling of the root in verse 6, and is picked up subsequently by Hannah to refer to her state of mind (16). Before the notation about the hostility from one woman to another, we learn that Elkanah "loved" Hannah. For all that the storytellers practice reticence in terms of inner life and feelings, it is not difficult to get an idea of the emotions flying around in this family! There are love, jealousy, and, on Hannah's side, silence and depression manifested in her abstaining from food and drink.

As expected from the setup for the story, the man is the first to speak:

1 Samuel 1:8

And Elkanah, her husband, said to her:
Hannah, why do you weep?
And why do you not eat?
And why is your heart down?
Am I not good to you above ten sons?[10]

Elkanah addresses Hannah at the point of her distress with four questions. It's clear that his words are hardly helpful with their threefold "why?" ending with a rhetorical question about his own worth to her (instead of her worth to him), drawing on her protective feelings toward him (feelings of a mother toward her child), and thus exacerbating the situation.[11] At best, his words are a clumsy

9. See, for example, Deut 4:25; 31:29; 32:16, 21; Judg 2:12; 1 Kgs 14:9, 15; 16:2, 7, 13, 26, 33.

10. The more common and more elegant rendering is "am I not better to you than ten sons?" With this more literal translation, I intend to highlight the repetition of the word "good," used by Elkanah again when he addresses Hannah for the second and last time (1:23).

11. Thus Fokkelman, *Vow and Desire*, 21. Lillian Klein (*From Deborah to*

attempt at comfort, although it is possible that they are meant to reassure her. The family in the ancient world was an absolute necessity for women's survival, and a childless woman was at risk not only psychologically but also socially and economically, since her husband could set her aside if he was not willing to accept her childless situation. It is thus conceivable that Elkanah's assurance of his love for her is meant to make clear that he has no intention of making her leave the household. It is worth noting that Hannah is the only woman in this material to be the explicit recipient of her husband's love and that her husband's speech is the one illustration of a man attempting to console a woman.

Whatever his intentions were, Hannah does not deign to answer her husband, and while on the face of it her silence could betoken her entering deeper into her depression, this moment is where the story takes a turn. Perhaps Elkanah's attempt at comfort have had the effect on Hannah of clarifying her need. She is depressed because of her lack of children and the constant reminder of this by her co-wife, and Elkanah's questions make clear that he is not worth more to her than even one son. Instead of appealing to her rival to cease her harassment, or to her husband as Sarai pled with Abram in regard to Hagar, calling him to account for the slights she experienced (Gen 16:5), Hannah resorts to a higher authority than that of any male in her surroundings. In the next breath, she gets up (subject of a verb of activity for the third time, in direct contrast to her former depression and passivity), heads for the sanctuary, bypasses Eli, who is sitting by the doorpost of the sanctuary, and pours out the bitterness of her soul to the only one she believes can solve

Esther: Sexual Politics in the Hebrew Bible [Minneapolis: Fortress, 2003], 49) interprets Elkanah's words even more negatively as "verbal attacks" which disclose "a man who is threatening, angry and punishing beneath the surface." See also Yairah Amit ("'Am I Not More Devoted to You than Ten Sons?' [1 Samuel 1:8]: Male and Female Interpretations," in *A Feminist Companion to Samuel and Kings*, ed. Athalya Brenner [Sheffield: Sheffield Academic, 1994], 75), who considers Elkanah a "man who never matured . . . indifferent to Hannah's pain" and "guilty not only of insensitivity to his wife's feelings but also of disregard for her future" since without children she would be poor if she died. Amit points out the praise for Elkanah generally issued by male interpreters.

her problem. From that moment on, Hannah stays in the center of the story until the last words of her thanksgiving prayer (2:10), and the elaborate setup with the fulsome introduction of her husband appears to have laid a false trail. Although not entirely off the stage, Elkanah will return only on the sidelines of the action.

Act I, Scene 2: Hannah Arose (1 Samuel 1:9–18)

The identity of the nonperson is not merely defined by suffering, but also through their resistance and action.[12]

1 SAMUEL 1:9–11

9 Then arose Hannah after the eating in Shiloh,
and after the drinking—
and Eli, the priest, was sitting on a chair
by the doorpost of the temple of Adonai.
10 She was bitter in her soul
and prayed to the Holy God
and wept and wept.
11 She vowed a vow and said:
Adonai of Hosts,
if you look, look well, at the affliction of your maid,
remember me, and do not forget your maid,
and give to your maid the seed of men,
I will give him to Adonai all the days of his life,
and a razor will not touch his head.[13]

12. Lieve Troch, *Verzet is Het Geheim van de Vreugde* (Zoetermeer: Boekencentrum, 1998), 194, author's translation.

13. Alter (*The David Story: A Translation with Commentary of 1 and 2 Samuel* [New York: Norton, 1999], 5n11) notes that the Nazirite (see Samson) is a person especially dedicated to God—no haircuts, no alcohol. Eli thinking Hannah is drunk is thus ironic. The NRSV follows a Qumran reading of this verse in translating, "Then I will set him before you as a Nazirite, until the day of his death; he shall drink neither wine nor intoxicants and no razor shall touch his head." Alter also notes the directness and simplicity of Hannah's

The verb "she arose," in the Hebrew text and in this translation, comes first in verse 9 and stands in opposition to her refraining from action in verse 7. This point is where Hannah's turn to agency and personhood in her own right begins, in contrast not only to her own previous passivity but also to the passivity of the one who exercises authority in God's name, the priest Eli who is *seated,* whom she ignores. She *arose* to turn, with the language of a classical lament, to the one she and everyone around her holds responsible for her fate, the one on whom she calls as "Adonai of Hosts." She *arose,* still captive to her bitterness and continuing to weep, to pray in the sanctuary, a location mentioned for the first time in the scene. As she prays, she pleads with the Deity to *pay attention, to remember* and *not forget,* referring to herself as the lowliest of beings in relation to the most mighty of beings: *your maid* (3×).

Before the words of her prayer, however, the narrator notes that she "vowed a vow," evoking the one person who so far in the Histories engaged in a similar exchange with God, Jefta (Judg 11:30). Like Jefta's prayer, Hannah's begins with the conditional "if." If you, God, do this, then I will do that. Like Jefta she vows a vow, and like Jefta she dedicates her child; unlike Jefta, however, her promise of dedication is for life rather than death, a life dedicated to God. Thus, both Hannah and God will benefit if she indeed gives birth to a son, explicitly stipulated in her request for male offspring (lit. "the seed of men"). She does not pray for a sign or any token that God will indeed remember her and grant her what she asks, but she goes on praying. It is a remarkable moment in the life of this woman, who stands up for herself and bargains with the most Holy God, "Adonai of Hosts" (11). This description for the God of Israel is used in verse 3 in connection with Elkanah, but from Hannah's mouth appears for the first time in Scripture as an address. In Fokkelman's words, here, Hannah attains her "true strength."[14]

When speech arrives in a story, tempo slows to a crawl. In the few lines of the introduction (1–5), years move past with all they

---

prayer ("If you give . . . then I will give") and draws attention to the change to "lent" in v. 28.

14. Fokkelman, *Vow and Desire,* 33.

entail to set the background, until Elkanah addresses Hannah at the point of her distress, and in the next phrase she gets up. The pace moves from years to days to one day to one moment, with the focus on one person regarded through a scrim of tears and depression who is now heard making one of the hardest bargains a person can make. For those living in an overcrowded world, it may be difficult to enter into the mindset of a community and culture where childlessness was a serious disability in view of the threat of infertility to its survival.[15] It is certainly motherhood Hannah needs and longs for, but it is especially her validation in the eyes of her family and community, for whom, no matter how much Elkanah loves her, she is not a valid contributor. In her family, she is a victim of mockery, in the community a woman of no worth. Her submissive self-designation during the prayer is not for a rhetorical purpose only.

As the tempo has slowed down, space has shrunk with it. Events that began in the wider world, in the "hill country of Ephraim," and moved to a town, Shiloh, are now taking place within the confines of a structure with one person at the center, Hannah, loved but in great need. Meanwhile, the one person with authority in this place, Eli the priest (now given his proper title) is on the sidelines. The placing of Eli at the doorpost of the sanctuary on a seat or throne, after his mention in v. 3 without his title, has cast

15. Childlessness even today may cause a sense of deprivation and isolation, even in a social context where there is awareness of overcrowding, and certainly in large parts of the world elsewhere. A difference is that for ancient Israel, survival of the people depended on the ability of women to produce enough healthy offspring to guarantee an ongoing population. Famine, epidemic and endemic parasitic diseases left women, weakened through constant child bearing, more vulnerable to dying at an early age. See Carol L. Meyers, "The Roots of Restriction: Women in Early Israel," in *The Bible and Liberation: Political and Social Hermeneutics*, ed. Norman K. Gottwald (Maryknoll: Orbis, 1983), 289–306; Athalya Brenner, *The Intercourse of Knowledge: On Gendering Desire and Sexuality in the Hebrew Bible* (Leiden: Brill, 1997), 65. Also consider population figures in the discussion of B. S. J. Isserlin, *The Israelites* (Minneapolis: Fortress, 2001), 95; Johanna W. H. van Wijk-Bos, *Making Wise the Simple: The Torah in Christian Faith and Practice* (Grand Rapids: Eerdmans, 2005), 41–42.

him in an ambiguous light. His conclusions about the woman, who is still intensely praying while only moving her lips and not making a sound, does nothing to alleviate our doubts about his astuteness. Not only does he conclude she is drunk, but when he opens his mouth, it is to directly accuse her and issue a command to sober up (14). To give him the benefit of the doubt, in light of the goings on at Shiloh coming to light in an upcoming scene, his assumption may not have been so out of place. Yet the man with the obligation to represent God to the distressed petitioner in his presence fails miserably in his task, joining the company of those who have mistreated Hannah or inadvertently exacerbated her pain. Instead of receiving a reply from Adonai or a divine messenger, she gets more abuse from one of God's representatives, and for a brief moment it looks as if the forward movement that began with Hannah's getting up and continued with her courageous bargain with God may be halted. She was still distressed, weeping as she prayed. What will she do now in response to a rebuke from God's representative? Everything points to a likely return to her former condition of passivity and depression.

1 Samuel 1:14–16

15 Then answered Hannah and said:
No, my lord!
A woman hard-pressed in spirit am I.
Neither wine nor alcohol have I drunk,
but I poured out my soul before Adonai.
16 Do not take your maid
for a worthless woman,
because from abundant distress and torment
I spoke until now.

That she resists expectations and perhaps her own inclinations in response to Eli's rebuke is clear from her first word: "Then answered Hannah and said: No" (15). Her no is testimony to how far she has come already, even before receiving reassurance from God or God's representative before her. She expresses her state of mind, her abstinence from alcohol, and her activity of prayer. There is no pouring of wine here but rather a pouring out of her "soul before Adonai." Nor does she stop there but makes clear he should not take her for a "worthless woman" because she spoke out of her anxiety and torment (16). There were those before who acted as "worthless men" (Judg 19:22; 20:13), and soon such characters will come back in the story (1 Sam 2:12). A worthless person, only here in the feminine, connotes not only someone with a lack of value but someone who is actively wicked (Judg 19:22; Prov 16:27). Hannah's disavowal of the designation implies that of all people, Eli should know what constitutes such a person! Clear and direct, twice admonishing Eli with a negative ("no my lord"; "do not take your maid") before stating her disposition and actions, she does not reveal the reasons for her downcast spirit, nor does she explain the request she has just made in the sanctuary. Eli, convinced of her sincerity, reassures her either with a wish or an assertion of God granting her request (the Hebrew can be read either way), and Hannah departs with a final polite phrase, having the last word. She proceeds to take nourishment and is no longer downcast.[16]

Eli's assurance in verse 17 is in Fokkelman's words "so general that the priest could unleash this pronouncement on almost any cultus participant without causing a sensation or being in bad style."[17] Yet he has spoken words that anticipate the future: "May the God of Israel give your request that you asked from him" (17). Literally, the line reads, "your asking that you asked." In Hebrew, the verb "ask" is *sha'al,* the root of the name Saul, or *Sha'ul*, "the one asked for," which is the form placed in Hannah's mouth with intricate punning

16. The Hebrew phrase literally means "her face was no longer," and most translations follow the Septuagint in translating that she was no longer sad.

17. Fokkelman, *Vow and Desire*, 51. Alter (*The David Story,* 5n14) compares the situation to what he identifies as an "annunciation motif which here is purposefully distorted. Eli should be playing the role of man of God or divine intermediary but he gets it all wrong. . . . When he prays/predicts a favorable outcome . . . he has no idea what she has asked. So Eli is a parody of the annunciating figure of the conventional type-scene—aptly introducing a story in which the claim to authority of the house of Eli will be rejected and displaced by true prophetic guidance in the person of Samuel."

later in the story (27). Hints at the future king of Israel have begun in the narrative.

Once Hannah takes charge of her actions, the phrase beginning "she arose" (9) may not strike us as all that unusual. People are always getting up in the Bible. It's an action performed hundreds of times. With a singular female subject, however, the form is not as common, and Hannah's arising puts her in the company of Rebekah, Tamar, Deborah, Naomi and Ruth, Abigail, Esther, and the proverbial valiant woman in Proverbs, all women who take on formidable and at times daring tasks (Gen 24:61; 38:19; Judg 4:9; Ruth 1:6; 2:15; 3:14; 1 Sam 25:41–42; Esth 8:5; Prov 31:15). Not every woman on this list provides an example of admirable behavior, as there are also the younger daughter of Lot (Gen 19:35), one of the prostitutes before Solomon (1 Kgs 3:20), and Queen Mother Athaliah, who has her family murdered (2 Kgs 11:1). The phrase does not so much testify to agency that demands approval as it points to initiative, good or bad, against the odds. Yairah Amit considers Hannah's leaving the family after the meal an act of "resistance and protest" by a woman "who is isolated within her family" and "deprived of being understood even by her husband."[18]

Furthermore, in every other context, the verb begins a sentence in which other activity follows, so that in the second half of verse 9, one would expect a verb that placed Hannah inside the sanctuary: "she went," "she stood," or a similar expression. Instead the line veers to Eli, who is "sitting," thus uniquely and sharply contrasting two characters and putting Hannah's activity in stark relief. The next verb with Hannah as subject, "she prayed," allows for no grammatical distance between her *arising* and her *praying*. The three verbs in verses 10–11 referring to the activity of an individual woman are mentioned only in regard to Hannah: "she prayed, she wept, and she vowed a vow," emphasizing the uniqueness of her activity.[19] Her reply to Eli is

18. Amit, "Am I Not More Devoted," 75–76.

19. Not surprisingly, the Rabbis comment elaborately on Hannah, her prayer, and her words to Eli, considering her to be an example of how to pray and deriving numerous regulations for both manner and content from her prayer (Berakhot 31a–b). "She prayed" with the Hebrew verb used here occurs again in 2:1, and Hannah refers to herself as having "prayed" for Samuel at the end of the first chapter (1:27). In addition, the preposition *'al*, used in

direct, with clear descriptions following her two negatives: "No . . . a woman hard-pressed in spirit am I. . . . Do not take . . . because . . . I spoke." Hannah is bold and well-spoken, and we shall see that, even after her exchange with Eli, she will continue on the path she began to walk when she arose.

What exactly did Hannah promise to give to God? It is clear that she dedicates the life of her son, with whom she is not yet pregnant, to the service of Adonai—another unique moment in the life of a childless woman—but other aspects are less explicit. The childless woman is a familiar subject in biblical narrative, and Hannah shares her condition with Sarah, Rebekah, Rachel, and Samson's mother, two of whom also lived in a hostile relationship with a co-wife. None of these are said to pray to God for relief from their distress. Sarah blames God, Isaac prays for Rebekah, Rachel complains to Jacob, and Samson's mother receives a visit from a divine messenger. All of them, including Samson's mother, are said to be "barren," but the text states about Hannah only that "she had no children."

While Hannah's experience is often compared to that of Samson's mother, especially in her dedicating her son-yet-to-be to God, it is the divine messenger who dictates that Samson will be a *nazir* of God (Judg 13:5). The two stories share the phrase "a razor will not touch his head," but the word *nazir* and abstinence from alcohol are not mentioned in Hannah's narrative, an omission filled in by the Qumran and Septuagint versions of the text and followed by some translations, such as the NRSV. We remain uncertain whether the text intended to have Hannah dedicate her potential offspring as a *nazir*; what is clear is the child's dedication to the service of God, which she declares to be "all the days of his life."[20] Reference to ab-

---

the phrase "she prayed to Adonai" in 1:10, is unusual (lit. "she prayed upon Adonai"). The preposition is used in this particular way in only one other place, in Ps. 18:42 (41), where the verb is "they cried." The notion conveyed in both cases is a prayer that presses upon God in an intensive way.

20. For strong arguments that the text does not intend to identify Samuel as *nazir*, see Matitiahu Tsevat, "Was Samuel a Nazirite?" in *Sha'arei Talmon: Studies in the Bible, Qumran, and the Ancient Near East Presented to Shemaryahu Talmon*, ed. Michael Fishbane, Emanuel Tov, and Weston W. Fields (Winona Lake, IN: Eisenbrauns, 1992), 199–204.

stinence from alcohol does not occur until her reply to Eli, and it is in relation to herself (15).[21]

The rules for vows regarding a Nazirite are spelled out in Numbers 6:1–21, and its stipulations are for individuals, male or female, who dedicate themselves for a limited period of time. In the case of both Samson and Samuel, their mothers explicitly spell out the status as lifelong (cf. Judg 13:7). David Jobling argues that it may be the very dedication to God Hannah desires rather than just pregnancy, and certainly rather than a son for her husband. On the other hand, in light of subsequent information about the deplorable situation at the sanctuary in Shiloh (2:12–17), it is possible that she hopes her son in a position of leadership will bring change to the way things are.[22] Others question Hannah's faith in a God who would entertain the kind of bargain in which she engages.[23] We may question Hannah's perspective on a God who would demand such a sacrifice of a mother, and it may well be that Hannah's character and her views are flawed. It is her agency and initiative that stand out in the story rather than her flawless character, two traits that position her as one of the strong multifaceted female characters in the Bible. The full scope of the narrative presents her as complex human character.[24]

21. Fokkelman (*Vow and Desire*, 47) argues that Hannah's abstaining from the general "eating and drinking" gave her the idea that she could do something creative with her withholding, and she decided "to make it into the spiritual preparation for the Nazirite, in imitation of the mother of Samson."

22. David Jobling, *1 Samuel*, Berit Olam (Collegeville, MN: Liturgical Press, 1998), 133–35.

23. Danna Nolan Fewell and David M. Gunn (*Gender, Power, and Promise: The Subject of the Bible's First Story* [Nashville: Abingdon, 1993], 138) offer such a critical take on Hannah and her vow, asking what sort of view of God Hannah has that she engages in this negotiation: "What sort of god does Hannah have faith in? A god who only gives when he gets something in return? A god who requires a mother to give up her child in order to live up to society's conditions of value?" Of course, people then most likely believed in such bargains, and people may still do so today. Although we may tend to dismiss the concept, what stands out in this text is the powerful pressure Hannah puts on the Deity.

24. Judging Hannah to "serve the heteropatriarchal agenda in her longing for a child" and considering her to exhibit "dutiful adherence to the hetero-

Act I, Scene 3: The One She Asked For (1 Samuel 1:19–28)

All that follows as a result of this story, all that Samuel will achieve . . . is the result of Hannah's vow and would not have occurred without her.[25]

The tempo picks up in a brief introductory unit (19–20), with the family returning home to Ramah and with pregnancy and birth-giving taking place in two lines (20a and b), in which at least nine months go by. Four verbs with the couple in charge (19) are concluded by three with Hannah as subject: "She became pregnant, she gave birth, and she called" (20). Clamped in between these phrases, the act of intercourse ("Elkanah knew Hannah") and God's remembering ("Adonai remembered her") take place—human and divine activity together result in Hannah's conceiving. Continuing her agency in the story, Hannah does the name-giving and, as Eli did earlier, uses the root "ask" (see p. 25 above): "And she called his name Samuel,/ for from Adonai I asked him" (20).

Her boy's name, Samuel, is ordinarily connected with the Hebrew root for "listening" and the word "God." Hebrew naming, however, often includes artistic referencing and allusion. We note that the name Samuel (*Shemu'el*) contains the three consonants of the verb for asking (*sha'al*), so the allusion to asking happens in the sound repetition: [*vattiqrah*] *shemo Shemu'el, ki me*[*'adonai*] *sha'alti*.

---

sexual imperative" is shortsighted in its lack of recognition of the ancient Israelite socioeconomic context and the different ways in which Hannah breaks through the standards of that context. See Deryn Guest, *When Deborah Met Jael: Lesbian Biblical Hermeneutics* (London: SCM, 2005), 132. Rather, we may conclude with Laurel C. Schneider ("Yahwist Desires: Imagining Divinity Queerly," in *Queer Commentary and the Hebrew Bible*, ed. Ken Stone, JSOTSup 334 [Sheffield: Sheffield Academic, 2001], 218) that the story of Hannah is among those "queerest stories in the Hebrew Bible" in which "women . . . managed to have a voice at all, women who managed to survive and/or overcome with some kind of chutzpah their barrenness, widowhood, slavery, rape, virginity, abandonment, marriage, ugliness, or other signifiers of their male-derivative identity, economic dependency and status."

25. Jobling, *1 Samuel*, 136.

In the next unit (21–28), action flows back and forth between Ramah and Shiloh, with years elapsing between verses 23 and 24. The moment has arrived for husband and wife to engage in opposite action, one "going up" and the other "staying" on account of the fact that her firstborn will in the end "stay" in the presence of God. She is not ready to relinquish him to the precinct of the sanctuary in Shiloh until she can no longer put it off. Hannah thus shaves off at least three and possibly five years from the time he is born until he will serve God at the temple. Elkanah consents to everything, telling Hannah to do "what is good" in her eyes (23); he, who once asked if he was not "good for her more than ten sons," may be resigned to the fact that Hannah is capable of deciding what is best for her and her child. Beyond the statement about his love for Hannah at the beginning of their story, we are not told about his feelings.

Hannah's feelings may be surmised from her actions. She bargained with God in Shiloh and made a promise, a promise of which the fulfillment is perhaps turning out to be more difficult than she anticipated, as is sometimes the case with bargains made in desperate moments. The section in verses 21–23 spirals around verbs for *staying* and *going/bringing, nursing* and *weaning.* The entire section is enclosed in the phrases "the man Elkanah went up" (21) and "the woman stayed" (23). It is possible that the limit of the weaning period was as much as three years, but it may well have been longer, as he could stay on the breast part of the time while she moved him to semi-solid and solid foods.[26] Once *she goes* to Shiloh, the boy will *stay* there.

Each verse has a reference to Adonai, an indication of the devotion to which both Elkanah and Hannah are now more than ever

26. Everett Fox (*The Early Prophets: Joshua, Judges, Samuel and Kings* [New York: Schocken, 2014], 285) assumes the three-year period, as do many others. But see Johanna W. H. van Wijk-Bos, *Reading Samuel: A Literary and Theological Commentary* (Macon, GA: Smyth and Helwys, 2011), 29: "Three years would be a minimum, but she may have stretched the period of weaning so she could keep him with her." Also see Alter, *The David Story*, 8n25: "Given the late weaning time in the ancient world, and given Hannah's likely impulse to postpone that difficult moment, one might imagine the child Samuel to be around the age of five."

inclined. There is mention of Elkanah's vow in verse 21, most likely a votive offering in thanksgiving for their newborn son. Both characters mention the name of God, Adonai, each time they speak, and Hannah uses it four times altogether in the scene. In close proximity to the name of God is the word "sacrifice." It occurs twice in verse 21, and Hannah refers implicitly to sacrifice when she observes that their son will remain in the sanctuary once she brings him there (22). Hannah refers to Samuel as "the boy," a word that will be repeated with intensity in the next units, while the narrator calls him "her son."

Finally, the moment has arrived when both are ready:

1 Samuel 1:24-28

24 She brought him up with her after weaning him
together with a three-year old bull,
half a bushel of flour, and a skin of wine.
And she brought him to the house of Adonai at Shiloh,
and the boy [was] a boy.
25 And they slaughtered the bull
and brought the boy to Eli.
26 And she said: Please, my lord,
by the life of your soul, my lord,
I am the woman who stood here with you praying to Adonai.
27 For this boy I prayed, and Adonai gave to me
my request that I asked of him.
28 So now I myself lend him on request to Adonai;
all the days of his life he is lent on request to the Adonai.
And she bowed down there to Adonai.[27]

27. With Alter (*The David Story*, 8n28), I accept the Qumran version of the verb "she bowed down" based on the fact that Hannah continues to be in charge of the verbs and that the change in a text from feminine to masculine is more likely than vice versa. On the other hand, it is possible that the singular masculine subject of the Hebrew text, "he bowed down," intends to refer to Eli. So Fokkelman, *Vow and Desire*, 72. The scene is framed by the act of prostration, first by the couple (19) and at the end by an individual, either Hannah or Eli.

The first sentence begins with her *bringing* the boy to Shiloh, opening an episode in which she subsequently *brings* Samuel to the sanctuary ending with her *bringing* him to Eli. The text repeats the fact that she had weaned him in verse 24, a notation also ending the preceding verse, thus underlining the significance of that particular activity during this period. Altogether "wean" occurs four times between verses 22 and 24.

Besides her son, Hannah takes with her to Shiloh materials for animal and food offerings—a sign not only of the family's comfortable economic circumstances but also of the fact that her *bringing* of Samuel constitutes a sacrifice of major proportions. To her autonomous action of arising, praying, and undertaking a religious vow in the sanctuary without male assistance, Hannah now adds the power of independent sacrificial action. In the words of Carol Meyers, "The validity and autonomy of Hannah's actions, as an example of family religion, should not be questioned."[28] Samuel's name is used only at the time he is born, and apart from the repeated mention of "son" (20, 23), he is called "the boy" (*na'ar*, a young boy, a lad). The phrase in verse 24 echoing this fact, "and the boy was a boy," means to emphasize his youth, drawing attention once again to the tearing of the mother-child bond while also making one wonder in view of what follows how a young boy would fare in the household of Eli and his two sons.

With her statement to Eli, Hannah reminds him of their previous encounter—something he has likely forgotten in the years that have elapsed—twice stating that she *prayed* and that *this boy* is what she *prayed* for, augmenting the times this verb is used with Hannah as subject. She also reveals the vow she has made, pointing to her bringing him to Eli as the fulfillment of her pledge. In this response, she plays with the root "ask," already used once by Eli and Hannah herself (17, 20), finishing up with the form of the verb that is the name of Saul, *Sha'ul.* Fokkelman writes, "Hannah makes the word 'ask' the key word, expands it and explores its possibilities in a vir-

28. Carol Meyers, "Hannah and Her Sacrifice: Reclaiming Female Agency," in *A Feminist Companion to Samuel and Kings*, ed. Athalya Brenner (Sheffield: Sheffield Academic, 1994), 102.

tuoso chain."[29] The playful and sophisticated wordplay assigned to Hannah by the narrator speaks volumes in terms of the narrative regard for her character and is also just about impossible to translate. In Alter's words, "The English here is forced to walk around an elegant pun in Hebrew."[30]

Asking/praying and *getting/giving* are key to an understanding of the chapter. One may get what one asked for, but it may not be easy to live with the getting and the giving. Hannah stands uniquely in the center of this back-and-forth, and in this way, one woman and a family's ups and downs anticipate and interweave events to come on the national stage. The *asking* will eventually originate with the entire people who will also be *given* what they asked for, but the road with the one they *asked* for will not be a smooth one. In addition, family interactions refracted in their positions of power and inferiority, here depicted on a small scale, will form an integral part of the interlaced stories of Samuel. Elkanah, Hannah and Peninnah will not offer the last portrait of dysfunction and mistreatment.

The fact that Hannah, in the story's opening the weakest and least likely person to play an important role, becomes the central figure once she goes into action may also be viewed as a metaphor for the Israel-God relationship, which in the Bible is often cast in familial terms. Robert Polzin observes parallels between Hannah's lack of a son and Israel's perceived need for a king, with both Hannah and the people living in contexts of hostility and both facing a situation of survival.[31] In all that has transpired, Hannah has shown herself to be an agent of change both in her own situation and in the larger context of her people. She is a facilitator of crucial connec-

29. Fokkelman, *Vow and Desire*, 71.

30. Alter, *The David Story*, 8n28. Translated literally, the text of vv. 27–28 reads: "Adonai gave me the 'asking' I 'asked' of him./ Even I myself 'lend him as asked' to Adonai;/ all the days of his life he is 'lent as asked' to Adonai." In Hebrew, the words "he" and "Shaul/Saul" stand next to each other: "He is Saul to Adonai." See van Wijk-Bos, *Reading Samuel*, 24.

31. Robert Polzin, *Samuel and the Deuteronomist*, 26. Polzin also views Elkanah's referring to Adonai establishing his word in 1:23 as fitting in the larger story line and creating a "central ideological puzzle in 1 Samuel" because of Saul's house not being *established* (29).

tions between an individual and God, anticipating a promise of restored connections between God and people and, on the social level, between her chaotic context and the desire for leadership among the community. In addition, with her second prayer, she signifies prophetic presence.

Act I, Scene 4: A Song of the Heart (1 Samuel 2:1–10)

. . . word pictures painted with a texture that is profoundly multivoiced, speaking of many things at once, often mutually conflicting accents.[32]

1 SAMUEL 2:1

My heart exults in Adonai.
High lifted my horn in Adonai.
Wide open my mouth against my enemies,
for I rejoice in your deliverance.

Into the voice of this once mute and depressed woman the narrator puts the words of her last prayer, a profound example of a psalm of joy in God's power and presence, resounding forward in time for Christian understandings to the voice of Mary as she sings her rejoicing (Luke 1:46–55). Hannah's prayer divides into three main parts, making use of stock language we find in the Psalms and creating from it strong statements of praise for the God of Israel (1–3), who wields divine power to lift the brokenhearted and deprived (4–8), to end in renewed praise to a God from whom all strength derives—including that of the royal leader yet to be (9–10).

The opening strophe moves from a declaration about personal joy—the only place in the poem to use first-person singular pronouns and a first-person singular verb (2:1: "my heart," "my horn," "my mouth," "my enemies," "I rejoice")—to praising God's incomparable holiness (2:2: "There is none" [2×], "there is no rock"), to admonishing those who speak in arrogance (2:3: "Talk no more"),

32. Polzin, *Samuel and the Deuteronomist*, 36.

the only time the speaker employs the address form. Some of the vocabulary is rare and occurs only in a poetic context, such as the verb "exult" with which the prayer opens, "my horn" in the second line, and the word for "arrogance" in verse 3, but there is no obscurity in meaning as Hannah begins by praising Adonai, whose name she uses altogether eight times in the prayer. Her theme is celebration in the face of those who opposed her, "my enemies"; specifically, she is glad about her deliverance by God's power.

The next verses unfold naturally from these opening lines: First, she praises the incomparable nature of this God in holiness, in uniqueness, and in trustworthiness. The holiness of God in the Bible can be described as belonging to the nature of a Deity who is transcendent, awesome, and not human, but God's holiness in biblical Israel is always at the service of the creation and human creatures. Logically, Hannah ascribes her deliverance to God's holiness. The line "there is none beside you" creates a fence against trust in other supernatural powers that could be resorted to for help (especially in cases of childlessness), which were no doubt consulted in many households of the period.[33] The rock image is a standard metaphor in Hebrew poetry for trust and reliability. Adonai is the incomparable helper of this woman in distress.

The subject of "the enemies" is taken up in verse 3 in direct address and warning: "Talk no more so very proud,/ arrogance coming from your mouth." Pride and arrogance issue from those who ascribe power to other beings than God or who judge a co-wife unworthy because she did not produce children for household and community. Literally, the first line reads, "Do not multiply speaking tall, tall!" A "high" or haughty countenance betrays the false confidence of the wicked (Ps 10:4); the believer may express distaste for those who speak evil of their neighbor with "high" (i.e., haughty) looks and a proud heart (Ps 101:5); a pious person proclaims that her heart is

33. In this early period, households possessed shrines, and it is likely that Hannah and her family appealed to household deities, including fertility goddesses, for aid with her predicament. See Oded Borodowski, *Daily Life in Biblical Times* (Atlanta: Society of Biblical Literature, 2003), 24–25; Isserlin, *The Israelites*, 255–56.

not "too high" (Ps 131:1). Similarly, a "high" heart is abhorrent to God (Prov 16:5). Literally, size will play a role in the election of Saul (1 Sam 9:2; 10:23), and it will not save him from failing to establish his royal house. When he is faced with a new candidate for kingship, Samuel is admonished by God not to be impressed by the tall stature of David's brother Eliab (1 Sam 16:7); also Goliath stands "tall" (1 Sam 17:4), and we know what happened to him. The warning points to the fact that all this arrogant talk is known to God, who weighs people's actions, including their interactions.

Hannah's exulting heart and highly lifted horn are set in distinction from the arrogance and pride of those who spoke against her. Her admonishment in verse 3 is in the plural, and we may safely assume that Peninnah was not the only person in Hannah's community who made her feel like a "worthless woman." Even Eli, at first encounter, had not valued her at her true worth. Once her heart had been down (1:8), now it overflows with joy. Her mouth, once not open for speech or taking food but open only for weeping, is now wide open in triumph. The image of the horn is significant in the poem, as it not only symbolizes Hannah's personal power but returns in the final verse with a royal reference (10). Also, the verb "to lift" (*rum*) is key, occurring four times in all (1, 7, 8, 10), alluding in this first mention to the town of her origin *Ramah.*[34]

For Hannah, however, the issues are not only between her and her immediate environment. In what follows, the imagery broadens to include the power of God and God's dealings with humanity in a wide, general context. The middle section of the prayer (4–8) thus speaks especially of God's actions vis-à-vis the downtrodden, those who are counted to have no worth, the ones who in the Bible especially have God's ear and attention. In 4–5, the only strophe which makes no mention of God, the subjects are in contrasting categories: "the heroes/warriors" versus "those who stumble," "the satisfied" versus "the hungry," and the "barren one" versus "one with many children." Paired with these opposites are verbs of contrast ending with the one heretofore fertile now *withering* or *languishing*, a reference elsewhere only used in the prophets, often metaphorically

34. In Hebrew, the phrase about the horn reads *ramah qarni.*

for land and fields.[35] The entire chain ends in the verb *to wither/ languish* (5), a strong expression that points to something or someone at the point of death. While the direct referent appears to be the concrete situation of Hannah and Peninnah, the imagery also draws on a metaphoric comparison to a place or a community on the verge of collapse. Jeremiah 15:9 thus says of the city of Jerusalem under siege, "One who has borne seven languished,/ gasped away her life."

Not surprisingly the next strophe (6–7) begins with an explicit reference to death.

1 Samuel 2:6–7

6 Adonai causes death and causes life;
takes down to Sheol and brings up.
7 Adonai impoverishes and enriches;
brings low, also lifts up.

In contrast to the preceding verses, these lines depict only the action of Adonai in eight verbs without objects. They stand out against the almost leisurely descriptions of verses 4–5, where the recipients of the reversals are the subjects. Here, the God of Israel is described as the one with absolute power over death and life as well as over social and economic positions.[36]

The *lifting up* (*rum*, see above), the last word of verse 7, leads naturally to the *raising up* as first word in the following strophe (8), with *lifting* repeated as its parallel. The recipients of this benevolent action are explicitly mentioned: *the poor* and *the needy*. The first half of this strophe is almost identical to Psalm 113:7–8, except that the fourth line veers in a different direction.[37] Where the psalm re-

35. The verb occurs in only 14 verses and elsewhere refers to a context of total collapse. Cf. Isa 16:8; 24:4, 7; 33:9; Jer 14:2; 15:9; Lam 2:8; Ezek 16:30; Hos 4:3.

36. Fokkelman, *Vow and Desire*, 92: "The systematically sustained ellipsis of objects signifies that his activity is not bounded but universal, affecting everyone."

37. Psalm 113 is a psalm of praise. It also exhibits similarities to 1 Sam 2:1–10 by pointing out the incomparable qualities of God as one who regards

peats the seating next to nobles, Hannah's prayer mentions "a seat of honor" given as an "inheritance." The word "seat" in Hebrew is also used for "throne" and at this point steers the poem in the direction where it will end, hinting at the elevation of one person to kingship. A reference to the cosmic nature of Adonai's power closes this part of the recital. Fokkelman writes, "The throne upon which the poor has now been put cannot be shaken, for the writer shows where its legs rest: the broad basis of divine creation."[38]

The final strophe (9–10) begins with a general statement and gradually narrows down to one person, the king anointed by God. In the general statement, God's faithful ones are contrasted with the wicked (God's *hasidim* with the *resha'im*)—those who love Adonai, who are devoted to God's service, with those who perpetrate persecution and evil against the weak and needy. The guarding of the feet of God's faithful is a stereotypical image in the Psalms, where God pulls the believer's feet from the net (Ps 25:15), where her feet stand on level ground (Ps 26:12), where the believer praises God for setting his feet in an open space (Ps 31:9[8]), and where God makes the believer's feet as those of the deer (Ps 18:34[33]). God's faithful ones are those who stand in opposition to the wicked. Seemingly in a non sequitur, the subject moves to the *strength of the warrior*, the one whose bow is broken in pieces in verse 4. This time, Adonai will break the warrior's adversaries in pieces.[39] The struggle taking place on earth against the king is reflected in the cosmic response of God, who thunders and "judges the ends of the earth." This lofty image involving the world descends to the individual on whose behalf the display of God's might is taking place, "his king" // "his anointed."[40]

---

the depths and the heights (Ps 113:6). In addition, Ps 113:9 refers to God "establishing the barren woman of the house as a glad mother of children." Also see vv. 7–8: "Who raises from the dust the poor,/ lifts from the ash heap the needy/ to seat them with nobles,/ with the nobles of his people."

38. Fokkelman, *Vow and Desire*, 95.

39. I understand the lines of vv. 9c and 10a to be a pair in which Adonai's strength undoes the power of the adversaries of the "man" who is not a warrior by his own strength. It is God who does the fighting and gives the strength (10d).

40. "Anointed" (*meshiakh*) for Israel's kings is used especially in the

The *horn* of the king *lifted* by God together with Hannah's *horn lifted* in jubilation forms the frame around the prayer.

Fokkelman calls Hannah's song "a study in power," considering it a "poetic preparation" for the problems that lie ahead in the narratives of Samuel, which deal with the embodiment of might and power in the monarchy.[41] Extending this idea, we are still pondering the question raised at the end of Judges: If everyone does what is right in their eyes when there is no king, will the presence of a king guide the people in the right way and thereby guarantee harmony and well-being in the land?

Act I, Scene 5: A Family in Shiloh Redux (1 Samuel 2:11–26)

Where is Hannah?[42]

The focus in the rest of the chapter is on the Elide family in Shiloh, where Hofni and Pinhas are priests serving both God and people ill. A brief narrative description puts everyone in their location: Elkanah back in Ramah and the *boy* Samuel in service to Adonai under the eye of Eli, a notation that serves to set both priest and boy apart from the sons, who, referred to as "the sons of Eli" (they are not named in this chapter until v. 34), are immediately identified as "worthless men," scoundrels (*beney beliya'al*; cf. Judg 19:22; 20:13; 1 Sam 1:16; see p. 25 above). Throughout the description, Samuel will be put on the stage in contrast to them, the distinction becoming sharper each time (11, 17, 25). Off the bat, Samuel is said to "serve" Adonai, while the sons of Eli "did not know" Adonai.

The description of the priests' behavior is characterized as their "justice" (*mishpat*), here pointing to a practice, and clearly not a just

---

books of Samuel. In the Torah, it is used for the priest, and outside of Leviticus and Samuel it occurs ten times in the Psalms, with only a few attestations elsewhere in the Bible. The *horn,* a metaphor for strength, is also the instrument used for anointing (1 Sam 16:13).

41. Fokkelman, *Vow and Desire,* 105. Together with others, Fokkelman understands 1 Sam 2:1–10 as linked to the prayer of King David in 2 Sam 22.

42. Fokkelman, *Vow and Desire,* 111.

one. The misrule of the sons of Eli spreads like a pool around the sanctuary, also involving their servant, called "the priest's boy," and those bringing the sacrifice, who are forced not to leave for the Deity what is required but instead to leave it to the worthless priests. In ironic contrast to the offenses of the priests, a remarkable series of cooking utensils and implements pass by one's eyes in verses 13–14. Although we can't be entirely sure of their precise nature, there is something like a three-tined fork, a cauldron, a pot, a vat, and a kettle. Alter writes, "Eli's sons are represented in a kind of frenzy of gluttony poking their three-pronged forks into every imaginable sort of pot and pan."[43] The action is followed by a threatening exchange between servant and the one bringing the offering, refusing to burn the fat as offering to Adonai (see Lev 3:1–17, esp. v. 16). The priests thus deprive both God and people of what is theirs. The entire section is framed in references to the priests:

1 Samuel 2:12, 17

12 Now the sons of Eli were worthless men;
they did not know Adonai.
. . .
17 And the sin of the boys was very great before Adonai,
for the men treated with contempt the offering of Adonai.

Sons who have no knowledge of, no *intimate acquaintance* with, the Deity, called *boys* in the final comment in counterpoint to Samuel, are of course *men*—men who are contemptuous toward God and people, dealing with sacrifices as if they were treats especially reserved for themselves. The transgression is considered to be a major one, "very great," for they treat sacrifices with "contempt."[44] Samuel, in verse 18 called "a boy," was most likely the only one who

43. Alter, *The David Story*, 12n14.

44. The relatively rare verb "to treat with contempt," often translated as "spurn" or "scorn," occurs only once more in Samuel, in reference to David's crimes against Bathsheba and her husband (2 Sam 12:14). Elsewhere, it is almost always used for human behavior toward God.

really was a boy. He appears once more in his role of servant of God wearing clothing appropriate to the role of priest.

The narrative returns to focus on Samuel and his family (18–21). A brief description revisits Hannah and her care for Samuel. She brings him a small coat or mantle every year when "she went up with her husband." We hear no more words from Hannah, but she is in charge of three actions of care for her young son, and she is the implicit subject of making sacrifice (19). In his turn, Eli blesses her and prays for additional offspring for the couple "in the place of the requested one" Hannah "lent" to Adonai (20). The last information about Hannah is that she gave birth to five other children.

The coat for Samuel is called a *me'il*, a word used for priestly vestments in Exodus 28–39, together with the ephod. It was an outer garment, and in the Historical Books we find it only in Samuel, where it becomes a significant symbol of authority and an identifier of protagonists.[45] Again, the domesticity of the depiction contrasts with the untoward behavior of Eli's sons, which surely resulted in an atmosphere of uncertainty and fear among the worshipers at the sanctuary. I assume that Hannah paid more than one annual visit to Shiloh, since sizing a growing boy would be a necessity even for an outer cloak. In view of the uncertain circumstances at Shiloh, she likely kept a closer eye on Samuel than explicitly mentioned in the text, which as usual provides only the most economical detail. The description of Samuel and his family is enclosed in the phrases "Samuel served before Adonai" (18) and "the boy Samuel grew up with Adonai" (21). The verb used for growing up also means "to become great," so that more than one way of growing is here alluded to. The expression "with Adonai" expresses the closeness between young Samuel and God, in distinction to the distance between Eli's sons and the Deity. The statement will be reinforced in verse 26, where Samuel is said to continue to grow "in favor with Adonai and people."

45. Saul will tear a piece from Samuel's cloak in 15:27; Jonathan gives his cloak to David in 18:4; David in turn takes a piece from Saul's cloak to use as proof that he spared his life in 24:5[4]; Samuel is identifiable by his cloak when called up by the shaman of Endor in 28:14. It is a more specific piece of clothing, directly connected to status, than the more general *simlah*.

In the next unit, we hear directly from Eli as he reproaches his sons for their misbehavior (22–25). The repeated emphasis on Samuel's youth creates a stark contrast with the recurring mention of Eli's age, which strikes a negative note: Eli is "very old." Old age in periods when average life expectancy was extremely low could be seen as a blessing, but in the Historical Books it can also allude to weakness and infirmity of body and agency, as it will for Eli (3:2; 4:18) and eventually for Samuel (8:1).

Not violation of sacrifice but violation of women is what Eli hears about, "women who did duty at the entrance to the Tent of Meeting." What type of service the women performed and what brings about mention of the Tent of Meeting in this part of the story is not clear. Generally, biblical commentators assume that women were excluded from service at a sanctuary. Yet the verb used in connection with this group, *tsava'*, when not denoting military service, is found as an idiom for the Levites who qualified for certain tasks in the sanctuary work force (e.g., Num 4:3; 8:24).[46] It seems at least possible that at a stage before priestly roles and functions were strictly reserved for one gender, there was participation of women in some way in sanctuary activities. The phrase could then be a trace of an early period when women were perhaps in charge of a part of the sacred apparatus. That they were present at Shiloh in a professional capacity and were violated by the priests raises the question whether Hannah herself had been vulnerable to this type of abuse.[47] Sexual

46. Most standard translations render the verb *tsava* "assembled," while Alter (*The David Story*, 13) offers the reading "the women who flocked to the entrance," an interpretation that appears especially gender biased. The same bias comes to the surface in Koehler Baumgartner's lexicon with the observation that the Exodus 38:8 text "definitely concerns mundane work, keeping the entrance clean, and this could also be true for Samuel" (*HALOT*, 3:994). Fox (*The Early Prophets*, 289) more accurately translates "women who were acting as-a-workforce at the entrance" with a note that explains the occupation as "serving at various tasks."

47. For a discussion of the "women who did service at the entrance to the Tent of Meeting," see Carol Meyers, "Guilds and Gatherings: Women's Groups in Ancient Israel," in *Realia Dei: Essays in Honor of Edward Campbell Jr.*, ed. Prescott H. Williams Jr. and Theodore Hiebert (Atlanta: Scholars Press,

activity with women who had a type of service at the sanctuary also hints at the possibility that Eli's sons treated the women who were present in an official capacity as prostitutes, which raises the specter of sacred prostitution, an activity condemned in Deuteronomy 23:18[17]. In any case, the narrative has added sexual sin to that of theft, and the priests have thus transgressed against God and people in multiple ways. Eli reproaches his sons for their behavior in a speech filled with useless and rhetorical questions to which the sons pay no heed. They are as contemptuous of their father as they are of God and what belongs to God.

It is easy to condemn Eli's speech as weak and ineffective, but in his speech the text offers a glimpse into the often fraught parent-offspring relationship that plays a role in many Samuel narratives. Eli will not be the last father to be at his wits' end in dealing with unruly sons. He begins by asking *why* they do these things but immediately loses focus, resorting to language about his *hearing things*. Rather than accusing his sons of doing "wicked things," he refers to things he has *heard*, thereby leaving an opening for his offspring to deny all these evil reports: "Why do you do such things that I hear

1992), 154–84. The phrase about the women is lacking in the Septuagint and one of the Qumran scrolls, but it is more likely to have dropped out than to have been imported later. Perhaps the Tent of Meeting occurs here because the entire expression is a type of technical phrase by which women who did service at one of the sanctuaries were known. Their presence in this way in the text caused obvious anxiety in later rabbinical commentary. See Dalia Marx, "Women and Priests: Encounters and Dangers as Reflected in 1 Sam. 2:22," *Lectio Difficilior* 1 (2011). Others understand the women to be a type of military guard. See Wilda Gafney, *Daughters of Miriam: Women Prophets in Ancient Israel* (Minneapolis: Fortress, 2008), 155; and Robin Cohn, "Women at the Entrance to the Tent of Meeting," *Women of the Bible for Thinkers* (blog), March 9, 2010, http://www.robincohn.net/women-at-the-entrance-at-the-tent-of-meeting. The verb is indeed used mostly for military service, and the noun derived from it means "army." *Adonai Tseva'ot* is "Adonai of the Armies/Hosts." Rabbi Sylvia Rothschild ("Vayakel Pedudei: What Women Do and Why Women Are Rewarded as They Carry the Burden of Faith into the Future" [blog], March 21, 2017, https://rabbisylviarothschild.com/2017/03/21/vayakhel-pekudeiwhat-women-do-and-why-women-are-rewarded-as-they-carry-the-burden-of-faith-into-the-future/) also comments on this phrase.

about,/ these wicked things about you from all these people?" (23). One can almost see the astonished look on the faces of the accused and hear their "Well, Dad, you know how people talk!" Yet Eli ends with a serious enough threat, for his pointing to the impossibility of intercession on behalf of those who offend against God means also that he himself will not intercede on behalf of his sons. It comes as no surprise that the sons, who have no respect for God—or for men and women for that matter—do not listen to their father. The father has *heard* too much while the sons do not want to *hear* any of it.[48] The narrator connects their refusal to listen with God's intention to "kill them" (25). In direct counterpoint to Hofni and Pinhas, Samuel continues growing in favor with God and people. The waxing of Samuel and the waning of the house of Eli are closely connected.

Act I, Scene 6: The Rise of Samuel (1 Samuel 2:27–3:21)

Scene 6, Part 1: A Failing House (1 Samuel 2:27–36)

The divine demand for human decision is shown here at the height of its seriousness. . . . It is to this personal decision . . . with its part in the power of fate-deciding that the prophetic announcement of disaster calls.[49]

Details of family relations open up in what follows to a grand perspective on times past and future, houses falling and rising. At the same time, the focus is on a particular family/house, and the tempo of activity comes to a standstill at the moment of the long speech of 2:27–36. The speech is addressed to Eli rather than his sons, holding him entirely responsible for what has transpired. The matter concerns Eli and his *house.* Unlike Eli reproaching his sons, the "man of God" makes sharp and decisive points in addressing Eli, voicing accusations and announcing punishment in a series of rhetorical

48. The root *shama'* does duty for both the English "hear" and "listen"; it is hearing in the sense of heeding. It occurs four times in vv. 22–25.

49. Martin Buber, *The Prophetic Faith* (New York: Harper and Row, 1960), 104.

questions (27–29) concluded with the "therefore" clause of verse 30. God's promises were clear, and the transgressions, elaborating on the narrator's comment in verse 17, are equally clear: The priests "trample" on the sacrifices to God and fatten themselves on what people give to God (29).[50] God's commitments are reiterated following the conjunction "therefore," putting into stark relief the new promise to cut down the power of the house of Eli.

1 Samuel 2:30–31

30 Therefore—oracle of Adonai, the God of hosts:
I certainly said that your house
and the house of your father
would walk before me for good.
And now, oracle of Adonai: Far be it from me!
For those who honor me I will honor,
and those who despise me will be of no account.
31 See, the days are coming
that I will cut off your strength
and the strength of your father's house
so no one will be old in your house.

The speech is so filled with invective and threat that it is difficult to absorb.[51] Its threatening and cruel tone may have rendered it problematic in the tradition and caused the extreme difficulty of the Hebrew. Some things are clear: To the earlier charge of treating sacrifice with *contempt* and *trampling* it underfoot (2:17, 29) the charge of despising God is added.[52] In addition, the pun-

50. The verb "trample" occurs in only one other place and means "to kick against" (cf. Deut 32:15). In both texts, it is used as a metaphor for treating with disdain.

51. Literally, the lines in v. 31 read, "I will cut off your arm and the arm of your father's house." The word "arm" is often used in the Hebrew Bible as a metaphor for strength. Yet we miss the ferocity of the expression somehow when the word "strength" is substituted.

52. The expression "despised me" with the root *bazah* ("to despise") occurs a few times in Samuel from one human to another but is notably

ishment will include a gradual diminishment, almost like torture: No one will become old (here considered to be a blessing!), not everyone will be cut off, Eli's house will survive in a weakened state, and, just to bring the point home, as a sign that the beginning of the end is imminent, Eli's two sons will die on one day. In the meantime, God will make sure there will be another who will become a "true" priest, a new house, and Eli's house will bow and beg before him (36).

The speech is cast in terms of prophecy, proclaimed by "a man of God," in the Historical Books a term reserved especially for those who function as prophets.[53] Moreover, it begins with the words "oracle of Adonai" (*ne'um* [*'adonai*]), which is stereotypical phrasing for prophetic speech in the Bible. The speech is rendered in the first person singular, as if God were directly addressing Eli, which makes its tone and content all the more difficult to absorb. Sarcasm and threatening speech are not alien, however, to prophetic utterance. Following Martin Buber's understanding of the nature and function of prophecy in ancient Israel, we should not understand the prophets to announce immutable decrees. Rather, the prophets intended to face their hearers with a choice, and their words should be interpreted as directed to an actual, specific situation. "God does not deliver into their hand a completed book of fate with all future events written in it. . . . They spoke into the power of decision that resided in the moment, and in such a way that the message of disaster touches this power." Buber understands the "primal theological principle" about the divine-human relationship formulated in the creation stories in Genesis as illustrative of the belief that created humanity has been granted the real power of decision and also the ability to oppose God's will. This facet of the human will comes into full force when faced with prophetic speech.[54] The choice of repentance in the sense of a turning away from the condemned practice and making a radical turn toward God with all this entails is thus

used again for David *despising* God in the aftermath of his crimes against the Bathsheba-Uriah family in 2 Sam 12:9, 10.

53. Samuel, in his role as prophet, will be so identified in 1 Sam 9:6, 8, 10.

54. Buber, *The Prophetic Faith*, 103–4.

always before the audience.[55] Of such a turn we hear nothing from Eli or from his sons. We will meet only passivity on the one hand and more untoward behavior on the other in the future.

Scene 6, Part 2: A Revelation in the Sanctuary (1 Samuel 3)

Samuel . . . finally appears in chapter 3, entering the scene as a boy (v. 1) and exiting a prophet (v. 20).[56]

From the fall and the rise of a priestly house and the roar of prophetic speech, the text moves to the intimate space of sleeping quarters in the sanctuary. Two verses tersely paint the scene (1–2). Everyone is in their place, both Eli and Samuel lying down for the night. An introductory sentence announces that Samuel is still in service to God under the supervision of Eli, while the divine word is "rare," literally "precious," in those days and visions have not "broken through." To break through connotes violence, overcoming obstacles, leaving the impression that the misdeeds taking place in the holy precincts form a blockade against God. Linking the statement to the immediately preceding prophetic speech against Eli, we surmise that an occasion such as the recorded prophecy was rare and that what is to happen to Samuel is equally special, elevating him to his role of divine representative. Logically, then, the chapter ends with the affirmation that "Samuel was a true prophet of Adonai" (20), God's revelation through the word having come directly to Samuel in direct counterpoint to the opening of the chapter (21).

55. The model for this interpretation of prophetic speech in the Bible is, of course, Jonah, who serves for Buber (*The Prophetic Faith,* 104) as *the* parable to illustrate the point of announcements of disaster calling people to the moment of decision. The Ninevites are able to accomplish a true "turning," upon which God "turns." Both turnings are away from violence. Buber is careful not to understand these two as automatic, as if human repentance would automatically bring about God's repenting of punishment, but one must step into the possibility of the "who knows" of those of Nineveh in Jonah 3:9.

56. Polzin, *Samuel and the Deuteronomist,* 49.

We also learn in the first unit that Eli is virtually blind, that there is still light from the "lamp of God," and that the Ark of the Covenant is in the sanctuary. There are darkness and light: no vision from God and blindness on the part of the human being in charge, but the lamp of God shines where the boy Samuel is in service to Adonai. The abrupt appearance of the Ark, last encountered in Judges in Bethel (Judg 20:27) and before that in Joshua at the ceremony between Ebal and Gerizim (Josh 8:33) is startling but needed for what will follow in the next chapter. It is of course *the* symbol of the presence of God.[57]

The middle section of the episode shows the most activity, with God calling to Samuel and Samuel consistently running to Eli in a fog of misunderstanding, probably because he is used to tending to his master in the night (4–10). Not only Samuel but also Eli is slow to pick up on what is really happening. Samuel does not yet have the knowledge (7), and Eli's literal blindness may be a metaphor for his lack of insight. The third time, Eli understands and instructs Samuel how to respond if the call comes again. "Then came Adonai and stood/ and called as at other times:/ Samuel, Samuel!" (10). Once Samuel provides the satisfactory response, he gets an earful. The expression that God "stood" is unique and makes clear in how high an estimation Samuel is held by the Deity, affirmed at chapter's end with the assurance that God is with Samuel and that not a word from him is without its results (19).

Samuel receives a shortened version of the prophetic announcement from the previous chapter, and one wonders why such a clear and severe speech needed repeating. On this second occasion, however, the destruction of Eli's house appears to have come closer, as if another decision has been made about Eli. While there may have been an opening for repentance earlier it is now too late for any atonement (14). The immediacy of the matter about to happen

57. In Joshua, it may have been located in Shechem, the location of Joshua's solemn assembly in chapter 24. The Ark was portable, and the towns of Bethel, Shechem, and Shiloh are not so far apart in the hill country of Ephraim that it could not have moved from one place to another, especially in turbulent times.

is made clear by the announcement "Look, I am doing a thing in Israel" (11) followed by the unusual phrase that it will cause ears to ring.[58] This time, it is also clear that the cause of God's wrath is Eli's unwillingness or inability to restrain his sons. Second, the emphasis in this episode is on Samuel, his trustworthiness, and his standing with God, reaffirmed at the close of the chapter. Samuel is already stepping into the shoes of the one who delivers a prophetic word, taking the place of the "man of God" in the earlier episode. He is also stepping into Eli's role as the one to receive direct divine communication and guidance.

Samuel reveals to Eli what God told him only after being pressed by Eli not to *hide* anything. The verb "to hide," mentioned three times in two verses, carries the uncomfortable echo of destruction and effacement.[59] Eli does not protest, and his reply to Samuel conveys resignation to God's intentions. While one house is sinking, another rises, and the words of Hannah's song regarding the reversals God brings about have turned out to herald future events (2:6–9). The final verses emphatically make clear young Samuel's status in the eyes of God and people (19–21). While the main action of the chapter takes place in one night, bringing the reader no further than the next morning, the closing comments cast the tempo forward into the future, ending with Samuel as a grown man.

1 Samuel 3:19–21

19 So Samuel grew up, and Adonai was with him
and let not fall any of his words to the ground.
20 And all Israel knew from Dan to Beersheba
that Samuel was a true prophet of Adonai.
21 And God continued to be seen at Shiloh,[60]

58. A phrase announcing God doing a thing occurs in Exodus as an announcement of one of the plagues (Exod 9:5, 6) and will later come to David when God announces to David that while he acted in secret, God will "do this thing before all Israel" (2 Sam 12:12).

59. See Exod 9:15; 23:23; 1 Kgs 13:34; Job 4:7; Ps 83:5[4].

60. I maintain the root "to see" in the expression, usually translated

for Adonai was revealed to Samuel
at Shiloh through God's word.

"The scarcity of God's word, the dimness of sight, and the barriers to a break-through on God's part have been lifted by the end of the chapter."[61]

Act I, Scene 7: Descent into Loss (1 Samuel 4)[62]

The emphasis on sound without sight coincides with the complete lack of insight, indeed the utter confusion, that surrounds both camps.[63]

Chapter 4 divides neatly into halves: a first section with activities on the battlefield at Eben-Ezer/Aphek (1–11) and a second with events in Shiloh (12–22). In the first half, we meet the massed armies of Israelites and Philistines. Among the Israelites, unnamed leaders are spokespeople who convince the army to bring the Ark into the battle. At the end, Israel is roundly defeated for the second time, and the Ark is captured by the Philistines. The sons of Eli who accompany the Ark are the only named characters in the episode and die in the course of the engagement. The second half concentrates on the reception of the bad news in Shiloh, first by the townsfolk and then by Eli and his daughter-in-law. Both Eli and his daughter-in-law die upon hearing the news of the death of sons and husband and the capture of the Ark, the daughter-in-law after giving birth to a son. The pace of the narrative alternates, with battle scenes described in the usual snapshot fashion, slowing down for speech and closeup views of elements the narrator considers important. In the second half, the tempo slows down to a considerable degree in counterpoint

"appeared," as it underlines the importance of sight and its meaning in this passage.

61. Van Wijk-Bos, *Reading Samuel*, 44.

62. Walter Brueggemann, *Ichabod toward Home: The Journey of God's Glory* (Grand Rapids: Eerdmans, 2002), 2: "The first sweeping move of this narrative in 1 Samuel 4 is Israel's *descent into loss*."

63. Polzin, *Samuel and the Deuteronomist*, 58.

to the runner who brings the news to Shiloh, zooming in first on Eli and his interchange with the messenger and then on the wife of Pinhas in her birthing pains.

Scene 7, Part 1: Death on the Battlefield (1 Samuel 4:1–11)

Deep into loss.[64]

An opening sentence continues with the same focus that ends the previous chapter, on Samuel, whose word is "to all Israel."[65] In view of this announcement, Samuel's absence from the proceedings both on the battlefield and inside Shiloh is conspicuous. The lacuna raises the issue of things going wrong on the battlefield *because* Samuel's counsel has not been requested or heeded.[66] Samuel will prove himself in another episode not to be alien to the battlefield, stepping into his role as judge (7:3–17). For the moment, he disappears from the story, which concentrates on matters pertaining to the Ark following the introduction of its location in chapter 3. After the events in the first chapters that took place in one specific place, the sanctuary in Shiloh, with a small cast of characters, the scene opens up unexpectedly to a wider scope, the plain west of Shiloh, and on armies in battle formation with a large number of mostly unnamed participants.

64. Brueggemann, *Ichabod toward Home*, 2.

65. It is possible to consider the first phrase of chapter 4 as the final clause of the preceding chapter, with its focus on Samuel, as I do in my commentary on Samuel (van Wijk-Bos, *Reading Samuel*, 47). Taking it as the opening phrase of chapter 4 sets the sequel in a more stark light in view of Samuel's absence from the story.

66. Such is the argument pursued by Frank Spina in his article "A Prophet's 'Pregnant Pause': Samuel's Silence in the Ark Narrative (1 Sam 4:1–7:2)," in *HBT* 13 (1991): 55–73. Spina argues that 1 Samuel 4:1 can be read as a temporal clause: "When Samuel's word came to all Israel, Israel went forth to battle," putting into stark relief the wayward actions of the Israelites. The truncated phrase indicates that "Israel's precipitous action had the effect of making the prophetic voice *pause*" (66).

The first two verses function as an introductory unit, setting everyone on the scene in their place, Israelites at Eben-Ezer and Philistines at Aphek. We are aware that the Philistines are still very present in Canaan, as Samson had only made a beginning of putting an end to the problems caused by this people (Judg 13:5). While occasionally Israel engages in military conflict with enemies outside the land in 1 Samuel, the Philistines will take up the space of an ever-present hostile and aggressive near- neighbor, the uncircumcised over against whom Israel identifies itself and with whom it is involved in continuous fighting until the time of King David. They have the upper hand in terms of technology, possessing iron tools and weaponry as well as chariots for warfare, and they are said to prevent Israel from having access to this more advanced material (1 Sam 13:19–22).[67] A discussion of some sort of peace process never arises; apparently, the idea of peaceful coexistence in the same territory was not a part of the conceptual framework of the time.

In chapter 4, it looks as if the Israelites have taken the initiative: "They went out to meet the Philistines in battle" (1). The Philistines respond, and almost in the next breath, Israel is struck a devastating blow, resulting in a great number of dead.[68] Information about battle tactics or leadership is lacking, but it becomes clear that the defeat is not decisive, because the troops stay in place and prepare to fight another day. Only the first round has been unsuccessful.

The leaders, indicated with the general title "elders," wonder why God let this happen. They hold God personally responsible for the defeat and decide that things will go otherwise if they have the Ark with them.

67. Alter (*The David Story*, 21n1b) suggests that the reasons for their eventual demise may have been related to the loss of the strategic advantage of chariots as they went up into the high country. It is difficult to conceive of armies taking chariots into the hills, however. It is clear from the accounts that there was a lack of central administration among them, each city having its own chief or king. The lack of strong cohesive leadership could have contributed to their eventual defeat.

68. The number 4000, as the later 30,000 (4:10) is most likely an exaggeration, a stereotypical phenomenon in conquest accounts.

1 SAMUEL 4:3

The people came to the camp,
and the elders of Israel said:
Why has Adonai struck us today before the Philistines?
Let us take for ourselves from Shiloh
the Ark of the Covenant of Adonai;
when it comes into our midst
it will save us from the hand of our enemies.

The idea is not so far-fetched. Had the Ark not accompanied the Israelite armies entering Canaan? Had it not been the sign of God's presence at the miraculous crossing of the Jordan and the collapse of Jericho? What worked then will surely work again! The Ark, after all, symbolizes the presence of Adonai, and it will be as if God in person is in the midst of the army to deliver it.[69] But in the conquest stories, the initiative for the presence of the Ark came from Adonai, and no one thought of *taking* it, let alone having some corrupt priests in charge of this most holy of objects. But that is exactly what happens. When the Ark of the Covenant of Adonai of Armies is brought from Shiloh, Hofni and Pinhas are the only individuals singled out by name in this part of the story. They are "with the Ark of the Covenant of God" (4). Great rejoicing in the Israelite camp is the result.

A swift turn in perspective gives a close-up of the Philistine camp and its reaction to the jubilant cries of Israel. First shown cowering in fear, crying "woe," and sounding helpless, eventually they brace themselves and "man up" to fight (9). We will hear more from these Philistines who are so informed about the Deity of Israel that they know this is the God who struck Egypt a devastating blow (8). They refer to the Israelites as "Hebrews," a designation with possible negative connotations that we find in the Bible a relatively small number of times as a label by hostile outsiders or as a self-deprecating term used by Israel for itself when in a position of

69. The final phrasing of v. 3 can also be translated "when he comes into our midst/ he will save us," making God rather than the Ark the subject of the verbs, as the NRSV does.

inferiority (see 13:3, 7, 19; 14:11; 29:3). The verbal root that echoes in this name is that of *crossing*, or *transgressing*; these are the "illegals" of the period. In 1 Samuel, one hears this name especially from the Philistines, who in their turn are called "uncircumcised," or literally and more graphically "foreskins" (see 14:6; 17:36; 31:4; 2 Sam 1:20). They engage in battle once again, and this time the Israelites suffer a decisive defeat (10–11). The short report packs seven verbs into two phrases: "the Philistines *fought*./ Israel *was struck down*;/ they *fled* . . ./ There *was a great defeat*,/ *fell* . . . *taken*/ . . . *died*." The defeat of Israel is accompanied by the Ark being *taken* (11). This last *taking* is thus the result of the *taking* of the Ark from its place without consultation of or approach to the God whose presence and power it represents. Hofni and Pinhas die, as foretold by the man of God in chapter 2, and their names close this part of the story of loss.

Scene 7, Part 2: Death at Home (1 Samuel 4:12–22)

Clear to the bottom of loss.[70]

All is hushed at Shiloh.[71]

News reaches Shiloh, roughly twenty miles to the east, brought by a Benjaminite covering the distance in one day. He first announces the defeat to the town, which bursts into lamentation, heard by Eli who is "sitting beside the road." The story allows a glimpse into Eli's state of mind so that we know he is afraid and the source of his fear. Evidently, Eli is deeply afraid, "his heart trembled," not because his two sons have gone to the battlefield but "on account of the Ark of God" (13). It is clear that Eli is cognizant of the whereabouts of the Ark, and we are left to wonder whether he protested when his sons came and helped carry it to war or whether he stood idly by. We already know Eli is old (2:22) and that his eyesight is poor (3:2).

70. Brueggemann, *Ichabod toward Home*, 2.

71. Herman Melville, "Shiloh: A Requiem" (1862). In this poem, the reference is to the US Civil War battlefield in Tennessee.

At the time of the defeat, we hear that he is 98 years old and that he is now totally blind.[72] The narrator does not reveal how many years have passed, but if we view the text from the vantage point of Samuel as grown up and in full possession of his powers (3:19–21), perhaps a decade has passed since he received his revelation in the sanctuary when he was young, and there has been no improvement in the situation at the sanctuary.

Clearly, Eli is sitting where he is—as it turns out, beside the city gate (18)—to be the first to hear what happened, but the runner has passed him by, perhaps in too much of a hurry to notice the old man on the side of the road. In an echo of the Philistines' questioning the noise in the Israelite camp, Eli asks what the uproar is all about, probably sending someone to inquire, for in the next breath the messenger is at Eli's side. When asked about the news, the runner responds with a repetition of the necessary elements of verses 10–11, so that the fleeing, the great defeat, and the death of Hofni and Pinhas are all mentioned, ending with the taking of the Ark. Upon hearing the word Ark, perhaps even before he gets news of its *taking* (see v. 19: "as he mentioned the Ark"), Eli falls from his seat and dies. To everything that we know about him, the narrator adds that "he was heavy." In Hebrew, the root for heavy connects to the word for glory/honor (*kaved/kavod*), a word that has already played a part in Hannah's song (2:8) and in the words of the prophecy to Eli (2:30), in which Eli received judgment on account of giving more *kavod* to his sons than to God. Alter writes, "the leader who might be supposed to represent Israel's glory exhibits only deadly heaviness."[73] He also apparently served as Israel's judge, a note appended to his death announcement. In this respect, too, Eli may have been lacking; little noticeable leadership has been evident on his part.

72. The expression in Hebrew in v. 15 is that "his eyes were set [lit. stood], he could not see." The condition sounds like cataracts of some sort, or perhaps glaucoma. The word for cataracts in some languages, such as Dutch (*staar*), is related to a root indicating immobility of the eye.

73. Alter, *The David Story,* 25–26n21. The note that he served as Israel's judge appended to the death announcement comes somewhat as a surprise.

The Ark is taken, multitudes of Israel are dead, Hofni, Pinhas and Eli are dead, and the story of loss is not yet finished. A shift in perspective takes us among Eli's family and to the birth of a grandchild (19–22). The pregnant wife of Pinhas also hears the news and gives premature birth. Once again, verbs follow one another in a tight knot ("she heard . . . she collapsed . . . she gave birth . . . she lay dying"), putting birth and death in close proximity. Ignoring the encouragement of her attendants with the news of a son, she speaks words to name her son: Ichavod, a name also connected to glory. Perhaps it means "no glory" or "where is glory?" It also connotes woe, which resounds in the naming.[74] Three times, her dying words echo with the word "glory": "no glory," "exiled is the glory," and once again "exiled is the glory from Israel." The verb usually translated "departed" should read "exiled," for these words spoken by a heretofore invisible and unnamed woman sound loudly into the future of Israel. Those who told the story centuries later were, after all, writing from the experience of exile and the loss of the Ark of the Covenant, destroyed during the destruction of Jerusalem and the burning of the Temple in the second decade of the sixth century (2 Kgs 25:8–18). So far in these chapters, the stature and renown of Samuel has not sufficed to quell the troubles of the Israelites besetting them from both inside and outside. Brueggemann calls the account with Eli's daughter-in-law as its focus "truth-telling all the way down" and asserts that one "may take heart and substance from this ancient account" in which it is said five times, "the Ark of God has been captured." The truth-telling also involves telling truth about its leadership and facing the reality that unjust practices among the leadership bring disaster to the people.

74. Alter (*The David Story*, 25n21) considers this sort of name, "inscribing the national catastrophe in her son's name," to be "most peculiar." There are other examples of this in the Bible, however, and it may be less unusual than one assumes (cf. Isa 8:3; Hos 1:6, 9; 2:25[23]). In more recent history, the renowned seventeenth-century Dutch poet Tesselschade (lit. "damage at Tessel") was so named by her father because one of his ships was wrecked at the island of Tessel three months before her birth in 1593.

Shiloh, so much at the center of these early chapters, departs with the taking of the Ark. We hear no more of it in Samuel, although there is also no mention of its destruction by the Philistines. Most likely, with the disappearance of the Ark and its major priestly staff, corrupt as it may have been, the Shiloh sanctuary fell into disuse and the city virtually disappeared from the map. Many years later, the prophet Jeremiah will prophesy that the temple in Jerusalem will be a ruin, the same fate as that once met by Shiloh (Jer 7:12, 14; 26:6, 9). The silence of death hangs over biblical Shiloh as it did over the nineteenth-century battlefield in the United States in Herman Melville's poem. Samuel, "the requested one," born at the beginning of the story, has his counterpart in the prematurely born baby "No Glory."

Act II: Who Can Stand before This Holy God? (1 Samuel 5:1–7:1)

This is a story that holds together seriousness and comedy. It is black (death) comedy.[75]

The ark is the property of nobody but God.[76]

Two chapters (5–6) center on the captured Ark and its adventures in Philistine cities; the Ark constitutes the main agent in what follows, surrounded by a crowd of nameless Philistines. What seemed to be a glorious victory for the Philistines turns into a tale of disaster and death when their trophy sows destruction wherever they take it. The result of their capture of Israel's most holy object is a detailed deliberation not so much about the question of its return to Israel but about *how* they will return it. The consultation results in the careful construction of objects to bring with the Ark to a town on the edge of the hill country, Beth-Shemesh. Once it arrives there, the unrest created by the presence of the Ark is not finished,

75. John Goldingay, *Men Behaving Badly* (Exeter, UK: Paternoster, 2000), 44.

76. Fokkelman, *Vow and Desire*, 249.

and, as if unable to stop its path of destruction, it kills inhabitants of Beth-Shemesh. Echoing the actions of the Philistines, the Israelites invite Kiryat Ye'arim, another city located deeper in the hills, to provide a place for the Ark, and there it finds a resting place for the time being.

Satirical touches pervade the story: Philistines, who are unable to take advantage of their military victory, succumbing to a box made of acacia wood, their god dismembered in its own sanctuary, in their panic sending the Ark from city to city, and finally returning it to its people with a great panoply of objects and a parade of officials. The Ark is not a safe object to have around either for the outsider or the insider in this story, and the negative consequence of the notion that Israel's God could be manipulated into delivering rescue becomes abundantly clear. Too close a proximity to the Ark is dangerous, even life-threatening.

The narrative takes us inside Philistine territory, where we witness Philistine action and reaction in an unusual extensive shift in perspective. We will encounter this shift again in 1 Samuel, a book permeated by Philistine presence, but never quite to this degree. The narration leaves the Israelites ignorant of the havoc the Ark creates among the Philistines. One imagines that the Israelite side has its hands full with the aftermath of the defeat at Eben-Ezer and the deaths of its leadership. At the end of the story, the blow dealt by the Ark to the population of Beth-Shemesh leaves an opening for still more lessons to be learned about what it means to be God's covenant people.

What Is the Ark?

In secular use, the word *aron* means a chest or box (see Gen 50:26; 2 Kgs 12:10, 11). In a sacred context, it is usually translated with the word "Ark," and various religious ideas are attached to it. In the usage of the Priestly writers, it is a box that contains the testimonies, or the two tablets with the Ten Words of the Covenant. The Ark is then called the Ark of the Testimony (Exodus) or the Ark of the Covenant (of Adonai). In another tradition, the

Ark functions as "a symbol of divine leadership to the Israelites departing from Sinai," specifically as a representation of God's military leadership (Josh 3–4; 6; see van Wijk-Bos, *The End of the Beginning,* 73–82, 93–97).[77] The Ark can also be viewed as a pedestal or footstool for the Deity, from which God rises to aid the people in battle (Num 10:35). All these traditions cling to the Ark in 1 Samuel 4, in which it receives a great variety of names.[78] As it was at times in the Joshua texts (Josh 3–4, esp. 4:13), in Samuel, the Ark is a representation or a manifestation of the presence of Israel's God (see p. 48). Because it was moveable, it is embedded in a tradition that emphasizes the transitory character of God's presence, according to Samuel Terrien pointing to "an intermittent and elusive presence of the Godhead."[79]

For an aniconic religious tradition like that of biblical Israel, divine representational value attached to any physical object can be viewed as problematic. These chapters in Samuel testify to these problems: The Israelites are wrong in assuming that the Ark's presence will automatically bring them God's help in battle; the Philistines are wrong, too, in assuming that there is no divine power attached to the Ark when they win the day and defeat Israel. Brueggemann asserts that the story of the Ark in 1 Samuel 4–6 is told to truthfully reflect the capture of the Ark and thereby the capture of Israel's God and also to teach about things happening that are unseen and unheard by Israel, changing the situation of despair. They told the story just like this because "there is no room for complacency, even when coming home; this home-coming, home-bringing God remains dangerous and beyond grasp."[80]

77. Hans Jürgen Zobel, "אָרוֹן," in *Theological Dictionary of the Old Testament,* ed. G. Johannes Botterweck and Helmer Ringgren (Grand Rapids: Eerdmans, 1974), 370.

78. In 1 Sam 4, the Ark is identified as the Ark of the Covenant of Adonai, the Ark of Adonai, and the Ark of God; in 1 Sam 5, the Ark is called the Ark of God, the Ark of Adonai, and the Ark of the God of Israel.

79. Samuel Terrien, *The Elusive Presence: Toward a New Biblical Theology* (New York: Harper & Row, 1978), 186.

80. Brueggemann, *Ichabod toward Home,* 107.

Act II, Scene 1: The Ark in Exile (1 Samuel 5)

The victors are being deceived once again. A Trojan horse situation arises and they rapidly discover that by bringing in the ark they have brought catastrophe upon themselves.[81]

A short chapter deals with the adventures of the Ark in Philistine territory and the problems it causes there. There are four units (1–5, 6–8, 9–10, 11–12), beginning with emphatic repetition of activity with the Ark as object. *The Philistines took . . . and brought it* (2×) . . . *placed it* (1–2), and finish by sending it *around* (8–10). All the commotion ends with a "cry" that "rose to heaven" (12). The units are filled with references to the "heavy hand" of God—using the word related to *glory* (see pp. 55–57 above) to great effect—devastating the cities' inhabitants and sowing panic.

First, the Ark is brought to Ashdod, about thirty miles south and a bit east of Eben-Ezer, avoiding the hill country and nearness to Israelite regions. The first lines show clever sound rhymes, noticeable even in translation with its repetition of the *a-o* sounds: "Ark of God," "to Ashdod," "Ark of God," "Dagon," "Dagon" (1–2). Once the Ark is placed next to Dagon, everyone goes home. They "rise early the next day," and Dagon has fallen face down before the Ark. With a deft touch, the narrator makes the audience look into the sanctuary together with the Philistines with the repeated "and look!" (3, 4). This time, the Ark is called "the Ark of Adonai," evoking the presence of Israel's God (3). Dagon was the fertility and grain deity of the Philistines, who features also in Judges at the end of the Samson story (Judg 16:23–25). It is worth noting that the narrative does not speak of an *image* of Dagon but of the god himself, so that the resulting expression is "Dagon was fallen" (3, 4), and reference can be made to *his head and both his hands*, reinforcing divine identification with the image and at the same time its humiliation before the Ark of the God of Israel. The hands probably lay near or on the threshold, because it is the threshold the priests of Dagon henceforth avoid stepping

81. Fokkelman, *Vow and Desire*, 248.

on.[82] These cut-off *hands* of the powerless Dagon also highlight the power of the *heavy hand of Adonai* that *weighs* upon Ashdod and later on Gath and Ekron (9, 11).

The narrator skips over the possible restoration of Dagon to his rightful image and place to recount in the second unit (6–8) how God with "heavy hand" strikes the people of Ashdod with tumors.[83] The Ashdodites gather all the chieftains of the five cities to ponder the question "what shall we do with the Ark of the God of Israel?" The name of the Ark has changed to include Israel, raising the possibility that the devastating item may have to go back to where it came from. Not yet ready to take this radical and humiliating step, they send it on instead to the next city, Gath, a bit closer to Israelite territory. Gath too suffers from the *hand* of God, which strikes them with the same disease suffered in Ashdod, so they send the Ark on once more, this time to Ekron, where the people cry out that the Ark has come around to kill them.

1 Samuel 5:10

And they sent the Ark of God to Ekron,
and when the Ark of God came to Ekron,
the Ekronites cried out:
They brought round to me the Ark of the God of Israel
to kill me and my people!

Cries have gone up several times already: a shout of jubilation at the arrival of the Ark in the camp (4:5), the Philistines' cry of "woe" on hearing about the proximity of the Ark (4:7), and the inhabitants of Shiloh's cry of grief after the defeat of Israel (4:13). Once again, it is

82. Fokkelman, *Vow and Desire*, 254, 256.

83. It is unclear whether the affliction consists of tumors or hemorrhoids (so Qere), but if we go with tumors, it may indicate an early outbreak of bubonic plague. Opinions go back and forth on this possibility. Even though we are not to take the narrative literally, epidemic disease would have been common enough, and if this was an infectious disease, the tale of something like plague wreaking havoc in Philistine cities in Israel's early days could handily be connected with another story dealing with a temporary stay of the Ark among them.

the Philistines' turn to "cry out," this time in distress and grief, using a verbal root that connotes a cry for help like the one used by the town of Shiloh. The *striking* they had feared on the eve of battle is only now brought home to them (4:8; cf. 5:6, 9, 12). Where earlier they were able to take courage and defeat the visible enemy, there is at this point only the invisible hand of God at work. The use of the first person in the lament of verses 10–11 ("kill me," "my people") zooms in on the personal level of the disaster.

Once again, the city chieftains gather, this time for the clearly stated purpose to "send the Ark of the God of Israel away." The question of what they should do with the Ark has received an answer. Sending it around to different cities has not worked, and the only solution is to send it back to "its place" (11). The unit ends with a repetition of the cry of those in Ekron. All the *taking, sending, bringing, placing,* and *sending round* has come to the inevitable *sending away.*

Act II, Scene 2: The Ark Returns Home (1 Samuel 6:1–7:1)

The whole point is that everybody has to keep their hands to themselves.[84]

Chapter 6 opens with the statement that the Ark was in Philistine country for seven months, a recap of the entire time the Ark spent in different cities, the days it took to transport it, the deliberations, and the execution of the plan. All of it must have taken up a serious amount of time with the construction of a cart and the fashioning of objects to be put next to the Ark. The first sequence (6:1–12) paints a picture of careful consultation on the part of the cities' leaders with the appropriate staff, priests, and diviners, until all is prepared and they walk behind the cart on the way to Beth-Shemesh.[85] Unlike the Israelites, who acted hastily under corrupt religious guidance in bringing the Ark to the battlefield in the charge of Hofni and Pinhas,

84. Fokkelman, *Vow and Desire,* 249.

85. Beth-Shemesh is a good choice in terms of distance and territory, located as it is about 8–10 miles away on the edge of the hill country, deeper into which transporting a cart would have been impossible.

the Philistines act with deliberation and care. Once it has become clear that hanging on to their religious trophy is untenable, they consult their religious experts as to what to do with the Ark of the God of Israel (6:2). They could, after all, have tried to destroy the Ark, sent it back without ceremony, cast it into the sea, or engaged in various other destructive options. Instead, a ritual return is designed, with symbols of their disease and perhaps the creatures that are thought to have caused it on a specially constructed cart. The diviners and priests preach a little sermon, admonishing the Philistine leaders to "give the God of Israel glory," with the word *glory/heaviness* once again coming into play.[86] They warn about the uselessness of "hardening their hearts" as the Egyptians once did, referring to episodes at the time of the Israelites' liberation from Egypt and to what the God of Israel did at that time, making a fool of Pharaoh.

The touch of using cows that leave their young behind and yet go straight on the road to Beth-Shemesh is particularly striking, especially since the text uses the word "children" (*beneyhem*) for the calves. Parents and their young have been central to much of the narrative, together with sacrifice. These mother cows, guided by the hand of Adonai no doubt, go straight to the Israelite town, sacrificing their instinct to return to their young and ultimately become themselves the sacrifice.

1 Samuel 6:10–12

10 And the men did so.
They took two milch cows
and tied them to a cart,
and their young they restrained at home.
11 And they put the Ark of God on the cart
with the chest with gold mice
and the images of their tumors.

86. A good deal of the word-play in vv. 5–6 is difficult to render into the translation, with the Hebrew making frequent use of the root *kavad* ("to be heavy") also in the reference to the hardening of the heart, of which the opposite is "lighten," along with the mention of God "lightening" his hand.

12 Straight off the cows went
on the road to Beth-Shemesh;
on one lane they went and went lowing.
They veered neither right nor left,
with the kings of the Philistines behind them
until the border of Beth-Shemesh.

The emphasis on the bellowing of the poor cows as they leave their young behind drives home the point that they go "straight on" against their nature. Alter writes, "They mark with maternal lowing their distress over a journey they cannot resist."[87] All in all, the idea of using the cows as proof that it was indeed Israel's God, symbolized by the representation of the Ark, who caused devastation among them, testifies to Philistine ingenuity and respect for this foreign Deity.

The perspective shifts in the second half of the scene (6:13–7:1) to the Israelites in Beth-Shemesh, who "lifted their eyes and saw the Ark" (6:13). Rejoicing is the reaction of those in the town at the edge of Israelite territory and the hill country. The Levites lower the Ark, and the wood of the cart together with the cows is offered up as a sacrifice to God. Three times the narration mentions sacrifice (6:14–15), emphasizing its importance. Besides the Levites, there is no reference to priestly activity, and in verse 14, the inhabitants, "the men of Beth-Shemesh," are in charge of bringing the offering. The Ark is deposited on "a great stone," an object with threefold mention in this section. Stones were natural places either for sacrifice or as a sacred witness and therefore a natural place for the Ark.[88] It is likely that an aura of sanctity clung to the stone that remains "to this day" in the field of Joshua of Beth-Shemesh, even after the departure of the Ark (6:18).

Every city and village of the Philistines is represented in the offering; sacrifices have been made, and the Ark is set in an appro-

87. Alter, *The David Story*, 32n12.

88. For a stone as a votive object, see Gen 28:22; 31:45; 35:14; Exod 20:25; Josh 8:31, 32; 24:26, 27. For a stone as a sacred witness, see Gen 31:46; Josh 4:3, 5–9, 20–21. In Gen 49:24, God is named the *Even Yisrael*, the Stone of Israel.

priate place; everything should be alright again; except it is not. The destructive rampage caused by the Ark's presence is not over, and the inhabitants of Beth-Shemesh ("House of the Sun") are *struck down* by the hand of God as the Philistines were struck. *Striking* is repeated three times in one sentence (6:19).[89] As once the Philistines did, the Israelites ask where the Ark should go and find a quick solution, sending it to Kiryat Ye'arim. The narrative assigns the cause of the divine punishment to the fact that the people of Beth-Shemesh have "looked upon the Ark," which makes one wonder whether they perhaps touched it and looked inside. Yet the text does not elaborate, and the question of the reason for the Ark's path of destruction continuing even among God's covenant people remains open.

As was the case with the Philistines, the Israelites send the Ark to another town, inviting those of Kiryat Ye'arim ("Forest Town") to come and get it without revealing what has happened to them and implying that having the Ark in town would be a great honor. Once it is put there in the house of one Abinadab, the Ark comes to rest with a person in charge of guarding it (7:1).[90] One wonders if the Ark, a chest made of wood, was more at home in a town named after trees. As others have observed, apparently the issue did not arise whether to send the Ark back to Shiloh, which is most likely a testimony to the town's decay at this time, whether as a result of actual destruction or through natural deterioration after the battle at Eben-Ezer.[91]

It seems unfair that Israelites, belonging to God's own covenant people, should receive the same treatment doled out to the Philistines. We are reminded that, at this point, leadership in Israel on a religious and political level is sorely lacking, notwithstanding the note at the end of chapter 3 regarding Samuel's stature. A warning embed-

89. The figure of 50,000 dead in Beth Shemesh is impossibly high in view of the town's small size. A number of translations read seventy, omitting the 50,000. The latter could be a result of the usual exaggeration in biblical numbers, but the numbering here is odd without a copula between seventy and 50,000.

90. The guardian of the Ark is named El'azar ("God Is Help"), a name with the same connotations as the town of Eben-Ezer ("Stone of Help").

91. Alter, *The David Story*, 35n21.

ded in the episode is that the Ark is not anyone's property. Fokkelman writes, "The Beth-Shemesh incident includes the lesson that the ark is the property of nobody but God, and is not, therefore, that of the covenant people." Their distressing discovery is that the divine punishment they experience puts them in "one and the same category as the Philistines: that of mortals who are punished numinously."[92]

Act III: Samuel's Word Was to All Israel (1 Samuel 7:2–8:22)

Samuel is a general who makes war by prayer.[93]

With its uncomfortable ending begging the question of the status of the Israel-God relationship, the Ark stories open up naturally into chapter 7, in which Samuel takes center stage. The chapter fits well as the closing account of the stage of military engagement with the Philistines, with its victory over the Philistines as a counterpoint to the defeat at Eben-Ezer, providing a strong link with the preceding events. It also fits with chapter 8 into one act, in which Samuel, who appears in 7:3 out of nowhere as if he has been present the entire time, is firmly in the center of the action. On the other hand, the account fits oddly into its immediate context, with its emphasis on idolatry and with phrasing and ideas that belong to the Deuteronomic treasury of word choice and theology. In addition, the total victory over the Philistines, who are said to never again "enter Israelite territory . . . all the days of Samuel" (7:13) is hardly consistent with the rest of Samuel, in which they remain a constant threat into the time of King David. The section may have been inserted by the editors to highlight the role of Samuel and depict an ideal restoration of the God-Israel relationship. The prominence of divine leadership and activity on behalf of the people also offers a salient counterpoint to the following chapter and the people's desire for human governance.

92. Fokkelman, *Vow and Desire*, 249.

93. P. Kyle MCarter Jr., *I Samuel: A New Translation with Introduction, Notes and Commentary*, AB 8 (New York: Doubleday, 1980), 148.

Chapter 8 is pivotal to the account of kings and kingship, because in it the people voice their strong desire for a king "like all the peoples" have (8:5). Both Samuel and God disagree that this will be of benefit for Israel but succumb in the end to the people's wish. Chapter 8 rounds off the career of Samuel as sole leader of the people. Although he will stay in the picture and play a crucial role in what follows, the major protagonists thereafter will be Saul and David. Like chapter 3, the episode contains no action, consisting of speech notable for its strong critique of the office of kingship. Even before the kings arrive in the land, a large warning sign has been set up by God's prophet.

Act III, Scene 1: God's Thunder at Mizpah (1 Samuel 7:2–17)

What is Samuel really?[94]

A first unit (1–6) begins with a precise marker of time passing by: The Ark stays in its forested hill town for twenty years and the "entire house of Israel lamented after Adonai." This estrangement between Israel and God is of some duration if we take the first six chapters into account, beginning with corrupt religious practices in Shiloh, the rejection of Eli, and a general absence of divine vision and instruction, continuing with the mistaken notion that Israel can manipulate God into help against national enemies through the presence of the Ark. The verb used for "lament" is rare, related to a noun for a wail or dirge of bereavement (cf. Jer 9:16[17], 17[18], 18[19]; Amos 5:16; Mic 2:4).[95] Its use here causes one to wonder what is going on with Israel. If this is the type of lamentation following loss, then why lament now that the Ark has been returned? Have relations between Israel and God not been restored? Is not Samuel, whose word comes to all Israel, in their midst? Has not the Ark been restored to a safe place and proper guardianship? Is everyone still

94. Fokkelman, *Vow and Desire*, 298.

95. Buber (*Bücher der Geschichte*, 167) has the German equivalent of "sighed after"; so also Fox, *The Early Prophets*, 308.

doing what is wrong in God's eyes and what is right in their own eyes? After the loss of Shiloh, is there no place to bring sacrifice? Do the Philistines continue to harry them? Perhaps all of these are part of the reality, but the point of the notation just here is that the people have become aware of a loss of contact with God and of alienation marking the relationship, and they grieve because of this. Likely, they also experience continued Philistine domination because of a lack of divine assistance.

Samuel addresses the people (note use of the expression "the entire house of Israel" in vv. 2 and 3) at the point of the breach in the relationship. His speech begins with the conditional "if" and ends with "he will deliver you from the hand of the Philistines" (3), a testimony to the fact that such deliverance has not been forthcoming. The conditions laid down by Samuel include a *return to* the God of Israel and a *turning from* foreign gods, with a specific mention of the Astartes, a reference to indigenous goddess religion. The concern with avoiding the worship of Canaanite deities is especially prominent in Deuteronomy, and we find it also in the final chapter of Joshua.[96] At the same time, the emphasis on devotion to Adonai with the *heart* is also at the core of Deuteronomic ideology. We met the charge of worshiping Canaanite gods also in Judges, but it is unusual in Samuel, and there has been no reference to it so far—not even in terms of the description of corrupt practices at the sanctuary in Shiloh or the accusations made against the house of Eli. The same concern will surface in chapter 12, again voiced by Samuel at the end of his career. At this point, the people do as Samuel demands (4).

Next, Samuel gives the directive to gather "all Israel" at Mizpah, a few miles from his hometown of Ramah, deep in the hill coun-

96. Archaeological testimony suggests the worship of deities other than Adonai in households, especially of gods guaranteeing fertility of land and people, was likely common during the centuries leading up to the exile. The notion of serving only one god was alien to the surroundings of biblical Israel, and it took firm root in the formation of the religion that preceded Judaism only gradually, made all the more difficult by the prohibition of visible representation of the Deity. See Josh 24:20 and 23 for identical phrasing in relation to setting aside the worship of "foreign gods."

try of Ephraim, and promises to "pray on their behalf," apparently not entirely satisfied with the people's renewed devotion to Adonai (5). So far, the only person to have engaged in prayer has been his mother, Hannah. Samuel's promise of intercessory prayer precedes the people's acts of contrition, which conclude with the comment that Samuel "judged" the people (6). This moment and its reoccurrence in 12:20 and 23 are the only instances of prayers of intercession in Samuel and underline his priestly function. After Samuel speaks of prayer and before his action of "judging," the people engage in appropriate gestures of repentance. There is no explicit mention yet of actual praying on Samuel's part.

The scene at Mizpah is interrupted in the next unit (7–10) by the announcement that the Philistines, on hearing the news of an Israelite assembly, gear up for battle. The community asks once again for prayer, and Samuel obliges with both sacrifice and prayer. The verb in verses 8 and 9 for praying has turned to "cry out," the same root used in chapters 4–6 by Philistines and Israelites in distress (see pp. 61–62 above). Deliverance from the Philistines is still high on the agenda, with the threat of their military actions against Israel once again apparent. This time, there is no mention of a real fight. Rather, God employs loud thunder against the Philistines, and as before, when the Ark was in their midst, the Philistines are "struck" by God and in a "panic," so they flee. We are reminded of Hannah's declaration that God breaks adversaries in pieces and thunders against them (2:10). All Israel has to do is the mopping up.

And so it goes: Pursuit of the Philistines and their defeat follow in a unit (11–14) that ends with the declaration that the military might and excursions of Philistia against Israel have come to an end (13) and that peace reigns supreme also between Israel and the indigenous population (the Amorites, 14). A stone set up by Samuel marks the spot to commemorate the occasion of Israelite victory at Eben-Ezer ("Stone of Help"), where they had earlier suffered defeat (ch. 4). The entire chapter ends with a description of the circuit Samuel travels as long as he lives to administer the small region between Bethel, Gilgal, and Mizpah from his home in Ramah, roughly a territory of twenty miles across. The expression "he judged" occurs in each of the three verses of the concluding unit (15–17).

It looks as if the editorial voice closest to that of Deuteronomy placed the episode here for the purpose of detailing Samuel's career as a prophet, priest, and judge. In the first unit, he speaks as a prophet and acts as judge (6); next, he performs priestly actions (8–10); finally, his role as judge receives triple emphasis (15–17). The narrator does not hesitate to assign all three labels to Samuel and in this way make him a true successor of Moses and Joshua, looming large in Israel's history and depicted as a worthy leader of the Israelites. Yet the discrepancy between this record and the rest of Samuel in terms of the continuing Philistine threat is clear. What follows will be far removed from the numinous defeat of the Philistines and the harmonious ending with a restored peace and Samuel in charge. Israel is at home, Samuel returns home (where his parents lived and where he may have gone after the decimation of Shiloh), and the Philistines stay home. The purpose of placing the episode cheek to jowl with the next scene, in which the Israelites, far from settled and at peace, clamor for a royal leader, may be to testify to the ambiguity regarding kingship that pervades the Historical Books, even the Book of Samuel. Who needs a king when a God-appointed leader is in charge and peace reigns supreme?

Act III, Scene 2: All about Justice (1 Samuel 8)

Shemuel is both the last of the old-time practitioners of theocracy (rule of God) and the first of the prophetic critics of human kingship.[97]

1 SAMUEL 8:1–6

1 And when Samuel was old,
he set up his sons as judges over Israel.
2 The name of the firstborn was Joel
and the name of the second Abijah—
judges in Beersheba.

97. Fox, *The Early Prophets,* 311.

3 And his sons did not walk in his ways
but turned after profit,
took bribes,
and turned justice on its head.

4 And all the elders of Israel assembled
and came to Samuel in Ramah.
5 And they said to him:
Look, you are old
and your sons do not walk in your ways;
now, set up a king over us,
to act as judge like all the peoples.

6 And the thing was evil in the eyes of Samuel,
that they said: Give us a king
to act as judge over us.
And Samuel prayed to Adonai.

With chapter 7 as background for the prevailing situation, chapter 8 takes an abrupt turn with its introductory note that "Samuel was old" and that his sons, whom he had made "judges of over Israel," were corrupt (3). Up until now, the information that someone is "old" has not been positive, and the act of installing his sons as inheritors of his office strikes a false note. Judgeship was not usually hereditary but rather occurred through divine appointment. Although the sons, each with a name that refers to God, are not declared to be scoundrels (*beney beliya'al*) as were Hofni and Pinhas, they are greedy like those two, out for profit, and like the venal sons of Eli, they pervert *justice.* Samuel, having created a hereditary judgeship and apparently even more blind to his sons' shortcomings than Eli, has his own weakness: He is *old,* and his sons' failings are pointed out to him by the leaders of the community, who come to him in Ramah. Rather than a judge, they want a king to rule over them "like all the peoples." The noun "judge" and the word "justice" are related, so in this opening unit, the pivotal issue of the chapter is emphatically introduced. It is and will be about *justice.*

Samuel brings the demand, which is wrong or evil in his eyes, to God in prayer, and the text skips immediately to the divine reply (7–9) without reporting the content of his prayer. From God's speech, we may surmise that Samuel's report was not positive and that he may have lamented the way the people are dismissing him. God's speech is framed by the admonition for Samuel to *listen* to the voice of the people—in other words, do for them as they ask (7, 9)—with a divine complaint wedged in between. God's response is not entirely coherent and runs along the following lines: Samuel would be wrong to consider himself rejected by the people, for they have rejected God by their request for a king, as they have done habitually by their idolatry. The issue of idolatry, on the face of it put to rest in the preceding episode, is thus raised once again. It is used here to return to the point, at first negated, that the people have indeed rejected Samuel also. The final lines include the caveat that although Samuel must consent, he must also tell the people about the *justice* of the king.[98]

And so Samuel does (10–18). The text has it that he "said all the words of Adonai," but only the part of justice according to Samuel's insight is recorded here, leaving the reader to guess if he spoke about rejection at all or about other parts of justice God may have had in mind, like royal responsibilities and restrictions on absolute rule. From Samuel's perspective, what characterizes a king above all is that he will *take*. Justice in biblical usage is above all a quality of God, but it's also a quality that God demands of God's covenant people. God's justice in Torah usage means that the God of Israel exercises specific care for the lowly, the ones who cannot take care of themselves, the widow, orphan, and stranger. For the community liberated from bondage, it means that they are required to follow God's example (see Deut 10:17–19) and make it a priority to care for those who experience deprivation. In marked distinction from this kind of justice, a king will *take*; he will take sons and land and harvest and metals and daughters and fields and seed and even their

98. The word *mishpat*, which I have translated with "justice" to keep the repetition with "judge" intact, can also be translated with "practice," "mode of operation," or "habitual behavior." Alter, *The David Story*, 42n11.

servants and animals, and the people themselves will become servants or slaves (the word is the same in Hebrew). And what then? "You will cry out on that day/ before your king you chose for yourselves./ And Adonai will not answer you on that day" (8:18). They will have to lie in the bed they made for themselves together with the king they made for themselves. It is a bitter and unforgiving speech with an entirely negative picture of kingship.

The elders will have none of it, and their answer is a straightforward "No!" (19). This time, they spell out more clearly what they are looking for in a king, which turns out to be a military leader to fight their battles (20). Chapter 7's rosy picture of peace in Samuel's days and lack of enmity among peoples is forgotten. The new king/judge will offer a consistent military presence. Samuel returns to God with the people's reply and is once again told to *listen* to the voice of the people. The last lines of the chapter introduce renewed tension.

1 SAMUEL 8:22

And Adonai said to Samuel:
Listen to their voice and king them a king![99]
And Samuel said to the men of Israel:
Go, each man to his city.

One might have expected Samuel to go and act on what God is telling him to do—not only to *listen,* but to find a king; instead, Samuel instructs everyone to go home. It does not sound as if he is exactly following through on God's directive, and this creates an expectation for what is to follow. In fact, God will have to practically put the right candidate under Samuel's nose when one is located, and even then, Samuel's reluctance to engage in the adventure of kingmaking will be all too evident.

99. This somewhat awkward expression in English is a literal rendering of the Hebrew, which uses the root for king in both verb and noun. So Buber (*Bücher der Geschichte*, 171) and Fox (*The Early Prophets*, 39). Renderings in the Greek versions also faithfully reflect this significant doubled use of the word *king.*

Act IV: Everybody's Looking for Something (1 Samuel 9–12)[100]

God is shown as having decided that if Samuel will not go to Saul, Saul will have to come to Samuel.[101]

Kingship is established in chapters 9–11 in a circuitous way with a threefold appointment of the candidate and a number of characters undertaking searches.[102] The searches take place within the regional boundaries of Samuel's activities recorded at the end of chapter 7, and events take us outside of this perimeter only once, during the battle with the Ammonites in chapter 11. Saul, ostensibly looking for his father's donkeys, ends up looking for a prophet/seer and finds a royal office. Samuel, told by God that the one God has in mind for kingship is on the way to him, looks for Saul but anoints him in secret and does not engage in a public declaration of Saul's kingship until quite a ways down the road. Finally, the people, as individuals and in groups, are throughout a part of searches, first for the donkeys, then for the seer, and finally also for a king. That Saul is three times declared to be the looked-for king may point to three different traditions regarding the rise of Saul to the monarchy, but they are here braided together into an intricate whole, filled with fortuitous encounters, some sought and some unforeseen. Finally, the people join in making Saul their king, and all the searches end with Saul and "all the people of Israel" rejoicing (11:15).

Saul, in Hebrew *Sha'ul,* is the one "asked for" (see pp. 25–32 above), but the roundabout way in which he gains the throne, combined with the air of mystery and secretiveness that imbues part of the narrative, casts the endeavor into some doubt. Is he indeed *the one,* or is there another more suited to the mind and heart of both people and God? We are informed about the reluctance with which both God and prophet are undertaking this new adventure in chapter 8 and re-

100. From "Sweet Dreams Are Made of This" (1983), lyrics by Annie Lennox and David Stewart.

101. Polzin, *Samuel and the Deuteronomist,* 90.

102. For a detailed analysis of the structure of 9:1–10:16, see Fokkelman, *Vow and Desire,* 356–61.

minded once again in chapter 12, the final account of this act and of the entire cycle, how much the people are risking divine displeasure by demanding a king. Kingship is portrayed by Samuel as a concession on God's part and a doing of the *wrong* thing on the part of the people. The prophet's final words are that they have put themselves and their king in danger of being "swept away," making use of an uncommon verb with ominous echoes of the destruction of Sodom and Gomorrah (Gen 18:23, 24; 19:15, 17) and the rebellion of Korah in the wilderness (Num 16:26). Samuel will appear on the stage again but is no longer the main actor in the story; he is the last judge, and his final words are far from propitious in regard to the future of the people and their land.

Act IV, Scene 1: A Handsome Man of Benjamin (1 Samuel 9:1–10:16)

On the one hand business-like, on the other hand magical and mysterious; on the one hand against kingship, on the other in favor of it . . .[103]

The first scene of Act IV is filled with a large cast of characters, groups as well as named and unnamed individuals. The opening (9:1–4) introduces "a man of Benjamin" with an elaborate ancestry, but the introduction sets the reader on a false trail; for not this man but his son, Saul, will be in the center of the story. Saul's father is Kish, a name connected to "gift" but with a sound that also evokes a root meaning "obdurate, difficult, stubborn," hinting perhaps at difficulties down the road. The father is described as "a man of substance" (1), and the story presents a domestic problem: Kish's female donkeys have wandered off, and he instructs his son to go looking for them with one of the servants. Donkeys, who may live in herds in the wild, were used by

103. Anne Marijke Spijkerboer, "Geheimzinnigheid en Geheimenis in 1 Samuel 9–10," in Amsterdamse Cahiers voor Exegese en Bijbelse Theologie, ed. K. A. Deurloo, B. P. M. Hemelsoet, F. J. Hoogewoud, K. A. D. Smelik, and R. Zuurmond, vol. 11 (Kampen: Kok, 1992), 35, author's translation. The opening lines share features with 1:1, including the introduction of a man with his ancestry who will not be in the center of the story. Both narratives also share a concern with a fresh start.

farmers mostly for transportation and occasional plowing. It is possible that in the donkeys, we encounter the first group on the lookout for something, since a herd of female donkeys, "jennies," is usually led by a male, "jack." While the jennies look for their jack, Saul and his lad look in vain for the animals, crossing and recrossing the difficult terrain of the hill country of Ephraim. Four times, verses 3 and 4 repeat the verb "to cross," twice echoed by the phrase "they did not find them."

When they arrive in the region of Zuf, Saul is about to give up, but his young servant convinces him that help may be in the neighborhood, for he has heard of a "man of God" in "this town," a man who knows everything.

1 Samuel 9:5–8

5 They came to the region of Zuf,
and Saul said to his lad with him:
Come, let us return,
lest my father stop worrying about the donkeys
and become anxious about us.
6 And he said to him:
Look now, there is a man of God in this town,
and the man is honored.
All that he says really arrives.
Let us go there;
perhaps he will tell us our way
by which we came.
7 And Saul said to his lad:
Look, we go and what shall we bring the man?
For the food in our bags is gone
and we have no gift
to bring the man of God.
What have we?
8 Again the boy answered Saul and said:
Look, I happen to have
a quarter-shekel of silver.
I will give it to the man of God,
and he will tell us our way.

Zuf, an unfamiliar region we have heard mentioned once before, when Elkanah was introduced in the first chapter, will slide out of the story as unspecified as it has appeared. Saul, concerned his father will begin to worry about them rather than about the donkeys, is for turning back, but his servant, perhaps less eager to return home empty-handed, suggests they go and find help elsewhere. Thus, the search, begun for stray animals, turns into one for "a man of God." Together, the alien region, the unknown town, and the anonymous forecaster (referred to three times as the "man of God") create an aura of mystery. Where is this town, and why is Samuel an unfamiliar name for these two? Are they among the few who have not heard that "Samuel was a true prophet of Adonai" (3:20)? Are they really searching with all their wits about them? Moreover, the servant does not suggest that the mysterious man of God will help them find the donkeys but that he will tell them their "way" (9:6, 8). The phrasing assigned to Saul's lad is ambiguous; the word "way" (*derekh*), used often enough in a literal sense, can also be used to mean *conduct, situation,* or *status.*[104] Some translations render the servant's words in verse 6 as "Perhaps he can tell us about the journey on which we have set out" (NRSV, NASB). Samuel will indeed reveal Saul's journey, although related to his future rather than the past, and in that sense the servant's words are prophetic.

It is clear from the conversation that Saul is the one who is at sea, asking questions, wanting to surrender the entire enterprise, and at the same time inadvertently uttering the word for prophet, *navi*, which also means "we bring" (9:7). The servant is the one who proposes a different solution and provides the few resources he possesses. This is hardly an auspicious beginning for a ruler in the making. Saul agrees to the proposal, but before taking the characters further on their road, the narrator interrupts the story by explaining that people in olden times used to consult a "seer" if they wanted to seek divine counsel, and that "seer" was the term for a prophet (9:9). This explanation, placed before Saul's agreement, reveals that the

104. A number of translations render *derekh* in v. 6 as "journey." Cf. also ch. 8:3 and 5, which use the word *derekh* in reference to the sons of Samuel who did not walk in their father's ways.

search is for Samuel, called a "true prophet" in 3:20, and anticipates the encounter of the two searchers with a group of young women, of whom they inquire regarding the whereabouts of "the seer" (9:11).

The next unit (9:11–14) opens with this question, to which the young women, who are on their way to draw water (and therefore most likely on the way "down"), provide an elaborate reply filled with references to movement and to "the height." The unit is enclosed in the framework of "going up" ("as they were going up the ascent to the town," 9:11 // "they went up to the town," 9:14), with three additional references to this verb in between (9:13 2×, 14). The first reply of the women would theoretically suffice, with its affirmative answer that the seer is indeed here just ahead of them (9:12), but they continue with a breathless recital filled with words for movement, with a predominance of the verb "to arrive" and repeated mention of causation: "Going up . . . he goes up . . . now go up," interspersed with "he arrived . . . you arrive . . . he will arrive" and "because . . . because . . . because . . ." indicating they are among the groups of insiders in the narrative who know things and give wise counsel.[105] Twice, they predict that Saul and the servant will indeed *find* the seer (13 2×). The unit culminates in the arrival of the two in the town and the first mention of the seer's name: "Here Samuel was coming out toward them, to go up to the height." A resolution to at least one of the searches is thus near.

All the *going up* and *arriving* underlines that there is one who has not yet arrived on the stage, the subject of a crucial search that has not been completed—the king to be "kinged" by Samuel on God's command. The narrator thus shifts perspective to Samuel in

105. Twice they refer to "the height" (*bamah*), a common place for sacrifice. The word *bamah*, though not etymologically linked, sounds like Ramah, Samuel's hometown, which also means "height." The high place was a frequent site for sacrifice. Alter (*The David Story*, 49n12–13) describes it as "a kind of open-air natural altar, perhaps sometimes with a structure erected alongside it." Fox (*The Early Prophets*, 318–23) translates with "sanctuary" throughout these episodes. We find *bamah* in 1 Sam only in this scene (8×), while in 2 Sam it occurs only in poetic contexts. Eventually, the "heights" will become synonymous with places of idolatry, and two-thirds of its uses occur in Kings and Chronicles.

the next unit (9:15–17) and tacks back to an announcement Samuel received directly from God a day earlier that someone is on the way for him to anoint, which then provides an opening for a new announcement when Saul comes into view, that here indeed is the one. The wording of the instruction in verse 16 is striking, referring to "a leader" rather than "a king" while picking up a phrase we encountered earlier in the calling of Samson: "to deliver my people from the hand of the Philistines" (9:16; cf. Judg 13:5). This task, begun by Samson, was seemingly brought to a conclusion in 1 Samuel 7:14, but the Philistine enemy clearly is still a threat. In addition, there is an echo of the encounter of God with Moses in Exodus 3 in the reference to the *cry* of the people that has come to God's attention (Exod 3:9), as well as of the period when the Israelites *cried* out to God under hostile oppression in the time of the judges (Judg 3:9, 15; 6:6, 7; 10:10, 14). Allusions to those events and the leadership that had once arisen spontaneously in Israel, combined with the note of a "leader" rather than a king, point to the strain ascribed to God and God's prophet regarding monarchy and carry on the voice in this material that does not regard monarchy in a favorable light. This negative view was first voiced by the protest of Gideon and by Yotam's fable in Judges 8:23 and 9:8–20, and subsequently raised by Samuel's protest in chapter 8. Once Samuel sees Saul, he receives verification directly from God that this is the one: "Here is the man of whom I spoke;/ he will control my people" (9:17).[106] While many translations read "rule" rather than "control," the verb means "to restrain/hinder." Deliverance or hindrance: Which will Saul be? And even more important, which will the monarchy turn out to be for Israel?

The entire scene is driven by discourse, exhibited especially by Samuel's exchanges with Saul, which take up most of the fifth unit (9:18–21) as well as the seventh (9:26–10:8), with Samuel as speaker. Samuel's address to Saul is filled with instructions and increasingly characterized by a predictive tone: You do this, then this will hap-

106. The pointer "here" (*hinneh*) is used strategically in the story to draw the listener/reader's attention to events in the scene (9:6, 7, 8, 12, 14, 17, 24; 10:2, 8, 10, 11).

pen. If Saul goes up to "the height" Samuel will send him off the next day and "tell him all that is in his heart" (show him his skill in acquaintance with his concerns?). The donkeys should not be on his mind, for they are found, a disclosure that provides a sample of what Samuel knows without having been told (i.e., that there was a search for lost donkeys). Samuel ends with a rhetorical question that implies that Saul and "all" his family are the focal point of "all the desire of Israel" (9:19–20).[107] This type of response is sure to throw Saul, who does not come across as someone with a great deal of self-confidence, off balance. He manages a reply that is self-deprecating in regard to the size of both his tribe and his clan (9:21), a response that may be one of standard politeness: Who am I? The narrative has already provided information that Saul's family is well situated, and the reality may indeed be different than what Saul says. Yet we remember the decimation of the tribe of Benjamin at the end of Judges, a story for which there may be at least some historical basis. Perhaps Saul mixes truth and etiquette. This is the second and last time Saul speaks to Samuel in the episode, both times with questions: Where and why?

A descriptive section follows, with all entering the place of feasting; sacrifice has apparently already taken place and people are ready to eat. Saul receives a seat of honor and is presented with a "portion" saved especially for him, reminiscent of the *portion* given to Hannah by Elkanah in the first chapter (9:23–24; cf. 1:5). The secrecy and hints at momentous events, without providing clarity,

107. The phrase in v. 20 is translated and interpreted in different ways. Alter (*The David Story*, 50): "Whose is all the treasure of Israel?" Alter considers this is a deliberately oblique reference to kingship: If all the choice possessions of Israel are to be yours, why worry about a few asses? He argues that *hemdah* is more often "desired/valuable thing" than "desire" (n20). Fox (*The Early Prophets*, 43): "To whom do all the riches of Israel belong?" NRSV: "On whom is all Israel's desire fixed?" JPS: "For whom is all Israel's yearning?" Buber (*Bücher der Geschichte*, 174) is clearly on Alter's side: "Wessen wohl ist alle Begehr Jisraels?" Fokkelman (*Vow and Desire*, 401): "To whom does [all] the desire of Israel [go out]? Is it not to you and to all your father's house?" Fokkelman understands the question to mean, "Everyone knows you are the one who is sought."

wrap everything in a shroud of mystery. In a reflection of enigmatic words and actions, the grammar of the Hebrew text in verses 24 and 25 participates in the obfuscation, resulting in a translation that can only amount to an educated guess.[108]

On their arising the next day, the text narrows the focus gradually to center on Samuel and Saul without the presence of the servant.[109]

1 SAMUEL 9:26–10:1

26 And they arose early at dawn
and Samuel called Saul on the roof:
Arise and I will send you off.
And Saul arose, and the two of them went out,
he and Samuel, outside.
27 As they came down to the edge of the town,
Samuel said to Saul:
Say to the boy to go on before us,
and he went on.
And you, stand still now
and I will let you hear the word of God.
10:1 And Samuel took the flask of oil
and poured it on his head and kissed him.
And he said: Is not Adonai anointing you
over his inheritance as leader?

We note the emphasis on the Samuel-Saul pair in verse 26. As if to make up for earlier omission, Samuel's name occurs in each verse, with the final words of verse 26 amounting to a redundancy. It is

108. Verses 24–25 are unclear, with translations resorting to variant readings. Alter and the Jewish Publication Society employ Greek variants. As Fox (*The Early Prophets,* 320–321) notes, "the Hebrew text appears garbled." At the end of the meal, everyone comes back down to "the town" and either someone "made a bed" for Saul on the roof or "Samuel spoke with Saul" on the roof.

109. Fokkelman (*Vow and Desire,* 408) points out the gradual preparation for the private conversation between Saul and Samuel, begun already in 9:24.

only now that Samuel claims to speak a word from God and refers to Israel's God, who is the subject of "anointing" Saul. It sounds as if greater clarity is reached with this phase, but rather than a declaration, Saul receives another rhetorical question: "Is not . . . ?" The questioning tone points to a lack of assurance on the part of Samuel and missing reassurance for Saul. A more appropriate fit would have been a statement from the prophet that hereby Israel's God anoints his chosen one to whom the desire of all Israel goes out. Instead, it sounds as if Samuel is still questioning the enterprise on which all are embarking. Once again, the title assigned to Saul during the anointing is "leader" instead of "king."

The text no longer reflects any puzzlement on Saul's part but moves to a long speech by Samuel filled with prediction and instruction (10:2–9), enclosed in verbs of movement: "When you go. . . . As he turned to go" (10:2, 9). The road ahead promises many encounters—with two men, three men, and a band of prophets—and a wait of seven days before Samuel will let Saul know what to do (10:8). Once again, some answers to questions are provided, but new questions arise. While Saul is assured that he will receive good news about his father's animals and sustenance for the road (10:2–4), there is mention of Philistines nearby (10:5), and while the presence of the spirit sounds empowering, the promise of ranting like a prophet (10:6) strikes one as likely intimidating, taking Saul into entirely unfamiliar territory.

Mostly, the speech serves to announce what will happen *to* Saul rather than what he will now undertake. Notably, a reference to deliverance from the hand of the Philistines is missing. Indeed, he is still to wait for word from Samuel as to what exactly he is to *do.* Saul remains a passive participant, receiving news and food, the spirit of Adonai, and a trance-like state, *being turned* into another man (10:6), and at the end of everything still *waiting* for word from his mentor in all these things. The seekers have found their seer and the seer his king to be, whom he only manages to declare a *leader*; it remains an open question whether the *people* have found their king. The final verse of the unit closes the encounter between Samuel and Saul and anticipates what is to happen next with the statement about God "transforming" Saul's heart and all "these signs" coming to pass (10:9). For the transformation of Saul's heart, the text uses a verb literally meaning "to overturn," an upheaval that takes place in the Bible in both negative and positive contexts (cf. Gen 19:21, 25, 29; Exod 14:5; Ps 30:12 [11]; Jonah 3:4).

The next unit (10:10–13), omitting most of the details foretold by Samuel, highlights the transformation of Saul into a ranting prophet (10:10–12), giving rise to the saying "is Saul also among the prophets?" The trance-state takes place in Gibeah (in Judges 19–20 a location of mischief and mayhem) under the influence of the spirit of Adonai, hearkening back to the state experienced by several judges (Judg 3:10; 6:34; 11:29). The phrasing here is identical to that used with Samson (Judg 14:6, 19; 15:14). In 10:11–12, we regard the occasion from the point of view of Saul's acquaintances (likely including relatives; in Hebrew, literally "all those who knew him from yesterday and the day before"), who express astonishment on finding Saul among the prophets. As Alter observes, the proverbial question seems to be a case of "extreme incongruity. . .—what on earth is a man like Saul doing among the prophets?—but at the same time points to a feature that is significant in the Saul story."[110] The bystanders identify Saul as "the son of Kish" (10:11). While Saul is thus located in his family context, an individual asks, "Who is their father?" (10:12), pointing to the prophetic function as one that takes place outside the family circle, thus placing Saul in a larger, more amorphous framework.[111] The transformation of the farmer's son who showed little self-awareness and spoke mostly in questions into a ranting prophet who, apparently not in control of himself, carries on in an obscure tongue, is not entirely reassuring about the form of leadership he will provide. The unit closes with the cessation of Saul's prophetic trance and his going up to the "height."[112]

The final unit (10:14–16) abruptly introduces an uncle of Saul, perhaps one who was among the acquaintances of Saul who earlier commented on his presence among the prophets. They have a short

110. Alter, *The David Story*, 56n10.

111. Fokkelman (*Vow and Desire*, 430) interprets this reference as signaling that "the divine and prophetic authority has ousted that of his father."

112. Some translations render it "he went home" (NRSV and NAB).

conversation, during which the uncle asks two questions. Saul gives concise replies, omitting detail and leaving out what one might think was the most important information. Upon the uncle's question as to where they went, Saul answers that they looked in vain for the donkeys and "came to Samuel," without assigning him any function. To the query regarding the content of Samuel's words, Saul reveals only that Samuel told him the donkeys were found and keeps quiet "about the matter of kingship." The absence of a name for the uncle is puzzling, while Saul's brevity and secrecy add to the mysterious nature of the scene. The closing phrase (10:16) can be understood in different ways. Either Saul did not speak of the matter of kingship *that* Samuel told him about, or he didn't speak *because* Samuel told him not to do so.[113]

While the donkeys were the ostensible reason for Saul's search, and also for the search for "a seer," neither he nor his servant ever asks the seer about the whereabouts of the donkeys. Twice they are said to have been "found" in the story (10:2, 16) without further information as to where or by whom. These donkeys are an important object of searching in the scene and appear to have significance beyond the immediately obvious. I suggested that they may be females who are looking for a male around whom they form a herd on their own (see p. 76 above). Thus, they may signify the people and their search for a leader. In his analysis of the meaning of the donkeys, D. Rudman argues that they represent the Israelites as an obstinate, rebellious people who need to be brought under control (cf. 9:17 above) and that as a metaphor they are analogous to sheep in the David story. While the people at the beginning of the monarchy are compared to donkeys "in need of discipline," they "end as sheep at the mercy of predators."[114]

113. The latter is the interpretation of Fokkelman (*Vow and Desire*, 435), who argues that such a reading makes for a closing phrase with more "force and substance."

114. D. Rudman, "The Commissioning Stories of Saul and David as Theological Allegory," *VT* 50 (2000): 529. See also van Wijk-Bos, *Reading Samuel*, 68.

Act IV, Scene 2: Caught among the Baggage (1 Samuel 10:17–27)

God and Samuel support the idea of leader/nagid, the people want a king/melekh.[115]

God and Samuel have found their king, it seems. Following the clandestine affair conducted by Samuel, Saul is selected to kingship in the second of the three scenes that involve his road to the throne, ostensibly concluding the search of the *people* for a king. A first section (17–21) describes the gathering of the people "before Adonai" initiated by Samuel once again at Mizpah (cf. 7:5–12), also a place for assembly and moments of crucial decision-making in Judges (Judg 11:11; 20:1). In contrast to the previous scene, the references to Adonai are abundant. Everything here takes place in the presence of Adonai, who is also an active participant in the event.

First, Samuel presents the people with a short speech before he has them sort themselves out in order to cast lots (17–20). The speech is in the form of a prophetic utterance with its opening ("thus says Adonai") and reviews in one sentence Israel's experience of deliverance by God, evident in its escape from Egypt and subsequently from the power of "all the kingdoms" that have caused its "evils and distresses."[116] In the next breath, Samuel accuses the people of *rejecting* God by their demand for a king. The mention of a direct rejection of God on the part of the people is unusual. Outside of this text, it is found only in Numbers 11:20, when the people question God's leadership, and in 1 Samuel 8:7 (2×), when the people express their desire for a monarch. In both Numbers 11 and 1 Samuel 8, the accusation is framed as a direct utterance from the Deity. Here, Samuel speaks for God but is also voicing his own opinion, one he has already uttered and will expansively lay out before the people in a final address in chapter 12. The harsh and unusual accusation of *rejection* highlights continuing resistance to the monarchy on the part of God and God's servant and throws a negative light on the process of casting lots.

115. Spijkerboer, "Geheimzinnigheid," 37.

116. So Fokkelman (*Vow and Desire*, 441), who reasons that by implication "the monarchial form of government is a catastrophe and an evil."

Moreover, the verb used for the selection is telling: Out of all the tribes, Benjamin is *caught*; out of the tribe, a specific clan is *caught*; and out of the clan, Saul is *caught*. The verb often translated "chosen" or "taken by lot" occurs in the biblical text most often of the capture of living beings, towns, or territory (so throughout Josh and Judg), and on the two other occasions where we find it in the context of lot-casting, it concerns the search for a culprit.[117] It is used three times in verses 20–21 with purpose. Lot-casting to *catch* someone who is wanted for a particular honor is not done, and thus this play of who will be *caught* keeps everyone in suspense, including Saul, who may have deduced he is singled out for some special punishment, especially after the scolding words uttered by Samuel. It should thus not be surprising that he goes into hiding.

At this point, the perspective shifts to the people, who on looking for Saul cannot find him and consult the Deity: "Did anyone else come here?" (22). The narrator omits any mention of consultative devices, with the result of a direct exchange between God and people without the mediation of Samuel. The people *ask* (*sha'al*) for *Sha'ul*, "the one asked for." The response of the Deity literally reads: "Here he [is] hiding among the gear" (22). In this short unit (21–23), it is all between God and people, who now take an active role in looking for and finding the one they have requested. The people "take" Saul so he can "stand" among the people, and we observe Saul's height together with them: "He was taller than all the people/ head and shoulders." This is the second time Saul's size is mentioned (see 1 Sam 9:2). Physical description is rare in biblical narrative, and Saul's height functions on different levels. On the height is where the people sacrifice, and Saul's initial road was to go up to the place of sacrifice. Saul's height is so striking that it is twice remarked upon. What is high may come down for a hard fall, and sacrifice is to play a role in the sequel—not to Saul's advantage.

117. Cf. Josh 7, the story of Achan's transgression, where it occurs eight times; 1 Sam 14:41–42, where it is used in reference to Saul's son Jonathan. Fokkelman's (*Vow and Desire*, 444) argument that the "drawing of lots was, perhaps, a neutral procedure in itself which could point out a guilty person one time, and another time offer a solution . . . in the case . . . of a candidate for high office" is particularly weak in view of the use of the verb *lakhad*.

The next short unit (24–25) makes use of the word for choice also, as Samuel, lifting the tension as to what is actually going on with the catching of tribe, clan, and individual, points to Saul and asks the rhetorical question whether the people see the one "Adonai has *chosen*," and the people acclaim him as king in response (24). We note that Samuel still does not use the title "king," and only the people welcome him as such. Samuel fulfills one more task by speaking of and writing down the justice of kingship, the *mishpat hammelukhah* (cf. 1 Sam 8:9), perhaps pointing to the instructions laid out for a king in Deuteronomy 17:14–20. In the coda to the episode, everyone goes home—the people to their houses and Saul to Gibeah, with a mini-army around him, "the valiant ones whose heart God had touched" (26). But there is still a sting in the tale in that it ends with criticism from another group, disgruntled by the prospect of "this one" as their king and deliverer. They are called "worthless fellows" (*beney beliya'al*) by the narrator, a recognizable designation in the story sequence (cf. 1 Sam 2:12). In the face of their disapproval, Saul keeps quiet, playing deaf rather than uttering protest. Literally, the text states, "He was like one keeping silent" (27). Samuel speaks, the people shout, and Saul stays silent, as he has throughout this part of the story. Disapproval and silence conclude the scene of the public election of the first king of Israel.

Act IV, Scene 3: Saul Put to the Test (1 Samuel 11)

The writer keeps him outside the resentful and embittered atmosphere surrounding the old prophet.[118]

Saul, until now somewhat of a question mark, comes into his own in the next episode, one that concludes with an affirmation of his kingship and rejoicing on the part of both the people and their king (15). The episode proceeds in four stages, with a short introduction of the problem (1–3), the reaction from Saul and the Israelites (4–7),

118. J. P. Fokkelman, *Reading Biblical Narrative: An Introductory Guide*, trans. Ineke Smit (Louisville: Westminster John Knox, 1999), 155.

the resolution of the issue (8–13), and the third and final appointment of Saul as king (14–15). The action in the chapter moves away from the narrow confines of the Ephraimite hills to the north and the Transjordan, expanding the space in which events are taking place. Surprisingly, the threat that will provide the test-case for Saul's leadership and his capacity to "deliver" does not come from the Philistines but from the other side of the Jordan, where Ammon besieges an Israelite Trans-Jordanian town, Jabesh Gilead. The Ammonite king, Nahash, threatens the inhabitants who want to initiate a pact with great violence and torture: Instead of making (lit. "cutting") a covenant, the enemy will *cut out* everyone's right eye. In a smart move, the citizens manage to get a concession of a seven-day pause in the assault to see if they can get help.

Ammonites appear from time to time as aggressive neighbors to Israel east of the Jordan who occasionally go on the warpath. They rise as enemies in the time of the judges, when they are defeated under Jefta's leadership (Judg 10:1–12:15), and this will not be the last time they play a part in the Histories. In both Judges and Samuel, negotiating with their leaders or their descendants proves resoundingly unsuccessful. Jefta, those from Jabesh Gilead, and later King David try this ploy (Judg 11:12–28; 2 Sam 10:1–4), and war is the result for each.[119] *Nahash*, the name of the Ammonite king, means "snake" in Hebrew and has connotations of divination. The snake in Hebrew lore is connected with wisdom, or wiliness, and also healing. This wily snake will indeed prove to be an omen for Saul in that he will turn out to function as the prod needed for the Israelites to affirm Saul as their first king. Why Nahash agrees to the seven-day delay is not clear, but it could be that this useless week of, to his mind, surely uncoordinated and scattered looking for help is granted because he thinks nothing will come of it and it will only underscore the disgrace of the Israelite town.

The messengers looking for deliverance come to Gibeah, where Saul inquires about the lamentation happening in the town in re-

119. In 2 Sam 10:4–5, it is worth noting that the son of Nahash, Hanun, inflicts humiliation on the Israelite messengers sent by King David with a message of peace and comfort, while the torture threatened by Nahash is meant as a "disgrace" (1 Sam 11:2).

action to the news. Rather than in a palace, we find Saul in the field behind the plow, a signal that his kingship has not truly begun, and upon hearing the news, he goes into a rage under the influence of the spirit of Adonai, butchers a pair of cattle, and sends the pieces around "to the whole territory of Israel" (7) with the threat that those who will not come out with him and Samuel will meet the same fate as his cattle. This action sends the terror of God on the people and they come out "as one man." The unit begins with lamentation in Gibeah and ends with the entire people going out to battle. Saul's state of mind and actions are reminiscent of judges who acted under the influence of the spirit of God. They also recall the cutting apart and sending around of the concubine on the part of the Levite in Judges 19:29. Moreover, both Gibeah and Jabesh Gilead are part of that story and its sequel, with neither town displayed in a positive light. The depiction of Saul mustering the people in just this way may be intended to paint Saul as a continuation of Israel's charismatic, spontaneous leadership. Moreover, in this role, Saul is the one who is able to resolve tensions between the territories to the west and those to the east of the Jordan, besides lifting the shadow of misdeeds and mayhem that has lingered over Gibeah and Jabesh-Gilead since the time of the judges. His calling on all the tribes "as one man" is a monarchial act, as if he has a standing army.[120]

Saul musters the army in verse 8, stationing it in Bazeq, roughly at the same distance from the Jordan to the west as Jabesh Gilead is to the east, and defeats the Ammonites in verse 11, with both events described in the briefest possible terms. In between, he sends word via messengers to the inhabitants of the town, who lull the Ammonite king into believing that they are on the verge of surrender so that Saul can deliver the strike against the Ammonite camp while it is unaware that anything is afoot. An exchange between people and Saul closes the adventure of Saul's first experience as war leader. The people want to kill those who spoke against Saul assuming the mantle of monarch, and Saul calms things down by declaring, "No one dies on this day, for today Adonai made deliverance for Israel"

120. The expression to come out "as one man" in preparation for battle is rather rare and found elsewhere three times, in Judg 20:1, 8, and 11.

(13). In contrast to the silent Saul at the end of the acclamation of his kingship in chapter 10, he comes to the fore as someone who will not take the life of Israelites needlessly and ascribes deliverance not to himself but to God.

Samuel, who is pictured as part of the undertaking, invites the people to Gilgal, a location important as a witness to God's delivering power in earlier times (cf. Josh 4:19–20), to "renew" kingship. From this point on, the people take over in making Saul "king before Adonai" and bringing sacrifice, with everyone rejoicing. The three-part journey of Saul to kingship has finally met with success. The narrative is silent about the emotions of Samuel on this occasion; we must wait until the next chapter to hear from the disgruntled prophet.

Act IV, Scene 4: The Wages of Sin (1 Samuel 12)

It does seem in character for Samuel that he would end up converting the coronation assembly into still another diatribe against the monarchy.[121]

Samuel's speech in this chapter is the counterpart and conclusion to his address in chapter 7, with a sharper tone and richer invective against the people who have had the temerity to opt for kingship. The location may be Gilgal, but I take the opening line of chapter 13 (v. 1a) as the coda to the speech and assume the text's intention is to indicate that Saul has been king "for a year at that time" (i.e., the time of Samuel's address). While the speech offers a retrospective both on God's delivering action and the people's ill-chosen path, it also opens up into what follows in the next three chapters with their twofold emphasis on the rejection of Saul as king. Its placement in the middle of the six chapters concerning Saul's kingship (9–11 and 13–15), before David is introduced, can thus be viewed as a deliberate choice at a key point on the path to kingship, raising objections not only to the specific king the people have chosen but to the entire enterprise. It is an option the people must live with but one that will not save them from disaster.

121. Alter, *The David Story*, 65n1.

Three parts make up the scene, which consists almost entirely of speech. Samuel opens with a lengthy defense of his own probity (1–5) to go on with a history lesson about all God has done for the people, who have kept sinning up until the present day (6–15), ending with a call for a divine demonstration of power that causes the people to fear and confess their wrongdoing (16–25). The scene is enclosed in the words of Samuel: "I kinged you a king" (1), and, "Both you and your king will be swept away" (25).

The listener/reader has followed Saul on his tentative path to kingship, and if they are not ready to rejoice, perhaps they have at least drawn a sigh of relief that he finally seems to have arrived and is able to take joy in the fact. Samuel's opening salvo hardly echoes these feelings.

1 Samuel 12:1–2

1 And Samuel said to all Israel:
See, I have listened to your voice
and all that you said to me,
and I kinged you a king!
2 And now, here is the king walking before you,
and I am old and grey,
and here are my sons with you.
And I walked before you
from my youth until today.

Twice, Samuel mentions the king, making it a triple reference by using the verbal root that means "to rule," in the form used to describe *making* someone king. Samuel points out the obvious fact that, now, here is the king in his position as leader while Samuel used to be the leader—the meaning of the idiom "to walk before you." These two observations enclose the reference to his sons, to whom he does not refer as leaders, seemingly a pointless observation because we know already that his sons are no better than the sons of Eli and have turned justice on its head (8:3). Still, there is an implied complaint that he has sons who are not appreciated! The tone of Samuel's initial words is like that of a parent who remarks they did all their offspring asked: "I did what you said, and now look what happened!" It's really all about Samuel. He goes on to build his own defense about not having *taken* anything from the people and he calls them to witness. The people verify that this is indeed so (5). The word *take* weighed heavily against the monarch of the future in Samuel's warning speech of chapter 8. It is exactly the opposite of what Samuel, the model of a righteous leader in his own eyes, has done. Twice, Samuel refers to God's "anointed" as present for the testimony (3, 5), so we must envision that Saul is among those attending the performance.

Samuel follows the verification of his own spotless career with a history lesson about all the good things Adonai has done for their ancestors, first in Egypt, then at the time of the judges, and how God rescued them every time they needed rescue (6–11). He recalls the people's confession during the previous era and their owning up to having served false gods (12:10). This litany is an almost exact repetition of the occasion in Judges 10:10 when the people cry to God that they "have sinned." At that time, there was little forgiveness on God's part, who replied with a sharp retort. Samuel recalls only the overall pattern of crying on the people's side and deliverance on God's side, with a mention of an assortment of judges.[122] The recital goes up to the present day and the ordeal caused by King Nahash, who according to this version came against the Israelites instead of just one city and who provided the occasion for the demand for a king. The upshot is that now they have their king: "And now, there is the king for whom you asked. There, Adonai has given you a king!" (13). The indignant words tumble over each other in a stutter of grief and resentment.[123] This part of the speech ends with a warning that

122. Different versions provide different lists of judges, some with four, some including Deborah and listing five characters.

123. Buber's (*Bücher der Geschichte*, 181) line divisions in verse 13 make the quality and tone even more clear:

Now there,
the king,
whom you chose,
for whom you asked,
there,
HE gave you a king!

the future, their own as well as that of their king, will depend on their faithfulness to God's voice and on following Adonai alone, for God will turn against them. Saul's joy must have turned into deep anxiety if he was present during this recital.

To top it off, Samuel calls on God for a demonstration of power through the arrival of rain during the early summer harvest, finally making clear that the people have done *evil* by choosing a king (17). It is not so much a question now of following the wrong gods, as they did in the past, but of making the wrong choice of leadership in the present. With all the threats and the disaster of rain on the wheat harvest, the people are cowering in fear and ready to confess.

1 Samuel 12:19–20

19 And all the people said to Samuel:
Pray on behalf of your servants
to Adonai your God
so we will not die.
For we increased our sins with more evil
by asking for ourselves a king.

20 And Samuel said to the people:
Do not be afraid;
you have done all this great evil,
but do not turn from following
Adonai, and serve God
with all your heart.

Both Samuel and the people, their joy in the king now forgotten, verify that their demand for a king was *evil,* Samuel once more identifying it as a *great evil.* It may be that everything will still turn out alright—*if* they watch their allegiance closely. Of course, Samuel will not join in sinning by ceasing to pray on their behalf, if only they stick to serving Adonai; but if not, all will be "swept away," both the people and their king (25).[124]

124. The verb for "swept away," here in the passive form, is a relatively

We can readily agree that the speech testifies to someone in an exceedingly bad mood about the turn of events. The language is heavily Deuteronomistic, with its focus on the continued existence of the people as dependent on their *serving* Adonai and avoiding idolatry, an issue not central in 1 Samuel outside of chapters 7 and 12. The idols are called "emptiness," a term applied to false gods in Second Isaiah (Isa 41:29; 44:9). The words of warning at the end echo loudly into the future of a people who were to lose their land and their royal rulers. The voice of Samuel, as unpleasant and truculent as it may be, is after all the voice of God's prophet, who issues words of warning in the mode of future prophetic speeches. Samuel's call is for the people to *listen* to God's voice rather than *rebel,* a term often used in respect to behavior during the wanderings in the wilderness. *Not listening* will be a key term of reproach that will come Saul's way in 15:11, 19, and 22 (2×), where his transgression will also be identified as *rebellion* (15:23). We close the curtain here on Samuel as a primary agent in the narratives. He will not be gone from the story and will still play a major role vis-à-vis Saul and his successor, but other leaders have now arisen, and the office of prophet will eventually take on great significance apart from central political leadership, pronouncing critique and dissent.

---

rare root used in connection with Sodom and Gomorra in Gen 18:23, 24; 19:15, 17; with the rebellion of Korah in Num 16:26; and with regard to divine punishment for idolatry in Deut 32:23. In the Historical Books, the only other occurrences are when David refers to the different ways that Saul will die (1 Sam 26:10) and to his own possible death by the hand of Saul (1 Sam 27:1).

Cycle II: A King on His Throne (1 Samuel 13–31)

In stories such as Saul's . . . even God's character is too enigmatic for us to take as exemplary.[1]

Just as it took three chapters to establish Saul in his kingship, it will take three to accomplish the destabilizing of his throne. As quietly as things started with a young man in search of his father's donkeys, so much are they in tumult once he has accepted his rule. At least, that is how the arrangement of the chapters shows the situation. The review of Saul's reign in 14:47–52 may give evidence of a different picture, but it is overwhelmed by the surrounding material, which displays Saul engaged in battles or planning for them—not only with the Philistines but also with Samuel and within his own family.

The placement of the material results in the impression that almost as soon as Saul is elected, he is also rejected. The sequencing moves deliberately to show increased alienation between Saul and all those around him: Samuel, his son Jonathan, and even the people, who oppose the king's intended action against Jonathan. Saul acts at times with deliberation and courage, but he also vacillates in taking action against the enemy and on behalf of his people, and altogether he does not appear to follow a steady course. A new candidate for kingship already waits around the corner and will be introduced in chapter 16.

Samuel declares Saul a failed king in the prelude to the Israelite-Philistine engagement at Michmash (13:13–14), a rejection more thoroughly verified by both prophet and Deity after the battle with

1. John Goldingay, *Old Testament Theology: Israel's Gospel* (Downers Grove, IL: InterVarsity Press, 2003), 587.

Amalek in chapter 15. In between these two denunciations, a lengthy account with Jonathan in the center of the action in chapter 14 raises questions about Saul's relationship with his eldest son. While the positive note on Saul's kingship includes that "he acted valiantly, struck Amalek, and rescued Israel from the hand of his plunderer" (14:48), the actual battle with Amalek results in an emphatic rejection of Saul's kingship by Samuel (15:23, 28, 35).

In chapter 16, the rejection of Saul by God is sealed by the anointing of David. This is the last chapter in which Samuel plays a significant role. David is introduced to the court of Saul in multiple ways, as musician-therapist and champion fighter (chs. 16–17), with Saul's envy aroused especially by the evidence of David's military prowess (18:6–16). Efforts by Saul's family members—his son Jonathan and his daughter Michal—to effect a reconciliation are in vain, and in the end David is forced to flee the court, initially living as a guerilla fighter in the Judean wilderness (chs. 18–20). During this period (chs. 21–26), the narratives cover the adventures of David as fugitive, with Saul often in hot pursuit but never quite able to catch him. On two occasions, David spares Saul's life (chs. 24 and 26). These episodes end with David joining the Philistines in chapter 27. In the final four chapters (1 Sam 28–31), the stories move back and forth between the two protagonists, each now with his own concerns and military engagements. Saul faces a superior force of Philistines in the north while David is off on a rampage of his own in the south. Saul finds his end on Mount Gilboa by his own hand in a battle ending with an Israelite defeat.

Act I: Caught in Kingship (1 Samuel 13–15)

It is not about the divine right of kings; it is about the divine right over kings.[2]

All the events of the first act take place on the battlefield; even the coda, with a review of Saul's rule in 14:47–52, refers to battles with

2. Anthony F. Campbell, S.J., *1 Samuel*, FOTL 7 (Grand Rapids: Eerdmans, 2003), 160.

various enemy peoples, including the Philistines, with a final mention of Saul's continuous gathering of an army and the note that the "war with the Philistines was bitter all the days of Saul" (14:52). These verses, occurring between two recordings of Saul's rejection, describe a more extensive and stable rule than one might conclude from both the preceding and the following episodes. Continuing battles were par for the course in these times and do not make Saul a negative exception. The final phrases about continuing war with the Philistines, to whom, as we know, Saul will succumb in a final military encounter, may be taken at face value as presenting the long-term conflict with this neighbor to the west. Twice the word for *valor*, or power, is mentioned both in reference to Saul himself and to the men he gathers around him (14:48, 52). We note also that in this final unit, his family members, including his daughters, receive mention by name, and he has only one wife. Although we will later hear of a concubine (2 Sam 3:7; 21:8–12), there is no sign here of a large harem, as was the custom in royal houses of the ancient world, including King David's, and which is denounced in Deuteronomy 17:17. The recital opens with the line "Saul caught hold of the kingship over Israel"(14:47), a phrase that may hint at complications, since it makes use of the verb *lakhad*, the same verb we met earlier for Saul being *caught* in the lottery for kingship. Saul was "caught by lot for kingship" and "catches" it, but perhaps the time was not quite right for his kingship or he was not quite the man for it.

On the whole, the brief description of 14:47–52 presents a mixture of comments that do not paint an overall negative picture of Saul. It would seem that the traditions concerning Saul are not unanimous and the editors let this matter-of-fact description stand side by side with two tales of a condemnation of his rule (13:13–14 and 15:23). Fokkelman especially takes this positive picture of Saul's reign seriously and judges that the text as it stands "makes it a priori impossible for the reader to remain locked in the naïve position of a condemnatory attitude to Saul, taking Samuel's side."[3]

3. J. P. Fokkelman, *The Crossing Fates*, vol. 2 of *Narrative Art and Poetry in the Books of Samuel* (Assen: Van Gorcum, 1986), 82.

Act I, Scene 1: What Have You Done? (1 Samuel 13:1–15)

Both Eli and Saul hear pronouncements of judgment, but in Saul's case, the sin which precipitates the punishment is not so clear.[4]

The initial phrases of the scene cause confusion as to the period in which the events take place. Saul can hardly have been king for two years during the events of chapter 13, with his son Jonathan a full-grown warrior, but so the second half of 13:1 would have it, most likely with the intention of having events as depicted here follow closely on Saul's first encounter with Samuel and the instruction to "wait for him at Gilgal" (10:8) and on Samuel's speech in chapter 12 with its negative judgment of kingship. Saul and his son Jonathan, who appears for the first time as one in charge of his own battalion, each have an army ready to go as Jonathan strikes out on his own and assaults either the entire Philistine post stationed near Gibeah (cf. 10:5) or one of its commanders (2–3). Saul has the ram's horn blown, rousing the people to pay attention to what has happened and to gather to "follow Saul at Gilgal" (4).

The Philistines, Saul, and the people (addressed by Saul with the derogatory term "Hebrews," perhaps to rouse them more swiftly in indignation) *hear* something of what took place, but they do not hear the same thing. The Philistines are, naturally, the first to take note of an assault on their own: "They heard of it" (3). Saul, who must have also *heard*, exhorts his people to *hear well*, with a double use of the root, upon which the Israelites *hear* and conclude that "Saul has struck the Philistine garrison," which has upped the ante in terms of Philistine-Israelite relations and brought Israel into bad repute.[5] The conclusion raises the question whether Saul intended to take credit for the assault or whether it was simply a matter of mistaken impression on the part of the Israelites. Whichever it may be, the scenes that follow

4. Peter D. Miscall, *1 Samuel: A Literary Reading* (Bloomington, IN: Indiana University Press, 1986), 87.

5. Literally, the text reads that the people conclude, "Israel stinks to the Philistines" (13:4).

do not show Saul and his son Jonathan acting in full accord with one another—a third example in 1 Samuel of fathers and sons existing in a tense relationship, anticipating future developments between the two.

The immediate result of what transpires at Gibeah is a rallying of the different sides for war (5–7). In the details of the preparations for war, the contrast between the two groups, Philistines and Israelites, is striking: The Philistines are listed with all their powerful weaponry and great numerical advantage while the Israelites, at the *sight* of the Philistines, go into hiding.[6] The phrasing thus opposes "thirty thousand chariots,/ six thousand cavalry,/ as many people as sand on the seashore" (5) on the one side to the other side hiding "in caves, among thorns, in dugouts and pits" (6), going so far as recording a flight to the other side of the Jordan (7). Notably, the text refers once again to the people as "Hebrews," underlining the contrast between the Philistines as war-mongering overlords and Israelites as cowering in fear.[7] The narrative places Saul in Gilgal, linking the text to Samuel's instruction in 10:8 that Saul is to wait for him there, combining the location with a wait of seven days to keep the appointment with Samuel. So Saul waits while his army disappears. The text says, "the people scattered," using a verb associated with armies on the run after a defeat.

1 Samuel 13:8–10

8 He waited seven days
for the appointed time of Samuel,
and Samuel did not come to Gilgal,
so the people scattered.

6. Exaggeration is no doubt a part of the picture, especially in the reference to 30,000 chariots. The picture of fighting with chariots in the hill country is hardly realistic.

7. The Hebrew word describing the people in v. 7 is "trembled." We are reminded of Gideon's admonition to the people in Judges 7:3 for those who were afraid and who "trembled" to depart.

9 And Saul said:
Bring me the burnt offering
and the sacrifice of well-being.
And he made the burnt offering.
10 And when he finished offering the burnt offering,
look, Samuel was coming,
and Saul went out toward him to hail him.

The implication of the seven-day wait is that it is toward evening before Saul decides to bring the sacrifice. The short description is framed between the absence and the presence of movement. First, there is Saul's wait and Samuel's delay (8), which ends in both characters moving toward one another, one of them at least in joyous anticipation, highlighted by the word "hail" (lit. "bless," 10). The rest of the encounter between Saul and Samuel consists mostly of dialogue (11–15). Samuel begins with a return to Saul's greeting that elsewhere occurs in the context of reproach. "What have you done?" God asks of Cain after he has killed his brother (Gen 4:10); likewise, Joshua asks this question of Achan upon discovering him as the culprit who violated the *herem* against Jericho (Josh 7:19), a parallel especially ominous in view of what is to follow for Saul.[8]

The accusation implied in the question must have thrown Saul off balance, and he engages in a lengthy explanation, ending with the statement that in view of everything that happened—Samuel not coming, the army melting away, and the Philistines just about to arrive on his doorstep—he restrained himself and made the sacrifice. Upon hearing this, Samuel roundly condemns the king in a scathing indictment because Saul has not kept God's "commandment," with the root for this noun repeated four times in two verses (13–14). He condemns Saul's actions as foolish and judges his transgression as so serious that in view of it, Saul's kingship will not stand—that is to say, he will not establish a royal house.

While Samuel clearly considers Saul to have violated a commandment, exactly what he has done wrong is less obvious. Is it

8. See also Gen 20:9; 31:26; Num 23:11; Jer 2:23.

the matter of bringing sacrifice? This is the direction in which the narrative would lead us if we follow the link to 10:8 and Samuel's instructions to Saul. Yet Samuel's speech does not mention Saul's bringing sacrifice as a violation, nor his failure to wait for him. Peter Miscall surmises that the violation of which Samuel speaks is that Saul let the army scatter and failed in taking on the Philistines. This explanation fits the divine intention to appoint Saul "to save" Israel "from the hand of the Philistines" (9:16) and to do what his hand finds to do once the signs have happened (10:7). "Samuel simply cannot believe that Saul is still at Gilgal preparing burnt offerings rather than engaging in full battle with the Philistines. Saul has blundered and revealed himself as unfit because he does not act on his own as king."[9] Different interpretations remain viable. It is true that Saul's hanging back in taking on the Philistine enemy, something of which he gave no sign in his battle with Ammon, will repeat itself and that the eventual victory will be partial and not exactly the result of his effective leadership.

It is hard to avoid the impression that no matter what the case is, Saul is being pushed into an untenable position. He was hesitant to accept the role assigned to him first by Samuel and subsequently by the people, he had to listen to Samuel denounce the people's demand for a king as "evil," and now he is excoriated for reasons that may have been no more clear to him than they are to the listener/reader. The ambiguity that surrounds the issue of kingship in Israel imbues the figure of Saul to the utmost. In the narrative, the denunciations that come his way clearly destabilize him and cause him to act in ways that do not testify to consistent leadership. Perhaps the only consistency is that this man, who accepted his role with diffidence and hesitation, loses clarity as to how to execute it once he has embraced it and is further undermined in his task by a prophet who, ostensibly zealous for the honor of the Holy God, appears often more eager to maintain his own status. Certainly, in this episode the denouncement of Saul appears to be of Samuel's rather than God's devising.

9. Miscall, *1 Samuel*, 87.

Act I, Scene 2: A Quake by God's Hand (1 Samuel 13:16–14:23)

Israel is held in an iron grip.[10]

In both this story and the one that follows, Saul is not portrayed to great advantage: inactively waiting in the first, as compared to the activities of his son, and putting the troops at a disadvantage on account of being famished in the second. The setup for this scene takes place in the final eight verses of chapter 13 (16–23). First, each contingent of the opposing forces is put in its location: Saul and Jonathan with their troops in Gibeah, which now number 600 rather than the three thousand of 13:2 (!), and the Philistines at Michmash, with the latter sending out raiding parties in three directions. The second part of the description emphasizes the desperate situation of Israel. They are deprived of smiths to forge the metal needed to make efficient weapons and tools to work their land. Thus, they have to pay the Philistines for the tools on which their livelihood depends (13:21), and at the same time they are on an unequal playing field when it comes to armed engagement.

This opening unit is permeated with the word "found": "no smith could be found," "no sword or spear was found," "they were found for Saul and Jonathan his son" (13:19–22).[11] It calls to mind the efforts of *finding* in the episodes leading up to Saul's ascent to the throne. Saul was *found*, but Samuel has declared that God is *seeking* another more suitable leader. The people are said to be *found* with Saul and Jonathan (13:15–16), and they too are in need of being *found* in order to constitute a nation. But instead they have disappeared, scattered across the hillsides and even across the Jordan (13:6–7, 11), just as the erstwhile donkeys were wandering around as objects of a search and perhaps on a search themselves. In contrast to the Israelites, the Philistines are clearly located in their different divisions and raiding parties, with a final note placing them again at Michmash (13:23).

10. Fokkelman, *The Crossing Fates*, 52.

11. It is noteworthy that the description in 13:19–22 adds economic features which were an additional advantage to the Philistines. Bronze weaponry is more expensive apparently.

Chapter 14 opens with Jonathan, who had initiated the earlier conflict (13:3), in charge of the action together with the lad who is his weapon bearer (14:1–15). We are reminded of an earlier time, when Saul went out together with his lad, albeit on a more peaceful mission, and of the distinct differences between the two characters. Saul's hesitations in the face of Philistine readiness for battle have become clear, and indeed the contrasts between Saul and Jonathan in this section are evident from the verbs of which they are the subjects: "Saul sat" (14:2) and "Jonathan had gone" (14:3). Neither the father nor the people know about Jonathan's departure to carry out a plan to "cross" to the Philistine garrison, a plan he and his lad put into effect at the end of the introductory section (14:4–5).[12] The son sounds already more adventuresome and bold than the hesitant and uncertain Saul of earlier episodes (chs. 9, 10, and 17) and the current one. Jonathan and his lad find themselves in the pass between two crags, by detail of name and location depicted as a forbidding and inhospitable landscape, a feature eventually emphasized by Jonathan's crawling up the hillside "on hands and knees" (14:13).[13] Jonathan proposes a plan that will expose them to the Philistines and a test to make them either go ahead with an assault or stay their hand (14:7–10). In his proposal, he puts the outcome of the plan in God's hand.

1 Samuel 14:6–7

6 And Jonathan said to the lad, his weapon bearer:
Come, let us cross to the garrison of these foreskins!
Perhaps Adonai will do it for us,
for there is no limit for God
to deliver, whether with much or little.

12. The text emphasizes Jonathan's secrecy especially in regard to his father by making the object the first word in the sentence: "His father he did not tell" (14:1).

13. Fokkelman (*The Crossing Fates*, 80) considers the detailed references to the two crags symbolic of the division between father and son in this episode. "The antitheses created by Saul are rigid and implacable and the confrontation between father and son rock-hard and grim."

7 And his weapon bearer said to him:
Do all to which your heart inclines you;
see, I am with you according to your heart.

For the second time, Jonathan announces his proposal "to cross" to the Philistine garrison, this time referring to them by the epithet often translated "uncircumcised," literally meaning "foreskins," assuredly not a complimentary label. It is used specifically for the Philistines in the Histories by Samson and his parents (Judg 14:3; 15:18) and by David in reference to Goliath (1 Sam 17:26, 36).[14] Jonathan is willing to gamble that God will come to their aid but undertakes the risk without such assurance, asserting that God can work by any means, powerful or not, anticipating David's words when facing Goliath.[15] In this regard, too, he stands apart from his father, who consults the Deity through appropriate cultic methods (14:17–19), thereby delaying military engagement. Jonathan plans to become visible to the Philistines and to go ahead with an attack if they invite him and the lad to come closer, for this will be the sign that God is with them.

All goes forward as planned, and the event is phenomenally successful. The success of the assault is only partly ascribed to the action of the two Israelites. Besides the weapon bearer killing and Jonathan striking down (14:13–14), the Philistines are described as *falling*, and a *trembling* comes on the field, with the entire Philistine garrison *trembling* and the earth *shaking* with a *god-almighty tremor* (14:15). There is thus more going on than two military heroes decimating a large troop. Further along, one hears of "a great

14. In 1 Sam 31:4, Saul uses it to refer to the entire people, as does David in 2 Sam 1:20.

15. The similarity between the two heroes is noted by others. See Fokkelman (*The Crossing Fates*, 81), who cites the phrase used by David in 17:47: "Not by sword or spear does Adonai bring deliverance,/ for to Adonai belongs the battle." We may think also of Hannah's claim that "not by strength is a man a hero" (1 Sam 2:9). Jonathan's speculation is also shared by the Philistines in 6:5 and elsewhere by the sailors and Ninevites in Jonah. The phrase "who knows" in that context expresses the same sentiment (Jonah 1:6; 3:9).

panic" and the final statement that "Adonai delivered Israel on that day" (14:23).[16]

The story takes us back to Saul, who is still stationary at Gibeah but whose lookouts become aware of the tumult in the Philistine camp (14:16). Saul is busy counting the troops, with the absence of his son and companion now evident. Meanwhile, the Philistine disarray grows, and Saul decides to suspend the consultation with the Elide priest Ahiyah to take advantage of the situation. He raises the battle cry, and all the soldiers who had gone into hiding come out and go in pursuit.[17] The scene ends with the comment about God's deliverance, but the battle is not over, for it "crossed to Beth-Aven" (14:23). The picture of Saul busying himself with forecasting, a descendant of the doomed house of Eli at his side (14:3), delaying while his son mounts a solo attack, is ominous. Even more serious rifts between father and son will open up in the next scene.

Act I, Scene 3: Caught by the Lot (1 Sam 14:24–46)

Try as he might to do the right thing, he invariably does the wrong thing.[18]

The opening statement of the first unit (24–30) that "the Israelites were hard-pressed on that day" is not consistent with the pursuit of the fleeing and panicking Philistines that ended the previous episode. It may be best understood as an observation for which

16. "Great panic" refers to the God-instigated confusion that indicates the Deity's involvement. The roots *hum*, *hamam*, and *hamah* all refer to noisy and tumultuous disarray. Cf. Exod 14:24; Josh 10:10; Judg 4:15; 1 Sam 7:10.

17. The Hebrew text of 14:18 twice refers to the Ark: "And Saul said to Ahiyah: Bring the Ark, for the Ark of God was on that day with the Israelites." Some translations substitute "the ephod." The Ark was not usually employed for divination, and its appearance here is anomalous. Yet the reference may be there to sound another alarm bell. The last mention of the Ark on the battlefield was in chapter 4, with all its dire consequence.

18. J. Cheryl Exum, *Tragedy and Biblical Narrative* (Cambridge: Cambridge University Press, 1992), 29.

the explanation follows. The troops are in distress on account of hunger because Saul has made them take an oath not to eat until total victory is achieved, with the result that they feel "faint" (28, 31). On the loose, outside of his father's command, Jonathan violates the oath by eating some honey, which refreshes him, and when told about his father's prohibition, he proclaims that his father "has brought the land disaster" (29) because in its weakened state the army is not able to deal the Philistines a definitive blow. The phrase for bringing disaster uses a rare Hebrew verb also put in the mouth of father Jefta reproaching his daughter (Judg 11:35), a link between texts casting the shadow of death on these events in the context of an unbearable chasm between parent and offspring.

A subsection (31–35) turns the attention to a violation of food ritual by the army as a result of their famished state. It records efforts by Saul to put the situation to rights by bringing sacrifice and restoring proper food consumption, including the construction of an altar and an oracular consultation about the advisability of pursuit. All these activities result in a renewed delay of the decisive blow needed to deal with the enemy. When the consultation yields no divine response, Saul concludes that someone has violated the food abstinence oath and swears to the death of the culprit, even if it would be his own son (36–39). Why did he make this declaration so specific? Was it not likely that especially Jonathan, who had not been present among the troops, would be the one to unwittingly go against the oath? Is this a signal that Saul has it in his heart to have his son killed with a legitimate excuse, perhaps as the man already chosen by God to replace him? Did not Samuel warn him that God was looking for someone after God's own heart (13:14)? Or is it simply that the vow involves the same rashness as the one Jefta made before he went to war? In Miscall's opinion, Saul is "in the company of both Jephthah and Samson," and like those characters is ruled "by strong and violent emotions."[19]

Saul's quick *decision* to finish off the enemy is replaced by a *question* regarding this decision and *ends in a possible determina-*

19. Miscall, *1 Samuel*, 93.

tion to finish off his own son. A lottery takes place, with the troops on one side and Saul with his son on the other, presumably to simplify the procedure. Jonathan is found out, the text repeating the word "caught" twice. Jonathan owns up to his eating of the honey and is willing to die, upon which Saul declares, "You must surely die," with a repetition of the verb "die" in the Hebrew text. Links with the episode of Achan in Joshua create an ominous context; as Joshua questioned Achan, Saul tells his son, "Tell me what you have done." Unlike Achan, however, Jonathan does not confess to any "sin" but simply declares what he did ("I tasted, yes I tasted," 43) and then stands ready to die. After Saul's verification of his son's fate, again invoking the name of God, the root "die" has sounded five times. It is picked up again by the soldiers, who have throughout been a party to all that has happened. First, when Saul announced the possible death sentence for Jonathan, they did not respond at all; now they throw the matter of death back at Saul by asking in disbelief whether this is the right fate for the person who initiated the victory over the Philistines.

1 Samuel 14:45

Then the people said to Saul:
Shall Jonathan die,
who worked this great deliverance in Israel?
Never! As Adonai lives,
not a hair from his head will fall to the ground,
for with God he worked today!
So the people saved Jonathan,
and he did not die.

Once Saul saved people who denounced him when he was chosen as their first king; now the people save his son, who was chosen for the fate of death. Though the outcome for Jonathan is the avoidance of death, the verb "to die" resounds through the episode, specifically in connection with Jonathan and reflecting back on Saul, in an eerie anticipation of the death that will eventually overtake them together.

Act I, Scene 4: Betrayed by Livestock (1 Samuel 15)

There is no room for Saul to find a way back into the role of the chosen king of Israel.[20]

The definitive rejection of Saul as king unfolds in one introductory section (15:1–9), a short report on Samuel receiving a divine revelation (10–12), and a long segment of dialogue between Saul and Samuel followed by the slaying of the Amalekite king, Agag (13–31), with a conclusive narrative coda restating the mindset of God toward Saul first revealed to Samuel in verse 11 (34–35). The scene is straightforward and clear, but for all that raises crucial issues and questions about Saul, about Samuel, and about God.

It all begins with Saul receiving word from Samuel to go after Amalek. To Amalek clings the hateful memory of its hostility toward Israel in the aftermath of the exodus from Egypt. As a people, they are actually descended from Esau and thus part of the ancestral family, perhaps an additional reason for the rancor experienced by Israel toward them. In the Histories, Amalek appears with an active presence as an enemy people only here and in 1 Samuel 30, where, although they were due by divine command for complete extermination (Exod 17:8–16; Num 24:20; Deut 25:17–19), they pop up again alive and well and ready for another go-around. First, Samuel issues the instruction to Saul to "listen to the voice of the words of Adonai" (1) and finally provides an emphatic and detailed order for total destruction of this enemy. The charge to apply the *herem*, total destruction (see van Wijk-Bos, *The End of the Beginning*, 46–48, 94–110, 138–42), is repeated through the explicit prohibition to *spare*, followed by the instruction to kill all humans as well as animals: "Put to death man and woman, child and babe,/ ox and sheep, camel and donkey" (3). Saul's campaign is successful, told with the usual exaggeration of numbers of soldiers involved and extent of the area conquered (4, 7), and ends with "Saul and the people" *sparing* the Amalekite king, Agag, and the best of the animals while consecrating to death only worthless property (9).[21]

20. David Hester, *First and Second Samuel*, Interpretation Bible Studies (Louisville: Geneva Press, 2000), 42.

21. As Susan Niditch (*War in the Hebrew Bible: A Study in the Ethics of*

A sudden shift in perspective puts the reader in the company of Samuel, who receives the news that God "repents" of having made Saul king because of Saul "turning away" from God and not following through on God's word (11).[22] Hearing this verdict causes Samuel to cry out in anger "all night long," and upon finding out Saul's whereabouts, he sets out for Gilgal. We note that Samuel does not receive a divine command to go and inform Saul about God's decision but only the stark announcement regarding God's change of mind. In verse 11, many translations render the verb for Samuel's reaction as "distressed" or "moved," but there is little doubt about the meaning of the Hebrew root.

We may wonder why Samuel is angry and with whom he is angry. Does he draw the conclusion that Saul has not followed his directives regarding the total extermination, and is he thus angry with Saul? Or, having already declared to Saul that his house will not establish an enduring monarchy and that God has settled on another candidate (13:13–14), is he angry at God for following through on this plan, hoping against hope, perhaps, that the choice of Saul would "stand" after all? Or is his anger directed at himself for having become too attached to this king, one whom he controls to a great degree? Earlier, he was angry with the people for making the wrong choice in their desire for a king. His crying out "all night" to Adonai indicates that his indignation is with God.

Neither Samuel nor God was happy with the people's demand for a monarch, but God directed Samuel to bow to the wish of the people, which he did in the end. Then Saul appeared, an unassuming but physically impressive candidate for kingship who finally man-

---

Violence [Oxford: Oxford University Press, 1993], 62) notes, action on Saul's part constitutes a misunderstanding of the "ban" and a devaluation of human life. "God's offering is that which is most valuable. To mix humans, the highest of God's breathing creations, with sickly or less valuable animals is to break the whole concept of the ban as sacrifice. Similarly, to offer all humans but spare the king, the prize as head of his people, and to offer the animals of lesser worth and spare the best is the opposite of what is required under the ban."

22. Literally, the expression is that Saul did not "maintain" or "establish" God's word—that is to say, did not act accordingly. We could translate that Saul did not "stand by" the instruction, thus forming an instructive repetition.

aged to embrace his role, and it looked as if people and God had found their king. Even though Saul will not establish a hereditary royal house, as long as Samuel is alive, he will be able to guide Saul, who, like a son, is more or less under his control. Now it sounds as if it is really over for Saul, and it is all too much for the old prophet. At the end of the scene the narrative notes that Samuel "mourned for Saul" (15:35). He is angry before the encounter and grieves after their exchange in the aftermath of the battle against Amalek. The loss of Saul is also Samuel's loss; his lack of success is also Samuel's. Much as a parent bemoans the failure of a wayward child, Samuel grieves the inadequacy of the one who once stood taller than all the people and who apparently has failed to live up to his high calling. Although there is no divine command to do so, Samuel goes looking for Saul, again acting more like a parent who feels the need to tell their offspring what they have done wrong. His anger takes the form of grief at the end of the encounter, while God once again is said to "repent" of having made Saul king (35). The exchange between Samuel and Saul at Gilgal is thus set in the frame of anger, grief, and repentance over the choice of Saul as king (11, 33–35).

In the meantime, Saul has done exactly what Samuel told him *not* to do, avoiding total extermination and *sparing* the king and some of the best of the cattle. In the lead-up to the battle, its aftermath, and the confrontation with Samuel, which takes up the largest part of the scene, a detail concerns the counsel of Saul to the Kenites to separate from the Amalekites because he does not want them to meet the same fate (6). Thus, the Kenites avoid the destruction that overcomes Amalek. The reason for his singling out the Kenites is an unspecified act of "kindness" (*hesed*), the quality that enabled Rahab and her family to be singled out for survival at the fall of Jericho. The mustering of soldiers and the battle take up all of three verses in the narrative (4–5, 7), with equal space devoted to the issue regarding the Kenites. Campbell surmises that the incident is here to "ensure a high moral purpose for the campaign,"[23] while Fokkelman judges the exemption of the Kenites to be "high-handed" and "irritating."[24]

23. Campbell, *1 Samuel*, 153.

24. Fokkelman, *The Crossing Fates*, 91.

The narrator may have included this sag in the taut exposition of the engagement with the Amalekites to anticipate what eventually happens. While the verb "to spare" is not used at this point, in fact Saul decides to spare a part of the population without instructions to do so. He is, after all, the king and the commander, and it is within his right to make this decision. In light of what follows, it is more ominous than irritating and a warning sign that more *sparing* lies ahead, of a kind that will go counter to divine instructions.

When Saul and Samuel meet, a long exchange takes place in which each of the characters speaks six times (13–31). The elaborate and lively dialogue draws the listener/reader directly into the encounter. Saul begins with the assertion that he did what God told him, "I have maintained the word of Adonai" (13), using the exact phrase that God gainsaid in his announcement to Samuel (11).[25] It sounds a bit suspicious, like a child claiming to have done everything right before the mother can accuse it of doing something wrong. Throughout his replies, Saul will protest too much. Samuel comes back with a sarcastic question about the sound of sheep bleating and cattle lowing, a dead giveaway that not everything has been destroyed. Saul had been instructed to "listen to the voice of the words of God" by Samuel (1), who now hears the sound/voice (the Hebrew word is the same) of the proof that Saul has not *listened* as he should have. *Not listening* to God's words lies at the heart of Samuel's accusation of Saul.

When Saul begins to explain matters, putting the burden of *sparing* cattle on the people, who saved the best for sacrifice, Samuel cuts him short: "Stop!" It's time for Saul to listen. At the end of this first accusation, he charges, "Why have you not listened to the voice of Adonai/ and fallen upon the spoil/ and done what is wrong in the eyes of Adonai?" (19).[26] Saul goes on protesting, this time revealing

25. The Hebrew text uses the verbal root *qum* (lit. "to stand" or "to arise"), which echoes loudly in these chapters, as it was the verb Samuel used to claim that Saul's kingship would not "stand."

26. The sequence of all the "a" sounds in these lines makes Samuel's accusation come out as one long wail: "Ah, ah, ah!" Susan Niditch (*War in the Hebrew Bible*, 62) derives the verb "swoop" from a root meaning to "wrap/cover," which communicates the notion of Saul becoming entangled in the spoil.

that he also spared Agag, the king of Amalek, in his anxiety taking credit for saving the king and blaming the troops for salvaging the best of the cattle for sacrifice. We are reminded that the intent of the *herem*, which in Samuel occurs only in this chapter, is to dedicate the victims to the Deity, making the claim of wanting to sacrifice the "best" anomalous. Samuel, in any case, will have none of it. Throughout, he has been speaking as a prophet, and now he utters his final devastating judgment in line with classical pre-exilic prophecy.

1 Samuel 15:22–23

22 And Samuel said:
Does Adonai take pleasure in burnt offering and sacrifice
rather than in listening to the voice of God?
Look, listening is better than sacrifice,
paying attention than the fat of rams.

23 For the sin of foretelling is rebellion
and iniquity and idols are obstinacy.
Because you have rejected the word of God,
God has rejected you from being king.

The exhortation that God is not pleased with blood sacrifice in itself goes to the core of preexilic prophetic utterance (see Isa 1:11; Jer 7:21–22; Hos 6:6; cf. Ps 50:8–13). More puzzling are the statements of verse 23, which equate rebellion with forecasting or divination and obstinacy with evil and idol worship. *Rebellion* is a word used for the behavior of the Israelites in the wilderness (Num 17:25[10]; Deut 31:27).[27] The prophet Isaiah equates refusal to listen with *rebellion*: "Indeed they are a *rebellious* people, deceitful children, children who do not want to listen to the instruction of Adonai" (Isa 30:9). The word here translated "obstinacy" really means insistent urging. It is used in Genesis 19 both by Lot's guests and by the townspeople

27. Out of the twenty-one times we find the word *meri* ("rebellion") in the Hebrew Bible, sixteen are in Ezekiel with the reference to Israel as a "house of rebellion" (e.g., Ezek 2:5, 6; 3:26, 27; 12:2, 3).

urging Lot to deliver his guests to them (Gen 19:3, 9) and in Judges by the father-in-law of the Levite (Judg 19:7). The intention of the insistent urging is not in itself always wrong but is unwanted or brings about unwanted results.[28] The utterance of Samuel is in poetic form, weaving words related to *sacrifice* into the first four lines, contrasted to *listening* and *paying attention*.[29] Bringing sacrifice without listening equals forecasting and idolatry and results in *rejection*. So far, Saul has not engaged in the actual practice of divination, but it is interesting that in Samuel's words it comes down to the same thing. In that way, the eventual consultation of the shaman of Endor in chapter 28 is a logical outcome of the path Saul is already treading.

In verses 24–31, Saul confesses his sin and repents, and when Samuel does not relent, he goes so far as to grab hold of Samuel's robe and tear off a piece, a gesture interpreted by Samuel as symbolic for the tearing away of Saul's kingship. For good measure, he adds that the kingship will go to someone "better" than Saul (see 13:14) while stating that the God of Israel is not a human being to have a change of mind, "to deal falsely or repent" (28–29).[30] The last declaration is especially interesting, as it flies in the face of the narrator's declaration that God "repented" of the decision to make Saul king twice in this chapter (11, 35). The notion that the God of Israel is able to come back from a decision, especially one of planned punishment, is expressed frequently enough in Scripture that we must ascribe Samuel's declaration to a personal perspective, due

28. The word is also used in Gen 33:11 of Jacob urging Esau to accept his gifts, in 2 Kgs 2:17 of Elisha's disciples looking for the body of Elijah, and 2 Kgs 5:16 of Naaman urging Elisha to accept a gift.

29. Burnt offering/sacrifice/fat of rams (15:22) contrasted with listening/paying attention. Most translations render the Hebrew *shama‘* with "obey/obedience." I have argued elsewhere that this rich concept in the Hebrew Bible becomes attenuated when rendered with "obedience." See Johanna W. H. van Wijk-Bos, *Making Wise the Simple: The Torah in Christian Faith and Practice* (Grand Rapids: Eerdmans, 2005), 18nn8–9.

30. The phrasing is interesting in that Samuel does not refer to "Adonai" but uses a term occurring only here as a divine title, meaning perhaps "the Glory of Israel." Miscall (*1 Samuel*, 111) wonders whether this title marks the statement as "maxim . . . a rhetorical flourish."

perhaps to his having cried out to Adonai for a whole night without success.[31] Saul implores Samuel not to leave his side for the sake of maintaining his status with the people, and Samuel relents but will no longer speak with Saul (31).[32]

The task still remains to dispatch King Agag, accomplished in a few sentences that paint a drama in vivid color (32–33), with Agag expressing hope that his demise is not yet near and Samuel taking the matter in hand himself, cutting him down "before Adonai," an act of ritual butchering accompanied with the words "As your sword has made women childless,/ so may your mother become childless above women."[33] In the Hebrew, the words "your sword" and "your mother" each come at the end of the phrase, directly connecting Agag's sword with his mother and making "your mother" the last word Agag hears. In the words of Campbell, "Samuel's act seems one of unparalleled savagery; today's equivalent: the prophet chopped the victim to pieces in church."[34] It is in any case a bitter conclusion to a disturbing episode in the life of Saul, Samuel, and the people,

31. See, for example, Exod 32:12, 14; Judg 2:18; Jer 18:8; 26:13, 19; Amos 7:6; Jonah 3:10; 4:2; Joel 2:13, 14. But see Num 23:19 for the opposite statement. On the concept of a divine change of heart as it occurs in the Bible, see van Wijk-Bos, *Making Wise the Simple*, 234–42.

32. The phrasing in 15:31 is ambiguous, using the term "return, come back" together with "behind, after." In 15:11 God declares to Samuel that Saul "turned away from me" using *shuv* together with *me'aharey*. The usage in 15:31 is more like Ruth 1:15, where Naomi admonishes Ruth to "turn behind your sister," i.e., to go back to follow your sister (see also Jer 34:11). Yet it is sufficiently rare to find "return" together with "behind" that it creates some ambiguity. Alter (*The David Story: A Translation with Commentary of 1 and 2 Samuel* [New York: Norton, 1999], 93n31) argues that *shuv 'im* and *shuv 'aharey* are antonyms and concludes that Samuel completes his rejection of Saul by refusing to accompany him to the cult." He thus translates "Samuel turned back from Saul."

33. The terse Hebrew lines show repetition and rhyme: *ka'asher shikkelah nashim harbekha/ ken-tishkal minnashim immekha* – "As it made childless women your sword,/ so may it make childless above women your mother." The root *shakhal* means to "miscarry" or to be "bereft of children." In the Bible, it occurs with "sword" as subject also in Deut 32:25 and Lam 1:20.

34. Campbell, *1 Samuel*, 156.

overshadowing a victorious battle on the part of Saul. The concluding statement (34–35) has everyone back in their place: Samuel in Ramah and Saul in Gibeah, with Samuel mourning and God repenting of his choice of Saul. As Fokkelman notes, the phrases include both death ("Samuel did not see Saul again until the day of his death," 35) and mourning, even though Saul is still alive. "We realize that Saul as king is dead; no stronger expression of the termination of the monarchy can be imagined."[35]

The Question of Saul

The story has a hard time demonstrating that Saul is at fault and an even harder time demonstrating that the magnitude of the wrongdoing justifies the magnitude of the price he pays.[36]

On his way to kingship, Saul comes across as a diffident young man who has a hard time finding his way, either to the lost donkeys of his father or to the seer and in the end to his kingship. He speaks little, and when he does, it is mostly to ask questions. He is from the beginning introduced as a "choice young man," handsomer and taller than anyone (9:2), an assertion repeated, particularly in regard to his size, following the selection process at Mizpah (10:24). Saul seems less than eager to accept any high office assigned to him, whether by prophet or people, questioning the judgment of Samuel when he first meets Saul and hiding among the baggage when chosen by lot (9:21; 10:23). He is able to exercise prudence by not speaking prematurely of Samuel's act of anointing (10:16) and kindness toward those who are not in favor of his appointment (11:13). He is an able warrior under the power of God's spirit (11:6) and is spoken of as a valiant fighter during his kingship (14:52). The narrative provides little detail of the latter, however, and hastens to describe the troubles that lead to Saul's fall from grace.

In the story Saul begins his downward slide almost as soon as he has reached the pinnacle of his career. His rejection from kingship is

35. Fokkelman, *The Crossing Fates*, 110.
36. John Goldingay, *Old Testament Theology*, 583.

announced on two occasions, first by Samuel in the name of God on the eve of a military engagement with the Philistines (13:13–14) and once again, this time more emphatically, with repeated declarations of rejection, after a victorious battle against Amalek (15:13–31, esp. vv. 23 and 26). In between these two episodes is a protracted battle with the Philistines in which Saul acts in turns too hesitant and too stern, wavering in pursuit of the enemy when they are on the run, putting the army on what appears to be an imprudent course of fasting, and overzealously pursuing religious ritual and oath fulfillment, even at the potential cost of his son Jonathan's life (13:16–14:46).

Samuel, who is informed by God that Saul is the man for kingship (9:16–17), behaves toward Saul in ways that must seem baffling in the extreme to this good-looking but awkward young man, first taking him to a meal where the best portion is saved for him, speaking with him alone and pouring oil on his head, and predicting a rapid-fire series of events to come in the near future, including Saul's "ranting like a prophet" (10:2–8), with the narrator noting that everything happened as Samuel predicted (10:9). It would have been enough to unbalance any young person, certainly one who appears as unsure of himself as Saul, who does not give evidence that he has resigned himself to the role Samuel and God picked for him. When the narrator notes that Saul does not reveal to his uncle what Samuel had told him about kingship (10:16), is a possible reason that he has not embraced his high calling? Why tell anyone about something that is not going to happen anyway?

When we encounter Saul after he is elected by lot, he is back at farm work behind the plow and needs the urging of the divine spirit to take on the mantle of military leadership (11:5–11). A tortuous path finally brings him to rejoice together with his people in his appointed role (11:15). Samuel, who tarried in the search for a candidate, has found his king but sees fit to engage in a long punitive discourse to the people on the issue of kingship after which the people confess their desire for a king as "evil," although they do not go back on their decision (12:19). In his speech, Samuel warns the people against "rebellion," something of which he will eventually accuse Saul and declare a cause for his rejection from kingship. We may surmise that Saul was among the crowd listening to Samuel's diatribe, which may well have taken place at Gilgal, where he was finally crowned. In any case, the narrator places the condemnation of kingship immediately following that occasion. Taking everything that has happened to him until the beginning of chapter 13, one could hardly expect to meet a king and military leader who is secure in his position, especially one who has been as hesitant as Saul. Saul's behavior in the episodes that follow should thus hardly come as a surprise. Having taken on something he hardly felt suited for, having finally been able to connect to his role with a degree of joy, he hears that the prophet turned kingmaker who came his way as a potential aid for a household conundrum and who surprised him by making him into a king views the entire enterprise of kingship as "evil."

Following Samuel's discourse in chapter 12, descriptions of Saul's behavior portray him as suffering increasingly debilitating episodes and unpredictable mood swings which are to last him his entire life. Further on, the narrator will ascribe Saul's instability to a bad spirit from Adonai (16:14). It is well known that in the ancient world, psychopathological problems were generally ascribed to demonic spirits sent as divine punishment. Such was most likely the case with Saul. His behavior will become more paranoid and unpredictable as time goes on, as he falls victim to onsets of devastating rage that drive him to commit assaults on defenseless individuals and groups.

Various traditions clung to Saul, the first of the kings of ancient Israel. His house did not establish a hereditary monarchy, and multiple versions of his personality and activities stayed alive, while at the same time an explanation for his failure needed to be found. The stories emphasize the fact that he was *rejected* by God, although the exact transgressions on his part are not always clear. Because we hear nothing about his inner life until chapter 18, Saul's personality remains opaque and conflicted: shy and modest, drawn on by powerful forces divine and human, forceful and yet hesitant, punctual in terms of religious observance yet going counter to instructions received from Samuel as God's mouthpiece. According to Cheryl Exum's observation, Saul, though guilty, "is not really wicked. The tragic vision gives rise to the uneasy awareness that the hero's punishment exceeds any guilt. The question is not why Saul is rejected. . . . The question is why there is no forgiveness."[37] In Exum's view, scholars who avoid this question are too eager to defend God.[38]

It may be useful to approach the question about God's rejection of Saul from the point of view of postexilic anxiety concerning divine *rejection*. We keep in mind that Saul is not rejected as a person but as a king, because as ruler he missed the mark somehow. Also, "kingship may not have been good for Saul himself. A certain instability in his nature, now leading to hesitancy and then to rash decisions, may have made him less and less able" not only to lead effectively but to function as a stable person.[39] Saul may have been, in Edwin Good's words, "a man not fitted for a job that should not have been opened."[40]

Ambivalence in the community in terms of divine approval of kingship, of Israel's kings, and of Israel as God's covenant people was likely a consuming issue at the time of the Babylonian exile and during its aftermath. Kingship in these narratives is thus approached from different angles, one of them as a concession on the part of Israel's God to a people who appear unable to find the right way of living together under God's guidance. This approach comes with the knowledge that, ultimately, kingship did not save the people from destruction and exile. Pressing questions resulting from the devastation came to the fore both in regard to the power of God and God's concern for the people who believed themselves in covenant with God. The prophets of Israel issued warnings before the Assyrian exile: "My God will *rejec*t them;/ because they have not listened to him,/ they will wander around among the nations" (Hos 9:17). On the eve of the Babylonian invasion, Jeremiah prophesied, "*Rejected* silver they will call them/ because Adonai has *rejected* them" (Jer

37. Exum, *Tragedy and Biblical Narrative*, 40.

38. The text appears to leave a good deal of the ambivalence surrounding the character of God in the story intact. For the editors and collectors, too, questions concerning God's role in the drama of Saul appear to be alive. Hence the conflicting statements concerning the possibility of God's repentance.

39. Johanna W. H. van Wijk-Bos, *Reading Samuel: A Literary and Theological Commentary* (Macon, GA: Smyth and Helwys, 2011), 88.

40. Edwin M. Good, *Irony in the Old Testament* (Sheffield: Almond, 1981), 58.

6:30), and, "Listen, oh land!/ Look, I myself am bringing evil upon this people/ . . ./ because to my words they paid no attention,/ and my instruction they *rejected*" (Jer 6:19). Especially striking is the plea in Jeremiah 14:

> JEREMIAH 14:19
>
> Have you *rejected*, yes *rejected*, Judah?
> Does your soul abhor Zion?
> Why did you strike us down
> and there is for us no healing?
> Awaiting well-being and there is nothing good;
> a time of healing and, look!, terror!

The book of Lamentations ends with a plea for restoration, unless God has indeed rejected God's people: "If you have indeed *rejected* us, your anger has become too much for us" (Lam 5:22).[41]

The notion of rejection is closely tied to the refusal to *listen* to God's instruction, and indeed this is the accusation Samuel hurls at Saul, reproving him for preferring "divination" and inappropriate "urging," probably indicating manipulation of divine power through magic or oracular means. In the Torah, divination is condemned in Numbers 23:23 and Deuteronomy 18:10, 14. In Samuel, "diviners" appear in Philistine culture (1 Sam 6:2), and Saul will resort to it during his consultation with the shaman of Endor (28:7–20).[42]

With the exile looming on the horizon, Jeremiah accuses the people of having relied on false prophecy and divination (Jer 14:14).[43] In the context of exile, Second Isaiah follows a lengthy condemnation of idol worship with a statement about God, who brings to

41. Cf. Hos 4:6; Jer 6:19, 30; 7:29; 8:9; 14:19. In the so-called book of consolation in Jeremiah (30:1–31:37), there is a denial of the very possibility of God rejecting the people (31:37). All these texts use the verb *ma'as* for "reject."

42. Elsewhere in the Historical Books, there is only a reference to divination in terms of the past in regard to Balaam (Josh 13:22) and in a narrative explanation of the cause for the Assyrian exile of the Northern Kingdom in 2 Kings 17:17, in a chapter that lists the sins of the people.

43. See also Ezek 13:6, 9, 23; 22:28.

naught the "signs of soothsayers and makes fools of *diviners*" (Isa 44:25). The question of *listening* to God's *torah* became acute for the community in postexilic Judah, a reason to highlight the failure of listening on Saul's part. *Listening* to God's instruction became one of the essential characteristics for the understanding of itself as God's people. Out of their traumatic experience arose the renewed conviction that, while kingdoms come and go and human kings come and go, the abiding presence of God is available for God's people in the *word* that comes to them more and more as *text*.

Act II: David at Saul's Court (1 Samuel 16:1–21:1)

Trauma also presents its own peculiar challenges to coherent story telling.[44]

The story of Saul while David is present at his court takes up five chapters, with David already revealed to the reader/listener as Saul's successor in the opening scene (16:1–13). David's appearance among Saul's entourage makes use of various sources, just as Saul's rise to the throne appears to originate in different strands of tradition. A number of tales with sometimes contradictory information clung to heroes of the stature of David and Saul. David is introduced as the chosen one of God anointed by Samuel, is subsequently invited to Saul's side on the counsel of Saul's servants, and finally comes out of nowhere as the hero to save the day in the face of a fearsome Philistine combatant. The collectors and editors evidently considered all of the material significant in shedding light on the protagonist and let the different voices have their say. The multiple perspectives lend complexity and interest.[45]

44. Danna Nolan Fewell, "A Broken Hallelujah: Remembering David, Justice, and the Cost of the House," in *The Fate of King David*, ed. Toda Linafelt, Claudia V. Camp, and Timothy Beal (London: T&T Clark, 2010), 105.

45. Although nothing "fishy or wishy" may be at the bottom of the multiple introductions of David, as Carol Fontaine ("The Sharper Harper [1 Samuel 16:14–23]: Iconographic Reflections on David's Rise to Power," in *The Fate of King David: The Past and Present of a Biblical Icon*, ed. Tod Linafelt, Claudia V.

For Saul, the three roads to kingship highlighted both his character and the difficulty embedded in the issue of the people's request for a monarch. David's anointing is revealed to the listener/reader but kept from Saul, an element which adds tension to the narrative. From the beginning, David is depicted as a man of multiple talents. While declared to be good-looking, he is not said to be tall as Saul was, and according to Saul's servants, he is both well-spoken and prudent, a musician and also a warrior.[46] He exhibits none of Saul's uncertainty and tentative posture but rather exudes self-confidence, including the conviction that God is on his side—particularly in his face-off with Goliath but also when going out onto the battlefield. A number of people, including Saul, love him at first sight, so that one concludes he emanates a kind of magnetic attraction. Saul and two of his children, as well as the people, are all said to *love* David. Notwithstanding all the love, or more likely because of it, David soon falls out of favor, and Saul not only makes a direct attempt on his life while he is at work soothing the king's disturbed psyche but devises plans to have him killed in a roundabout way. Saul's daughter Michal manages to help David escape the palace, but it takes more than one threat for David to understand that there is no place for him at Saul's side, and he finally resorts to living outside the bounds of the king's reach and starts a life as a guerilla fighter.

David's emotions do not come to the surface in this section; it is ambiguous whether this so-loved man loved anyone in return, for

---

Camp, and Timothy Beal [London: T&T Clark, 2010], 135–52) would have it, it is true that their multilayered quality puts a complex character on the stage, one of the most intriguing personalities of the Bible. About the incoherence between 16:14–23 and ch. 17, Edwin Good (*Irony in the Old Testament*, 74n23) observes, "Only one thing can be said with certainty. . . : the double accounts of David's entry into Saul's court did not bother the editor."

46. In this context, Alter's (*The Art of Biblical Narrative* [New York: Basic Books, 1981], 148 and 152 resp.) observation concerning discrepancies between chs. 16 and 17 still sounds persuasive. He writes that "both stories are necessary . . . for the writer's binocular view of David." He adds, "David will be the brilliant warrior-king . . . and for this identity the Goliath story is the fitting introduction. But he is also to figure as the eloquent elegist, the composer of psalms."

example. He is one of those people who draws all eyes, fills everyone around him with admiration and affection, brazen, glowing with youth and good looks, a star who can do no wrong, except in Saul's eyes. We will follow David on his long path from the time he first strides on to the pages of the biblical story through his life as exile and outcast to the days of his kingship and beyond. There is no life in the Bible that we are able to follow in closer detail than that of David, the son of Jesse.

Act II, Scene 1: A King in Sight (1 Samuel 16:1–13)

There was something God could see about him.[47]

Chapter 16 takes us first to Samuel, who is admonished by God to stop grieving over Saul and to get on with the task of anointing a new king. The divine instructions are quite specific—Samuel is to go to Bethlehem, to the house of Jesse—but they stop short of indicating the individual God has in mind among Jesse's sons, "for I have seen among his sons for myself a king" (1). This lack of detail will create a hitch for Samuel in the execution of his task. As with Saul, the new candidate for the monarchy will be anointed, and there will be a celebratory sacrificial meal, a meal that attracts only a passing mention. Unlike with the introduction of Saul, Samuel needs to take an active part in the search rather than waiting for the person of God's choice to turn up. In addition, the new king will be one who responds to God's need rather than the needs of the people. The emphatic "for myself" (*li*) returns in verse 3 with the instruction "anoint for me." The connection between God's wish and its fulfillment in King David is from the beginning tightly drawn. As the previous chapter centered on the verb *to listen,* chapter 16 has its focus on *seeing,* reaching its apex in the statement of verse 7 with a fourfold occurrence of the root. We stay with Samuel through verse 13, when the scene shifts to the house of Saul. First Samuel then Saul is at center

47. John Goldingay, *1 and 2 Samuel for Everyone* (Louisville: Westminster John Knox, 2011), 79.

stage in the episodes, while David does not speak at all. We see him through the eyes of the narrator but have no opportunity to judge his personality, which in biblical narrative is so often revealed via a character's speech.

First off, Samuel is terrified at God's command, realistically judging that Saul will kill him if he gets wind of the prophet's errand. God's cover story for Samuel is to make Jesse and his family the centerpiece of a sacrificial celebration. The ruse works both for Bethlehem's citizenry and the Jesse family in that Samuel gets to review the sons of Jesse in turn. While Samuel has good cause to fear Saul finding out the truth about his errand, the reasons for the frightened reaction of the Bethlehemites to Samuel's arrival are less obvious. The text uses the same verb found in chapter 13 for the *trembling* that overcame the army fleeing away from Saul in the face of overwhelming Philistine power and in chapter 14 when the Philistines were tricked by Jonathan into the belief they were met by a superior force (13:7; 14:15). It is a root used elsewhere in the context of military engagement (Judg 7:3; 1 Sam 4:13; 28:5). The connotations are of a panicky fear, at times caused by an encounter with supernatural events (cf. Exod 19:16, 18). Samuel comes, and all are atremble. News in the small-town environment of the time traveled fast, so it is possible that folks are aware of the split between Samuel and Saul and are afraid of getting caught in the crossfire. Word of Samuel's rage at Saul, together with his butchering of the Amalekite king, had probably done the rounds, and the Bethlehemites have no idea what he may be up to. Their question to Samuel is not about his welfare but whether his presence bodes well for the town: "Is your coming peace?" (4). Once reassured, the representatives disappear so that the focus narrows gradually, first to Jesse and his sons and eventually to his youngest son.

The details of sacrifice and sacrificial meal are mostly forgotten as Samuel, most likely still uneasy, is quick to judge the first one of the sons to come before him as the one he is to anoint. God has to set Samuel straight until the last son has passed before him and he has to declare for the third time that none of them are God's choice. The entire episode began by God's statement about *rejection*, a word that now echoes forth in the words "not chosen." The declaration made by God to Samuel in verse 7 goes to the core of the issue, picking up attributes that were notably Saul's when he was the *chosen one*. After settling on Eliab, Samuel is cautioned not to regard his appearance *or the height of his stature*, a feature highlighted about Saul when he was first introduced and on the way to his kingship (1 Sam 9:2–10:23). The caution is followed by a renewed use of the word *reject* with a motivational clause added: "Adonai does not see as a human sees, for humans see according to the eyes, and Adonai sees according to the heart" (7).

When the youngest of the sons finally comes into view, it turns out he is very attractive to Samuel's eyes: "ruddy with beautiful eyes, of handsome appearance" (12). While the description can be seen as a contradiction to the declaration of verse 7 since it emphasizes outer appearance rather than the heart, it is also possible that the emphasis in the description of David's looks is in implied contrast to Saul. David is "the youngest," but the Hebrew *qatan* can also indicate "little." It is the youngest and littlest, the one son whose existence was almost forgotten, of whom God states, "He is it!" (12). The anointing takes place in the family circle and, while not as secretive as Saul's, is still far from public. It is only when the divine spirit rushes upon David that his name is revealed (13). Unlike the same phenomenon reported of Saul, nothing is said about the effect it has on David. In the end, all are back in their place, David in Bethlehem and Samuel in Ramah, as if nothing had happened.

Act II, Scene 2: A Therapist in Sight (1 Samuel 16:14–23)

Little David, play on your harp.[48]

The scene opens at the court of Saul, who is now suffering from the departure of God's spirit and the arrival of a "bad spirit." He is surrounded by his servants and clearly in an agitated state. The reference to a "bad spirit" originating with God overcoming an individual

48. Traditional African American spiritual.

occurs in the Bible only in relation to Saul.[49] As early as the Talmud, Saul is declared to be unusual in his actions,[50] and in more recent times has been judged to have been insane.[51] It would be natural for the ancient world of which Israel was a part to ascribe delusion, paranoia and other mental instabilities to the work of a divine spirit.

1 Samuel 16:14–17

14 And the spirit of Adonai had turned from Saul;
then terrified him a spirit sent from Adonai.
15 The servants of Saul said to him:
Look, a bad spirit of God is terrifying you,
16 let our lord, please, speak to your servants before you
for them to seek a man, who knows how to play the lyre.
And when the bad spirit of God is upon you, he will play
and it will be well with you.
17 Saul said to his servants:
See me, please, a man who plays well
and bring him to me.

Saul's disturbance is placed very close to the notation of the anointing of David, whose receiving the spirit of God is directly contrasted with the departure of God's spirit from Saul. That his agitation is public is evident from Saul's servants taking the lead in advising him. As music was understood to be a means to soothe mental anguish, the servants counsel that Saul direct them to "seek a man," upon which Saul instructs them on *seeing* him a man in words

49. In 1 Sam 16:14, 15, 16, 23 (2×), 18:10, and 19:9. The "bad spirit" of Judges 9:23 is not sent to an individual.

50. TB Mo'ed Qatan 16b (New York: Schottenstein, 2004): "Saul was unusual in his deeds." The word *meshuneh,* in the older editions translated "distinguished," is clearly not to be understood in a positive sense but with the meaning of different from the norm, as the skin of the Ethiopian is different.

51. Yehiel Michel Wisser (Malbim) https://www.sefaria.org/Malbim_on_I_Samuel.18.10.1?lang=bi&with=all&lang2=en. More recently, Alter (*The David Story,* 98n14) has defined Saul's mental state as "psychosis . . . [with] fits of depression, later accompanied by paranoia."

reminiscent of the divine declaration to Samuel (16:1). Ironically, both God and Saul *see* for themselves the same man; the one who will arrive to make him well will be the one appointed by God to take the throne—if not from Saul himself, then from his heir. One of the servants has also *seen* the right man, who will be the wrong man for Saul. Once again, David's name does not come to the surface when one of the lads responds and speaks of "a son of Jesse" being skilled with the lyre. The short resume he provides combines all the factors that make him remarkable: a talented musician but also a powerful man—something observed earlier of the father of Saul—and a warrior, as well as a gifted speaker and a good-looking man with God on his side. Need anything more be said?

Although no name has been mentioned, Saul sends for David, who in his turn is sent by his father Jesse with gifts fit for a king in hand (19–21). Verse 20 details the donations that accompany David as "bread, a skin of wine, and a young goat," all of which are items brought by the men who encountered Saul in 10:3. The effect of the repetition is that David is beginning the same process Saul started earlier.[52] The omission of naming David until he is on his way to Saul's court may reflect the likelihood that everyone knows whom they are talking about. There is at least a suggestion in the narrative that word about what happened in Jesse's family in Bethlehem has gone around and that there was a David-admirer among Saul's household.[53] The first identification of David as he comes to Saul is that of weapon bearer, perhaps a kind of guise to cloak David's role in Saul's household from the world at large.

1 SAMUEL 16:21

David came to Saul
and stood before him,

52. Alter, *The David Story*, 99n20: "David then is beginning anew the process on which Saul launched."

53. Such an inference is also drawn by Alter (*The David Story*, 98n18), who raises the possibility of there being "a pro-David mole in the court of Saul."

and he loved him greatly,
and he became his weapon bearer.

There is one here *standing* who will be the undoing of the one before whom he stands, whose *fall* will be excruciatingly slow until he finally *falls* on his own sword. But who exactly loves whom here? David is the subject of the other verbs in the sentence (David came/he stood/he became) and grammatically fits the subject of "loved" with Saul the object. If that is the intention, it would be the only time David is said to *love* anyone in this cycle, while he is the object of others' love in a number of cases. If Saul is intended as the subject, it makes the sequel all the more heart-rending. Perhaps the note is intentionally ambiguous. There was love on someone's side, but nothing good will come of it. In fact, love and David do not make easy bedfellows, either here or in the sequel to his life as weapon bearer and court musician. In many cases, it will prove to become his own and others' undoing.

A final description (22–23) has Saul making the arrangement of David's position permanent with Jesse and David playing the lyre before the terrified Saul. Where the introduction to the scene presents God's spirit turning away from Saul and leaving room for the "bad spirit," the music eases Saul to the degree that the bad spirit turns away. Yet God's spirit is not said to return to Saul.

Act II, Scene 3: Appearance of a Champion (1 Samuel 17)

In this case the "Achilles heel" was Goliath's knee.[54]

But then an entirely different story of David's introduction to the royal household was at hand, and the editors wedged it in between the tradition about David as music therapist and the first surge of Saul's jealousy of David in 18:8. The long chapter that tells the tale of David and Goliath highlights David's skill and bravery in the arena

54. Ariella Deem, "And the Stone Sank into His Forehead: A Note on 1 Samuel XVII 49," *VT* 28 (1978): 351.

of warfare in the face of an overpowering opponent (as the previous episode did in a more summary fashion regarding his talent in the arena of music) while at the same time providing an elaborate example of his being well-spoken. It is possible that it was not really David who killed Goliath,[55] but characters that loom large in the history of a people tend to accrue to themselves lore that comes with the space they occupy in the imagination, and who does not love the way "little David," the underdog, dispatches the mighty giant of the Philistines? The chapter exhibits signs of originating in different traditions, the most obvious one being David's double introduction to Saul: once as Saul calls him in ahead of the duel (32–37) and again in the closing unit, with Saul oblivious to the earlier encounter (55–58). Such contradictions left intact in the one story of the final edition allow us to view David from more than one perspective.[56]

The events are told in detail as extravagant as the outfit of the champion, who looms so large that everyone, including Saul, sits cowering in their tents—except David, who comes onto the battlefield as an errand-boy sent by his father to look after the welfare of his brothers. The account emphasizes the fear of the Israelites, recording it twice, explicitly including Saul among the terrified (11, 24). Once again, there is the demand for "a man," and none is to be found until David, the youngest/littlest son of Jesse, turns up, too small to wear Saul's armor but, like Jonathan earlier in the story, willing to take a risk and trusting in the aid of the Holy One of Israel.

The scene is set on the page with perfect skill, with an alternating tempo shifting from description to speech, from habitual action to one-time occurrences that draw the reader/listener directly into the event. Spatial location is clearly determined throughout the

55. In 2 Sam 21:19, one Elhanan is named the slayer of Goliath.

56. Antony Campbell (*1 Samuel*, 188), who analyzes a "core" and a "variant story" in chs. 16–18, expresses bafflement at the desire of commentators to review the text as a single story. He paraphrases the gospel injunction "what God has joined together let no one separate" (Matt 19:6): "What the text has separated, let no interpreter join together." While Campbell offers an insightful analysis of possible antecedents of the tradition represented in 1 Samuel 16:14–18:16, the obvious response to his bafflement is that the biblical writers present the narrative as one and must have had reasons for doing so.

story, beginning with the placing of the two armies, each on a hill with a valley in between, where the champion, in Hebrew literally the "in-betweensman," takes his place to issue the challenge. Space continues to receive emphasis with the renewed introduction of David, at home with his father, then at the Israelite camp to bring provender to his brothers, among the soldiers, in Saul's tent, and finally as he approaches Goliath. Much becomes clear, but the account still leaves questions. Is David a naïve, brash young man who is willing to gamble everything, including his life, on the chance of outwitting the lumbering giant who faces him in the valley? Is the story an example of his trust in God, or is he a more scheming kind of fellow, out for the main chance and seeing an opportunity to better himself and achieve standing at the court of Saul? Does the truth lie somewhere in between? I will approach some of the issues raised in the story through a closer look at dialogue and speech, which take up a good deal of the chapter.[57]

The location of the two armies is on the hills facing the Elah valley between Socoh and Azekah at the western edge of the hill country, about twenty miles south-west of Gibeah and perhaps ten from Bethlehem (1–3). The champion's origin is nearby Gath, a short distance to the west in Philistine territory. He is introduced in the next unit (4–11) with elaborate detail about his battle gear. It's as if a one-man army walks onto the battlefield, his armor alone weighing 125 pounds and the shaft of his spear more than fifteen. Alter writes, "The thematic effect is clear: Goliath is represented as a hulking man of material military impediments—everything is gargantuan size or weight . . . with untypical specification."[58] While it has the desired effect on the Israelites, who are terrified (11), one wonders if the outfit is entirely useful and whether the detailed description, untypical in Hebrew narrative, aims to poke fun at this "in-betweens-man." Miscall asks, "Is this a powerful and fearsome warrior or a big oaf weighed down with armor and with little mobility?"[59] It is at this

57. For a detailed analysis of each unit in the chapter, see, for example, Fokkelman's discussion in *The Crossing Fates*, 145–208.

58. Alter, *The David Story*, 102nn5–6.

59. Miscall, *1 Samuel*, 120.

point not so much the sight of him as his *words* that paralyze the Israelites with fear. His voice, the first one heard in the story, takes up most of verses 8–10.

1 SAMUEL 17:8–10

8 And he stood and cried to the ranks of Israel
and said to them:
Why have you come out in battle ranks?
Am I not the Philistine,
and you servants of Saul?
Choose yourselves a man
who will come down to me!

9 If he is able to fight me and strikes me down,
we will be your servants,
and if I am able and strike him down,
then you will be our servants, and you will serve us!
10 The Philistine said:
I mock the ranks of Israel today!
Give me a man and we will fight together!

Goliath stands and shouts the challenge. He identifies his words as a mocking taunt (10), a term used especially in the context of battle and one that will be picked up by David and repeated four more times. He questions the use of the Israelites coming out with an army, applying the word "ranks," a key word picked up ten more times. He calls for "a man" to come and fight him. The challenge is clear: one man for one man, and whoever wins decides the victor. With his opening identification of himself and his enemies, he already insults the Israelites, calling them "servants of Saul" while he is "*the* Philistine," a servant of no one. Servant and slave are the same word in Hebrew, and so the old Greek translations render the word "slave." What Goliath says is that this rabble already amounts to little more than a bunch of slaves, and when he is the victor, they will only change overlords. For good measure, he adds that they will *do service* as slaves. Twice he calls for "a man," one the Israelites will choose for themselves, a new "chosen" one who will have to prove his mettle in single combat![60] With his last words, he repeats the challenge with the phrase "give me a man"—in other words, whomever they choose will be delivered to Goliath as prey. His words have the effect that everyone cowers in fear, beginning with Saul (11).

Enter David (12–19)—not a man but a *lad* as he is called throughout the episode (33, 42, 55, 58). He is the youngest son of one Jesse of Bethlehem, who has eight sons and is advanced in age, with three of his sons on the battlefield with Saul. David appears here as if we had not met him before, clearly identified by patronymic and tribe and as one who herds the flock of his father, sent on his habitual errand (15) to bring his brothers food and see if they are doing alright. Jesse is the second person to speak in the scene.

1 Samuel 17:17–19

17 Jesse said to David his son:
Take please to your brothers
this ephah of parched grain and ten loaves of bread
and run to the camp, to your brothers.
18 And these ten wedges of cheese
bring to the master of their thousand;
take account of your brothers' welfare
and bring back their token.
19 Saul and they and all the Israelites
are in the Oak Valley fighting with the Philistines.

David takes a load of food. The bushel of grain, loaves of bread, and wedges of cheese must have been loaded on a pack-animal, so the trip going through the hill country, although not much more than ten miles, may well have taken him the better part of the morning. We note that the emphasis in Jesse's commission is on the

60. With many versions and translations, I opt for the reading *baharu* in v. 8 rather than the MT *baru*, a verb that occurs only here with the supposed meaning "select."

brothers, who are mentioned in each verse. It's all about the brothers. One is reminded of young Joseph sent by his father to inquire after his brothers' welfare in the Genesis story. Those brothers did not have a good relationship, and we shall see that family relations in the Jesse household are perhaps not much better. Joseph went on a much more hazardous mission than foreseen by either him or his father in Genesis 37:13, while David's errand is to the dangers of the battlefield, which is not something that appears to give his father concern. Only the welfare of the brothers is of interest. Jesse mentions the armies fighting, which may indicate that word about Goliath's challenge has not reached Bethlehem and that he is worried about the well-being of his oldest sons. The provender sent along with young David is substantial. It will not do to define David as a "nobody." His great-grandfather was Boaz, a "man of substance" in his town (Ruth 2:1), and the provisions listed here give evidence of a family of some standing.

David arrives at the battle lines and does what he was sent to do, but then he hears Goliath and witnesses the fear he instills in the Israelite army ("When they saw the man, they fled before him and feared greatly," 24), and speaks for the first time since his appearance in the text. The image painted in 20–21 is that of Israelite and Philistine soldiers organized in battle formation, "ranks upon ranks." The orderly formation changes under the effect of the terrifying sight of Goliath, and we may picture the conversation between David and unnamed soldiers in the following dialogue to take place in the midst of the army's milling about.

1 Samuel 17:25–26

25 And an Israelite said:
Have you seen this man who comes up?
Indeed, to mock Israel he comes up.
But the man who strikes him down,
the king will enrich him with great riches,
his daughter he will give him,
and the house of his father
he will make tax-free in Israel!

26 David said to the men standing with him:
What will be done for the man
who strikes down this Philistine,
to turn away the shame from Israel?
For who is this foreskinned Philistine
that he mocks the ranks of the living God?

The unnamed soldier, addressing a group rather than an individual ("Hey, did y'all see?"), offers just the right phrases to get young David's dander up, calling the champion "this man who *comes up*," pointing to his *mockery* of Israel, and putting him in direct opposition to "the man who strikes him *down*," who has, of course, so far not appeared. The information that there is a reward for the one who will succeed in the challenge is new and fits perfectly with the folkloristic cast of the story.[61] Both in the ancient world and in more modern times, the promise-of-great-wealth motif belongs to the tale of the underdog taking on a larger-than-life threat. "Oh, I will give you silver and I will give you gold/ and my own fair daughter your bonny bride shall be/ if you will swim alongside of the Golden Vanity/ and sink her in the Lowland Sea!"[62]

David, in his query about the reward,[63] kicks the register up a notch by referring to Goliath twice as "this Philistine," the second time adding the adjective "foreskinned." In fact, the name Goliath has disappeared from the story, and he will henceforth be indicated by his ethnic origin, at times including references to his foreskin. In 1 and 2 Samuel, only Jonathan, David, and Saul refer to the Philistines

61. Alter (*The David Story*, 104–5n25) notes that the folkloristic motifs "have been historicized and to an extent even psychologized. The slaying of the giant becomes an emblem," not only for Israel but also for the "resourcefulness of the first dynastic king in securing power."

62. Lines from the ballad "The Golden Vanity." In this song, a young boy saves his ship and all on it by sinking the Spanish vessel threatening *The Golden Vanity*. Of course, the cabin boy dies in the attempt.

63. In the context of an army in confusion, the conversation need not be imagined as following a straightforward remark-response sequence, as the two may have spoken at the same time, with v. 27 serving as an affirmation about the reward from multiple sources.

in this way. David, in doing so, follows in the footsteps of Jonathan's daring exploit (14:6; see pp. 103–5 above). In the Historical Books, the Samson narratives provide the only other context in which the Philistines receive this unflattering label. David is comparable to both Samson and Jonathan. Not only does he similarly identify the Philistines this way, but he matches these other heroes in zeal and confidence in the face of the enemy's overpowering presence. According to David, the one who kills the champion will take away the "shame" of Israel. The word "shame" elsewhere implies the jeering taunt of those who take pleasure in Israel's oppressed status.[64] The shame of Israel redounds by extension on Israel's God; David thus identifies the target of the Philistine's taunt as "the ranks of the living God."

The focus narrows from David and a group of anonymous soldiers to two members of Jesse's family: David and one of his brothers.

1 Samuel 17:28–29

28 Eliab, his older brother, heard him speaking to the men,
and Eliab flew in a rage against David and said:
Why have you come down,
and with whom have you left
this bit of flock in the wilderness?
I am one who knows your presumption
and your evil impulses;
in order to see the battle you have come down!

29 David said: What did I do now?
Wasn't it just talk?

David's older brother has overheard the conversation and takes the opportunity to upbraid him, perhaps not an untypical reaction, as he may be concerned that David's life is in danger. On the other hand, sibling relations, especially among brothers, are often contentious in the Bible, and this exchange could be just another example

64. Cf. Josh 5:9; 1 Sam 11:2; Neh 1:3; 5:9; Pss 44:14[13]; 79:12; 89:42[41]; Isa 25:8; 51:7; 54:4.

of typical interactions. The previous chapter, too, did not leave the impression that David had high standing in the family—perhaps a trope to reinforce the motif of the least likely candidate unexpectedly coming to the fore and in the end assuming the most important position. Eliab begins with a question which he then proceeds to answer. His opening salvo, "Why have you come down?" is answered by his own "You have come down. . ." with the assumed motivation provided. "Why did you do this? Oh, I know why!" In between, he inserts an insult and accusation regarding David's tasks at home. Eliab's question about leaving the flock includes a comment about its size ("those few sheep") and the insinuation that David was irresponsible in leaving them, making use of a verb that implies abandonment.

Eliab's knowledge of David's true reasons for being at the camp is based on his acquaintance with David's intentions, literally in Hebrew: "I know your arrogance and the perverseness/wrongness of your heart." Here is someone who has looked into David's heart, a capacity assigned to God in the anointing narrative in chapter 16, and discovered nothing good, unlike what God saw there. David's reply begins with a question like Eliab's, which he then also answers with a rhetorical question that one can take to mean "I was just talking!" He refuses to engage with his brother further and turns to continue the conversation with other people, who all affirm what the first soldier told him (30). The conversations finally penetrate to Saul's inner circle, and Saul orders David into his presence.

1 Samuel 17:32–37, 39

32 David said to Saul:
Let no one's heart fail on his account!
Your servant will go and fight this Philistine!
33 Saul said to David:
You will not be able to go against this Philistine to fight him!
For you are a lad, and he is a fighting man from his youth!

34 David said to Saul:
A shepherd your servant has been of his father's flock.

And when the lion came or the bear
to take a sheep from the flock,
35 I came out after it, and struck it down
and rescued [the sheep] from its mouth.
And if it rose up against me, I grabbed it by its hair
and struck it down and killed it.
36 Even the lion, even the bear your servant struck down.
And this foreskinned Philistine will be like them,
for he has mocked the ranks of the living God!

37 David said:
Adonai, who rescued me from the hand of the lion
and from the hand of the bear,
will rescue me from the hand of this Philistine.
Saul said to David:
Go, and may Adonai be with you!
. . .
39 David said to Saul:
I cannot go in these, for I am not used to it.

Together with the discourse when he is face to face with the champion on the field, this is one of the longest speeches made by David, not only in these initial chapters but at any time in the cycle. In addition, the back-and-forth constitutes a true dialogue between him and Saul, the longest they will be allowed in the narratives. It is of some interest that the narrator assigns the first words to David on this occasion when he is, after all, faced with the king—even though it is a king who has joined his army in being terrified. David speaks about "the heart," encouraging everyone to take courage and by extension including Saul in this reassurance; he does not have to spell it out.[65] In a covert way, he counsels the king not to be afraid. Next, he volunteers for the mission. Saul ridicules the notion of this foolhardy adventure, calling David a "lad" as compared to Goliath, who from the time he was a "lad" was a fighting "man." This put-down gives David the opportunity to launch into his defense.

65. The Septuagint reads, "Let not the heart of my lord fail him."

With great eloquence, he portrays his own valor, fending off the wild animals that have come to threaten his flock. It is of some interest that he identifies himself as a "shepherd," a title often assigned to the monarch in the larger world of the Bible.

David reports his having killed ("struck down") marauding animals out to attack his sheep, first rescuing the sheep and then killing the predators if they persisted in the attack. First, he mentions a lion, and then adds a bear: "even the lion, even the bear."[66] The verb *strike down* echoes forth in his declaration like a trumpet call. In the end, "this foreskinned Philistine," whom he compares to the wild animals that are on the prowl around his flock, will become just like the carcasses of the beasts that fell under his hand. David claims to be brave and capable enough based on his experience. He does not express trust in God's help at this point but mentions again the insult against "the ranks of the living God." Whether he is speaking in truth about his exploits in the field, is exaggerating, or makes the whole thing up one does not know. It does not really matter, for it is the self-confidence of his recital that speaks the loudest, and it is this aspect which the narrative exhibits as part of the introduction of David as a warrior of valor, even if he is not of the stature of Saul.

Saul is apparently dumbfounded, for he does not reply, and David picks up the thread of the conversation to give witness to his trust in God. Nothing he has said is due to his prowess or courage, but rescue came directly from God. The word "hand" in Hebrew is often used as a metaphor for power, and so it is here. Neither lion nor bear has hands, but they do have great power, as does "this Philistine." God has brought rescue about and will bring it about again. This is apparently enough to convince Saul, who is ready to send him on his way with God's help. We note that the issue of a reward in the case of success does not arise between Saul and David.

66. The lion, as Emily Vermeule (*Aspects of Death in Early Greek Art and Poetry* [Berkeley: University of California Press, 1979], 86) has pointed out, was for "the Greeks and almost all their Mediterranean neighbors . . . the most skilled hunter himself, the most frightening object of the hunt, the representative of male ambitions to be courageous, dangerous, intelligent and successful." It is thus no small boast David makes, doubling it up by mention of "the bear."

All along, it must have been clear that David has no weaponry, so Saul offers him armor and a sword. This effort at matching the champion's gear is to no effect, for nothing fits David. Decked out in battledress, helmet, and bronze sword, he is unable to walk (38–39). David offers as an excuse his lack of familiarity with the equipment, but clearly everything of Saul's is too big for "little" David. He excuses himself by pointing out that he is not able to take on the task so encumbered by armor and weapon, for he is not accustomed to it. The verb "to go" literally means "to walk" in Hebrew, and so he points out that he cannot *walk* in all this stuff. The effect of the statement is that both David's first and his last words are about going in contrasting statements: "I will go"/"I cannot go." The negative statement opens up the question whether Saul understood him to forego the task altogether. The narrative does not linger in Saul's tent, however, and moves with David on the way to his duel.

He sets out with his shepherd's tools, his stick, and his sling, and he picks up some handy stones, which he puts in the sling.[67] The scene with David trying on his lord's gear vividly portrays the young man doing his best to make it work, putting on one piece of the outfit after another, perhaps taking a few steps. It is humorous but also carries the message that, for David, victory will not be gained by traditional weaponry, and thus he goes to meet his opponent with minimal equipment, emphasizing again the contrast with Saul, who, though well-equipped, is hiding in his tent.

1 Samuel 17:43–47

43 The Philistine said to David:
Am I a dog that you come to me with sticks?

67. In verse 40 the description is overloaded with words for David's gear: "He took his stick in his hand,/ and chose himself five smooth stones from the creek / and put them in the gear of the shepherd / that he had with him / and in the pouch,/ and with his stick in his hand / he approached the Philistine." The combined effect of the accumulation of words for equipment creates obfuscation, and the final line, which draws attention to the stick, highlights the fact that David's weapon is not the stick which is mocked by Goliath but is hidden elsewhere. See Fokkelman, *The Crossing Fates,* 178.

The Philistine cursed David by his god.
44 The Philistine said to David:
Come closer! And I will give
your flesh to the birds of the sky
and the cattle of the field.

45 David said to the Philistine:
You come to me with sword, spear, and javelin.
I come to you with the name of Adonai of Hosts,
the God of the ranks of Israel you mocked.
46 This day, Adonai will deliver you into my hand,
and I will strike you down
and sever your head [from you];
and I will give the corpses of the Philistine camp
this day to the birds of the sky
and the wild animals of the land,
and all the land will know there is a God in Israel!
47 And all this assembly will know
that not by sword or by spear
does Adonai bring deliverance,
for to Adonai belongs the battle,
and He will give you all into our hand.

When David meets Goliath in the valley, we first view him from the Philistine's perspective (42). What he sees is a good-looking boy who cannot possibly do him any harm, so he curses him by his gods and hurls insults at him in what may be a stereotypical taunt for the context, threatening to reduce him to carrion for wild animals. All he sees of weaponry is the shepherd´s crook, so he sarcastically asks if he is a dog to come after with sticks (43). David in his turn invokes the God of Israel in every challenging phrase. First, he picks up on Goliath's "you come to me" by listing Goliath's weapons, and then he contrasts it with his "I come to you," substituting instruments of war with the name of Israel's God. Adonai and the divine hand is the only defensive armament he claims, and Adonai will deliver the enemy into his hand. He follows this statement with three verbs in the first person: "I will strike," "I will sever," "I will give." Not only Goliath, but the bodies of his comrades will become food for the birds and the wild animals. The purpose of the exercise will be knowledge for the entire land and for the whole assembly of soldiers gathered on the hills. The land will be aware that there is a God in and for Israel, and the armies will know that this God does not need arsenals to bring about deliverance. "For not by power is a man a hero"—the words of Hannah's praise song echo forth in the lines assigned to David. Goliath indeed stands tall and speaks insolently, but he will be deprived of speech like the wicked of her prayer. He will be brought low while God gives strength to his anointed (1 Sam 2:3, 4, 9; see pp. 38–39 above).

The end comes as the giant lumbers forward and David runs to come close enough to sling a stone at Goliath's most vulnerable spot. This causes Goliath to stumble and fall ("He fell on his face on the ground," 49), upon which David cuts off his head with his own sword. Ariella Deem is most likely correct in deducing that the stone from David's slingshot hit Goliath at the shin-bone above the shin-guard just below the knee, where the greave, of necessity, had an opening. Being hit at this weak spot would not cause death but could easily occasion a stumble and fall forward, with the weight of the armor serving to make the fall especially hard and getting up quickly equally difficult.[68] Fokkelman comments, "His own armour turns against Goliath; how ludicrous now the whole catalogue of arms in the beginning." Fokkelman notes also that falling forward puts Goliath "into the praying position for the God of Israel. He has to fall like Dagon in 1 Sam 5:3–4."[69] David has indeed struck down the bragging gigantic enemy as he said he struck down the marauding animals preying on his flock.

The dispatching of Goliath is followed by Philistines fleeing in a panic with their corpses littering the roads while Israelites gather

68. Deem, "And the Stone," 349–50. Deem argues that the helmet of the Philistine warriors of that time covered the forehead, often reaching the bridge of the nose, and interprets the rare Hebrew word used in 17:6 and 49 as "knee armor" or "greave."

69. Fokkelman, *The Crossing Fates*, 186.

the plunder (52–53).[70] A renewed encounter between Saul and David closes the episode.

1 SAMUEL 17:55–58

55 When Saul saw David
going out to meet the Philistine,
he said to Abner, the army commander:
Whose son is the lad, Abner?
And Abner said: By your life, King,
I do not know!
56 He said: O King, you ask yourself
whose son the young man is.

57 When David came back
from striking down the Philistine,
Abner took him and brought him before Saul
with the head of the Philistine in his hand.
58 Saul said to him:
Whose son are you, lad?
David said:
The son of your servant Jesse, the Bethlehemite.

The exchange involves Saul, Abner, and David, and we are left to ponder its purpose. Were David's identity and background not mentioned before or during his earlier encounter with Saul on the eve of the contest (32–39), or were they forgotten afterward? If the seam between the different sources of David's arrival at the court is

70. An anachronistic note has David taking Goliath's head to Jerusalem while depositing the armor in his tent (54). At the time of the contest, Jerusalem was not yet an Israelite city, and most likely David would not have had a personal tent. In any case, it is clear enough that what we have before us in ch. 17 is at least two stories combined into one, as those who are most interested in the antecedents of the traditions in these narratives cogently argue (e.g., Campbell, *1 Samuel*, 184–89). The final editors were content to include the note about Goliath's head in Jerusalem as a pointer to the future and perhaps out of a desire to anticipate David's eventual kingship and residence there.

showing up again, why is the unit added just here, and why does it highlight these particular questions?

First, consistent within the chapter and previous presentations of Saul, the conversation with Abner shows him in a fog of uncertainty, back to where he was at the very beginning on his road to kingship, asking questions—perhaps about things he should have known. When he was with Saul in the tent earlier, David did not reveal his identity, and it is possible that proper introductions were not made which are now to be filled in. Saul's ignorance of David's name and background would explain his question to Abner. It is also possible that he did not count on the person clanking around in his battle gear in the tent actually taking on the task of fighting Goliath, in accordance with David's statement that he could not go. With Saul, we are in a place of misunderstanding and missed information.

In the ancient world of which Israel was a part, one's identity lay not so much in name as in parentage, so the question here is about David's father: not *who* but *whose* are you?[71] David is called the *boy* or *lad*, as he has been consistently. David responds with his father's name and place of residence, but the question still lingers: Who is this boy? The question still lingers for Saul, who knows nothing of the secret anointing, which David, to no one's surprise, does not reveal—a withholding of information that parallels Saul's own reticence at an earlier stage (1 Sam 10:16). The part of David's presence that will begin to disturb Saul—that he is a strong and confident fighter—has become evident in David's capacity to kill an overpowering enemy, but that is not all David is.

The question about David lingers also for the reader/listener. In one part of the discourses we reviewed, he is the brash young go-getter who will take on the challenge but wants to know what is in it for him. When reproached by his sibling, he refuses to engage, for that is not a battle he wants to take on. As he flaunts his skill in guarding his father's flock before King Saul, claiming to protect his sheep against predators, is there an underlying theme of the shepherd king who puts the protection of his people above everything?

71. For example, Boaz asks his field supervisor to whom Ruth belongs: *lemi hanna'arah*? (Ruth 2:5).

He is willing to trust in God but nevertheless enlists the weapon he knows best—the well-cast stone—to bring the giant to a stumbling halt, thus putting himself at God's disposal rather than manipulating the Deity to his side. When he announces to Goliath, "I come to you in the name of Adonai of Hosts, the God of the ranks of Israel," is it too much to read here also the announcement of a new day in kingship, a new king who comes to Israel in the name of its God, the one to enlist the "ranks of Israel" in battle with the Philistines, the one who will put their threat to Israel's existence to rest? If David is courageous, he is also eloquent and clever, tricking an enemy into a fight where wits prevail over superior force. It will not be the last time that David will employ this skill. Is he an ambitious young schemer who turns into a usurper king, with malice aforethought, rising to the throne by murdering all who stand in his way and executing his office in a less than perfect manner? Or is he the humble shepherd boy, one who pleases God's heart, who trusts in God, who comes from nowhere to serve Saul, and who then becomes the chosen king of Israel who establishes a lasting house, providing the model for the shepherd king to come in a time beyond time? Or is he something of both? All the aspects of David's complex character will be on display in the subsequent episodes.

Act II, Scene 4: The Turning of the Tide (1 Samuel 18)

Clothes and armour pertain to the honour of the man, make part of his soul.[72]

The section following the encounters in the context of David's duel with the Philistine giant is filled with observations about feelings. First of all, where David appears, love follows. The notation that someone or a group of people "loved" David occurs seven times in chapter 18. Love is, however, not the only feeling that predominates. There are also anger, suspicion, fear, and animosity, particularly on

72. Johannes Pedersen, *Israel, Its Life and Culture*, vol. 1 (Oxford: Oxford University Press, 1926), 279.

the part of Saul with regard to his therapist turned champion. In distinction from the scanty information about the motivations and feelings of Saul in previous episodes, the present chapter affords an abundance of insight into what Saul thinks and what he does. By contrast, we are not informed about David's state of mind and heart—whether he returns any of the feelings coming his way, be they of love or anger—but only about his actions. He also speaks relatively little, so that one is unable to deduce his disposition from his words.

The scene begins with a short section about Saul's son Jonathan as he forms a strong attachment to David (1–4). Jonathan's "soul was bound to the soul of David" out of his "love" for him. He shares with him his robe, his armor, and his weapons. In the context of these narratives, the robe has special, significant value, and the handing over of battledress and weaponry hints at Jonathan's early recognition of David's ascent to the throne. The center of the unit is taken up with actions of Saul and Jonathan toward David. Saul no longer lets David go back to his home but keeps him continuously by his side (2). While on the surface a benevolent gesture, perhaps even indicating a rise in David's status, this circumstance also sets boundaries around David's movements. Close to the throne, is he kept in a cage? Jonathan on the other hand draws David into a covenant, a lasting pact which he seals by the handing over of his royal accoutrements. Saul keeps David close, perhaps too close, while his son endows David with enduring loyalty.[73] The loyalty shown to David by Jonathan will indeed last for Jonathan's lifetime, against his own interests as his father's heir, and it will put him on a trajectory of tragic conflict with his father, to whom his loyalty is due. Jonathan never abandons devotion to either and is thus also an example of someone who refuses to let himself be divided between the two. He could have followed David in his eventual flight from Saul's residence, but instead he stays at his father's side until they die together

73. With others, I note the use of the singular form of the verb ("*He cut* a covenant with David," 18:3) rather than the plural, which would have indicated a more reciprocal agreement. The only time the covenant between the two is mutual is in 23:18.

on the battlefield. He will form his attachment to and bond with David at the price of his father's displeasure, as we shall see.

From the beginning of the descriptions about Jonathan's feelings and behavior toward David, it is clear that, for Jonathan at least, this relationship goes further than the bond of comrades in arms. In fact, the two are not shown as comrades in arms in the text anywhere. The text leads us in the direction of understanding the relationship between the two men as homoerotic—at least from the one side and perhaps reciprocated, as hinted at in David's words of his lament over the deaths of Saul and Jonathan in 2 Samuel 1:26.[74] David Jobling writes, "The . . . politically important claim stands that the Bible here shows itself able to say what it has to say through the dynamics of what appears to be a gay relationship."[75] With regard to Jonathan giving David his armor and weapons, we note that on this occasion there is no question of the offered equipment fitting the recipient as had been the case with Saul's gear (17:38–39).

The Goliath-David scene has prepared the reader/listener for the valor of David on the battlefield, a feature followed up in this scene with the repeated notation "David was successful" (5, 14, 15, 30) in his engagement with the Philistines. It is especially this aspect of David's presence that begins to hinder Saul, above all when the women who habitually greet returning warriors with song, music, and dance raise the number of David's slain above those of Saul: "Saul struck down his thousands,/ David his tens of thousands!" (7). While intensification of numbers in the corresponding line is typical of Hebrew poetry, indicating ultimate praise for both Saul and David, Saul becomes incensed and takes the comparison literally (8–9). He feels that the women have given greater honor to David and begins to cast a suspicious eye on David. Quickly, David's favored status in the house of Saul as his music therapist and the valiant

74. Further expressions of Jonathan's love for David may be found in chs. 18–20. Denial of the most obvious reading of Jonathan's role in David's life forces the reader to go against the plain meaning of the text.

75. David Jobling, *1 Samuel*, Berit Olam (Collegeville, MN: Liturgical Press, 1998), 102. For an insightful discussion of the Jonathan-David relationship, see Danna Nolan Fewell and David M. Gunn, *Gender, Power, and Promise: The Subject of the Bible's First Story* (Nashville: Abingdon, 1993), 148–51.

conqueror of Goliath, beloved by all who meet him, deteriorates as he becomes the focus of Saul's jealous anger.[76]

Logically, there is no reason for Saul's paranoid behavior, but on the other hand, the narrative has clued the listener/reader in on the fact that Samuel has already anointed David as the royal heir before Saul had even met him. Saul's suspicion has as its background that David presents a real threat to him and especially to his heir. Fokkelman writes, "The tragic thing is that Saul knows what he does not yet know and Saul does not know how very much he knows. He is trapped and no one can help him anymore."[77] Is it possible that Saul has heard something of the goings on in Bethlehem before David appeared at his side? Did the servant who had "seen the son of Jesse" (16:18) know more than he let on at the time, and did some information make its way to Saul's ears? At least eight people, perhaps more, witnessed the anointing of David in Jesse's house. It is not unlikely that Saul heard some version of the affair, something he is unable to verify in his current predicament, with Samuel keeping him at arm's length. Even a more stable and more confident person than Saul might have been driven to cast a suspicious eye on the youngster who came from seemingly nowhere, drawing people's attention and attachment like a magnet. Saul is not a particularly confident person, and his equilibrium, already undermined by Samuel, may have been shaken even more by his failure to take on Goliath while

76. A number of interpreters view Saul's jealousy toward David as arising from the same homoerotic feelings as his son's, partly based on the statement in 16:21–22 that Saul loved him greatly (see p. 127 above) and other hints in the text. See Sylvia Schroer and Thomas Staubli, "Saul, David and Jonathan—The Story of a Triangle? A Contribution to the Issue of Homosexuality in the First Testament," in *Samuel and Kings*, ed. Athalya Brenner, A Feminist Companion to the Bible, Second Series (Sheffield: Sheffield Academic, 2000), 28: "It is quite possible that the love relationship between David and Saul's son . . . has something to do with Saul's hatred." More recently, Randall Bailey ("Reading Backwards: A Narrative Technique for the Queering of David, Saul, and Samuel," in *The Fate of King David: The Past and Present of a Biblical Icon*, ed. Tod Linafelt, Claudia V. Camp, and Timothy Beal [London: T&T Clark, 2010], 66–81) has argued for same-sex love relationships between David, Saul, and Samuel.

77. Fokkelman, *The Crossing Fates*, 220.

being outdone in courage by a young sheep farmer. The chanting women uncover for him what he really feels about himself. Jealousy and suspicion send him over the edge so that he engages in his first attempt to murder David.

1 SAMUEL 18:10–12

10 On the next day, a bad spirit from God fell upon Saul,
and he ranted like a prophet in the house,
and David was playing the lyre with his hand
as he did every day, and the spear was in the hand of Saul.
11 Saul threw the spear and said:
I will strike David down to the wall.
And David eluded him twice.
12 Saul feared David,
for Adonai was with him
and had turned away from Saul.

The bad spirit from God causes Saul to go into a prophetic trance at home, and in his rage and his ecstatic state, he decides to kill David, throwing his spear at him. Curiously, he does not manage to even wound his target, who is without doubt in fairly close proximity. The disturbance of the spirit may have caused such agitation that his aim was uncertain, or he is divided in his heart as to his true intention, or David is exceptionally nimble. At this point, Saul's suspicion and anger turn into fear, a sentiment repeated two more times (15, 29), with the notation at the end of the chapter that Saul "increasingly feared David," turning "into his enemy all the time" (29). Instead of a loving though somewhat unstable mentor, David has found a fearful and vengeful enemy lord.

Saul, in the meantime, sends David out to the battlefield against the Philistines, hoping the enemy will be successful where he has failed, a thought voiced in verse 17 after he promises his oldest daughter Merab to David as a bride. It looks as if the king's "own fair daughter" will thus indeed be the award for David's courage and skill on the battlefield. Unaccountably, Merab is given as a wife to someone else—whether by Saul or others in the household is not clear. The verb "she was given" underscores the passive position of the women at this point in the story. It could be that mothers had, if not the ultimate power, a good deal of influence on marriage arrangements; Merab herself may have had some say in the matter. Or, Saul may have decided not to go through with his promise in order to keep David off balance and outside of the immediate family circle. In any case, the next candidate, Michal, appears more suitable, as she too is said to "love David," something that comes to Saul's ears, and this time he decides to follow through on his promise. His motivation is sinister, for he plans to set her up as a "snare" by asking for a bride price that is likely to cause David's fall by Philistine hands (21, 25). Michal's love for David will evidently simplify the matter of making her his wife. By implication, it is possible that one of the barriers to Merab becoming David's wife is a lack of love on her part.[78]

David is evasive in his reply to Saul regarding the offer of marriage to the first daughter, and the negotiations for Michal are less than straightforward from both sides, with Saul first inviting David to become his "son-in-law" (21), to which David does not respond. There is subsequently an intervention through Saul's staff to assure David of the high regard in which Saul and everyone holds him and to convince him to become the king's relative (22–23). David only accepts when Saul stipulates a bride price of one hundred Philistine foreskins. Unable to turn down a challenge, David presents double the amount, and so the deal goes through. Saul's hope that David will fall by the "hand" of the Philistines, repeated three times (17, 21, 25), cements his murderous intentions toward his champion turned rival. The consequence, alas, is that David only becomes more famous and his stature in Saul's household and the wider community grows by leaps and bounds.

David's only speech in the chapter comes in reply to the offers of a bride, first in regard to Merab, then Michal. Each time he uses the expression "son-in-law to the king" (18, 23). Initially, he underlines his low status: "Who am I and who are my kin,/ the clan of my father

78. In the book of Ruth, it appears that the mother had authority in deciding marriages for daughters (Ruth 1:8), and a young woman's feelings and desires are in the biblical text recorded at times as a factor in her acceptance of the man she is to marry (Gen 24:57).

in Israel?" (18). Later, to the servants, he says that to become related by family to the king is not "a light thing" (23). Both times, he speaks in rhetorical questions. With the offer of Michal, Saul invites David directly to "become my son-in-law today," a request repeated as a demand by the servants (21–22). The repetition underlines the family connection that will henceforth exist between Saul and David. From now on, David will be connected by ties of kinship as well as loyalty and love to the house of Saul, a factor that will make the resulting relationships more complicated for everyone involved. David will never just be the upstart outsider, for he is now inside the clan, and when Saul pursues his plans to assassinate David, he is engaged in plotting the murder of a family member. From David's speech, it is clear that he is none too eager to be so closely tied to Saul and his house. He has, after all, experienced at least one attack from the king and must fear future assaults on his person, while being part of the family will of necessity keep him close under Saul's eye.

Act II, Scene 5: A Narrow Escape (1 Samuel 19)

To go through the window is also a birth, that of the man who can go only per aspera ad astra.[79]

In this scene, two of Saul's children, the two who "love" David, come to David's aid. First, Jonathan, directly told by his father to kill David, tries to broker a reconciliation between the two (1–7), an effort that meets with initial success but ends in failure (8–10). The opening lines put Saul and his son in opposite camps vis-à-vis David.

1 Samuel 19:1

Saul spoke to Jonathan, his son,
and to all his servants to kill David.
And Jonathan, the son of Saul,
took much pleasure in David.

79. Fokkelman, *The Crossing Fates*, 264.

A desire to *kill* on the part of Saul stands in direct opposition to the taking *much pleasure in David* by Jonathan, whose relationship to Saul is mentioned each time his name occurs. While taking pleasure in someone or something can be used in a variety of contexts, it does occur in the context of male to female attraction in the biblical text (see Gen 34:19; Deut 21:14; 25:7; Esth 2:14; Song 2:7; 3:5; 8:4) and is here underlined by the word *me'od* ("much" or "very"), again pointing to the extent of Jonathan's commitment to David as one of a love partnership. Jonathan, after telling David of Saul's plans, speaks to his father about Saul's mistake in going after David, who contributes so much in the fight against the Philistines. He uses the word *transgress* to great effect, framing his plea in the words "let not the king transgress. . . . Why would you transgress?" (4–5). Saul is willing to go back on his determination, and David "was in his presence as before" (7). While this sounds like good news, we call to mind that "before" brought nothing good from Saul's side to David. Indeed, as soon as David is once again successful in battle with the Philistines, Saul once again is possessed of a murderous rage and tries to pin him to the wall with his spear. As he did before, David eludes the attack and gets away from Saul (10).

Michal, who until this moment appeared mostly in a passive role—*given* to David by her father—now takes an active part. While Jonathan has done his best to be peacemaker, perhaps in a desire to keep David in the neighborhood, Michal, more realistic, warns David that he will not survive the night and cooks up a scheme to delude the delegation sent to dispatch him (11–17). The vignette of her ruse is drawn in fine detail as she lets David down through a window, aiding him as Rahab once had Joshua's spies, and puts the image of a household deity adorned with goat hair in his bed. She buys time for David with her announcement that he is sick, and when the second group arrives on Saul's orders to bring David, bed and all, they discover the scam—probably as soon as they come anywhere close: "Look, the household gods in the bed and a braid of goat hair at the head" (16).

The presence of household deities in the compound of Saul elicits no comment from the narrator. We met such an image in Judges (17:5; 18:14, 17, 18, 20) and as a negative element in the speech of

Samuel to Saul after the defeat of Amalek (1 Sam 15:23). The word in Hebrew is *terafim*, connoting a plurality, and one encounters them elsewhere in the company of Rachel, who takes them from her father's house and hides them under her saddle (Gen 31:19, 34, 35).[80] Elsewhere in the Historical Books, their presence evokes negative judgment (2 Kgs 23:24), but in other places their existence in the lives of ordinary people is simply taken for granted. While we encounter Michal in her active role for the first time, it is striking that she sends her husband away while substituting a lifeless image for him in her bed—in the end, a bed that will not grant her offspring. To her father, she invokes an image of a bloodthirsty David who would have taken her life had she not helped him get away (17), playing on her greater vulnerability as a woman, which at the same time creates an ironic reversal of the real situation, in which David is the true victim of Saul's bloodthirstiness. Like Jonathan, Michal loves David, the only time in the Bible a woman is said to love a specific man, and she goes further than Jonathan in inventiveness and risk-taking. Though she is one of the children of Saul to survive her father's demise, her place in David's life gains her little reward, as the sequel of her story will show.

David does not speak in this scene. His only activity besides mowing down Philistines (8) is to "get away" (10, 12, 18). His choice of hideout is first the domicile of Samuel in Ramah, from which the two of them set out to a place called Nayot, perhaps a residence specifically for prophets (18). The location appears to be so filled with the ecstatic spirit that it catches everyone who comes near. Thus, three delegations sent by Saul fall into a prophetic trance (20, 21 2×), and when Saul himself appears, the same condition befalls him. This time, it reduces him to lie naked before Samuel (24); one can hardly imagine a more vulnerable figure, far removed from the tall young man who towered over the rest of the populace at the beginning of his leadership.

80. Scholars note the parallels between this short episode and the story of Jacob, including the role of the *terafim*, the goats, and the daughter who rebels against her father on behalf of her husband. Also, Saul's words to Michal resemble those of Laban to Jacob (Gen 31:26). Cf. Alter, *The David Story*, 120–121nn13 and 17.

Once again, we ponder the fate of Saul, who is now well into his downward spiral. Would it have been possible to act otherwise in the presence of David, even while assessing him as a potential rival to his son? Could he have made a pact, as Jonathan did, and together with David taken the Philistines to their final defeat? It is of course possible, but then would the story have been of the sort that gets a hold of the imagination even thousands of years later? Here he is once again in the company of Samuel, but with no communication between them. Here he lies down as he later will fall down in Endor at the moment of his deepest despair—not on the battlefield, but during his last grasp for a word of hope from his erstwhile mentor.

Act II, Scene 6: A Step away from Death (1 Samuel 20:1–21:1)

Banish from your mind any thought of sex when you read of Jonathan's love: it is essentially political, and though there was also a warm personal "affection," there was absolutely nothing more, honest.[81]

Unaccountably, we find David back in Saul's vicinity in a long episode that deals mainly with an exchange between him and Jonathan. The statements made by the protagonists in the scene and their actions are important for the rest of the David story, providing David's life as an outlaw with greater depth and background while at the same time highlighting Saul's instability. David will have to resort to survival in hiding, living by his wits and skill alone. He has allies at the court, but these alliances will be of no further help to him, and he will have to seek out others, even going so far as serving the enemy. Saul, who up until now has vacillated between jealous rage and lingering attachment for David, will transfer his rage to his own son. The scene, with its extended set of discourses, serves to slow

81. David Clines's (*Interested Parties: The Ideology of Writers and Readers of the Hebrew Bible* [Sheffield: Sheffield Phoenix, 2009], 241) critical comment of Kyle McCarter Jr.'s (*I Samuel: A New Translation with Introduction, Notes & Commentary*, AB 8 [New York: Doubleday, 1980], 77) interpretation of the Jonathan-David relationship.

down the pace of the action in the story, providing greater insight into the different personages involved, who all speak and act in ways coherent with the manner in which they have appeared so far. The exchanges between David and Jonathan put Jonathan in the center as the crucial person. In his position as covenant brother and lover to David, he speaks ultimately as a prophet, preceding Abigail, who will fulfill this function down the path. The language is in many places convoluted and difficult to translate, as if the characters speak in broken sentences, finding their words only haltingly. I divide the material into four parts.

Scene 6, Part 1: What Have I Done? (1 Samuel 20:1–11)

David appears before Jonathan and in their first conversation attempts to convince Jonathan that the danger to his life is real, proceeding from the assumption that Jonathan is still interested in reconciliation. At this point, the question arises why he chooses to approach Jonathan rather than his wife, who, after all, was effective in managing his earlier escape. It could be that David does not want to put his vulnerable spouse in further danger, while his friend Jonathan, as the male heir, has higher standing, is better able to defend himself, and can stand his ground with his father. It could also be that Michal's residence is a more dangerous hiding place. In a more negative take on his avoidance of Michal, we might conclude that the David of this part of the narrative has little interest in looking to Michal as his rescuer. She has come into the story and left it almost as quickly as she played a major part in David's adventures. She will not be the last woman who suffers this fate. Furthermore, Jonathan most likely has a more prominent place in David's heart than Michal, and it is important to David to hear from his friend that staying in Saul's neighborhood is too dangerous.

In his first address to Jonathan, David asks mostly questions: "What have I done? What is my guilt? What is my trespass?" (1). The three-times repeated "what" is the Hebrew word *meh.* With his plaintive *meh, meh, meh . . .* , David sounds like one of the sheep once under his care. *Meh asiti*? "What have I done?" David once asked this of his brother Eliab when he and the soldiers were discussing Goliath and his challenge. This is the same question in different circumstances, for what indeed has he done except to become a thorn in Saul's flesh by his very existence? No offensive action has raised the king's ire, only an offensive person. The questions are unanswerable and, in the discourse, serve mainly to establish David's innocence before Jonathan, an innocence which serves as an argument for the baseless nature of Saul's determination to end David's life. Jonathan's first reaction is one of horrified denial. If Saul has renewed his nefarious purpose, surely he, Jonathan, would be cognizant. His "Why should my father hide this matter from me?" sounds naïve, for Saul has every reason to hide his intentions from Jonathan, the sworn and loyal friend of David. David then logically brings up exactly that issue: Saul would not wish to cause distress to his son by revealing his plans, but in fact David is as close to being killed as ever, "only a step away from death" (3). Such insistence is enough to get Jonathan to pledge help where it is needed.

David then comes up with a plan that will potentially involve Jonathan in a lie.

1 Samuel 20:5–7

5 David said to Jonathan:
Look, it is New Moon tomorrow,
and I myself should definitely sit
with the king to eat.
Let me go, and I will hide
in the field until the evening of the third day.
6 If your father really misses me, say:
David has begged me
to run to Bethlehem, his town,
for there is a seasonal sacrifice there
for his entire clan.
7 If he then says: Good,
it means well for your servant.
But if he becomes really incensed,
know that he has determined evil.

New Moon is a time for ceremonial feasting and sacrifice. David states it was his plan to be present at the king's table, although one wonders about such a plan, but he proposes instead to hide. In the sentence, the domestic scene of *sitting* at table and *eating* turns into the precarious existence away from home in *hiding*, foreshadowing what is to come for David not only at this moment but for the foreseeable future. Once his absence is noted, much will depend on the king's paying attention and his reaction to the ruse David has constructed. There are a number of "ifs" in David's proposal: "if he misses me," "if he says," "if he becomes incensed." He adds a plea for Jonathan to act with loyalty on the basis of the covenant Jonathan initiated. As an afterthought, he states that if Jonathan thinks he is truly guilty of something, he might as well kill David himself.

What exactly is David planning? Does he truly think that Saul will have a positive reaction to his running run off to Bethlehem with Jonathan's permission? Or is all this designed to convince Jonathan of Saul's purpose so he can leave while his friend still thinks well of him and is aware of his father's designs, which may guarantee David an ally in Saul's household for the long term? I agree with Robert Polzin that it is difficult to take David seriously in the sense that he expects any "favorable utterance of Saul about him" or that such a word could be trusted. More likely, David's strategy is "to provoke Saul to an angry outburst that would remove Jonathan's misconceptions, not his own."[82] Jonathan's reply, following his shocked denial that he could ever be the one to take David's life, still sounds guileless, as he puts a conditional on his father's determination, of which he clearly still needs convincing (9). David is the one who pushes the conversation forward, for even Jonathan's goodwill and promise do not guarantee a way for David to become informed. To make a plan, they need to be out of earshot of third parties, and so Jonathan suggests they move outside. Already, having a conversation together has become too dangerous for the two of them, and at this point they can only continue outside, so they move to "the field,"

82. Robert Polzin, *Samuel and the Deuteronomist*, vol. 2 of *A Literary Study of the Deuteronomic History* (Bloomington: Indiana University Press, 1993), 180.

perhaps the same location where David was hidden at their earlier encounter in 19:3.

Saul is, throughout the conversation, referred to as a father—"your father" or "my father"—and only once as "the king." Of the fourteen times the word "father" occurs in this scene, eight of them are in this first unit, underlining the relationship between Jonathan and Saul, and pointing out that in opposing the king Jonathan stands in the way of his own father's desires. The covenant to which David appeals apparently overrides the natural loyalty and bonds of kinship between father and son. David will one day be a father himself and taste far more deeply than Saul the bitterness of a son's rebellion.

Scene 6, Part 2: A Pledge in the Field (1 Samuel 20:12–23)

While the two are in the field where David will once again hide, they continue their discourse, and Jonathan devises a plan whereby he will convey to David whether to stay or go. Jonathan pledges to sound his father out regarding David's absence at the feast and let David know of the outcome. If indeed Saul has evil in mind, he will make it known to David and let him go. "I will let you go and you will go in peace" are his literal words (13). But, as David needed his pledge earlier, Jonathan now needs a promise from David. His words relate to his own person and present condition, but they also reach into the future, for he asks David to swear loyalty to his "house for all time" (15), pointing to a period when Adonai will have destroyed all David's enemies, including, one presumes, Saul. In this way, Jonathan predicts David's rise to the monarchy at the cost of his own abdication. Once again, the matter is concluded with a covenant in the name of God. For good measure, the love of Jonathan is mentioned three times in the concluding words: "Jonathan swore again to David by his love for him, for he loved him as he loved himself" (17).

Then follows the manner in which Jonathan proposes to bring back news, all involving the shooting of arrows and their place near to or far from the lad who is there to pick them up (18–22). It is not so much the issue of the location of the arrows as what Jonathan will say, which would be overheard and must sound innocuous. The arrows involve *shooting* and *sending* them at a target in addition to *sending* an assistant to pick them up. If things have gone wrong, it is a sign that Adonai has *sent* David on his way. In this way, the arrows function as the symbols of David's departure from the royal residence and from Jonathan's life. I will return to the significance of the arrows below.

Scene 6, Part 3: Fathers and Sons (1 Samuel 20:24–34)

The initial lines of this unit place everyone in their different positions with great clarity, evoking a sense of peril similar to that of David's encounter with Goliath: The king *sits*, Jonathan *stands*, Abner *sits*, David is *missing*. The king is next to the wall with Abner at his side, while Jonathan's location is not noted so that the emphasis is on his standing position, indicating a certain watchfulness. Saul, whose thoughts are revealed at this point, as has been the case in the scenes immediately preceding, is aware of David's absence but initially makes an excuse on his behalf, ascribing it to a ritual cause. It is only on the second day that Saul asks Jonathan for the reason of David's absence, calling him "the son of Jesse" (27), a denigrating way of referring to his son-in-law and once faithful adjutant. Jonathan reports the urgent request David supposedly made of him—three times making use of the root for asking (*sha'ul*)—to follow his brother's directive and participate in a clan sacrifice in his hometown so he may visit with his family (29). Jonathan again uses the word for sending, adding to it the verb "get away," which is found three times in chapter 19 for David's escape from Saul. He makes it clear that David needed to be *sent* in order to *get away*.

As could be predicted, Saul is incensed and turns his anger on his son. Polzin identifies the information about David having gone to his family and hometown as "the detonator embedded in the message" David has proposed for Jonathan to deliver to Saul."[83] He declares Jonathan a "son of a twisted rebellion" for "choosing the

83. Polzin, *Samuel and the Deuteronomist*, 189.

son of Jesse."[84] The word "choose" (from the root *bahar*) is loaded because of its use in this cycle for Saul as the *chosen one* by God and people (9:2; 10:24; 12:13). He accuses Jonathan of shaming himself and the woman who gave him birth.[85] Saul rages at Jonathan that David's very existence is a threat to Jonathan as Saul's heir. He orders his son to fetch David and declares him "a dead man"; literally in Hebrew, the "son of Jesse" is now declared the "son of death." When Jonathan answers with the same question put to him earlier by David ("What has he done?"), it antagonizes Saul so much that he throws his spear at his own son.

1 Samuel 20:33–34

33 Then Saul hurled the spear at him
to strike him down,
so Jonathan knew that his father
was determined to kill David.
34 Jonathan rose from the table in hot anger,
and he did not eat food on the second day of New Moon,
for he was distressed over David
and because his father had humiliated him.

While the narrator omits any reference to the weapon missing its target or to Jonathan escaping, the result of the bungled attempt on his life is that he now knows his father's true intentions. Saul's hot rage is answered by Jonathan's equal anger. Jonathan has once before gone against the commands of his father, albeit unwittingly,

84. Fox (*The Early Prophets: Joshua, Judges, Samuel and Kings* [New York: Schocken, 2014], 378n30) translates the first phrase this way rather than "son of a perverse, rebellious woman," arguing that Saul would hardly have insulted his wife. One could compare the outburst with the contemporary English phrase "you son of a bitch," insulting the mother together with the son. Either translation is possible, although I here prefer the interpretation of Fox.

85. "Do I not know you are choosing the son of Jesse to your shame and the shame of your mother's nakedness?" (20:30). "Your mother's nakedness," as Alter and others have observed, is violent language—"nakedness" referring to the genitals. Alter, *The David Story*, 128n30.

but he was afterward compliant even to the point of being willing to die (14:43). He knew before of his father's distrust of David and was willing to mediate between them. It takes the full knowledge of Saul's true purpose for him to become enraged. In addition, he does not eat. Not eating is a sign of a depressed spirit, and calls to mind Hannah (1:7), who was also humiliated by one inside her family circle. Jonathan's emotional state is a similar mixture of anger and distress, the very emotional turmoil David had suggested as the reason Saul had withheld from him what he had in mind for David (20:3).

It's all between fathers and sons in this scene, coming to a head in the episode at the dinner table. David begins the string of references by referring to Saul as "your father" to Jonathan, who continues to speak of "my father." Thus, in 20:1–3, we hear the repeated "your father," "my father," "my father," "your father," which continues in 6–12 with a second series: "your father," "your father," "my father," "your father," "my father," "my father," "my father." These two series end with Jonathan's statement: "See, Adonai is between you and me for all time" (20:23). Then, inside at the meal, Saul is described as speaking to "Jonathan, his son," whom he questions about "the son of Jesse." During Saul's outburst, the word "son" sounds four times, once applied to Jonathan and three times to David, twice calling him "the son of Jesse" (30–31). Saul points out that in siding with the wrong *son*, Jonathan is giving up his true filial loyalty to his father and his right to the throne as heir. Moreover, by allying himself with the wrong son, Jonathan has sided with a "son of death."

Saul's rage and the bungled attempt on his son's life are signs of his deranged state of mind, in which he rather than David becomes a threat to his son's life. On the other hand, his speech contains truth. It is indeed to Jonathan and his position that David poses the true threat, and by supporting David, Jonathan can be said to shame himself and his family. When Jonathan speaks against his father's command to bring David to him, he puts himself also on the side of death so that the throwing of the spear follows a dreadful logic on Saul's part. Instead of Adonai between Jonathan and David, Saul has put himself between the two. Jonathan will not bring David to his father, but he will also not stay by David's side, remaining loyal in his own way to his kin. Perhaps he would have increased the danger to David by leaving together with him, but that is beside the point. The king's position in this triangle is now the permanent obstacle to a continued relationship between the two lovers.

Scene 6, Part 4: Arrows in the Field (1 Samuel 20:35–21:1[86])

The device of using arrows for informational purposes can obviously only be executed in daylight, so Jonathan waits until morning before going out to the field accompanied by a "small lad" (20:35). What follows is a detailed replay of the method planned in 20:19–22 to apprise David of the true state of affairs (20:35–38), a narrative move that underscores the importance of this particular way of doing things. One does not have to be an expert in archery to consider shooting arrows into a field an odd and potentially dangerous exercise unless a target is set up, of which there is here no mention.[87] It does not seem that the arrows are truly necessary, since Jonathan knows David's hiding place and, as he did earlier, could simply meet him there. But arrows are weaponry, and the *sending* of the arrows may thus symbolize the danger that seeks David as a target. Arrows are used as symbols in the biblical text of attack by hostile powers, including the Deity (e.g., Pss 7:14[13]; 18:15[14]; 38:3[2]), and of victory in an episode between Elisha and King Joash of Israel (2 Kgs 13:14–19). They are also used as an instrument of forecasting by the king of Babylon (Ezek 21:26[21]). In a way, David himself will become like the arrow, needing to be *farther away*; he is furthermore the weapon directed at Saul and his house. Jonathan's words to the boy with him ("Hurry, quick, do not stand still!" 20:38) are in truth meant for David's ears and indicative of the urgency involved in the matter. The boy obeys his master's directives in ignorance of their

86. I am following the chapter divisions of the Masoretic Text of the Hebrew Bible, in which the lines that appear at the end of 20:42 in the NRSV and other English translations appear as 21:1.

87. In 20:19, Jonathan mentions shooting an arrow as if he were aiming at a target, but no target is present during the execution of the plan.

significance ("He did not know anything," 20:39), assuring that none of the information will reach Saul's ears.

David comes out of his hiding place and prostrates himself before Jonathan.

1 SAMUEL 20:41–21:1

41 The boy entered [the town], and David arose
from by the mound and fell on his face to the ground
and bowed three times.
Then they kissed one another,
and they wept together
until David wept a great deal.

42 Jonathan said to David:
Go in peace, because we two are sworn
by the name of Adonai,
saying: Adonai is between me and you
and between my seed and your seed for all time.

21:1 He arose and went,
and Jonathan came to the town.

No sound is heard from David apart from his weeping. Jonathan is the one in charge, the one before whom David bows and who sends him on his way with God's blessing. This is still only the beginning of the road David must go on, but it is the end of the road for the two of them, marked by the notation of their embrace, their kiss, and their tears. As Polzin observes, the statement that God is between the two of them is deeply ambiguous because "no matter how many oaths they make or how deep their love is for each other," Adonai is *for* David and *against* Saul and thus "remains 'between' David and Jonathan, who are thereby placed in an either-or situation."[88] Almost a century ago, Johannes Pedersen noted the tragedy of Jonathan when he wrote, "In reality there is no possibility of a

88. Polzin, *Samuel and the Deuteronomist*, 193.

solution of the conflict in the soul of Jonathan. The strife does not come from without, but depends on his being placed in two soul-relations which are at war with one another."[89]

Act III: The King and the Outlaw (1 Samuel 21:2–23:28)

David is never far away.[90]

Three chapters recount the initial attempts of David to flee from Saul, who will make fruitless attempts to overpower the fugitive and execute him. Nob, Gath, Adullam, Keilah, Zif—the places that harbor David on his path through the Judean wilderness and beyond follow one another, as there is no one place safe for our hero, not even a town he liberates from the Philistines. Most of David's peregrinations take place within a limited geographical area, around the hill country of Judah, south of Gibeah of Saul. The farthest he will get away is the wilderness of Zif, forty to fifty miles south. Saul, in the meantime, appears to have ears and eyes everywhere seeking David's whereabouts; so he sits and waits until he sees an opportunity to go after him.

Chapters 21–22 present an ongoing event beginning and ending at the town of Nob, with the insertion of two interludes (21:11–16[10–15]; 22:1–5). All the material reviews David's adventures, most likely originating in different traditions, making transitions rough in places; but as it now stands, one gets an overview of what life may have been like for someone of David's stature when it is open season on his person and someone like Saul holds the power. Evidently, the collectors of the various stories about this period in David's life thought it important to put them together in just this way, leading from one unarmed man fleeing Saul's court to the point where he has managed to gather a fighting force and considers his only security to be forming an alliance with Israel's archenemies, the Philistines.

89. Pedersen, *Israel, Its Life and Culture*, vol. 1, 283.
90. Van Wijk-Bos, *Reading Samuel*, 111.

We note that at several stages of David's life on the run, there are people ready to hand him over to the king. Once David has managed to gather a band around him (22:2), he becomes the leader of a small fighting force, men loyal to him who are ready to attack or protect as the situation demands. They fight off Philistine marauders at Keilah (23:1–5) but are perhaps not as welcome there as they had hoped. The reality of this kind of life is that large cohorts must be armed and fed. Even if the numbers of four to six hundred are exaggerated and there were only forty to a hundred men around David, the need for shelter and provisions would always be urgent. A band of loosely organized roving warriors around a skilled captain would most likely be a burden on the countryside they settled in or came through. The readiness of the Keilites and the Zifites to give David up to Saul and Nabal's eventual rude refusal to feed David's men strikes a realistic note under the circumstances.

Act III, Scene 1: The Search for Sanctuary (1 Samuel 21:2–22:5[91])

It is the shadow of Saul over the land, it is the terror of the royal side of power.[92]

The episodes begin with a focus on Nob, a city marked by the presence of a sanctuary and priestly descendants of Eli. In the opening, David arrives there to secure provisions of food and weaponry (21:2–10). Two episodes follow, the first an unsuccessful attempt by David to find shelter among the Philistines (21:11–16), the second a notation of a new hiding place and of David being joined by followers and his family, whom he then moves to a location outside the reach of Saul (22:1–5).

91. As noted above, I am following the chapter divisions of the Masoretic Text of the Hebrew Bible, in which the lines that appear at the end of 20:42 in the NRSV and other English translations appear as 21:1. In ch. 21, subsequent verses are one number higher compared to their counterparts in English translation.

92. Fokkelman, *The Crossing Fates*, 354.

Scene 1, Part 1: Flight to Nob (1 Samuel 21:2–10)

What David is about these days remains hidden from almost everyone around him in the story.[93]

The report of David's appearance at Nob is told mainly through his conversation with the priest Ahimelek, a great-grandson of Eli. The introduction of Ahimelek in the opening sentence sounds an ominous note in view of the doom of the house of Eli foretold years earlier. Ahimelek "trembled" to meet David as the elders in Bethlehem once did when Samuel made an unexpected visit (16:4), and as the elders did, he asks a question.[94] His question on the surface asks the same thing twice: "Why are you alone?/ Without anyone with you?" In reality, there may be another inquiry hiding underneath, and he may want to know two things: "Why are you here?" and "Where is everyone else?" People like David were usually surrounded by other men, cohorts with which to go on the warpath. We assume, then, that David turned up in Nob without an entourage and, as will be evident shortly, without weapons. The situation fits more aptly with the aftermath of David's flight in chapter 19, since there would have been ample time during his exchange with Jonathan in the episode immediately preceding to at least make sure that he did not leave unarmed. Most likely, the events at Nob are placed here to mark clearly the beginning of David's wanderings as a lone man without provisions or a company of fighters.

In his response to Ahimelek, David claims Saul has sent him on a secret mission, which is as much as saying, "I can't tell you why I am here, but it is of national importance," and which answers the question about his being alone. His company will meet him "somewhere" (3). The phrase "let no one know anything of the matter"

93. Polzin, *Samuel and the Deuteronomist,* 195.

94. "Such anxiety is no trifling matter. . . . It is not simply a matter of astonishment . . . or of attitude toward authority . . . rather, it is signal in the narrative from the outset that the action to follow will be fraught with consequences." Campbell, *1 Samuel*, 225.

recalls the lad with Jonathan who did not "know anything" (20:39). Secrecy indeed surrounds the "matter," about the nature of which David does not elaborate. He cloaks even the place of reuniting with his phantom troops in vague terms: "The lads I told only about a certain place." He could easily have invented a location, but specific information can be double-checked, and the very mysteriousness of his description may keep the priest off balance. Something this secret must be very important!

Without lingering on the issue of the mission, perhaps to maintain the fable of a company waiting for him somewhere or to deflect further questions from Ahimelek, David moves to the matter of food. Where there are troops, there is need of provisions. He needs so many loaves of bread and asks what the priest has "at hand" (4). Ahimelek still does not know much—not why David has turned up nor where his company is waiting for him—but he may know more than he lets on. The news that David is no longer in Saul's favor might well have spread in the surroundings of Gibeah, which is not far away. The reason that he "trembled" when encountering David is possibly that he fears being asked to provide refuge for a warrior who has become a fugitive. Sheltering those whom a government intends to liquidate is at all times a risky business, and the risk of helping David will turn out to be grave indeed for Ahimelek and his entire town. His response to David's request is that there is indeed bread, but only the special bread kept in the sanctuary—"the bread of the presence," as it will be described in verse 7—holy bread that is strictly reserved as food for priests (Exod 35:13; 39:36; cf. Lev 24:5–9; Num 4:7). One would expect Ahimelek to say, "There is only holy bread, and you know you cannot have that!" But he equivocates by raising the possibility of giving the bread to David on the condition that the men with David are in a state of ritual purity (5–6). David takes up the point elaborately in defense of the purity of "his troops," deflecting the priest again from the real issue that no matter what their state of ritual purity, the bread is not for ordinary folk. Only after he gets the food does he get around to what is probably the most important matter: securing a weapon.

1 SAMUEL 21:7–9

7 And the priest gave him the consecrated,
for there was no bread there
but the bread of the presence
removed from the presence of Adonai
to be replaced by warm bread
on the day it was taken.

8 And there a man of the servants of Saul
on that day was detained in the presence of Adonai,
and his name was Doeg, the Edomite,
a chief herdsman of Saul.
9 David said to Ahimelek:
Do you have here at hand
no spear or sword?
For neither sword nor gear
did I take in my hand,
for the king's matter was urgent.

In quick succession, the bread of the presence is handed over to David and David inquires as to the availability of weaponry, most likely the reason he has turned up at this particular place. When Ahimelek reveals that Goliath's sword is there, not "in the presence of Adonai" but hidden in wrapping and "behind" the ephod this revelation can hardly have come as a surprise to David, who may have had it transported there himself. There is nothing like that particular weapon in his opinion, and his request is almost brusque: "Give it to me!" The narrator does not bother to report that the priest indeed gives him the sword, and the story moves on, with David, albeit still on the run, now equipped with food and a weapon.

In addition to bread "in the presence of Adonai," there is a person in God's presence, an outsider who is "detained" at the sanctuary for an undisclosed reason. The story mentions only what is significant for what follows: the man's name and origin and his allegiance to Saul, whose name occurs here twice (8). In this way, as Antony Campbell observes, the story in 21:2–10 manages to be an introduction both to David's life as a fugitive and to the slaughter of the priests and people of Nob in chapter 22.[95] Following the gift of bread, the mention of a person closely attached to Saul raises tension and anticipates a sequel. The tension increases as it becomes clear that Ahimelek hands to David the gift of bread, necessary for life, and the best weapon available, necessary for striking down the enemy, in the presence of an eyewitness.

There remains a question as to the reason for David's visit in Nob. It was perilously close to Gibeah, and a priestly enclave is not a likely location to go looking for food. The likelihood is that the narrator intends to imply that the primary goal was the search for a weapon in a situation where David fled the court without armor (see the suggested sequence of events above, p. 164). It follows that David knows very well where the armor of Goliath is kept and that he came to Nob not armed with a sword but with the knowledge of where he could find a sword. Once he has what he wants, he is out of town in no time and on the way westward, where he may have been headed all along.

Scene 1, Part 2: Flight to Gath (1 Samuel 21:11–16)

Achish withdraws his visa and puts him on the first flight out of Gath.[96]

In this episode, the precarious nature of David's situation becomes abundantly clear, as he is said to be on the run. "He fled from the court of Saul and came to Achish, king of Gath" (11). He runs west to the first Philistine city in the plain, Gath. Trying to find refuge with the enemy of his pursuer is not a bad move, as it would put him outside of Saul's reach, and eventually David will be successful in this effort. For the moment, however, the attempt turns out to be David's first misstep, and for the first time he becomes afraid: "David feared greatly before Achish, the king of Gath" (13). The reason for his trepidation is that the servants of the court are on to his identity,

95. Campbell, *1 Samuel*, 227.
96. Goldingay, *Men Behaving Badly*, 157.

referring to him as "king of the land" and quoting the praise songs David received from the women on his return from the battlefield (12). Prophecy about what lies ahead for David thus arrives from Philistine lips, along with the repetition of the praise he once received at the side of Saul for the battles he fought with Philistines. The servants may thus be putting their leader on notice that here is a very dangerous person, an archenemy of his people.

Indeed, it would have been a prime opportunity for Achish to do away with an opponent who will eventually hand devastating defeats to his people. The king, however, is somewhat slow to get moving, and before he can take any steps, David puts on the act of someone who has lost his senses, scrabbling at the gate and drooling in his beard (14). Literally, the text reports that he "pretended to be mad in their *hands*," implying that at this point he is in the power of the king's servants, perhaps, as some translations have it, "in custody." This spectacle evokes an outraged reaction from the king.

1 Samuel 21:15–16

15 Achish said to his servants:
Look, you see the man is crazy;
why did you bring him to me?
16 Do I lack crazies
that you should bring this one to act crazy to me?
Why did you bring him to me?
Would this one enter my house?

Three times he repeats words referring to insanity, and three times he asks why they would bring such a person into his presence.[97] David, who is the subject of most of the verbs in the episodes of these chapters that concern him, is here the assumed object of the action of *bringing*, but in fact he has come to Gath on his own. So Achish has it wrong, which works to David's advantage. Alter calls

97. The root for madness and raving is *shagah*, which produced the word *meshuggah*, with only six occurrences in the Hebrew text of the Bible. The root for "bring" is *bo*, "to enter," and actually occurs four times in the speech.

this "an extraordinary moment in the story of the founding king of Israel: David, the glamorous young hero of the preceding episodes, is prepared to do whatever is necessary in order to survive, even if it means making himself appear as the most shunned of humankind."[98] It shows that David is quick-witted enough to let go of his wits in order to get out of a predicament. The short episode displays him as able to take advantage of an extremely precarious situation, and at the same time the narrative has inserted an experience that will have an eventual follow-up at a later stage in David's career as an outlaw.

Scene 1, Part 3: Flight to Adullam (1 Samuel 22:1–5)

David . . . belongs to no society except one that gathers around him.[99]

In the next breath, we find David in the cave of Adullam, east of Gath at the border of the hill country, where his family joins him. In addition, he is able to gather a small fighting force, not men of great renown but those who are hard up—embittered men with debts and grievances (2). In the words of Joel Baden: "The Bible makes no attempt to sugarcoat the fact that David surrounds himself with a band of misfits and outlaws. Given his whereabouts he had little other choice."[100] The text assigns David the role of the men's "leader" (*sar*), a term used often for military leadership. Under Saul's command, David had been the *sar* of a thousand men, and although it's a bit of a step down to have only four hundred around him, gradually David is gaining strength.[101] We observe also that this time David's

98. Alter, *The David Story*, 134n15.

99. Goldingay, *Men Behaving Badly*, 157.

100. Joel Baden, *The Historical David: The Real Life of an Invented Hero* (New York: HarperCollins, 2013), 86. In a similar vein Goldingay (*Men Behaving Badly*, 157) writes: "In the classic pattern, the potential leader of a revolution gathers round him other people disillusioned with the government who have nothing to lose by associating with someone who may bring about political and economic change."

101. Most likely, we must take for granted that all the numbers of the fighting forces are exaggerated. In his article on David and Keilah, Nadav

family comes to him, no doubt for safety. It is a role reversal from the youngster who had not been deemed worthy to appear before Samuel, *sent* as an errand boy to his brothers on the battlefield and subsequently receiving a public dressing down by one of his siblings (17:17–18, 28–29).

This time it is David who does the *sending*. He brings his family members to the other side of the Jordan, to Moab, where he requests shelter from the king for them. By his own words, he himself will wait to find out what God has in store for him (3). Soon enough, a divine directive comes to him from a prophet, who tells him to move from Moab and go into the "land of Judah." Neither Adullam, on the border between Philistine territory and Judah, nor Moab is a suitable hiding place, and David moves to the forest of Hereth. While the precise location of this place is unknown, we may assume it to be in the hill country of Judah. It is worth noting that David is the one receiving prophetic advice, another sign of his rising in stature even while he is on the run from Saul (5).[102]

In each brief episode, David is moving from one place to another: "David came" (21:1); "David arose and fled . . . and came" (21:11); "David went from there and got away" (22:1); "David went and came" (22:5). The different expressions show development in regard to his status. From impecunious unarmed refugee in Nob he moves, on the run from Saul, into the arms of Israel's enemies—for the time being an inauspicious move, but one that will ultimately work out—subsequently to a hiding place that works as a center for gathering a sizeable force around him, and eventually to a shelter closer to the residence of Saul. We can agree with Fokkelman that the purpose of inserting the vignettes about false refuge in Gath and

Na'aman ("David's Sojourn in Keilah in Light of the Amarna Letters," *VT* 60 [2010]: 96) observes that forty to one hundred armed and organized men would constitute a "strong military force that required the mobilization of powerful armed forces to crush it."

102. Outside of this passage, the prophet Gad appears in 2 Samuel 24:11–19[10–18] during the account of the census and its aftermath. Here he comes out of nowhere, perhaps not receiving antecedents because the emphasis is on the divine guidance received by David. Possibly, we have here a shorthand account of what was once a longer story.

safe refuge in Moab and the Judean forest is to establish that David has entered a modicum of safety and that he is guided by God in his endeavors.[103]

In addition, references to *king* abound in 21:1–22:5. First, there is Ahimelek (4× in 21:1–9) the priest of Nob, whose name means "my brother [is] king," followed by two references to *King* Saul (21:3, 9), then to *King* Achish (21:11, 13), designations that surround a mention of David as *king* (21:12). Finally, there is the *king* of Moab (22:3, 4).[104] Altogether, we find *king* eleven times in twenty-one verses. David moves from king to king, and is once, albeit mistakenly, so designated himself. All of these may be considered signposts for the path to kingship on which David has set his feet.

Act III, Scene 2: Massacre at Nob (1 Samuel 22:6–23)

David is prudent in speech all right, and it saves him—but it kills Ahimelek, who is not prudent in speech.[105]

One of the most horrific scenes in Saul's career follows in the episode that directly links up with David's visit to Nob (21:2–10[1–9]). It opens with a notation that "Saul heard" about David's location and his gathering an entourage. As of this scene, through chapter 26, there will be constant references to both Saul and David getting to know each other's plans and whereabouts, at times through named sources but often simply with the observation that they "heard," "saw," or "were told." The lives of royal pursuer and outlaw move in tandem, and the picture is of a constant back-and-forth of spies and

103. Fokkelman, *The Crossing Fates*, 378: "Saul can no longer change the David-line, but it also reflects the fact that the narrator first wants to bring David in calmer waters. That in turn is evidence of how David's fate is guided by the Deity."

104. Although within the context of the David history a refuge in Moab is not outside the realm of possibility in view of the origin of David´s great-grandmother Ruth, it is unlikely that at this point the Judean outlaw would have discourse with a royal leader.

105. Goldingay, *Men Behaving Badly*, 156.

informants on both Saul's and David's side, reminding us that the theater of activities is geographically small. Yet the terrain is difficult and affords plenty of opportunity for David to elude the pursuers.

The sequel to the Nob episode, this time with Saul in the center, stands out because in it, Saul is stationary in contrast to the events that follow. When the narratives report that Saul "heard" or "was told" in chapters 23–26, Saul usually moves into military action against David, albeit without success. Here, Saul "heard" and stays put; "he sat," which remains the case throughout the rest of the scene until its dreadful end. Saul sits in his own residence in Gibeah "with his spear in his hand," elsewhere a sign of aggressive activity just around the corner (cf. 18:10; 19:9). Furthermore, the incident is marked by speech, with action happening only at the end. What Saul has heard is knowledge of David's location and also that there are men with him. In other words, it looks as if David may be gathering a fighting force. This information drives Saul into irrational rage.

Saul begins by accusing his clansmen in a speech that betrays both his state of disarray and his manipulative power.

1 Samuel 22:7–8

7 And Saul said to his servants
gathered around him:
Listen now, Benjaminites:
Sure, to all of you will the son of Jesse give
fields and vineyards;
he will make all of you leaders of thousands
and leaders of hundreds.
8 For all of you conspire against me;
and no one informs me
that my son is in covenant with the son of Jesse,
and none of you is bothered on my account
or discloses to me that my son set up
my servant against me to lie in wait today!

Saul appeals directly to his kin, in Hebrew literally "the sons of the right hand" (*beney yemini*), avoiding David's name and consistently calling him "the son of Jesse" (*ben yishay*). "All of you" (3×) think to benefit, "all of you" stand accused with "no one/none of you" in counterpoint. All of you are in league against me, no one tells me anything, while my own son (*beni*) has made a pact with this scoundrel about which no one told me, and no one even cares about me, while my own son (*beni*) is in league with this character and set up the whole thing, making my servant into an enemy. It is all highly irrational. Of course, someone must have told Saul something, both about David's movements and about Jonathan's strong bond with David. How would he know otherwise? It is irrational that all of it is about him, Saul, who finds himself outside the loop of information, a victim of a conspiracy! It is also manipulative, because such a speech is sure to raise the indignation of someone to counter these accusations!

On cue, Doeg pops up with a reply—Doeg, who is an outsider, an Edomite, rather than one of Saul's own folk. We met Doeg earlier during the David in Nob episode (21:8[7]), when he apparently witnessed a great deal while detained at the sanctuary during David's negotiations with Ahimelek (22:9–10). Of all that went on there, he first mentions that Ahimelek, whom he calls "the son of Ahitub," inquired from Adonai on behalf of "the son of Jesse"—in other words, he acted in his priestly capacity to seek an oracle. It is likely that Saul hears nothing beyond this incendiary information, designed to add fuel to the fire of his rage, because such guidance is precisely what is lacking in his own life.

We do not know if Doeg speaks the truth, nor will it become clear from Ahimelek. What matters here is the effect the revelation has on Saul. It causes him to gather another group around him: "Ahimelek and *all* his father's house, the priests of Nob, they *all* came to the king" (11). Saul throws at him the same accusations he aimed earlier at his servants: conspiracy and enabling "the son of Jesse to lie in wait against me" (13). Making an inquiry of God on David's behalf is wedged in between the accusations, and it would be easy for Ahimelek to not address that specific issue at all.

Instead, in his reply (14–15), Ahimelek does everything to aggravate Saul further rather than presenting him with a diplomatic and soothing answer. First, he praises David to the skies, calling him the most trusted servant of Saul, his son-in-law, the head of the bodyguard and honored in Saul's house. He then addresses the issue of making divine inquiry directly rather than avoiding it.

1 SAMUEL 22:15

Did I just now begin to inquire for him of God?
Perish the thought!
Let not the king impute anything to his servant
or all my father's house.
For your servant knew nothing of all of this,
neither small nor great.

Although not prudent, it is a clever and high-handed answer, appealing to Saul's better nature. Surely, Saul can see the unreasonableness of his attitude! And if Ahimelek must go down, he will do so with all flags flying. He was, after all, in total ignorance, unlike Saul who knew almost everything. What Saul does not know and what we do not know from this answer is if the priest, who is the first one to mention David by name (14), truly sought an oracle on David's behalf, because in effect he says, "If I indeed made an inquiry, then so what? I have done this all the time for someone so trusted by you, King, so much a part of your household." With his reply to the king, Ahimelek, in Fokkelman's words, decides to die "with his head held high and a completely clear conscience."[106] I believe that in so doing, he also may hope against hope that there is still in Saul a part that will respond to the qualities of David he has highlighted, but as Jonathan found out earlier, it is now too late for that type of appeal. No matter his intentions, Ahimelek's words spell his doom.

The horrific scene that follows is too painful for contemplation. When Saul's own servants refuse Saul's order to kill the priests, an action that carries a strong taboo, Doeg takes it upon himself to mow them down and in a frenzy of bloodlust also puts to the sword all the inhabitants of Nob, "men and women, infant and babe, ox and

106. I ultimately agree with Fokkelman (*The Crossing Fates*, 401), who argues this point exhaustively.

donkey and sheep" (19), executing total destruction on Saul's own people—the same destruction Saul himself once failed to complete on Amalek (15:8–9). Joel Baden writes, "It demonstrates the depth of Saul's anger: the destruction of Nob is an explicit bastardization of the Israelite law of *herem*. . . . In his rage, Saul has twisted Israel's laws and customs."[107] According to Baden, all of this fits in with Saul's denigration and the elevation of David in the text.

The killing of everyone in Nob, together with all its priests (thereby fulfilling the predicted doom over the house of Eli), is not quite the end. As often happens in such stories, someone survives—in this case a son of Ahimelek, Abiatar, who, like David earlier, "got away . . . and fled." He seeks refuge with David, who grants him asylum wholeheartedly, assuring him complete protection (20–23). For the time being, the narrator withholds the information that Abiatar has managed to bring along the ephod (23:6), meaning that David now has not only priestly support but also the help of the official means to acquire divine counsel, gaining another advantage in his life as an outlaw. To Abiatar's news that Saul has killed the priests of Adonai, David replies that he had a notion Doeg would be up to no good when he saw him at Nob. He then declares: "I myself turned against the life of all your father's house," taking responsibility for what has happened at Nob.[108]

The Question of Saul and David

A miasma of misery hangs over this episode, a low point in the life of Saul as he causes the decimation of an entire town under his rule. The events accounted leave a stench of vengeful slaughter in the air but also a question. Could even Saul, who fell into murderous

107. Baden, *The Historical David*, 85.

108. With others, I maintain the verb form *sabboti* from the root *savav* means "to encircle, turn." It is also used in Saul's speech in 22:7–8 and for the verb with which Doeg begins his execution. The narrative here puts the same verb in David's mouth because he rightly assumes the responsibility for putting Ahimelek, his house, and the entire town at risk by turning up there.

rages as we know, until now aimed at individuals—persons he had, moreover, a right to suspect—have gone so far as to have an entire town murdered, taking reprisals, in the manner of all wicked tyrants, on the innocent for the perceived transgressions of an enemy? The question arises whether this picture fits with the image of Saul constructed within the story world presented by the narrator.

Where is the kernel of veracity around which this story about Saul and David turns? Let us assume that there was indeed an Israelite town that fell victim to a massacre, that the memory of it lingered, and that it was a place associated with the name of David—perhaps one where he sought refuge during his time on the run from Saul. To whose benefit was it to have the entire population of this town erased from the land? Could the possible perpetrator indeed have been David, as testified to by his own words (22)? David, albeit not in charge of a large force, had enough fighting men to slaughter an unsuspecting and unarmed crowd of people. Was he desperate enough to eliminate any witnesses of his whereabouts so close to the residence of Saul at this moment in his career when his life hung in the balance? Is Doeg a handy point-person for the storyteller because he is, after all, an Edomite? It all depends on how characteristic we judge the speech and actions of Saul in this episode to be of the person we have known so far. Can we imagine that on account of his doomed house, like the house of Eli, it did not really matter if the storytellers ascribed one more deed, be it ever so grossly wicked, to the man who was going downhill anyway?

With others, I ascribe the narratives in 1 Samuel 16–31 to a source generally favorable to David, and it is in this context that Saul is portrayed committing what Campbell calls "a shockingly sacrilegious act."[109] Saul in these recitals is the "man of blood," an epithet later hurled at David by Shimei Ben Gera (2 Sam 16:7–8). But perhaps it is not so clear who exactly is the bloodthirsty man, and we are left with our uneasiness and the fragmentariness of our knowledge.[110]

109. Campbell, *1 Samuel*, 235.

110. "We have no other reference to this act of Saul's; similarly, we have

Act III, Scene 3: Rescue and Betrayal (1 Samuel 23[111])

We are given this picture in which David is the deliverer, Saul the destroyer, and the people fickle.[112]

In the next chapters, Saul and David move in and out of each other's orbit. Constant reporting to Saul has him on the move to pursue David, and the same takes place with David, keeping him a step ahead of the king. "They told Saul that David had come to. . ." and "David got to know that Saul. . ." or phrases like these recur throughout the tale. Chapter 23 tells of David coming to the rescue of a town that eventually is ready to betray him under the threat of Saul's impending arrival. In addition, there is another group with whom he has found shelter, which is eager to hand him over. Not everyone is in favor of David, and certain people—perhaps most—stay loyal to their king. In spite of the king receiving constant information, David consistently eludes Saul. Between Saul and David, it is a matter of whose power will prevail, in the story indicated by the frequent use of the word "hand." Throughout, David is assured of divine support and guidance while such aid eludes Saul.

Together with the chapters that follow, the events include an acclamation of David's kingship. This anticipatory announcement began with the Philistines during his flight to Gath (21:12[11]), is continued in chapter 23 with a pronouncement by Jonathan (17), and will be repeated in subsequent material, even by Saul. The Jonathan-David encounter with its affirmation of friendship and loyalty (16–18), sandwiched in between potential and actual betrayals of David, represents a strong counterpoint to its context. While it cements the bond between the two men, it does not change their respective situation, with each returning to his place at the end of it.

---

no story of his putting the Gibeonites to death (2 Samuel 21:1. . .). We are reminded of how fragmentary our knowledge is" (Campbell, *1 Samuel*, 235).

111. I am following the chapter divisions of the Masoretic Text of the Hebrew Bible, in which the verse that appears as 23:29 in the NRSV and other English translations appears as 24:1. This verse will be considered as the first verse of the next act.

112. Campbell, *1 Samuel*, 238.

In the opening unit (1–6), David receives a report about a Philistine assault on Keilah, a town on the border between Philistine and Israelite territory, a bit south of Adullam. Word is that the Philistines are "looting the threshing floors," meaning they are after the town's food supply, with potentially disastrous results for the inhabitants. David asks for divine advice, which he receives; he asks twice because his men, not without reason, are afraid to venture that far out of Judah. They are already scared enough in their home region—how much worse will it get if they risk coming closer to enemy terrain! (4). Twice, David receives an affirmative response, with the second one adding the detail that God will "give the Philistines" into David's "hand." And so they go on their expedition, reported as six hundred strong (13), and conclude it successfully.[113] David is here the *liberator* in contrast to Saul the *destroyer* of a town. It is at this point that the narrator reveals Abiatar had escaped Nob with the ephod (6), the oracular device used by priests to receive divine counsel. The earlier report of inquiries by David to Adonai leaves it up in the air whether he simply asked on his own, but we should probably understand the reference in verse 6 to mean that he made use of the device now in his presence. David will take explicit recourse to inquiry with help of the ephod in the sequel.[114]

The threshing floors were outside the walls of the town, so David's troops may have indeed been able to chase off the marauding Philistines, who possibly came out with a light force, never counting on meeting a greater threat than unarmed civilians. Or it could be, as Joel Baden argues, that David waited until the Philistines had done

113. On the size of David's fighting force, see pp. 169–70n101 above.

114. The ephod was both an oracular device and a linen garment worn by priests. The reference in 22:18 is to the garments of the priests. Fokkelman (*The Crossing Fates*, 423) is of the opinion that the inquiries of God by David in vv. 2 and 4 are made without the help of the ephod because "the elected one is not dependent on having an oracular device." I read the text in a less linear way and assume some ambiguity in the references where the ephod is not mentioned explicitly. Verse 6 may be seen as a notation that sheds light on the means by which David achieves his oracular results. Although David prays in the narratives in 2 Sam, one does not get much of a sense that he is in direct communication with God in the manner of Joshua, for example.

their work and left, then positioned himself as the one who drove away the Philistine plunderers.[115] If the latter is the case, there is no question of David in any sense "saving" Keilah (2). The true course of events may lie somewhere in the middle. David and his men may have waited until the last moment to chase off Philistine stragglers and present themselves as liberators. For David and his followers, a town is a preferable base to hiding in the Judean hills. The Keilites are, however, less than eager to embrace their savior, which provides some foundation for the notion that the true state of affairs was a bit less overwhelming than the striking of "a great blow" against the Philistines reported in the story. The Keilites will turn out to be ready to hand David over to their rightful king.[116] As Na'aman points out, the character of bands like David's was "by nature predatory and a threat to the villages in the vicinity," which "explains how the news of David's sojourn at Keilah soon reached Saul" while also accounting for David's willingness to come and take care of the marauders.[117]

Saul finds out about David's current refuge and in response decides that God must have abandoned David to deliver him into Saul's power and that it will be easier to find him in a town "behind gates and bars" than out in the open. The next section tells of Saul's decision to lay siege to Keilah in order to flush David out, with David fleeing when he discovers Saul's intentions and Saul ultimately turning away from his purpose so the chase is fruitless (9–13). While Saul is gathering "all the people to battle," David makes another inquiry of Adonai. His perturbation is evident from the double question he poses: "Will the masters of Keilah surrender me into his hand?/ Will Saul come down as your servant heard?" (11–12).[118] The oracle responds only to the

115. Baden, *The Historical David*, 88.

116. Baden (*The Historical David*, 89) argues that David's men would have been a burden on the town, "sapping their resources," and that the townspeople would have feared retribution from Saul if they gave shelter to David. "It was in their best interest to make clear that they were not aligned with David."

117. Na'aman, "David's Sojourn in Keilah," 96.

118. We note the expression "masters of Keilah" (*ba'aley ke'ilah*). The "masters" of a town in theses texts generally have a negative connation (see Judg 9 throughout; Judg 20:5 for the "masters of Gibeah"; cf. Josh 24:11; 2 Sam 21:12). In 1–2 Sam, the expression occurs only here and in 2 Sam 21:12.

second question so that the painful issue of betrayal must be raised again (12). The divine answer to both questions is affirmative: Saul will come, and those of Keilah will hand David over.[119] The marshaling of the troops by Saul must have taken some time, so David has plenty of time to leave Keilah, and Saul has time to halt his efforts once he finds out that, once again, David "got away" (13).

A narrative comment in verse 14 draws attention to the fact of David's new retreat, this time to the south, the wilderness of Zif in the Negev, and Saul's relentlessly chasing him without success: "Saul sought him all the time,/ and God did not give him into his hand." The comment provides a breathing space in the midst of anxious episodes, and into this space steps Jonathan, who apparently has no need of informers to find out David's location. The text simply reports that "Jonathan . . . went to David at Horesh." Their meeting (15–18), the last time these two will be together, allows Jonathan to encourage David, to commend him as king, and to speak of himself as a future second-in-command (17). Only Jonathan speaks in the episode, and his words have the weight of a predictive announcement. Poignantly, the short section refers to him as "the son of Saul," and he speaks twice of "Saul, my father" (16–17). The meeting concludes with a renewal of their bond: "They cut a covenant before Adonai" (18)—this time a mutual act (cf. 18:3; 20:8).

The situation becomes tense in verse 19 when the Zifites approach Saul to reveal David's sojourn among them, inviting Saul to come and get him (19–28). Thanking them elaborately, Saul charges them to find out more details so he will know exactly where David can be found and go on the warpath. Saul's instructions for more information are odd in view of the facts seeming to be sufficiently clear regarding David's location. Further searches will cause a delay, providing David with an opportunity to find out about Saul's

119. The text plays with the words "to shut" and "surrender" by using the same root, *sagar*. In the form used in v. 7, it means to "shut in" or "close up," while in vv. 11–12 (in the *Hif'il* form), it has the sense of "secluding" in order to separate. David who has "shut himself" in the town of Keilah will thus be "shut out" by the townspeople. In English the meaning of the *Hif'il* is here best rendered by "surrender" with the result of losing the pun.

impending arrival. Perhaps aware of this possibility, Saul sets out right away, with David already located northeast of Zif in Maon.[120] This is precisely where Saul seeks him out, and he comes very close to catching David.

1 SAMUEL 23:26–28

26 Saul went on one side of the mountain,
while David and his men went on the other side;
and David hurried in panic to go away from Saul,
while Saul and his men were closing in on David
and his men to capture them.

27 Then a messenger came to Saul, saying:
Come quickly for the Philistines are raiding the land.
28 So Saul came back from pursuing David
and went to meet the Philistines.
Therefore, they call that place
the rock of separation.

This is the only time that David is said to be in a panicky haste during his flight from Saul. He "hurried," with a rare verb used one other time in the Samuel texts (2 Sam 4:4) and elsewhere in the Psalms of panicked anxiety regarding God's presence (Pss 31:23[22]; 48:6[5]; 104:7). Saul and his men, meanwhile, are "closing in," to "capture / grab" them. Both verbs are of some interest. The first also means "to surround with a wreath or crown," with its derivation directly referring to a king's "crown." Even at the direst moment, the text hints at David's impending kingship. Rescue comes in the nick of time via a "messenger" to Saul who calls him back to his true task, liberating his people from the Philistines. In Hebrew, the word for messenger (*malakh*) can also refer to a being sent by God, in standard English translations an "angel." At the same time, the word is also close to the noun meaning king (*melekh*). It is a rare moment

120. The thread of the Zifites' return is picked up again in 26:1, where they once again provide exact information.

when an individual messenger brings word to Saul, and possibly the narrator indeed implies that God's hand stayed the king, who is coming too close to finding his prey, as well as once again implying David's future kingship through wordplay.

Act IV: In the Presence of the Enemy (1 Samuel 24–26)

All the day long they injure my cause; against me all their devisings are for evil. (Ps 56:6[5])

Chapters 24–26 form a triptych with close encounters between Saul and David on the side panels and a meeting of David with an outsider in the center. Each panel depicts a challenge to David in the proximity of an enemy, and in each case he refrains from violence. Each panel also provides an announcement that refers to David's future kingship. The panel on the far right (ch. 26) seemingly ends in reconciliation between the king and his rival, but the two will thenceforth stay on their separate paths.

The encounters are painted in vivid detail; all three display deep emotions on every side. Doubt, grief, anger, awe, love, and lust for vengeance overcome the different characters. There is no question that these are among the liveliest of the descriptions of David's life while he is on the run, living outside the margin of established social life with his band of fighters. The stories serve to establish David as able to abstain from unnecessary violence in counterpoint to the picture of Saul in chapter 23. They also paint a portrait of David as the one in charge while, by all rights, he should be the one in fear for his life. Do the episodes serve the purpose of affirming that David indeed did not raise his hand against his rightful king, God's anointed—an issue that is repeatedly mentioned? Or does the question of a possible reconciliation between the two hover over the stories?

David stays in hiding, for the most part in Saul's neighborhood, and the two never engage in armed conflict against each other. Twice, they have an encounter, initiated by David, when they exchange words filled with emotion, even love. Indeed, there is no time in the text when Saul directs harsh words at David while in his presence. He thinks angry thoughts—murderous thoughts—and nurses jealous rage; he speaks disparaging and accusing words *about* David in his absence, hurls biting mistrustful words at his son and his kinsmen. Yet when face to face with his erstwhile beloved adjutant and therapist, he changes his tune entirely. It is, however, to no avail. For when all is said and done, only Saul's death will bring an end to the struggle between the two. As David himself states, "God will strike him down, or his day will come and he will die, or he will go down to battle and be swept away" (26:10).[121] When the sun sets on Saul's last words to him, words of blessing (26:25), they depart from one another still estranged, and in the next breath David decides that he will "surely perish at the hand of Saul" (27:1).

A central feature shared by the three chapters is a statement about David's future kingship, first made by Saul, then strongly implied by Abigail, and then by Saul again. Saul makes the first declaration, following in the footsteps of his son Jonathan (23:17).

1 Samuel 24:21[20]

And now, look, I know
that you will surely be king,
and the kingship of Israel will stand by your hand.

The introduction "and now" is especially strong in the speeches between David and Saul, drawing emphatic attention to what follows. Saul, who at this point uses the words for king and kingship three times, declares what Jonathan had already told David: He *knows* what lies ahead for David, and he sounds resigned to it.[122]

Abigail, who in chapter 25 is trying to prevent bloodshed in her household, makes the longest speech regarding David's future office,

121. With the expression "he will be swept away," the text employs the same verbal root as at the end of Samuel's speech in 1 Sam 12:25 (pp. 93–94n124 above).

122. In Hebrew, the phrase here translated "you will surely be king" repeats the root: "You will be king, yes king." Fox (*The Early Prophets*, 397) translates, "You will reign as king, yes, king."

referring throughout the second part of her plea to David to the fact that Adonai will build David a "lasting house" and that his enemies will be taken care of by the Deity.

1 SAMUEL 25:30–31

30 And when Adonai has done to my lord
according to all the good he spoke to him,
and has set you up as a prince over Israel,
31 this will not be for you a stumbling block,
and a heartache for my lord,
to have shed blood without cause
to gain victory for himself.

Abigail thus argues that for David himself, it would be a wound in his psyche (here his "heart") if he acted violently when there was no need for it and it was only in order to triumph over someone. She is the only one who appeals to David's better nature, where in the other encounters David himself is keen to plead his own exoneration.

The third declaration comes when David has once again proven to Saul that he is no threat to his life. Saul, who is allotted few words in this section, confesses that he has done wrong and ends their exchange as follows.

1 SAMUEL 26:25

Saul said to David:
Blessed are you my son David;
in all that you do you will surely succeed.

The three proclamations constitute signposts pointing to what lies ahead for David. The collectors who finalized the narratives and their placement in the text before the announcement of Samuel's death and Saul and David's final parting highlight the fact that friend and foe alike are aware of David's future as Israel's successful king and that this future is God-willed and God-blessed. David's kingship is a done deal; it is, as they say, not a question of if but when.

Act IV, Scene 1: In the Wilderness of Engedi (1 Samuel 24[123])

It is not that Saul is insincere. It is that he no longer knows how he really wants to deal with David.[124]

Four verses take us into the heart of the matter, with Saul locating David and then unwittingly finding himself at David's mercy instead of the other way around, most likely because of a need for rest, for which he enters the very cave in Engedi where David and his men are staying (1–4).[125] It appears to David's gang a prime opportunity (5–8)—a divine omen that the king is now in their hands—and they urge David to go get him! David instead cuts off a piece of the king's cloak. This is no minor matter, for the royal cloak betokens the very rule of the king, and so David rues his action. Rather than feeling regret for his failure to dispatch his royal opponent, he shakes in his boots because he has so dared violate "Adonai's anointed" (24:7 2×).[126]

123. As noted above, I am following the chapter divisions of the Masoretic Text of the Hebrew Bible, in which the verse that appears as 23:29 in the NRSV and other English translations appears as 24:1. In ch. 24, subsequent verses are one number higher compared to their counterparts in English translation.

124. Jobling, *1 Samuel*, 92.

125. The Hebrew expression "to cover his feet" is usually taken to mean that Saul went to relieve himself in the cave and is so rendered by many translations. The expression occurs only in one other place, on the occasion of the assassination of Eglon (Judg 3:24), and even there it is not clear what it means. In the case of Saul at Engedi, it seems absurd to assume anyone would use a cave for a toilet and privacy, since anyone, including a king, could find a better surface, like soil, for the purpose of urination or other physical needs and gain privacy by natural protection of bush or tree. A more logical interpretation is that Saul is going to sleep, for which one might cover the feet (cf. Ruth 3:7, where Ruth uncovers the feet of the sleeping Boaz). The Syriac version translates it this way. In addition, it is highly unlikely that David would be able to cut off a piece of Saul's cloak undetected while the king is relieving himself, but it would be understandable if he were asleep. Finally, the rocky terrain around Engedi could make it especially needful for Saul, who is no longer young, to take a power nap.

126. Fokkelman (*The Crossing Fates*, 455) suggests that by refusing to kill "Adonai's anointed," David formulates and perhaps institutes a taboo. "As a

He prevents his men from going after Saul, giving Saul the opportunity to exit the cave.

There is still tension in the air, because David may have prevented his followers from going after Saul, but he may himself yet have a change of heart. This possibility is soon put to rest by what follows in the major portion of the chapter, a section of speech and response between David and Saul, with the longer portion going to David (9–16). The gist of his flood of words is that he is being maligned by those who speak ill of him to the king, for he had the opportunity to kill him and did not do so.

1 SAMUEL 24:12

And, my father, see now, see
the edge of the cloak in my hand;
for when I cut off the edge of your cloak,
I did not kill you;
know and see that in my hand there is no evil or rebellion,
and I did not sin against you,
and you are stalking me to take my life!

He addresses Saul as "my father," which could simply be a respectful form of address but is nevertheless striking and could equally harken back to a time when the two men were in a close relationship. Twice he avows, "I did not kill you"/"I did not sin against you" (12), and he furthermore pledges he will not do so in the future: "My hand will not be against you" (13, 14; cf. 11). He ends with a self-deprecating comment and commends his case to God.

In his response (17–22) Saul, overcome by emotion, is at first able to choke out only a few words (four in Hebrew) and weeps for the first time in these accounts, bringing to mind Jonathan and David's tears at the end of chapter 20. Between them, he declares David to be the more righteous (18), and as Jonathan did, he exacts

result of the anointing the monarch is given a share of God's own holiness and becomes untouchable. That is so important to David that he speaks of this explicitly three times (24:7; 26:9, 11 and again in 2 Sam 1:14, 16)."

an oath from David in regard to his descendants (cf. 20:15). Only father Judah in Genesis 38 makes this type of declaration to another character as he declares his daughter-in-law Tamar more righteous. Both men provide as the reason for their statement that they did something wrong; in Saul's case, he confesses that he has rendered David "evil" in return for good (18). The episode ends with David swearing to Saul not to cut off his line, and the two go their separate ways. The emotional and confessional statement by Saul leaves the impression that he will now give up chasing David.

Act IV, Scene 2: The Things That Make for Peace (1 Samuel 25)

Abigail's eloquence is voluble, meandering, and brilliantly persuasive.[127]

Before one can find out if Saul will indeed no longer go on the warpath against David and whether the fragile peace between them will hold, another adventure comes in between, recounting an altercation of David with one of the locals: Nabal of Maon, a man of standing and wealth. First, however, the narrative writes the death notice of Samuel (1). It will be repeated in chapter 28, where it serves its own purpose, but here it appropriately follows the avowals of David's kingship by both Jonathan and Saul. Nothing more can now be done, and Samuel, who has not played a role of significance since chapter 16, may go to his grave. The verse mentions mourners but does not say if David was among them. He may well have been, still counting on the goodwill established by Saul at Engedi, for in verse 2 he is said to be on the move again, from Engedi to Maon.[128] It is in this neighborhood, where Saul once nipped close at David's heels (23:24–26), that the events of chapter 25 take place.

127. Fewell and Gunn, *Gender, Power, and Promise*, 156.

128. I opt for the reading "Maon" with the Septuagint version, because Paran makes little sense, although there could be a purpose on the part of the narrator in placing David so far into the Sinai peninsula. See Joseph Lozovyy, *Saul, Doeg, Nabal, and the "Son of Jesse": Readings in 1 Samuel 16–25* (London: T&T Clark, 2009), 65.

In the lead-up to the main incident, a rich and boorish man, Nabal, refuses to reward David and his cohort for protection granted to the shepherds of Nabal's many flocks and sends David's emissaries on their way with harsh words (2–11). He is most likely a Saul supporter and will have nothing to do with "servants who break away from their lords" (10). Upon receiving this news, David flies into a rage and orders his men to gird on their swords (12–13). To give Nabal his due, the "gift" requested by David sounds much like the price Nabal will have to pay for continued protection from David's band, and we could call the exchange, in modern terms, a protection racket in which Nabal refuses to engage.[129] The story is, however, told from a perspective of support for David and continues with the report from one in the household who is on David's side in the affair.

One of the servants in the household tells his mistress, Nabal's wife Abigail, of the altercation between her husband and David's men and speaks of his master in disparaging words, calling him a "scoundrel" (*ben beliya'al*). We have met men who were identified this way earlier in the stories (cf. 2:12; 10:27), and usually the designation bodes ill for the person who receives the label. Abigail has been introduced as someone with a good mind and beauty, in contrast to her husband, whose name means fool and who is described as "harsh" and "ill-behaved." He is from the tribe of Caleb, a *calibi*—in this case likely a pun on the word for "dog" in Hebrew (3).[130] Abigail's sensible mind and attractiveness will all be called on in her encounter with David. She is indeed smart enough to pack up plenty of provisions for David's men before she goes on her way with her servants without telling Nabal.

A large portion in the sequel is devoted to her speech to David, which serves as an outstanding example of how to sway a hotheaded male from his chosen path of violence (23–34). That David is indeed so minded is made clear in the verses that lead up to their meeting, when he swears he will not leave a single "wall-pisser" alive

129. It is so identified by André Caquot and Phillipe de Robert, *Les Livres de Samuel* (Geneva: Labor et Fides, 1994), 307.

130. The variant for the word in the Septuagint indeed reads "dog-like."

come morning, verifying the anxiety of the servant that it will not go well for everybody in Nabal's household (22).[131]

Abigail's speech takes up eight verses and is a high point of oratory and clever persuasion. First, she puts herself in the position of a supplicant, described in the text in triplicate: "She fell before David on her face/ and bowed to the ground;/ she fell at his feet" (23–24). As Alter points out, this first move puts her in a "highly dangerous situation" in the face of David's threatening words and attitude, which the reader/listener has heard but which are unknown to Abigail.[132] She must have read her man well, or been quite aware before this moment of his reputation and counted on his hesitancy to hurt an unarmed woman—one who is, moreover, unknown to him. She does not take up time with introductions, however, as her first words constitute an apology, taking all the responsibility on herself and pleading with him to let her speak and to listen to her (24). Then she shifts into high gear with her appeal to David, who is so far above this Nabal—this man whose name is *fool* and who *is a fool*, a *scoundrel*, as her servant has already called him—that David should simply pay him no attention. As a follow-up to her denouncement of a man she does not once call her husband, she adds that she had not been aware that messengers from David were in her household, implying that things would have gone otherwise had she been there! In this way, she accomplishes introductions of herself as well as Nabal, each in their proper frame.

Next, she calls down a curse on the enemies of David and wishes that they will all be brought down to the same low stature as her husband, "fool" (26), and before she utters these condemning words regarding both David's enemies and her husband, she thanks Adonai for having prevented David from "committing a crime by the vengeance of your hand" (26). In the end, her husband will turn up dead, so that in effect she wishes death on David's enemies in anticipation. Oh, and yes, my lord, here is a present which can be given to the men who are loyal to you (27).

131. The word for "male" ascribed to David is a vulgar epithet for a male, used elsewhere in 1 Kgs 14:10; 16:11; 21:21; 2 Kgs 9:8.

132. Alter, *The David Story*, 156nn23–24.

Abigail could stop here, and it might be enough, but she has a few more things to say. First, she makes clear that she has no doubt about David's future, for "Adonai will make for my lord a lasting house" (28), underscoring it by stating that someone like David fights on Adonai's behalf, and no "evil" should be found in him all his days. She returns to her point about the enemies.

1 SAMUEL 25:29–31

29 When a human being arises to pursue you
and seek your life,
the life of my lord will be bound
into the bundle of the living with Adonai, your God;
but the person of your enemy will be flung
as from the pocket of a sling.
30 And when Adonai has done to my lord
according to all the good he spoke to him,
and has set you up as leader over Israel,
31 this will not be for you a stumbling block,
and a heartache for my lord,
to have shed blood without cause
to gain victory for himself.
And when Adonai has done good to my lord,
then remember your maid.

The unnamed "human being" of verse 29 is clearly a reference to Saul. Furthermore, she declares that this pursuer will be cast from the slingshot while David himself will be safe with God.[133] Her imagery is particularly apt in view of the ability of David to wield this particular weapon, as shown in the contest with Goliath (17:49). Just in case David has not gotten the point, she speaks of him as one whom God will "set up" as a "leader over Israel," using the term *nagid* earlier employed of Saul (9:16), and repeats the important idea that it will not cause him pain to have "shed blood

133. The "bundle of the living" in the text is probably the equivalent of the "book of the living" (Ps 69:29[28]; Exod 32:32–33).

without cause." David is the focus of her speech except for the one reference to herself at the end.

As Ellen Van Wolde points out in an essay detailing the fine points of Abigail's speech, "the source domain structured in Abigail's discourse reflects the relationship between David and Nabal, whereas the target domain reflects the relationship between David and Saul."[134] In other words, while her surface text speaks to the threatened confrontation between her husband and David, the subtext addresses the very real threat posed to David by Saul. This idea is reinforced by her use of the general *adam* ("human being") when she speaks of someone pursuing David in the second half of her speech, inaccurate in terms of Nabal but on target as a reference to Saul. Van Wolde also argues that in speaking on multiple levels, Abigail functions as a prophet and that David receives her words as such. Assigning Abigail a prophetic role lifts her declarations above those of Jonathan and Saul in the surrounding chapters. There was, after all, a prophet around, Gad, who issued advice to David when he first fled from Saul (22:5) but who makes no pronouncements regarding David's future kingship. Also, both Jonathan and Saul request a specific pledge from David in return for their assent to this future role (cf. 20:42; 23:16–17; 24:23[22]), whereas Abigail makes only a general reference to a future reward for her present efforts. Together with Hannah and later the wise woman of Tekoa, Abigail is one of the women who address the future of a God-appointed leader and in this way anticipate the prophet Huldah in late-seventh-century Jerusalem at the time of King Josiah (2 Kgs 22:14–20). After Hannah, and with the exception of Michal, women characters have been missing from the stories. Abigail thus stands out both for her singular appearance and the importance of her words.

David's response (32–35) is brief in comparison to Abigail's speech, but with his first word, "blessed," he allays all fears that he will proceed with his planned violence. He blesses Adonai and utters a twofold blessing over Abigail, for her discretion and for staying his hand from "entering into bloodguilt" (33) in order to gain the upper

134. Ellen van Wolde, "A Leader Led by a Lady: David and Abigail in 1 Samuel 25," *ZAW* 114 (2002): 365–66.

hand, repeating the phrase used by Abigail (31), although he omits the words "without cause," probably still convinced that his side was the proper one. He ends by sending her off in peace, affirming that he has heard her plea and granted her request: He will refrain from violence. Literally, the Hebrew has, "See, I have listened to your voice and lifted your face" (35).[135]

The end comes quickly for Nabal, who is dispatched in three verses:

1 Samuel 25:36-38

36 Abigail came to Nabal,
and look he had a feast in his house,
like the feast of a king;
and Nabal's heart was happy,
and he was very drunk.
And she did not tell him anything,
small or great, until morning light.
37 When in the morning the wine left Nabal,
his wife told him these things,
and his heart died within him,
he was like a stone.
38 In ten days Adonai struck Nabal,
and he died.

The short comments showing Nabal at a feast fit for a king and dead within a short span of days—or even the next morning—contain three further references to Abigail: "Abigail came to Nabal. . . . She did not tell him anything. . . . His wife told him these things." At the close of the story, as at the beginning, Abigail appears in relation to Nabal. While the verb "to come" (*bo*) occurs often enough of entering a space or presence, it is also used of sexual intercourse with a male subject. Of the relatively few instances of the verb with

135. The expression "to lift the face" of someone can either have a positive or a negative meaning. For the former, see Gen 19:21; Job 42:8–9. For the latter, see Lev 19:15 2×; Deut 10:17.

a singular female subject, there are times when the subliminal context is sexual (Ruth 3:7; 2 Sam 13:10), and here it puts Abigail in a framework of the conjugal relationship. In the next verses, her name disappears and she becomes "his wife" when she tells her husband what has transpired, while he is no doubt suffering a hangover of major proportions. This sequence causes one to wonder. Throughout the story, Abigail has come across as insightful and very good with words. We assume that her delay in revealing her adventures is deliberate, waiting for Nabal to be in his right mind before she presents him with her story; or does she wait until he is in his right mind and particularly vulnerable? Of course, we do not know *what* she told Nabal since the narrative leaves it at the vague "these things." The language of his demise hints at a possible stroke and subsequent death, with the responsibility laid at God's door. Intriguing household scenes are thus kept from our knowledge because the narrative's focus is on David and on Abigail's words in relation to him.

In addition to her prophetic role, Abigail acts as a peacemaker. As I have pointed out in an earlier work on this material, the voice of the peacemaker is rare in this world of male warrior culture, and Abigail's is thus a "formidable offer of peacemaking . . . with no emulation in the context of her world."[136] It is a voice the narrator considered significant enough to maintain as a part of the stories of David's rise to kingship. David thinks well enough of her to enter into negotiations with her as his bride (39). She formally agrees to the proposal and follows David's messengers to become his wife (42). The reader/listener must decide for herself if the change in her status turns out to be a just reward for her attempts on behalf of David and her household.

Two brief notes (43–44) close the story, both on continuation of families: Ahinoam of Yizreel and Abigail *became* David's wives, while Michal has been *given* to become the wife of one Palti'el, an event of which more will be heard in the future. Samuel, the kingmaker and prophet of Saul and David's day, is dead at the opening of this story, although his voice is not quite gone. David is gaining

136. Van Wijk-Bos, *Reading Samuel,* 137–38.

his own family and his and Michal's lives no longer flow in the same direction. Danna Fewell and David Gunn identify these final notes as casting a shadow over Abigail. David "will not have one wife but several. And no wife will be first in his house. . . . Abigail, whose options are now closing, will have to learn to live in their shadow."[137] This is, after all, not Abigail's story, "it is David's; he begins it, its encounters are with him, he ends it."[138]

Act IV, Scene 3: Encounter in the Hills of Hachilah (1 Samuel 26)

One is not a complete villain and the other is not an angel of light.[139]

One other story creates a counterpart to chapter 24, with a description of a second encounter between Saul and David, although this time not at close quarters. To put to rest the idea that the reconciliation of the earlier encounter at Engedi had taken hold, the introduction to the main event of chapter 26 presents Saul ready to go after David and David taking initiative to pay Saul a visit (1–6). The Zifites are once more reported as willing to betray David. Like the Keilites, like Nabal, there are people who either out of self-interest or because of loyalty to Saul are ready to hand him over to Saul, either directly or by providing Saul with his location. Very quickly, the text moves us to the heart of the matter, a final confrontation between the king and the king to be. In the first six verses, the names of the two fall thick and fast, alternating in quick tempo, here Saul, there David. In contrast to chapter 24, David actively seeks out the spot where Saul is rather than coming upon him unawares. Saul is noted as lying asleep in this episode (5), told in elaborate detail like the events of chapter 25. With David, we view Saul asleep in the midst of his men together with his cousin Abner, his commander.

137. Fewell and Gunn, *Gender, Power, and Promise*, 157.

138. Campbell, *1 Samuel*, 258.

139. Moshe Garsiel, *The First Book of Samuel: A Literary Study of Comparative Structures, Analogies and Parallels* (Ramat-Gan, Israel: Revivim, 1985), 124.

The action begins when Abishai, David's nephew, offers to go with David to Saul in his camp.[140]

The adventure takes place at night (7–12). When they arrive at Saul's camp, with another notation of Saul *lying asleep*, Abishai urges David to take care of the matter right there and then, for surely this means God is delivering Saul into David's power. Abishai offers to do the deed, but David turns him down, protesting that Saul is Adonai's *anointed*, as he did in 24:7, 11 [6, 10]. He then makes his declaration that either God will kill Saul or Saul will die a natural death or "be swept away" in battle (26:10; see pp. 93–94n124 above). Abishai speaks in direct counterpoint to Abigail. Instead of urging David to stay his hand and avoid engaging in unnecessary bloodshed (25:26, 31, 33), he recommends that David kill his *enemy* (8). As Abigail did (25:29), David declares that God will take care of the matter. David is not here to engage in an act of vengeance, although he has more cause to do so now than in the case of Nabal, but he needs to confront Saul one more time. To that end, he takes Saul's spear and his water jar (26:11–12), items symbolic of Saul's power and his life. Just at this junction, the narrator reveals that God had put everyone in a deep sleep, a *tardemah*—the sleep that comes from God, as in the Garden of Eden when God created the first human being's counterpart (Gen 2:21), or when God entered into covenant with Abraham (Gen 15:12). After the death of Nabal, it is in these particular episodes the second time that God directly intervenes in the events. Death and a deep mysterious sleep are related, and the sleep that has caused Saul to be prone anticipates both his fall before Samuel at Endor (28:20) and his final fall in the battle at Gilboa (31:4). This allusion makes the disappearance of spear and water all the more meaningful.

David first makes sure to be at a safe distance before he awakens not Saul but Abner (13–16). He addresses Abner scornfully, chiding him for not guarding Saul, "the anointed of Adonai," appropriately and mockingly asking him where he thinks Saul's spear and water jar could be. When Saul also awakens, the rest of the exchange is between David and Saul (17–25). As before, Saul inquires if it really is

140. We will hear more in a sequel of Abishai, together with his brother Joab, David's commander. They are sons of Tseruyah, David's sister.

David's voice he hears (cf. 24:17[16]), but this time he does not weep. As before, David asks what he has done for the king to persecute him so. He accuses those who have aroused Saul's ire against David, curses them, and blames them for depriving him of being able to live in the land God gave to the people, "the inheritance of Adonai" (19). Saul admits his mistake.

1 SAMUEL 26:21

Saul said: I have done wrong.
Come back, my son David,
for I will do you no more wrong,
because my life was precious in your eyes today.
Look, I have been foolish and erred greatly!

Twice, Saul confesses his wrongdoing, and in between the two acknowledgments he begs David to return. Upon hearing this, David returns Saul's spear but not his water jar, and he does not come any closer to the person of the king. His final words pertain to his own well-being rather than to Saul's, and to the extent God will protect him in the same way he, David, has protected Saul. Before each goes his separate way, Saul blesses David and announces his future success.[141]

Act V: The Roads Diverge (1 Samuel 27–31)

What is the sense of the arrangement that we find in the actual text?[142]

As a testimony to the continuing breach between Saul and David, the two will no longer move in and out of each other's orbit, and

141. The words of confidence in David´s future on Saul´s part are strongly and uniquely worded: "You will surely do and will surely be able," with a doubling of the verbal root and the omission of grammatical objects. Fokkelman (*The Crossing Fates*, 551) observes that the omission of complements points to the "unlimited nature of David's success."

142. Fokkelman, *The Crossing Fates*, 556.

their paths diverge. In spite of Saul's avowal of repentance and the conveying of his blessing on David, no true reconciliation has taken place. When their roads separate, the stories also stop following a consecutive timeline carried forward by each chapter; rather, Saul's and David's stories weave in and out of one another as they lead up to the Philistine-Israelite battle in the final chapter. Three episodes focus on David as he first finds shelter from Saul's relentless pursuit with the Philistines, while two segments specify Saul's descent into fear and despair until his final moments on the battlefield, segments that are separated by the David episodes. The visit of Saul to the necromancer at Endor (28:3–25) fits time-wise as a lead-up to the battle scene at Gilboa in chapter 31 but is instead inserted between David's flight to the Philistines and his adventures while in service to Achish, the king of Gath, in chapters 27 and 29, with the next account in chapter 30 taking David back to Ziklag, the town assigned to him by Achish. The effect of the placement is that the account of Saul's descent is "embedded in the progression of David's vicissitudes," with the "Saul-thread pulling the reader consistently to the North, and David's activities take place in the South, thus creating the greatest distance possible between them."[143] In addition chapters 30 and 31 present the ascent of David and the descent of Saul in stark contrast: David is successful against the Amalekites (30:17–20), the ones symbolic of Saul's failure (15:1–35), while Saul suffers defeat at the hand of the Philistines (31:1–13), the enemy forces from whom he was expected to deliver Israel (9:16).

The narratives provide only a general overview of battle scenes, while there is a good deal of conversation among main characters and even inner reflection—on the part of David for the first time, but also of the Philistine king, Achish. Saul's visit to the necromancer at Endor is told in close detail, as are David's adventures on his return to Ziklag, which in his absence has been raided by Amalekites (28:3–25; 30:1–31). Locations for the different parties are precisely indicated, with the Philistines and Saul moving north while David moves further and further south, so that the final scenes find the two geographically separated as far as possible, symbolizing their contrasting fates.

143. Fokkelman, *The Crossing Fates*, 537.

Act V, Scene 1: Flight to Gath, Part 2 (1 Samuel 27:1–28:2)

The text portrays David as driven into mercenary service rather than having freely sought it.[144]

Four verses introduce the renewed attempt of David to find refuge in Gath (27:1–4). His decision is based on his reflection that Saul is bound to get the better of him some day, and the only recourse left is to "get away, yes get away to the land of the Philistines" (27:1). Through this insight into David's thoughts, a first since he was introduced in chapter 16, the move to King Achish of Gath is provided with a reasonable motivation. As Campbell observes in the quotation above, it makes David's mercenary service with the Philistines something he feels forced into. It is a serious matter for Israel's model king to have served with the archenemy of Israel, perhaps also thereby joining the worship of Philistine deities, and it is therefore important to provide a solid reason for an act that could easily be viewed as treachery.[145] In fact, the narrative will offer a second mitigating factor to clear David from the taint of having "crossed over" to the enemy (27:2). At the same time, by this action, David gives substance to his earlier complaint that he is being "driven out from having a share in the inheritance of Adonai," being constrained to "serve other gods" (26:19). He and his band join King Achish of Gath—everyone together with his immediate family. The introduction ends with the note that Saul gives up pursuing David once he knows that David is in Gath.

Even if we consider the figure of six hundred men in David's company an exaggeration, a largish group of fighters together with their nearest and dearest constitutes an overwhelming pres-

144. Campbell, *1 Samuel*, 273.

145. I agree with Alter (*The David Story*, 168n2) who notes that the account of David's stay with the Philistines bears the "mark of an authentic memory" since "no one would invent out of whole cloth such a traitorous act for its mythical king."

ence and a burden on the modest towns of that day. It is thus not surprising that King Achish readily grants David's request for a town of his own, about twenty miles almost directly south of Gath (27:5–7). We are not told what those of Ziklag thought of the arrangements, only that Ziklag endured as a property of the kings of Judah until "this day." The account of the granting of Ziklag ends with a note of the length of the period David served with the Philistines: a year and four months (27:7). This comment too, a rare time-marker in this material, can be seen as limiting the degree of David's disloyalty, setting a firm boundary around this phase of his life.

With Ziklag as his base, David goes on military expeditions to fight Canaanite and related peoples, including Amalekites, rather than Israelites, killing everyone so there will be no opportunity to tattle to his Philistine boss, to whom he tells a different story (27:8–10). The verb used for David´s military expeditions literally means "to strip, lay bare" and is used of stripping off clothes (cf. 18:4; 19:24). The list of plunder includes "flocks" and "cattle," and in addition, no doubt, David and his troops lay the countryside bare, stripping it to provide for their maintenance. Achish falls for David's story about raiding in Judean country and believes that David will be bound to his side "forever" (27:12), an ironic comment for all who are aware that David will ultimately overpower the Philistines (2 Sam 8:1; see also 2 Sam 21:15–20).

The first two verses of chapter 28 move the action ahead to the moment the Philistines are mustering troops in preparation for a battle with Israel. Achish tells David with an emphatic statement that he will be going with him to the battlefield: "You surely know that with me you will go out with the troops" (28:1). To this David replies that Achish "knows well" what he as the king's servant "will do." Each man makes use of the verb "to know," while in reality the Philistine king does not really know what David is doing or what he might do. Perhaps in awareness that he cannot be entirely sure of David's loyalty, Achish decides to keep David close by and appoints him as his bodyguard for "the whole time" (28:2).

Act V, Scene 2: The Sound of Silence (1 Samuel 28:3–25)

The witch of Endor has cast a spell over biblical commentators.[146]

First, the narrator repeats the obituary note of Samuel (28:3; cf. 25:1), this time in the context of a prohibition issued by Saul on the practice of necromancy and forecasting by means of calling on the spirits of the dead. These practices are forbidden in the legal material of the Torah (Lev 19:31; 20:6, 27; Deut 18:11), but may all the same have been prevalent, and Saul has sought to put an end to them. It is the spirit of the deceased Samuel which will come into play in the story that follows. The scene is set by the gathering armies of the Philistines, in the north near Shunem (4–5), with the Israelites encamped at Gilboa and Saul in a panic at the sight of the enemy camp: "He was afraid and his heart trembled greatly" (5).[147] Such a reaction seems unusual for an experienced warrior, but Saul was recorded to be afraid when he faced the Philistine champion, and he has equally feared David (17:11; 18:12, 29). Saul consults with Adonai, but there is no answer via any of the approved means of consultation (6). The three-times repeated Hebrew word *gam*—"*even* by dreams, *even* by Urim, *even* by prophets"—calls forth only a resounding silence from God's side.[148] As Kenneth Craig argues, silence following a question *is* an answer, and one should identify the question accordingly, a question "answered with silence."[149] As earlier in 14:37, the only other occasion in the story of Saul in which he explicitly does not receive an answer from Adonai, Saul tries to force the issue.

Unlike in 14:37, it is not clear at Mount Gilboa what Saul has asked God about; the narrative omits this information, fur-

146. Pamela Tamarkin Reis, "Eating the Blood: Saul and the Witch of Endor," *JSOT* 73 (1993): 3.

147. The heart of Saul "trembles," as once the elders trembled on encountering the prophet Samuel on his way into Bethlehem and as the priest Ahimelek trembled at the sight of David turning up at the sanctuary in Nob.

148. For a similar phrase, see 1 Sam 14:37, where Saul inquires of Adonai if pursuit of the Philistines is in order: "And he did not answer him on that day."

149. Kenneth Craig Jr., "Rhetorical Aspects of Questions Answered with Silence in 1 Samuel 14:37 and 28:6," *CBQ* 56 (1994): 222.

nishing instead detail about the means of inquiry, because it is precisely the *means* by which Saul seeks counsel that are at issue in the chapter. When he does not get any response from God, Saul asks his servants to find him a woman who is a necromancer, literally "a mistress of the pit" (*baalat ov*, 7). Specifically, he commands them to *seek* him a woman. The verb "to seek" played an important role when Saul began his journey to find his father's straying donkeys, one that ended when he found his kingship (see pp. 74–94 above). At another important juncture, Saul's servants offered to seek a *man* able to soothe the king's agitated spirits (16:16). As they did at that time, they have the information he needs (7): a *woman* in Endor. The fact that the servants are quite ready with the information is probably a sign that the practice was still widespread. Seeking recourse to consulting a necromancer is a serious infraction on Saul's part, going against rules he has set for the entire land. We are reminded of the indictment Samuel issued to Saul after the battle with Amalek that "the sin of divination is rebellion" (15:23). Divining is precisely what Saul will ask the necromancer of Endor to do.

The residence of the necromancer, usually rendered "Endor" in English translations, is assumed to lie about ten miles north of Gilboa, which would necessitate Saul and his men skirting the Philistine camp at Shunem, a trip not without its hazards. *Eyn dor* in Hebrew is literally "the spring of the [former] generation," hinting at the practices of necromancy that go on there.[150] The woman's title contains a word, *ov*, which may indicate a groove or pit or other opening in the ground made for the purpose of calling on the spirits of the dead. We note that Saul asks specifically for a *woman*. Since this is the only narrative in the Bible that describes an encounter with a necromancer, we do not know if practitioners habitually were women or what the purpose might be of this specification. The woman remains unnamed throughout the narrative, appearing only as "the woman," with the result that the opening and the closing of

150. The epithet traditionally assigned to the woman at Endor is "witch," but she is rather one who works through calling on the spirits of the dead and is thus more accurately a "medium" or "necromancer."

the story contain the word "woman" eleven times, lending the story a pervasive female presence.

Saul, in disguise, and two of his men arrive at the woman's place at night, and Saul asks her to call up a spirit.

1 Samuel 28:8–11

8 He said: Divine for me please with the pit [*ov*],
and bring up for me the one I tell you.
9 The woman said to him:
Look, you know what Saul has done,
that he cut off the pits and spirit workers from the land.
Why do you entrap me to kill me?
10 Saul swore to her by Adonai, saying:
As Adonai lives,
no guilt will come to you on account of this thing.
11 The woman said: Whom shall I bring up for you?
He said: Bring me up Samuel.

Saul asks the woman to "divine" or "conjure" for him, using the word for a prohibited practice, the one Samuel employed when he raised the issue of the "sin of divination" against Saul following the battle against Amalek (15:23). He demands that she "bring up" (lit. "cause to ascend"), the idea being that the spirit of the dead ascends from the pit, the *ov*. The woman objects, suspecting perhaps that someone has been sent by Saul to catch her in the unlawful procedure, but Saul swears a strong oath that she will bear neither guilt nor punishment, the word *avon* meaning both the guilt as well as the consequence incurred for a transgression. Twice more, the expression "bring up/cause to ascend" is heard, from the necromancer and from Saul, causing the exchange between the two to be framed by this verb and underlining the action that is to take place.

At this point, one expects a description of the calling up of the spirit, but instead the narrator leaves a gap in the information and draws the reader/listener directly into the vision of the prophet granted only to the woman, who does not recognize the apparition before her. We are told that she "cried in a loud voice" when "she saw

Samuel," but she addresses the king, charging him with deception and declaring "You are Saul!" (12). Saul tells her not to fear, but the being that has come up is apparently hidden to him, for he asks her what she sees and to describe it. The narrator informs us that "the woman saw Samuel," which she identifies as "a mighty being coming up from the ground" (12–13).[151] While we see Samuel, the woman sees a mighty being, does not know it is Samuel, and recognizes Saul; meanwhile, Saul sees only the woman. He decides the being is Samuel by the woman's description of "an old man wearing a cloak" (14), the same cloak he held onto and tore (15:27). The next section (15–19) presents the speeches as if they occur directly between Samuel and Saul, but it is likely that the necromancer stays in the picture and gives voice to Samuel's words in view of the fact that Saul does not seem to have any direct contact with the being that "came up from the earth" and has to let the woman describe what she sees.[152]

Saul makes obeisance, but Samuel's first words are not promising. He asks Saul why he has been "roused" and "made to come up." Saul describes his situation, with the enemy ready to fight him and the silence of a God who has turned from him, as one of "great distress." He explains that he has called Samuel "to let me know what I should do" (15). It is a strange question which leaves a wide opening for a reply. What exactly does Saul have in mind? Is he asking whether to take a stand or flee? Does he want to know if he will survive and the Israelites will be successful? Is he asking if he should belatedly call on David to join him against the Philistines? Or is that exactly what his fear is about? He knows that David has joined with the enemy. Is he now afraid that with David at their side,

151. The Hebrew word for "mighty being" is *'elohim*, lit. "god" or "gods," a word that can also be used for something or someone mighty or very big. Tikva Frymer-Kensky (*Reading the Women of the Bible* [New York: Schocken, 2002], 311) translates, "I saw the divine coming up from the earth."

152. I agree in this respect with Susan Pigott, who argues the point in her essay "1 Samuel 28: Saul and the *Not* So Wicked Witch of Endor," *RevExp* 95 (1998): 438. So also Frymer-Kensky (*Reading the Women of the Bible*, 312) who observes that the necromancer "channels the words of Samuel's ghost." Others assume that the necromancer disappears. See, for example, Alter (*The Story of David*, 175n15) who determines that the woman's role is "minimal."

the Philistines will be invincible—that he will have to face David on the battlefield? All these concerns are possible, and Samuel steps into the opening provided by the question, bringing it down in the end to the issue of Saul's survival. Adonai, he points out, is not only silent but has turned away from Saul and is now against him, his "foe" who "tore" the kingship from Saul's hand and gave it to David (16). Basically, Samuel repeats the earlier charges he made against Saul when he spoke of "rebellion" as the "sin of divination" and of not heeding God's voice in the matter of Amalek (15:19–28). Frymer-Kensky writes, "The very act of necromancy is mute testimony that Samuel's earlier words have come to pass."[153] The punchline speaks at last to a question Saul may have on his mind but has not uttered: He will indeed not survive.

1 Samuel 28:19

God will deliver both Israel and you
into the hand of the Philistines.
Tomorrow, you and your sons will be with me.
Also, the camp of Israel
Adonai will deliver into the hand of the Philistines.

Twice, the prophet's spirit mentions the defeat of Israel. Not only Saul but all his people will go down with him, all doomed because of Saul's failure. Not surprisingly, Saul falls defeated on the ground, as the text has it, "full length," harkening back to the once high stature of the man who now lies defeated on the ground in a foreshadowing of what is to come on the morrow (cf. 9:2; 10:23).

The story could have ended here, but the necromancer comes back into the picture, demanding that Saul take some food. She reminds him that she listened to his voice and that he now has to listen to her (21–22): "Let me put before you a bit of food and eat." While he first refuses, he gives in after both she and his servants pressure him. The man who did not "heed" the voice of Adonai "heeds" the voice of the woman whose skill is equal to idolatry, en-

153. Frymer-Kensky, *Reading the Women*, 313.

gaging in a craft he himself outlawed. She slaughters a calf and prepares bread, setting food before the men, and "they ate" (25). Many commentators speak approvingly of this act of seeming kindness on the woman's part. Frymer-Kensky calls her "the very model of Israelite hospitality."[154] It is indeed possible that the woman's only motivation is to perform an act of kindness toward a man who is at the end of his rope.

A peculiar aspect of the description in verse 24 is that specifics are provided for how she prepares the bread but not what she does with the meat. This gap in the information causes speculation for some that the meal she prepares is something other than simply a strengthening repast. The necromancer could have prepared a "mantic sacrifice to the dead," including "the stringently proscribed eating of blood."[155] In other words, the absence of a description of her preparing the meat indicates that she served up raw meat. Pamela Tamarkin Reis makes the case for this, as she opposes the idea that the necromancer's act of feeding Saul is in any way protective or motherly. The woman is "not a model of motherly protectiveness but of mother wit, professionalism, resourcefulness and daring."[156] The strongest argument in favor of a reading that the meal is some sort of sacrifice is the verb used for slaughtering the calf she has in the house: *zavakh*, in the Hebrew Bible most often—and in the Samuel texts exclusively—reserved for the slaughter of a sacrifice. We must leave possibilities open, as the storyteller has left gaps in this narrative, either out of scruples about describing forbidden practices or out of ignorance. It remains conceivable that the woman necromancer provides for Saul what Samuel did not, a measure of comfort to gain strength for what he will face in the morning.

Near the end of his life, Saul shows the same uncertainty he exhibited when he began his search for his father's animals. He

154. Frymer-Kensky, *Reading the Women*, 314. See also Alter, *The Story of David*, 78. Campbell (*1 Samuel*, 284) writes, "The text offers a remarkable image of caring by the medium and the men." Fokkelman (*The Crossing Fates*, 622) calls her a "mother figure."

155. Reis, "Eating the Blood," 4.

156. Reis, "Eating the Blood," 4.

speaks in questions, he does not know what to do, and he finds a prophet who tells him what lies ahead. In Michael's opinion, the Endor story portrays Saul in parody: "The narrator makes Saul a tragi-comic character who is deemed a misfit in the company of the prophets."[157] It is indeed possible for the reader/listener of today to perceive irony in the situation at Endor. The question is if the narrative intends this irony or has another purpose with the placement of the story and its detail. The story is one about a forbidden practice, called "detestable to Adonai" in Deuteronomy 18:12. In 2 Kings 17:17–18, divination is listed among the ways Israel provoked God and so caused its exile. Thus, the theological voice that aligns with Deuteronomy reviews the tale of Saul and the necromancer on the eve of the demise of Israel's first king with an eye toward the eventual demise of both kingdoms. The spirit of Samuel speaks doom not only for Saul but for the entire enterprise of kingship (cf. 2 Kgs 9:22; 17:17–18; 21:6; 23:24).

The event of eating a meal almost at the end of the story of Saul remains striking, as it concludes the dealings of Saul with the necromancer at the "well of the former generation." The presence of this important woman closes the larger story that began with Hannah in 1:1–2:10. At Shiloh, also, partaking or not partaking of food was an important element of the story. In addition, the beginning of Saul's career is marked by a sacrificial meal, at which he is an important guest in 9:22–24, so that meals, perhaps both sacrificial, open and close the trajectory of Israel's unfortunate first king. If it is correct to assume that the necromancer of Endor voices the words of Samuel, then it is also correct to assume the woman speaks with a prophetic voice regarding the immediate future of Saul. Matthew Michael remarks on the remarkable "fusion of the domains of prophecy and witchcraft/divination" within the same passage.[158] The voices of two

157. Matthew Michael, "The Prophet, the Witch and the Ghost: Understanding the Parody of Saul as a 'Prophet' and the Purpose of Endor in the Deuteronomistic History," *JSOT* 38 (2014): 332. Michael asserts that Saul is at this point also "tragically represented as a misfit in the company of kings."

158. Michael, "The Prophet, the Witch and the Ghost," 317: "It appears the world of the prophet/seer is completely fused with the world of the witch/

women thus frame the stories of Samuel and Saul: Hannah, who speaks prophetically of the one "asked for" (*shaul*) and becomes the mother of Samuel ("God has listened"), and the necromancer at Endor who voices the speech of the one who accuses Saul of not listening to God and announces his impending death.[159]

Act V, Scene 3: Like a Messenger of God (1 Samuel 29–30)

This all seems a bit too fortuitous.[160]

Following the report in chapter 27 on David's crossing over to the Philistine side and the announcement of the massing of Philistine armies, the detour to Endor on the eve of the Philistine-Israel battle has left a question hanging in the air regarding David's role in the upcoming course of events. What exactly is David planning to do? If he is joining Achish to go north, is it his intention to join the Philistines and fight his own people? At first blush, it seems to be that way, for the Philistines are mustering their armies at Aphek, and David is there together with his master, King Achish. Aphek is still about thirty to forty miles south of the Jezreel Valley, and with this episode (29:1–5), we are some days removed from the scene of

---

diviner, thus allowing them, in spite of their apparent conflict, to stay together momentarily in the same cultic space."

159. Michael ("The Prophet, the Witch and the Ghost," 327) also points to the presence of the young women in 9:11–13 who point Saul to the seer, Samuel, who is "going up," anticipating the presence of the necromancer at the end of Saul's life. It is true that these are the only occasions where women form the bridge between Saul and Samuel, but there is virtually no presence of women outside of these two occasions in the Saul story, with the exception of Michal.

160. Baden, *The Historical David*, 108. Baden considers the account of David's return to Ziklag improbable and a part of a "biblical cover-up": "Where was David while the Philistines were killing Saul and his sons? By all rights, he should have been right there with them. And—despite, or perhaps precisely because of the Bible's emphatic statements to the contrary—we may conclude that this is exactly where he was" (109).

the battle. As the different cohorts with their royal leaders file by the Philistine officers, they notice a group they mark as outsiders following Achish, stand-outs perhaps on account of a difference in dress or some other feature of outward appearance, and ask, "Who are these Hebrews?" In effect, they are inquiring what these "worthless" people are doing here.[161] When Achish reveals the presence of David, recommending him in strong terms, they become furious and demand that Achish send him back where he came from. For them there is no question but that David will turn against them in the heat of the battle. Their view of David is still rooted in the early days when he fought Philistines on Saul's behalf and the women sang Saul and David's triumphs (over Philistines!) in their victory songs. Surely, they reason, nothing would please Saul more than for David to come back with "the heads of these men," the term "heads" likely intended as a euphemism for the foreskins once presented to Saul by David (18:25–26).

In his excuses and orders to David (28:6–10), Achish actually calls on the name of Israel's God and declares David "good"—that is, "without evil"—but "not good" to the Philistine kings, which causes an interesting back-and-forth of this identification. Is David "good" or "bad" for Achish, for the Philistines, for Israel? Whatever question lurks underneath the surface, there will be nothing to do for David but to go back. David protests once again in this string of stories, asking what he has done, and Achish once again declares him "good," going so far as calling him "a messenger of God." If it were up to him . . . but unfortunately, it is not, so they had better make haste, "rise early in the morning" and depart.[162] It takes a huge decision away from David, who now will be so far removed from the battlefield that no one can accuse him of having had a hand in the demise of King Saul.

161. For the usage of the term "Hebrews" for the Israelites, see pp. 53, 98–99 above.

162. In Achish's speech, he varies the ones who are asking for David's expulsion from "kings" (29:6, 7) to "officers" (*sarey*). The narrative actually refers to the "officers" commanding Achish to send David back (29:4). If the variation is for a purpose, it may be that Achish wants to make clear that all the higher-ups, including the kings, are involved in this decision.

Once David has come back to Ziklag, there follows an adventure told in slow motion involving a raid on the town by the Amalekites, with the women and children taken captive and the town burned down (30:1–8). The story contains some detail of special interest, even if much of it is an account constructed to highlight the ascent of victorious David in contrast to the failing defeated Saul. This is the first time that David is on the receiving end of armed struggle in which his own people have been victimized, and he is "in sore distress," a state echoing how Saul described himself to Samuel at Endor (28:15). Not only has he wept with his men "until they could weep no more" (30:4), but his people are rebelling—in fact, they want to stone him, a harbinger of events to come when David, in advanced age, has a shaky grasp on the throne (2 Sam 15:13–14). In contrast to Saul, however, who resorts to finding counsel outside the boundaries of what is permissible, David is presented as finding strength in "Adonai his God" and engaging in successful consultation with the Deity through the presence of Ahimelek and the ephod (30:7–8).

In an interlude, the troops who have joined David in pursuit of the Amalekites and the retrieval of their hostages come across an Egyptian youth escaped from his Amalekite master who is able to reveal the details of the Amalekite raid and leads the Israelites to the location of the Amalekite camp (30:9–15). In fine detail, we watch the Amalekites enjoying their spoils, lying sprawled about, not suspecting a thing. As there was in the Endor episode, there is a focus on eating. The Egyptian youth is famished and is fed and given drink (30:11–12), which revives his spirit—a statement absent after Saul is fed by the necromancer. Meanwhile, the Amalekites are described as "drinking and feasting" on the plunder (30:16). David is, naturally, successful in killing everyone, with the exception of 400 escapees (30:16–20), but especially he manages to "rescue": "Then David rescued all that Amalek took, and his two wives David rescued" (30:18). In a final gesture of generosity, he refuses to listen to those who would deprive the men who had not joined in pursuit from a share of the plunder (30:24), a practice which became standard in Israel according to the narrative note (30:25). Not only his own men but other towns and comrades receive gifts of plunder from David's hand as he goes overboard in sharing (30:26–31), perhaps with an eye to his future in the midst of the people, who have now experienced not only his leadership but also his openhandedness. This king is not one who *takes* according to the warning issued by Samuel (8:11–17), but instead he *gives* liberally from what he has. His reasoning in doing so is impeccable: He gives only from what *God has given* (30:23) and acts in this capacity truly as a "messenger of God," the title bestowed on him by King Achish.

Act V, Scene 4: Death Abounds (1 Samuel 31)

A battle has been looming on the horizon since the beginning of chapter 28, and finally it comes about in this scene. The battle itself is given short shrift, taken care of in one sentence in the most general of overviews. The Philistines are the subject of "fighting," with the Israelites fleeing and falling slain on Mount Gilboa. Even in the context of the habitual silence in the Bible regarding the minutiae of armed conflict, this note stands out for what it includes and leaves out. There is no mention of the Israelites *fighting* or even of their *defeat*, a subject that was at least a part of the short battle summary in 4:10. The entire short chapter has its focus on *death*, especially the death of Saul. The first part of the chapter is filled with words for death and destruction: "the slain" (1, 8), "to fall" (1, 4, 5, 8), the rare verb "run through/pierce" (*daqar*) (4 2×), the root "die" (5, 6, 7), and "abuse" (4), a verb used in connection with the mistreatment of the concubine in Gibeah (Judg 19:25). First, Saul's three sons die, including Jonathan. Then the archers find him, and he is already in death throes by verse 3.[163] The perspective shifts to Saul's in verse 4.

163. I retain the verb *hil* of the Masoretic Text rather than reading "he was wounded" with the Septuagint and many modern translations. *Hil* means "to writhe" or "tremble" and can be used of labor pains (Isa 13:8; Jer 4:19). Here it could either indicate fear or a bodily shaking from having been hit by the arrows.

1 Samuel 31:4–6, 8

4 Saul said to his weapon bearer:
Draw your sword and run me through with it,
lest these foreskins come and run me through and abuse me.
And the weapon bearer was not willing,
for he was very afraid.
Then Saul took the sword and fell upon it.
5 When the weapon bearer saw
that Saul was dead,
he too fell upon his sword
and he died with him.
6 So died Saul with his three sons
and his weapon bearer
and all his men on that day together.

8 On the next day, the Philistines came
to strip the slain,
and they found Saul
and his three sons
fallen on Mount Gilboa.

Saul, his life ending, asks his weapon bearer to run him through so it will not be the Philistines—"these foreskins" (note the epithet used by Jonathan and David in 14:6; 17:26, 36)—who will do the work of dispatching and "abusing" him. When the weapon bearer refuses out of fear, Saul falls on his own sword. So sets the sun on the first king of Israel, Saul, son of Kish, a man of Benjamin who came to his kingship hesitantly, but once having a hold of it could not let it go; a man who was sent by God, according to the narrative, to "deliver" God's people from the hand of the Philistines (9:16), who spends his last moment in defeat by those very people; a man who once stood taller than anyone else (9:2; 10:23), fallen for the last time. When asked by the people to appoint them a king, Samuel pointed out that they were making the wrong choice, and God told Samuel he was right but to go ahead anyway. In choosing Saul as the first deliverer-king, God apparently made the wrong choice, a divine mistake; or the mistake was that God works only through the human tools available, and Saul proved to be the wrong tool.

Saul intends to prevent abuse of his body by the enemy, but they abuse him anyway (8–10). The Philistines come, cut up the bodies of Saul and his sons, and send the head of Saul around "to bring the good news" (9), hanging his body on the wall of a town about eleven miles to the southwest of Mount Gilboa, Beth-Shan. It is from there that those from Jabesh Gilead, at one time beneficiaries of Saul's military prowess, come and retrieve what can be retrieved, giving at least the bones a decent burial (11–13). Throughout his life Saul has had supporters, and at his death they do not desert him, his weapon bearer and the Jabeshites among them. The story of the one who was "asked for" (*shaul*) by a woman who fasted in depression about her inability to give birth, ends in a fast of seven days by men who mourn the death of one who came against the odds to deliver them.[164]

David and the Death of Saul

Where was David while the Philistines were killing Saul?[165]

The final five chapters of 1 Samuel depict the roads of David and Saul, intertwined until this point, diverging so that in the end David could not be farther away from Saul and still be in Israel. The tradition that David had joined the Philistines remained alive in Israel, and, logically, the thought would occur that when Saul died on the battlefield, David was present as a mercenary in the service of one of the Philistine kings. Is the sending away of David by Achish in chapter 29, together with the events around Ziklag in chapter 30, an elaborate construction to obfuscate the role of David in Saul's death? To Joel Baden's view, the picture of David as he is on the run from Saul is that of the "unscrupulous outlaw, willing to do whatever

164. Fokkelman (*The Crossing Fates*, 628) suggests that the seven days are a counterpart to the seven days Nahash the Ammonite allowed Jabesh Gilead for a deliverer to turn up, a deliverer who turned out to be Saul.

165. Baden, *The Historical David*, 109.

it takes to survive and gradually gain power."[166] Baden considers it likely that David was present on Mount Gilboa and had at least a hand in the death of Saul, even if he did not personally perpetrate the deed. Whether constructed entirely out of the imagination of the story tellers or reflective of at least a partial truth, especially in terms of David's whereabouts, the shifts in focus from David to Saul and back, together with the detailed account of David's revenge on the Amalekites, who have destroyed his town and taken his family hostage, serve the double purpose of describing the ascent of David in contrast to the fall of Saul and of removing the possible taint of Saul's death being laid at David's door.

Robert Polzin points out the multilayered nature of the phrase "this is the plunder of David" (30:20). While on the surface it points to everything David "brought back" (30:19), in the long run it may also allude to the reality that "Israel's share in the spoils of David's kingship ultimately turns out to be exilic in nature." Polzin thinks it was not David's presence at the battle but his absence from it that was the cause of Saul's death. "The king, who hid himself among the baggage when called upon to rule (10:22), is replaced by one who stays by the baggage (30:24) as he waits for a chance to rule."[167] In the end, then, it makes perhaps not much difference whether we place David physically at the scene of Saul's final battle, for even by absenting himself from the engagement he secures not only Saul's death but the defeat of Israel and a Philistine takeover of a part of the region. In the meantime, the passing away of one king does not mean there is immediately another. Israel is not yet proclaiming, "The king is dead, long live the king!"

166. Baden, *The Historical David*, 115.
167. Polzin, *Samuel and the Deuteronomist*, 222.

Cycle III: Ascent to Kingship (2 Samuel 1–8)

Some yearn for simplicity in their Scriptures.[1]

Eight chapters describe a period of seven and a half years while David is king over Judah in Hebron, followed by the extension of his reign to all of Israel until he is settled in Jerusalem with his first campaigns of defense and aggression behind him and is able to dispense "justice and righteousness for all his people" (8:15). The road to David's kingship does not run smoothly but involves civil war with two kings in the land in the first part of the story (1:1–4:12). Establishment on the throne includes two anointings (2:4; 5:3), notably without reference to a prophet or priest. Altogether, David is anointed three times: once by Samuel (1 Sam 16:3), once by "the men of Judah" (2:4) and finally by "the elders of Israel . . . in the presence of Adonai" (5:3).

In Act I (chs. 1–4), David faces another contender for the throne, one of Saul's heirs, and the country is divided in opposite camps, causing military strife (2:8–32), plots and counterplots by major characters (3:7–39), and a final resolution through the assassination of David's rival Ishboshet (4:1–12). As the opening of chapter 3 puts it: "The war was long between the house of Saul and the house of David" (3:1). In fact, the accounts in the first four chapters of 2 Samuel only provide a sketchy overview of all that must have transpired in a period that lasted more than seven years. That it was a time filled with mayhem and violence is clear from even the

1. Antony F. Campbell, S.J., 2 *Samuel*, FOTL 8 (Grand Rapids: Eerdmans, 2005), xiii.

scanty reports. Every chapter contains reports of death and murder; funerals and mourning are the order of the day, starting with the lament over Saul and Jonathan's death (1:11–12), continuing with the murder of Asahel by Abner (2:23) and Abner's death at the hands of Joab (3:27), ending in the assassination of Ishboshet by his servants (4:6). In all cases, the narratives place David at a distance from the bloody incidents; in fact, the portrait of David in the first act of the cycle is less that of commander than of onlooker and commentator on events. The oratorical skill that already set him apart when he was chosen to be Saul's music therapist comes to the fore more than his talent on the battlefield. He takes initiative only at the beginning of the period (2:1–4). David is, in Fokkelman's words, not "the hero but the receiver" with "everyone working for him" and "David constantly the beneficiary of all this effort." It is exactly this absence of action which in Fokkelman's view acts as "a force-field, making particles behave in an ordered fashion."[2]

The emphasis changes in Act II (2 Sam 5:1–8:18), when David engages in a great deal of aggressive military activity. First, he wins his capital, Jerusalem—until this point not a city in Israel's possession—by assault on its inhabitants (5:6–9) and takes on the perennial threat provided by the Philistines (5:17–25; 8:1). He then engages in wars of expansion against Edomites, Moabites, Arameans, and Ammonites (8:2–12). He is still fighting the Ammonites when the next chapter in the saga of David begins. Chapters 5 and 8, with their focus on armed conflict and a vague timeline, bracket two episodes in which the tempo slows down, first with an account of David's efforts to transport the Ark of the Covenant to Jerusalem (6:1–19) and second with a report consisting for the most part of speech after the narrative note on David's desire to build a sanctuary (7:1–29).

Except for the cursory mention of David's wives (3:2–5; 5:13–16), his sister Tseruyah (2:13, 18; 3:39; 8:16), Saul's concubine Rizpah (3:7–8), an unnamed caretaker of one of Jonathan's sons (4:4), and an opaque reference to female gatekeepers at Ishboshet's residence (4:6), Saul's daughter Michal is the only individual woman who steps

2. J. P. Fokkelman, *Throne and City*, vol. 3 of *Narrative Art and Poetry in the Books of Samuel* (Assen: Van Gorcum, 1990), 145.

out of the shadows of powerful men, in which women and concubines have their place, to take on both an old role as David's wife (3:13–16) and a new one as his critic (6:20–23). Her appearance is, however, brief and negative in terms of her relation to David. This is a meager tally for women and their importance in the rise of David to kingship!

Act I: War between Brothers (2 Samuel 1–4)

Will the sword devour forever? (2 Sam 2:26)

The narratives begin with renewed attention on the manner of Saul's death as it is reported to David and David's reaction to it in poetic form. As we did at the beginning of the Samuel texts, we find here a character who gives poetic expression to deep feelings. Poetry is soon left behind as David is crowned king in Hebron, with one of Saul's sons, Ishboshet,[3] set up as a rival king across the Jordan in Mahanaim. The two factions engage in bloodshed and a long struggle that concludes with the killing of Ishboshet, who appears to be little more than a puppet in the hands of his relative, general Abner. Only one vignette of what must have been many armed conflicts presents itself in chapter 2. Occasionally, we receive glimpses of David's mental state and at other points must speculate on his disposition from reported actions and dealings with his servants. We view events from inside both David's household and Ishboshet's.

As pointed out above, this stage in David's ascension to the throne is marked by bloodshed in combat (Asahel, 2:23), in rivalry (Abner, 3:27), and in bed (Ishboshet, 4:6), each of the victims struck in the belly.[4] While some observe the "gory" nature of this death, it

3. The name of Saul's son was likely originally Ishbaal and is so rendered by the NRSV. *Ish boshet*, meaning "man of shame," would be an unlikely name for anyone, while the element "baal" may have been considered offensive for certain editors. In 1 Chr 8:33, there is a son of Saul, Eshbaal, who is presumably the same.

4. The group engaging in a kind of blood sport in ch. 2 strike each other in the side (2:16).

is probably related to the type of weapon employed, a dagger, which is easier to conceal than a sword and more suited for stabbing. Only Abner, in the midst of a battle, uses a spear. Abner and Ishboshet are killed in a surreptitious manner comparable to Eglon in the Ehud story (cf. Judg 3:16–21). Kin-strife and gruesome assassinations thus mark the beginnings of David's kingship.[5]

Act I, Scene 1: A Story and a Song (2 Samuel 1)

Rejection and election have assumed the form of defeat and victory.[6]

A story and a poem open 2 Samuel as they did 1 Samuel. The context and themes, however, could not be more different. Whereas in 1 Samuel a woman and the hope of giving birth took center stage, followed by a prayer of triumph and thanksgiving that assigns power to a God who supports the lowly, here men recount the brutal business of war and death and celebrate the power of war heroes and their weaponry.

Scene 1, Part 1: A Messenger Comes to Ziklag (2 Samuel 1:1–16)

Is he lying or telling the truth?[7]

It begins with a messenger arriving at David's town, Ziklag, bringing a new report of Saul's death and carrying Saul's crown and armband to prove the truth of his news. In the course of his exchanges with David, he turns out to be an Amalekite who dealt Saul the mercy blow to put him out of his misery. His lively story pulls us into Saul's

5. Everett Fox, *The Early Prophets: Joshua, Judges, Samuel and Kings. A New Translation with Introductions, Commentary, and Notes* (New York: Schocken, 2014), 431.

6. Fokkelman, *The Crossing Fates*, 631.

7. Robert Polzin, *David and the Deuteronomist*, vol. 3 of *A Literary Study of the Deuteronomic History* (Bloomington: Indiana University Press, 1993), 2.

final moments, when he begged the Amalekite to finish him off because he had little life left in him (7–9). The news throws David and his men into a bout of serious mourning: "They wailed and wept and fasted until evening" (11–12). When the Amalekite explains he is a "stranger" (*ger*), perhaps counting on special treatment from David, David's reaction to his news may come as a surprise. The Amalekite gets the deathblow from one of David's servants instead, with David calling down a curse on him because he dared to end the life of the "anointed of Adonai" (16).[8]

The Amalekite's story is odd, not only because it contradicts the account provided by the narrator in 1 Samuel 31 but also because it is hardly likely that David had not already heard of the Israelite defeat and the death of Saul and his sons, which the Philistines had been at pains to broadcast far and wide, and which was known even on the other side of the Jordan (31:9–10). Yet David is portrayed as receiving the messenger's story while still in complete ignorance of the disastrous events in the north. Furthermore, the idea that an Amalekite would run for three days to bring David the crown and armband of Saul, whose death he had just caused, is highly unlikely, even within the story world created by the compilers of 1 and 2 Samuel. A number of scholars elaborate on the issue of the veracity of the Amalekite's story, but historical truth can hardly be the point of this account.[9] David evidently believes what he has been told. I

8. The identification as stranger (*ger*) is important because it indicates a category of outsiders, those from different ethnic groups who have come to stay and live within Israel. Laws protecting this category of people are more frequent in the Torah than any other prescription for the social context, occurring in every major law code, extending from prohibitions against oppressing them (Exod 23:9) to the prescription to love the stranger as one loves one's self (Lev 19:34; cf. Deut 10:18), with many specific prescriptions between these poles. See Johanna W. H. van Wijk-Bos, *Making Wise the Simple: The Torah in Christian Faith and Practice* (Grand Rapids: Eerdmans, 2005), 25–33, 179–201.

9. So, for example, Fokkelman, *The Crossing Fates*, vol. 2 of *Narrative Art and Poetry in the Books of Samuel* (Assen: Van Gorcum, 1986), 640; Polzin, *David and the Deuteronomist*, 5; Pamela Tamarkin Reis, "Killing the Messenger: David's Polity or Politics?" *JSOT* 31 (2006): 171. Alter (*The David Story: A Translation with Commentary of 1 and 2 Samuel* [New York: Norton, 1999],

agree with Campbell who argues, "The most that can be said without doubt is that 2 Sam 1:10 and 16 portray a different understanding of the manner of Saul's death than that given in 1 Sam 31."[10]

Saul is dead, and David is not yet king. Getting handed Saul's regalia is a first step on the way, while at the same time the story underlines again that David had no hand in either the death of his erstwhile protector turned pursuer or in robbing him of his royal insignia. Every time a death occurs in these first chapters, the story distances David from bloodshed, making clear he did not grasp for kingship but that it was handed to him, so willed by God. It is hardly to be believed that the narratives assume David to have become oblivious of his own anointing by Samuel (1 Sam 16:13), surely no everyday event in the life of the youngest boy in Jesse's household. As readers, we have known that as long as Saul was alive, there were two who were "anointed" in the land. Now, there is only one left, and new tension arises around the question of how David is going to lay claim to his kingship. One thing the narratives emphasize multiple times: When he gets there, he will do so as one who is innocent of the bloodguilt that presently clings to the Amalekite.

In an interesting twist, the David who listens to the messenger is in question mode, reminiscent of young Saul when he set his first steps on the road that would lead him to his throne. David asks the messenger where he came from, how the battle went, how he knows that Saul and Jonathan are dead, and then once again where he is from, probing more deeply into his identity. The messenger only gradually reveals he is an Amalekite, which puts another ironic twist on the narrative.[11] Amalekites are listed in the Bible as Israel's

---

197n10) calls it a "sensible conclusion" that the Amalekite is lying. The motive would have been to bring "the new king" Saul's regalia, a reading ignoring the fact that in the biblical account David is not yet king of anything and possibly still allied to the Philistines. Reis ("Killing the Messenger," 171) argues for the choice of 1 Sam 31 as the true tale: "By biblical convention, the narrator always tells the truth and knows everything." But see Campbell (2 *Samuel,* 18), who argues that "the judgment to be passed is not one of historical fact but one of plausibility within the horizon of the narrative."

10. Campbell, 2 *Samuel,* 19.

11. A number of commentators observe similarities between this scene

archenemies (Exod 17:8–16; Num 24:20; Deut 25:17, 19) and have had a particular function in Samuel, notably in the battle when Saul neglects a total follow-through on the ban (1 Sam 15:2–35) and further in the account of the destruction of Ziklag in David's absence (1 Sam 30). Within the context of the story world, it comes as no surprise that the young man does not immediately reveal his identity but comes to David as a mourner, in torn clothes and with dirt on his head, like the Benjaminite who brought news of the defeat of Israel at Eben-Ezer to Shiloh and Eli (1 Sam 4:12). The symbolism of an Amalekite killing an Israelite king could hardly be more powerful. Saul once failed to complete the ban on Amalek, upon which Israel's prophet killed the Amalekite king. Here, an Amalekite, one of Israel's most hated enemies, claims to have dispatched Saul. Of course, he is not to survive the adventure; David will make sure of that, completing on the messenger his act of vengeance on the entire people. In addition, killing him ensures that David keeps himself free of any association with Saul's death in the manner in which the stories have consistently presented him in the lead-up to the battle at Gilboa.

The point of the story is that David, until this point in ignorance, receives news about Saul's death from an Amalekite who declares himself to be the person responsible for that death, which absolves David from any part in that drama. In addition, he is handed Saul's royal insignia by the Amalekite, who, guilty of the blood of Adonai's anointed, receives the deathblow, pointing the accusing finger away

---

and the one where Eli receives the news about the defeat of the Israelites at Eben-Ezer in 1 Samuel 4:15–17. Yet the focus on identity is entirely different in the report to David and crucial to both the report and to the way it is received. The first question from David ("Where have you come from?") could pertain to identity also, although it is not answered that way but taken literally as to the immediate place of origin. I do not think the Amalekite is hiding his identity, as he makes it plain almost immediately in telling the story of Saul's death. That David asks the question again points to the fact that the lad's Amalekite identity is central to the story. This is contra Pnina Galpaz-Feller's ("David and the Messenger: Different Ends, Similar Means in 2 Samuel 1," *VT* 59 [2009]: 207) opinion that the messenger "obscured his Amalekite origins in his long and detailed description of Saul's death."

from David and in addition from any other Israelite.[12] David can thus position himself to officially mourn the death of Saul and his son Jonathan, even though the latter had not figured in the messenger's story.

Scene 1, Part 2: David's Lament (2 Samuel 1:17–27)

Language and imagery flicker between positive and negative connotations.[13]

If you can't say anything real nice, it's better not to talk at all is my advice.[14]

2 Samuel 1:19–27[15]

19 The splendor, O Israel,
on your heights slain.
How have fallen the mighty!

20 No, do not tell it in Gath,
nor announce it in the streets of Ashkelon,

12. Joel Baden, *The Historical David: The Real Life of an Invented Hero* (New York: HarperCollins, 2013), 111–12: "The story about the Amalekite . . . is designed to explain how David came to have Saul's crown and armlet. . . . Whether Saul died by his own hand or by that of the Amalekite, David's hands are clean." Baden also assumes that whoever took the items and brought them to David was in league with him, most likely one of David's men.

13. Tod Linafelt, "Private Poetry and Public Eloquence in 2 Samuel 1:17–27: Hearing and Overhearing David's Lament for Jonathan and Saul," *JR* 88 (2008): 517.

14. From "Please, Don't Talk About Me When I'm Gone" (1930), lyrics by Sidney Clare.

15. I render the poem here in the short lines that represent the divisions in Hebrew, staying as literal and close to the Hebrew as possible to reflect repetitions, word order, and rhythm. The introduction to the poem (1:17–18) states that David instructed the song to be taught to those of Judah and that it was also written in the "book of Yashar," a document we find referenced also in Josh 10:13. It is one of the lost works of which there may be many.

lest they rejoice
the daughters of Philistia;
lest they exult
the daughters of the foreskins.
21 Hills of Gilboa, no dew,
no rain upon you, bountiful fields.
For there was cast off
the shield of the mighty,
the shield of Saul
not anointed with oil

22 From the blood of the slain,
the fat of the mighty,
the bow of Jonathan
did not recoil,
the sword of Saul
did not return empty.
23 Saul and Jonathan—
beloved and dear,
in their life and their death
not separated—
more than eagles swift,
more than lions mighty.

24 Daughters of Israel,
weep over Saul,
who robed you
in scarlet and finery,
with gold ornaments bedecked you.

25 How have fallen the mighty
in the midst of the war;
Jonathan on your heights slain!

26 Distress is upon me over you, my brother.
Jonathan, very dear to me,

wondrous your love to me,
more than the love of women.

27 How have fallen the mighty,
have perished the weapons of war.

The lament is called a *qinah* in Hebrew. The short lines of this type of poem, a dirge for fallen warriors, echo the sobs of the grieving person. It begins with a double-voiced reference to an ornament or a gazelle, identical words in the Hebrew (*tsevi*). We want to keep the ambiguity intact—a gazelle can be slain whereas an ornament cannot.[16] The poem is a so-called "apostrophe"—a poem in the form of an address—and its subjects are not mentioned by name until verse 21, which gives the lines a powerful tension. All one knows in the initial strophe and the lines immediately following is that something splendid lies slain, literally "pierced" on the heights of Israel, and that the mighty have fallen.[17] The reader recalls the importance of the verb to "fall" in connection with Saul, of course, but so far nothing is spelled out.

The second strophe (20–21) begins with emphatic negations followed by the names of the locations. *Not* in Gath, *not* in the streets of Ashkelon, should the news be proclaimed—the exact opposite of what took place according to the description of the aftermath of the battle (1 Sam 31:9).[18] Since women were the ones to welcome victo-

16. Polzin (*David and the Deuteronomist*, 19) draws attention to the meaning of *tsevi* as "ornament," specifically in prophetic literature where it refers to "land" (*erets*, Jer 3:19; Isa 23:9). He makes a connection between this phrase and the utterance by the dying wife of Pinhas in 1 Sam 4:21 that the "glory has gone into exile." It is entirely possible that these echoes and others were overheard in David's lament at the time the compilers inserted the poem into the narratives.

17. For line 19c, I keep the verb at the front, as it is in the Hebrew line, so that "fallen" immediately follows "how," keeping it close to "slain" in the center line, while "splendor/gazelle" and "mighty" frame the introductory verse in a so-called chiasm.

18. The same verb, *basar*, is used for the bringing of news in 1 Sam 31:9 and here.

rious warriors home, the attention turns to the Philistine women, the ones to rejoice in the victory of their kinsmen. Joy for one group is grief for the other, and the address moves to inanimate nature in Israel as the counterpart to the Philistine women. The hills of Gilboa and their fields are to enjoy no life-giving moisture.[19] Finally, the subject, Saul, appears by name, although indirectly because the emphasis is on the "shield" (*magen*) of the "mighty" which lies rejected and dusty, unanointed.[20] The repeated reference to Saul's "shield" is surrounded by the verbs "rejected" and "not anointed," terms that reverberate in the history of Saul, the fallen, rejected from his anointing.

Once Saul is named, he gets full attention, and he is joined by Jonathan. The third strophe (22–23) turns from lament to praise of the dead, pointing first to Jonathan, then twice to Saul, and then back to Jonathan. The poet follows the cast-off shield with the weapons which were always successful, the sword of Saul and the bow of Jonathan. These two are called "beloved," "dear," and "not separated" and compared to swift and strong animals of prey: the eagle and the lion. Of course, these are exaggerations. We know that the sword of Saul and the bow of Jonathan were not always effective as the stories have related. Saul failed to kill the Amalekite king with his sword, which finally caused his own death, either by his own hand or by another, and Jonathan's bow was particularly ineffective in the episode with David in the field. The two were at odds about David a number of times, and Saul once tries to kill his son. Such is the way with a eulogy at a funeral, even though there is no funeral here—at least not yet.

In contrast to the indirect address to the Philistine women in verse 20, in the next strophe (24), the Israelite women are directly admonished to "weep" over Saul because of the largesse he bestowed upon them. It may sound to us like an off note in this otherwise eloquent poem, but special garments and jewelry were likely hard to come by for ordinary women and underline the king's generosity.

19. We note the force of the negatives in the second strophe: no, not, nor, lest, lest, no, no, not.

20. Shields in the ancient world were made of leather and kept supple with oil. Saul's shield lies neglected on the battlefield where he fell.

Once again, the refrain is heard about the fall of the mighty, with the variant line in the middle about the war and the final line with a focus on Jonathan alone. The final strophe reflects the only personal feelings of the poet toward one of the "slain," Jonathan. Using the first person, the speaker declares his distress over the death of his "brother" and expresses his emotions about Jonathan's love, "wondrous . . . more than the love of women." The poem ends with a repeat of the refrain on the fall of the mighty, concluding with a lament about the loss of the weapons of war. In Hebrew poetry, the second line often restates the first, intensifies it, and gives it focus. The "weapons of war," then, are not just the literal weapons used by Saul and Jonathan, but they are embodied by the heroes—the mighty themselves who have perished.

The poem could be spoken by almost anyone as a typical dirge over the death of fallen warriors, except for the personal lines directed to Jonathan. We observe that even at that point, the poet speaks of experiencing the love and not of reciprocal feelings toward Jonathan. We do not know if David was the composer and speaker of the lament, but it makes little difference. By tradition, David was a musician and poet. It is a possibility that the dirge over Saul and Jonathan goes back to him and equally possible that the editors of the material assigned it to him. The only lines directly applicable to David are in verse 26, and even those would not necessarily have to come from him.

The poem is much admired by scholars and is indeed a fine and unique example of this type of ode. In a perceptive article on the lament, Tod Linafelt has analyzed its content in terms of the double voice he hears in it, both positive and negative, with the second level of meaning a "consistent denigration of Saul's kingship and a disqualification of Jonathan as a potential successor to his father's throne."[21] Joel Baden judges the lament to reach "extreme limits of

21. Linafelt, "Private Poetry," 517. Especially interesting is Linafelt's reading of the lines on Jonathan's love, which he understands to be indeed homoerotic but not as a celebration. "As rhetoric, as words 'supposing an audience,' David is careful to cast his relationship with Jonathan in such a way as to preserve his own dominance and heterosexual reputation. It is Jonathan who

biblical apology. He hardly could be more effusive in his posthumous praise."[22] In my view, one need not take too cynical a view of the material, expressing as it does traditional praise for the fallen war heroes, in this case a king and his son. This lament is not a prayer, the name of God is not mentioned, God's care and concern and power are not praised. It is in its own way an appropriate leave-taking by David of a man with whom he was unable to cut his ties completely, even if we judge him to be indirectly responsible for his death.

Act I, Scene 2: One Throne, Two Kings (2 Samuel 2)

The Old Testament and pacifism make uneasy bedfellows.[23]

I divide this scene into two parts, with the first (1–11) focused on David and the second (12–32) on soldiers and generals. First, there is David's relocation to Hebron and his being established as king there, followed by an announcement of his kingship to Jabesh Gilead, the town whose people had come to save what they could of the bodies of Saul and his sons to give them a burial (1 Sam 31:11–13). In the meantime, the Saul faction has not sat idly by, and Abner, a familiar name from the Saul narrative (cf. 1 Sam 26:7–16), has made a countermove and established one of Saul's sons as king in a town across the Jordan. The second part provides a close-up of the kinds of skirmishes that may have been par for the course during this period when David ruled only Judah. A number of people die, with the focus on one victim, Asahel, whose funeral closes the scene.

---

loved David . . . not David who loved Jonathan" (523). Polzin (*David and the Deuteronomist*, 17) also hears a negative voice in the lament, with a special focus on "the heights," in Kings especially places marked by idolatry. Polzin also points to the use of the root for "pierce/slay" as having the double meaning of "pollute, defile." Polzin concludes that the language of the lament "is chosen precisely for its prophetic and cultic power to foreshadow the fall of Israel and the idolatrous role of its kings in bringing about this disaster."

22. Baden, *The Historical David*, 114.

23. John Goldingay, *Men Behaving Badly* (Exeter, UK: Paternoster, 2000), 184.

Scene 2, Part 1: A Move and a Message (2 Samuel 2:1–11)

Clearly, Abner did not organize a kingdom in a day. Equally clearly, David's transfer to Hebron and his anointing did not happen in a day either.[24]

The scene opens with David ready to "go up" to one of the towns in Judah, and upon questioning Adonai, he is told to "go up" to Hebron, one of the few instances of his being in motion in these first chapters. The emphasis on "going up" is reminiscent of the opening of Judges, in which Judah and Hebron also played a prominent role. We encountered Hebron also in Joshua as a town assigned to Caleb (Josh 15:13; cf. Judg 1:20) and recall the association of David's wife Abigail with the Calebites through her husband Nabal (1 Sam 25:3). In addition, Hebron is associated with Israelite ancestral tradition, notably as the burial place of Sarah (Gen 23:2, 19). Hebron was, for its time and place, an important city, perhaps the most significant in the hill country. As Baden observes, "There could be no more symbolic place to be anointed than in the ancient royal city of Hebron."[25] The connection with the opening episode in Judges and the use of the verb "go up" bring with them connotations of warlike action, and it may not be entirely without force that David comes to settle in Hebron, a possibility taken for granted by some scholars.[26]

For David, as it was for the settlers of Judges, Hebron is a strategic city where he can stay put for the time being, apparently having ended his service with the Philistines. His household accompanies him, evident from the mention of his wives, followed by the company David brings with him—his band, who all come with their households. David's wife Abigail is here named "wife of Nabal the Carmelite" (2), as she was in 1 Samuel 30:5 during the raid on Ziklag. The notation most likely serves to establish David's rights to settle

24. Campbell, *2 Samuel*, 29.

25. Baden, *The Historical David*, 119.

26. Campbell (*2 Samuel*, 27) leaves the issue of force open, and Baden (*The Historical David*, 120) assumes it: "David's move to Hebron is less a mere relocation and more an act of aggression."

where his wife already has ties through her first husband, who in 1 Samuel 25:2 is said to belong to the Calebites, with "business in Carmel." Hebron is also one of the towns where David earlier sent a share of the plunder he gained in attacking Amalek (1 Sam 30:31). Laconically, the narrative announces that "the men of Judah came and anointed there David as king over the house of Judah" (4). From grieving in Ziklag, David is king in Hebron almost in the next breath. There is no mention of any further dealings with the Philistines, nor with the inhabitants of Hebron or of how the men of Judah came to "anoint" him, a matter usually left to specific functionaries acting on divine guidance in the Historical Books. Once Saul, for example, was anointed by Samuel, all Israel "made Saul king," with the anointing already a fait accompli (1 Sam 11:15; 10:1). Equally, David was anointed by Samuel (1 Sam 16:13). Perhaps the narrator uses the verb to make clear that the "men of Judah" consented in the anointing of David, or perhaps, as Baden believes, they were forced into the act by David as a quid pro quo on account of his earlier distribution of gifts.[27]

That David has his sights on a larger territory for his rule than little Judah is clear from a delegation he sends to Jabesh Gilead (5–7). In his message, he heaps praise on the inhabitants for respecting the remains of Saul, an act he calls one of loyalty/devotion (*hesed*) offering them reciprocal action in turn. Just in case they would misunderstand him, he adds, "I will do you some good," before he reminds them that Saul, whom he calls "their master" rather than "their king," is dead and he, David, has been *anointed* as king of Judah. Jabesh Gilead is in the far north, across the Jordan from the battle between Saul and the Philistines. It is a significant and strategic city for someone trying to extend his rule. We recall that this town had once experienced the wrath of their kinsmen because they refused to join in violent action against Benjamin (Judg 21:9–13) and that Saul was a Benjaminite. It was also the place once saved by Saul from Ammonite aggression (1 Sam 11). In any case, David's offer must have fallen on infertile ground and is met by a deafening silence.

27. Baden (*The Historical David*, 124) argues that the "men of Judah" were the leaders of the communities summoned by David to acknowledge his de facto leadership.

Instead, we are informed about another event in the Transjordan: the installment of a second king, Ishboshet, one of Saul's sons, who is "made" king by general Abner, who was Saul's cousin and one of his commanders. With Ishboshet, there is no talk of anointing but a blatant "Abner brought him . . . and made him king over . . . all Israel" (9). Clearly, Ishboshet is king in name only and sits on his throne by the grace of Abner. The ease with which Abner makes his countermove witnesses to the fact that there is as yet little evidence of one unified nation ready to support David as their king. Saul has mostly reigned within a small contingent of tribal alliances and kin. The kin-strife already a threat in Joshua 22:1–34 and emerging in Judges through the absence of unity and through tribal war (chs. 20–21) is once again ready to raise its head. If David's aim is to enlarge his kingdom, he has his work cut out for him. The notation of the time he rules in Judah as seven and a half years testifies to the difficulties he faces.

Scene 2, Part 2: The Field of Knives (2 Samuel 2:12–32)

Evidently something has been lost from the text.[28]

The meager reports on important events of this period in the first part of chapter 2 are followed by an account which appears to omit important details and to linger on a specific incident that will have long-term consequences. First, Abner and Joab meet with their troops at Gibeon (12–16). The text does not mention a purpose for their movements, and it is quite possible that neither has a military encounter in mind. A chance encounter is argued by Loring Batten, who suggests that both Abner and Joab were "stationed along their respective borders to keep the peace and prevent incursions."[29]

28. Loring W. Batten, "Helkath Hazurim, 2 Samuel 2, 12–16," *ZAW* 26 (1906): 94.

29. Batten ("Helkath Hazurim," 91), in face of the verb-form used in v. 13, suggests that Joab goes out first to protect the border and that Abner comes across the Jordan in response to protect Benjamin, so that the two come

Abner suggests a "play" or a "contest," to which Joab agrees. The incident gets attention in verse 16.

2 Samuel 2:16

Each grabbed the head of his neighbor,
and his sword in the side of his neighbor,
and they fell together.
They call the name of that place:
Chelkat Hatsurim [field of knives], which is in Gibeon.

The text explains the name of a place, but it is far from clear *what* exactly happens. It sounds as if each has a sword or dagger and, while grabbing his opponent's head, sticks him in the side so that all twenty-four fall down dead. But the second line of verse 16 is missing a verb, raising the question as to the exact nature of the event. It is very possible that ancient Israel knew of this type of ritualized combat, but that assumption does not help us to understand the situation any better.[30] Batten argues that a number of words, such as "play" for the contest, which is never used in bloody combat, and "neighbor," which is not suitable for an enemy, coupled with taking hold of one's opponent's head indicate that no bloody combat was intended but some sort of friendly athletic competition. Most likely, to his view, the twelve contestants provided by Abner, were left-handed Benjaminites who created a bloodbath by sticking daggers they kept hidden until the right moment into the sides of

upon each other accidentally at the pool of Gibeon "not for offense but for defense." In the Historical Books, "to go out," especially of troops, as is here the case, is often for the purpose of war and expressed explicitly with that purpose (cf. 1 Sam 4:1; 7:11; 17:8; 18:5, 16; 28:1), but here there is no specific purpose mentioned.

30. Niditch, *War in the Hebrew Bible: A Study in the Ethics of Violence* (Oxford: Oxford University Press, 1993), 95. Alter (*The David Story*, 205n16) mentions that depictions from the ancient world show men "in precisely this posture." See also Otto Eissfeldt, "Ein gescheiterter Versuch der Wiedervereinigung Israels," *La Nouvelle Clio* 3 (1951): 110–27; "Noch Einmal: Ein gescheiterter Versuch der Wiedervereinigung Israels," *La Nouvelle Clio* 4 (1952): 55–59.

their challengers.[31] The Judeans would then be the subject of the line "they all fell together." This treacherous act so enraged the troops of Judah that battle ensued. On the other hand, as shown in ancient bas-reliefs, the contestants may indeed have grabbed the opponent's head and both sides may have used swords. The only surprise in this case would be that all the contestants died. A contest of this sort was used to decide the victor, and in the case of the twenty-four, the matter is left undecided, so a battle must take place.[32]

As is often the case, the narrative provides no detail of the military struggle but states merely that the "men of Israel" were "beaten before the servants of David" (17). We notice that in this section, David is not assigned the title "king," the issue of his rule being far from settled. Also, for the first time in the stories about him, he is absent from the battlefield. Instead, his general, Joab, until now mentioned only once by the side of his brother Abishai (1 Sam 26:6), comes to the fore as commander of David's troops. Joab's two brothers, Abishai and Asahel, are here also, and all three are identified as the sons of Tseruyah, David´s sister. Tseruyah's name occurs fifteen times in the books of Samuel, always in relation to one or more of her sons, and we know nothing else about her than that she was the mother of the three mightiest warriors in David´s employ. As Campbell points out, it is "extremely rare" in the Bible that a man is named with his mother's rather than his father's name, as is the case with Joab and his brothers. In Chronicles, Tseruyah is listed as David's sister (1 Chr 2:16). Campbell suggests that she may have been "a prominent woman, eclipsing her husband" and that she was "likely to have been a formidable woman."[33] At one time, in any case, her name must have resounded in the context of the narratives as a well-known figure.

Abner is on the run, pursued by Asahel, who runs like a "gazelle in the field" (18). Everything stops when Abner addresses his pursuer and tells him to veer from his chase. When Asahel does not comply,

31. Batten ("Helkath Hazzurim," 93) also observes that the side is not where one strikes in combat but is rather "the spot aimed at by an assassin."

32. Eissfeldt, "Noch Einmal," 55.

33. Campbell, *2 Samuel*, 48.

Abner begins to argue that he does not want to kill him and face the wrath of Joab (22). When Asahel refuses to give up, Abner strikes him with the butt of his spear in the belly so hard the spear comes out on the other side "and he fell and died there" (23). Apparently, Asahel was a great runner but not such a great fighter. The picture the scene paints is interesting in the way it presents a reluctant Abner, who would rather see his pursuer turn to other business than have to kill him. The bloody death of Asahel is such a shock that it stops Joab's troops in their tracks, but Joab and Abishai continue on (24). It is again Abner who cautions Joab to stop: "Do you not know the bitterness that will be afterwards?" Plenty of bitterness is to follow, immediately in the aftermath and much further down the path. As Alter writes, "This grim prognostication hovers over not only the continuing war but over the entire David story,"[34] and, we might add, over the entire history of the monarchial period in ancient Israel's life. The fleet gazelle's life is over, and they bury him in Bethlehem (32). It will not be the last funeral in this lead-up to David taking his seat on the throne over all Israel.

Act I, Scene 3: A Fragile King (2 Samuel 3)

David is looking like a winner.[35]

Twice, the chapter informs us that the battle between the rivals, the house of Saul and the house of David, was long (1, 6), but we hear nothing further of armed struggle in any of the chapters that lead to David becoming king of all Israel, except between individuals. Two incidents take place of which the first, though seemingly of minor importance, sets the second one in motion, one that results in the death of Abner—the third major event. Abner is all-important to Ishboshet, who needs him in order to remain in the saddle, and another chapter ends with a funeral and elaborate mourning. Throughout the events, David stays in Hebron, away from bloodshed. His

34. Alter, *The David Story*, 207n26.
35. Campbell, 2 *Samuel*, 43.

family has multiplied so that in the opening lines, the statement about David becoming stronger while the house of Saul grows weaker (1) is underlined by the elaborate listing of all David's wives and sons (2–5). He is now gathering something of a harem around him, testifying to his growing royal status. Both Ahinoam and Abigail are mentioned, as well as a third wife, Ma'acah of Geshur, apparently a princess. About Amnon, the son of Ahinoam, Absalom, the son of Ma'acah, and Adonijah, the son of Haggit, we will hear more. Three other sons are named, but they, like their mothers, drift out of the story as soon as they come into it.[36]

In verses 6–11, we get a glimpse into the household of Ishboshet, where Abner is accused by his master of having a sexual relationship with one of his father's concubines, Rizpah. The accusation enrages Abner, although he does not deny it; what galls him is to have a quarrel over "a woman." An ironic juxtaposition faces us. One household has many wives and male offspring, while in the other there is mention of only one woman, a concubine at that, who has become a cause for contention within the royal family. The act, if true, is of course not minor, because sexual possession of a member of the royal harem was laying a claim to power. Abner's rage may actually testify to the truth of the allegation, and he swears that he will switch sides to support David's claim over all of Israel (9). The narrator assigns to Abner knowledge about Adonai's choice of David as king—an unlikely piece of information for Abner to know—and uses the opportunity to declare David's right to the throne by putting this declaration in the mouth of David's most powerful enemy. The altercation leaves Ishboshet speechless and Abner ready to abandon a lost cause.

Without further hesitation, Abner opens a conversation and proposes to "make a covenant with David," upon which he will bring

36. Some identify Ahinoam as Saul's wife acquired by David and a significant factor in his rise to the throne, while Abigail, first married to Nabal, was David's sister (1 Chr 2:16), whom he took back from Nabal, usurping his status in Hebron. See Jon D. Levenson and Baruch Halpern, "The Political Import of David's Marriages," *JBL* 96 (1980): 507–518. Baden (*The Historical David*, 78–89, esp. 79) shares this opinion on Ahinoam and argues that David took her in an act of rebellion, which became the "precipitating event for Saul's attempt on David's life."

all Israel to David's side, a proposal to which David agrees on one condition (12–16). It would be helpful to know what exactly Abner has in mind with the "covenant," which most likely includes mutual agreements and conditions by which he must be carving out some role of standing and power for himself. Does he propose to become a vassal to David as de facto king of the north, as Baden would have it?[37] Or is his bargaining chip a position as David's general, replacing Joab? We do not know; all we know about is the condition David provides: He wants to have his wife Michal back at his side. The actual task is left to Ishboshet, who apparently sends Abner. The scene is pathetic.

2 Samuel 3:15–16

15 And Ishboshet sent
and took her from her husband,
from Palti'el, the son of Laish.
16 And her husband went with her,
going along weeping behind her
as far as Bachurim.
Abner said to him:
Go home! And he turned back.

When David demands the return of Michal, he refers to her as the woman whom he "betrothed with a hundred Philistine foreskins" (14). It is not for anything *she* has done for him that David commands Abner to bring her to him but because he remembers how much she cost *him* and because she is "the daughter of Saul." He does not say that she is the woman who saved his skin when her father first became determined to kill him or that she stuck her neck out for him and deceived her father on account of him. In 1 Samuel 25:44, the text reports that Saul "gave" Michal to another man, one Palti'el. Palti'el literally means "God [is] my deliverance." Perhaps Michal found a respite with her new husband; at least from this scene it is clear that he felt a deep attachment, as he follows her in tears.

37. Baden, *The Historical David*, 134.

Deliverance for Palti'el or Michal is hard to find. We do not hear from Michal; she is here a pawn in a play between powerful men. She will now be one woman among a growing number of women in David's household. Ironically, Abner, who did not want to have a dispute about a *woman*, has become David's errand boy to pry a *woman* from the presence of her reluctant husband, whom he tells in so many words to get lost (16).

True to his promise, Abner gets in motion to convince "the elders of Israel" to accept David as their king, using the argument that he will deliver them from the Philistines (18), the first time we hear them mentioned as an enemy still to be taken care of. After the defeat at Mount Gilboa, it is likely that they held sway over a good part of Israel, and the threat of their presence has not gone away. The promise that David will make an end of them must find a ready hearing, for all seems to go along fine. David gives a feast for Abner and his retinue, which Abner leaves with the assurance that he will take care of everything: All will come to David's side, who will be "king over all that your heart desires" (21). We note that he does not promise David will be king over "all Israel." In any case, the last word of this interlude is "peace."

For one of David's people it is, however, far from peace. In the next unit (22–27), Joab is coming back from a raid, returning home with booty to Hebron, which Abner has already left "in peace." Where did Joab go exactly to come back with plunder? The text does not say, but it points to the fact that David is still in need of having the necessary provisions gathered, by force if necessary, for his household and troops, his position in the land still far from secure. Of course, there are enough interested parties to tell Joab about what transpired with Abner: that he came and that the king sent him off "in peace," a term now heard for the third time in the short span of two verses. Joab will have none of it and gives David a piece of his mind, beginning with, "What have you done!" (24). No reply is heard from David, and perhaps Joab takes this as consent, for he has Abner brought back, perhaps by a ruse, and kills him in the gate by a thrust to the belly. The text declares that the murder was "for the blood of Asahel his brother" (27), and this may well have been a part of what was on Joab's mind, but it is not what he spoke of to David.

He clearly does not trust Abner and may also see him as a rival. And David? He does not reply to Joab or prevent him from interfering. What took place certainly must have had his silent permission.[38]

The first word he utters after he hears what transpired is "innocent." He protests that he has nothing to do with this bloodshed and calls down a curse on the "the head of Joab" and "the entire house of his father" (29). The narrator restates that Joab killed Abner out of vengeance, underlining the absence of guilt on David's part. Not only does David protest his innocence, but "all the people" dress in mourning, lamenting and weeping over the death of Abner (31–36). The elaborate rituals may sound puzzling, since this was the man who had, for a good long time, propped up the one person who could challenge David's kingship and before that had been Saul's general. But the mourning continues, with David composing a lament over Abner and the people fasting and firmly believing in their king: "All that the king did was good in the eyes of all the people." David calls Abner a "commander and a great man" and refers to himself as "fragile/weak," not able to stand up to "these men, the sons of Tseruyah" (39). Poor, weak David is just no match for "the doer of evil"; he will leave it up to God to take care of recompense. In the last section (36–39), the text emphasizes the approval of "all the people," in whose eyes all that the king did "was good." Yet

38. In his essay "Davidic Complicity in the Deaths of Abner and Eshbaal: A Historical and Redactional Study" (*JBL* 99 [1980]: 533), James VanderKam argues that the murder of Abner by Joab took place with David's tacit permission, as he counted on the fact that Joab would kill Abner without this in "any way tarnishing his image." Campbell (*2 Samuel*, 47) professes that the tenor of the story "strongly suggests that it would have been in David's interest to keep Abner alive." While this is true enough, there are interesting gaps in the story that leave it unclear exactly what Abner has in mind once David has claimed his throne and therefore leave the possibility open that Abner could pose a continuing threat, either to David, to Joab, or to both. Baden (*The Historical David*, 133) surmises that Abner intended to set himself up as the head of a vassal state in the north: "Abner would not have simply given up his power for nothing. . . . He would have supported David's nominal kingship in the north, but with himself as a vassal king, ruling over Israel." Fokkelman (*Throne and City*, 144) thinks it would have been "difficult for David to have given Abner anything less than the position of chief of general staff."

a chapter that emphasizes such total acclaim and earlier noted the "peace" (*shalom*) that surrounded Abner ends with the double mention of "evil."

Act I, Scene 4: A Disabled House (2 Samuel 4)

We have an intimation of mayhem and dismemberment that is an apt thematic prelude to the story of David's reign.[39]

The news of Abner's death causes a greater weakening of Ishboshet and the people who support him (1), and it results in Ishboshet's eventual demise. In the midst of this mayhem, domestic notes pervade the scene. First, there is a quite detailed description of two men, Ba'anah and Rehab, who as non-Israelites live with their kin as "strangers" and serve Ishboshet as commanders. Their introduction is followed by a note on a son of Jonathan, Mephiboshet, who has survived the disaster of Yezreel with crippled feet, dropped by his nurse in their flight.[40] The unit teems with names—Ishboshet, Abner, Saul, Ba'anah, Rehab, Rimmon, Benjamin, Jonathan, Mephiboshet—reflecting the chaotic character of what takes place. The only unnamed character is the female nurse who carried Jonathan's son in her flight and dropped him. While there is some lack of clarity in the Hebrew phrasing of how exactly the assassins entered the royal residence, their act is clear: they kill their master in his sleep, cut off his head, and take it with them to David.[41]

39. Alter, *The David Story*, 219n12.

40. Like *Ishboshet*, the "boshet" ending indicates shame, and like Ishboshet, the name most likely originally included a "baal" element: Mephibaal. Mentioning him here anticipates his future role in David's household (9:6; 19:24, 30).

41. Difficulties in the Hebrew sentence prevent a clear understanding of verse 6, which may contain another reference to female characters since it begins with the feminine plural pronoun. Alter (*The David Story*, 218) translates, "And look the woman who kept the gate had been gleaning wheat and nodded, and fell asleep." His translation reflects the text of the Septuagint. Altogether vv. 6 and 7 provide slightly different pictures of what transpires. Verse 7

If the two had counted on a warm welcome from David, they are sadly mistaken. On their announcement that they bring him "the head of Ishboshet, the son of Saul, your enemy who sought your life" (8), David recalls for them what happened when another messenger came with news about the death of Saul himself. Sarcastically, he notes that death was the reward for that particular bearer of "good news." How much more will he deal with guilty evildoers who have killed "a righteous man" while he was "in his house, in his bed." The intimate knowledge David displays about the location of the deed betrays the fact that spies had already passed on information about Ishboshet's demise. Death begets death, and the two are killed, their corpses displayed with hands and feet cut off, while Ishboshet's head receives a burial next to Abner. David's road to the throne has proceeded from murder to murder and burial to burial.

The civil war is over, but kin-strife is not at an end.

Act II: Consolidating the Monarchy (2 Samuel 5–8)

After his official crowning over all the people, David is on the move. His first act is to establish a capital, a story told in fragmented language, with the result that in a few verses David settles in Jerusalem. From there, he negotiates with foreign powers for labor and provisions to build his house so that he can go on his first military campaign against the Philistines (ch. 5). Once he has a capital, he also makes it a religious center by transporting the Ark into it, a feat he accomplishes with some difficulty (ch. 6). Finally, at rest in Jerusalem, David nurses a plan to build a temple as a fitting residence for the Ark, a project that is thwarted by God through the prophet Nathan, who appears on the scene for the first time. A long speech from God's side elicits an equally lengthy response from David, the first time we encounter him in prayer in these stories (ch. 7). A final chapter concerns a series of military campaigns of aggression, ending with a note on administrative and military assignments at

doesn't mention a particular body part, noting only that "they struck him down and killed him and removed his head."

his court (ch. 8). While the chapters are presented as occurring in a straightforward timeline, we should probably understand them as taking place at different periods in David's career. All events are marked by pervasive presence and activity on God's part.[42]

Act II, Scene 1: A Throne and a City (2 Samuel 5)

It was a smart choice.[43]

Three units make up the scene in which David becomes king over all the people, establishes a capital city, and goes to his first battles following the death of Saul, both against the Philistines. The three constitute essential steps in David's leadership over "all Israel": He is crowned as king (1–5), founds and settles in a capital without previous alliances to any Israelite tribe on the border between south and north, making it "the city of David" (6–16), and takes on the hated enemy with a strong presence in the land, the Philistines (17–25). The presence of Adonai is notable, especially in the encounters with the Philistines.

First, "all the tribes of Israel" come to Hebron and make a series of declarations to David: The first is about their close kinship, something that is not immediately evident. The second is about David, the one who "brought out and led Israel" during Saul's kingship—in other words, as commander of his troops—according to the narratives true only for a part of the time. The third statement is about Adonai, who personally announced that David would be "shepherd" and "leader over Israel." The title "leader" is applied to Saul (1 Sam 9:16; 10:1) as well as Saul's future replacement (1 Sam 13:14) and is also used by Abigail for David (1 Sam 25:30). We encountered "shepherd" as a verb for David in a literal sense when he first appeared on the scene (1 Sam 16:11; 17:15, 34, 40). It occurs here for the first time

42. Fokkelman (*Throne and City*, 155) details this and notes that there is "no other Act in the books of Samuel which so clearly puts God forward as agent."

43. Baden, *The Historical David*, 162.

as a term for royal rule, and its unique combination with "leader" underscores the power of the proclamation and the importance of the occasion.

Then the "elders of Israel" come to "the king in Hebron" and anoint "David king over Israel."[44] It is a momentous occasion, on which David is said to "make a covenant" *for* them, that is to say on their behalf, a pact of which we are not told the content.[45] A notation about the duration of David's kingship both while he was only king "over Judah" (seven and a half years) and subsequently in Jerusalem over "all Israel and Judah" (another thirty-three) closes this first section.[46] The description bears the character of an artful construction to make clear the acceptance of David as king by all the tribes, although unity may still be far off, as is hinted at in the two-part expression in 5:5: "all Israel *and* Judah."

Once David is king over all the people, the text sets him in motion to conquer Jerusalem, a city still inhabited by non-Israelites, which "he captured," putting the lie to the declaration of the Jebusites: "You will not enter here" (6–9). Entering and not entering sit at the center of this very complicated text, of which the end result is clear enough: David now resides in Jerusalem, now called the "stronghold" or "fortress" and renamed "the city of David" by David himself. Jerusalem resounds with enormous significance in

44. On the unusual event of a group of people rather than an official representative "anointing" a king, see p. 228 above. The text most likely uses the term here and in 2 Sam 2:4 to underline David's initial anointing by Samuel in 1 Sam 16:13.

45. David concludes a covenant *for* or *on behalf of the people*, not *with* them as many translations have it. That is to say, he pledges himself with specific promises, probably in terms of being their commander and leading the armies against the enemy, but the text does not specify.

46. James VanderKam ("Davidic Complicity," 528) explains the discrepancy between the time period of David's kingship in Hebron, also stated in 2 Sam 2:11 as seven and a half years, and the length of Ishboshet's kingship, set at two years (2 Sam 2:10), in light of the fact that David had already set himself up as king in Hebron "five and one-half years before Saul died," and the reigns of the two kings overlapped for the final "two years of David's residence in Hebron."

the history of peoples and faiths, but as far as we are aware, it was an exceptionally small town in David's time. Although strategically located, it "comprised . . . a small spur to the southeast of the Temple Mount, . . . little more than half a kilometer in length," while it was from "side to side no more than a quarter of a kilometer."[47] Its diminutive dimensions even in its day as compared to the cities of Mesopotamia and Egypt did not prevent the biblical writers from glorifying both it and its glorious king: "David continued to grow great, and Adonai of Hosts was with him" (10).

A great king needs a palace, and to this task David turns next, having himself a house built—the first of its kind in ancient Israel's history—with the help of foreign labor (carpenters and stonemasons) and using cedar and stone rather than the ordinary mud-brick of Israelite houses (11). As Baden remarks, "If David wanted a palace, Tyre was the place to turn."[48] While the "palace" cannot have been very large, it must have been spacious enough to accommodate a growing family, which for the first time begins to include "concubines." We call to mind the admonition in the Torah that the chosen king in Israel should avoid a large harem (Deut 17:17). The notation about David's family clearly anticipates the length of his reign rather than describing his initial residence there. Since he took concubines and wives "from Jerusalem," they must have included Jebusites. There has been no mention of erasing and killing the entire population of Jerusalem, and the addition of concubines to David´s household who are of Jebusite origin could be characteristic of a pact between the king and the local inhabitants, especially if they came from social and political circles that belonged to a powerful stratum in the hierarchy of the former city-state.[49] The concubines from Jerusalem are thus a token of David's political power.

47. Baden, *The Historical David*, 161. On the size of the land and Jerusalem, see van Wijk-Bos, *The End of the Beginning*, 23.

48. Baden, *The Historical David*, 164.

49. See Andrew E. Hill, "On David's 'Taking' and 'Leaving' Concubines (2 Samuel 5:13; 15:16)," *JBL* 125 (2006): 129–50. Hill argues that "the marriages to women belonging to the families of Jebusite power brokers were absolutely necessary. They were a means of securing the loyalty of both the cadre of 'civil servants' and the citizenry of Jerusalem to the new Hebrew regime" (131).

David's activities have not gone unnoticed by the Philistines. Baden, who believes that David was until this point a vassal of the Philistines, points out that David "crossed the line from useful mercenary to potential threat."[50] Even if David has been independent of Philistine vassalage until this time, his actions will have drawn the notice of his aggressive neighbor in the west. Now, Saul is no longer after David, but the Philistines have come to *seek* David. It may have been the first occasion on which Jerusalem proved its advantage as a capital—difficult to capture on account of its high altitude and with a good view of the surrounding countryside. Two battles take place (17–25), in both of which David is victorious with the direct help of Adonai. The location of the engagement is not any clearer than are the details of what happens. Baden believes that David met them in the hills, the usual interpretation of "the stronghold" (cf. 1 Sam 22:4, 5; 24:23[22]), because he would have the advantage over the Philistines, who needed open space for their chariots. The encounters are especially significant for divine engagement, proving that "Adonai of the Armies" (10) is indeed on David's side. The fight with the Philistines is not decisive, for the resistance against them will be a subject again in chapter 8.

In contrast to the preceding episodes, when David was king over Judah alone, he proves his mettle as a strategic thinker and military leader. He unites a kingdom out of a fractured and disunified people who have lived under two different kings, he conquers the small population of a non-Israelite city to make it his capital, and he wins two battles with the archenemy of Israel, the Philistines, probably partly through the choice of the locations where the fights take place. He gives credit where credit is due to Adonai, who "broke through" his enemies and handed David a victory.

50. Baden, *The Historical David*, 141. With this opinion, Baden follows the deductions of J. Maxwell Miller and John H. Hayes (*A History of Ancient Israel and Judah*, 2nd ed. [Louisville: Westminster John Knox, 2006], 168–69), who state that in the early years of David's career as king in Hebron, he "was an emerging regional chieftain with Philistine backing." Once David became king of Israel and Judah (5:1–3), the Philistines "appropriately regarded him as the enemy."

Act II, Scene 2: The Ark Returns Home, Part 2 (2 Samuel 6)

There is, then, an unpredictable danger, a risk, in seizing the ark.[51]

Securing Jerusalem as a capital with no previous tribal attachments was a stroke of genius on the part of David, but it had the disadvantage of having no associations of religious and historical significance. There is, of course, an item that embodies the tradition of the sacred presence of God with Israel, which, following its central place in the first six chapters of 1 Samuel, has lingered outside the view of the reader, barring an enigmatic mention of its presence in 1 Samuel 14:18 at the battle of Saul with the Philistines. There, the Ark was glimpsed fleetingly and to no effect, only to disappear right away. Eventually, the Ark in its proper location, the temple, lent the "city of David" its aura of central significance for the people's understanding of God's presence with them.[52]

The road home for the Ark from "the house of Abinadab in Gibeah," does not run as smoothly as David might have hoped. I divide the episode into three stages. In the first (1–12), David goes out with a large contingent of his troops[53] to *bring up* the Ark from Abinadab's house in Gibeah.[54] The distance of about ten miles is not

51. Polzin, *Samuel and the Deuteronomist,* 64.

52. Regardless of the importance of the Ark prior to David's monarchy, it eventually became the central religious symbol once it was moved to Jerusalem. Karel van der Toorn ("David and the Ark," *JBL* 113 [1994]: 231) argues that the Ark was a Saulide cult object and that David created national and religious unity around it.

53. We note the number 30,000 is identical to the number of Israelite dead in 1 Samuel 4:10. Both numbers reflect the usual exaggeration, but "the numbers three, 30, 300, 3000, 30,000 and 300,000 are above all associated with military forces" (Robert Rezetko, "David over Saul in MT 2 Samuel 6:1–5: An Exercise in Textual and Literary Criticism," in *For and Against David: Story and History in the Books of Samuel,* ed. A. Graeme Auld and Erik Eynikel [Leuven: Peters, 2010], 262). See Polzin, *David and the Deuteronomist,* 61.

54. In v. 2, the notation is *baaley Yehudah,* a name that in the Qumran scroll of Samuel reads "Baalah which is Kiryat Yearim in Judah." In the Masoretic Text, the words mean "the masters of Judah." The Hebrew text shows some difficulties and errors, as is not unusual in the Hebrew of Samuel. For

far, but it is difficult terrain, and perhaps with this in view, they load the Ark on "a new cart" and carry it off with appropriate personnel in front and behind (3–5). The picture is clearly drawn, including an elaborate listing of musical instruments, as David and all those around him "play" before Adonai.[55] Yet in spite of all the pomp and the musical accoutrements that surround the cart on which the Ark is transported, the first trip ends in the debacle of the death of Uzza, one of Abinadab's sons, who is guiding the cart (6–7). The incident brings to mind the experience of the people of Beth-Shemesh when the Ark arrived there after its sojourn with the Philistines (1 Sam 6:19).

All motion stops as the anger of Adonai that strikes Uzza elicits from David reciprocal emotions so that he leaves the Ark for the time being outside Jerusalem. We know that the Ark is not an entirely safe object to have around. In verse 6, it appears as if Uzza takes hold of the Ark because it is in danger of falling.[56] The explanation of his death in verse 7 ("on account of his. . .") contains an incomprehensible word in Hebrew, which does not bring us any closer to a solution. It is possible that the use of a "new cart," last seen when the Philistines brought the Ark back from its disastrous sojourn among them (1 Sam 6), was itself cause for the Deity to be quick to anger; in fact the word for this conveyance occurs in the Historical Books only here and in the earlier adventures with the Ark among the Philistines. The Ark is elsewhere outfitted with rings so it can be carried by poles, a detail described in Exodus

Ba'ala meaning Kiryat Ye'arim, see Josh 15:9. If we read "the masters of Judah," the words "from there" are more difficult. Yet here I read with Rezetko ("David over Saul," 268) that the Ark is in Gibeah, the residence of Saul. Such a reading explains the reference to the Ark in 1 Sam 14:18 as being with Saul.

55. The verb *sahaq* refers to making music. We encountered it in 1 Sam 18:7 in the context of the women who welcome victorious warriors home. For a discussion of musical instruments and movement during the procession with the Ark, see David F. Wright, "Music and Dance in 2 Samuel 6," *JBL* 12 (2002): 201–225.

56. I read the verb with the cattle as subject in v. 6 as transitive. The rare verb used here (*samat*) means "to drop" with an object (cf. 2 Kgs 9:33, for example). The direct object is missing in the line.

25:10–15. In the Deuteronomic tradition, the Levites are in charge of it, including its transportation (Deut 10:8; 31:9, 25; cf. Josh 3:6; 8:33). Was the cart the improper conveyance, and were the people taking care of it the improper personnel? No reference to a priest is to be found in the unit. A certain amount of neglect vis-à-vis the Ark and a too-nonchalant handling perhaps led to disastrous consequences.[57]

David's anger is most likely the other side of the fear ascribed to him, for if God could strike down one of David's servants, who is to say he, David, will not be next? For the first time, there is conflict between David and Adonai, with whom he has been on such good terms until now! He asks, "How will the Ark of Adonai come to me?" (9). It is worth noting that only after he is told that the house of Obed Edom, a man from Gath, and thus presumably a Philistine, is blessed on account of the presence of the Ark (11) is he willing to undertake the endeavor anew.

2 Samuel 6:10, 12

10 So David was not willing
to turn the Ark of Adonai toward him,
to the city of David.
And David diverted it
to the house of Obed Edom the Gittite.
. . .
12 It was told to King David:
Adonai has blessed the house of Obed Edom
and all that is his
for the sake of the Ark of God.
So David went and brought up the Ark of God
from the house of Obed Edom
to the city of David with gladness.

57. In 1 Sam 7:1, the inhabitants of Kiryat Ye'arim are said to consecrate one of Abinadab's sons to guard the Ark, but the phrase does not make his position clear. A comparable situation is perhaps to be found in Judg 17:5 where a man consecrates his son to be priest, but there the term "priest" brings clarity to the situation.

If a Philistine benefitted from the presence of the Ark, surely the "city of David" would experience no harm! The stay of the Ark in the house of Obed Edom is framed by the contrasting statements of David not being willing to bring the Ark closer and his decision to go and bring it up after all. In the meantime, we pay attention to the fact that the first stage of David's attempt to bring the holy relic into his city ends in strong emotions of anger and fear, and in death.

The second stage (13–19) records a successful entry, with the impressive spectacle of the Ark (now carried by people), sacrifices, and David in a type of ecstasy of whirling and shouting.[58] Rather than the noise of all the musical instruments of the earlier occasion, there is now the sound of the shofar, the ram's horn. Once inside Jerusalem, in this chapter consistently called "the city of David," the Ark is placed in a tent especially put up for it by David while David once again brings offerings. The role of David in this section is kingly and priestly. As a priest, he wears the linen ephod (14), brings the sacrifices, and blesses the people. His royal act is the largesse he bestows on all the people.

In the midst of these festive proceedings, the perspective shifts to someone who views them from her window: Michal looks down and sees her husband carrying on and despises him completely (16).[59] Michal is, however, not called David's wife but "the daughter of Saul," an identification that creates new tension in the narrative. At this stage, we only know about Michal that David had her brought back, separating her from her protesting, grief-stricken husband Palti'el (2 Sam 3:14–16). There is no word about the reception she received from David. The text does not make clear if she is obligated to stay inside as a member of the royal harem or if she is inside by choice. The verb for her "looking from a window" is not the usual Hebrew

58. Verse 13 implies that the Ark is carried in the way it was intended when it mentions "the carriers of the Ark."

59. The verbs used for David's movements in the procession are difficult to interpret precisely, although it is clear that some kind of dance is involved. Fox (*The Early Prophets,* 453) translates "leaping and whirling"; Fokkelman (*Throne and City,* 196) has "leaping and clapping."

for seeing but one that occurs in other places within contexts of dishonor or disaster. Notably, we find it in Proverbs as the speaker watches a naïve young man fall into the clutches of an adulterous woman (Prov 7:6–27).[60] The moment when we look down on David with Michal not only creates a hiatus in the progress of the Ark but leaves tense anticipation for its sequel.

The sequel arrives with David's homecoming, the last unit in the scene (20–23), when Michal steps out of her confined space to greet David.

2 Samuel 6:20–22

20 David returned to bless his house,
and Michal, the daughter of Saul,
came out to meet David, and she said:
How glorious the king of Israel today,
who exposed himself today in the eyes of the maids of his servants;
as exposed as the exposure of a worthless person!
21 And David said to Michal:
Before Adonai—
who chose me above your father and his whole house
to appoint me as leader over the people of God, over Israel—
I will indeed play before Adonai!
22 I will demean myself even more,
and will be low in my own eyes,
and with the maids of whom you speak, I will find glory!

Michal does not wait for David to enter the house but makes her accusation in the open, in public. David has other matters on his mind and is in fact on his way "to bless his house" but is caught by Michal's scathing reproach. Her words begin with a reference to

60. Abimelech looks out the window and discovers that the woman he had taken into his household is really the wife of Isaac (Gen 26:8); Sisera's mother, whose son has already been dispatched by Yael, looks out the window anxiously wondering about the delay of Sisera's return (Judg 5:28).

"glory," or "honor," a significant word we encountered in the first chapters of 1 Samuel (see pp. 55–57 above). If we translate the first sentence with "how honored the king of Israel was today," we could understand the phrase at face value as an appreciation of all David accomplished. Michal soon puts any misunderstanding of her meaning to rest with the triple reference to the king "exposing himself" and comparing him to a "worthless person."[61] Not only did he expose himself, he did so in the eyes of the female servants. In his reply, David points out that he was chosen by God above her father and his whole family and that he will do as he likes, both before God and before the maids. By implication, he states that he will have sex with whomever he wants to!

The speech of the two characters is enclosed in the references to "glory." Once, a woman died giving birth and lamented that the "glory" was gone in exile from Israel in reference to the capture of the Ark (1 Sam 4:21–22), and she too used the root here translated with "exposed" (*galah*). Michal's words resonate with meaning far beyond her immediate context, for in her speaking of David's *higgalot niglot* (shameless exposure) one hears echoes of the *galut,* Israel's exile. When the writers compiled these narratives, the glory had been exiled from Israel indeed, the religious and the royal glory. The account of the Ark's glorious entry into Jerusalem contains somber notes, referring to death and a dying house. The last words about Michal from the narrator refer to her lack of children "until the day of her death," making "death" the last word in the story, echoing the result of the first attempt to bring the Ark into the city. The segment of Michal's exchange with David reflects more than a declaration regarding the "old order," which is a thing of the past; it also casts a long shadow forward over the fate of the house of King David, the people, the land, and the Ark.[62]

61. The word *req* literally means "empty" and can be used for people of no account, worthless fellows (cf. Judg 9:4; 11:3; 2 Chr 13:7).

62. Campbell, *2 Samuel,* 68: "The rejection of the old order is most sharply expressed in the exchange initiated by Michal."

Queen Michal

There is a David story, but there is not a Michal story.[63]

His heart was a cluttered room. He would sing in the morning, and kill in the afternoon and make love to a woman in the evening. . . . I didn't live easily with him.[64]

When we first meet Michal, if one can be said to meet her in a text which is filled with silence about her person and experiences, she is said to *love* David (1 Sam 18:20) at a time when everyone who sets eyes on him loves him. Michal is only one of the elements in the surfeit of love coming David's way, but she is the only *woman* in the crowd and the only woman in biblical narrative who "loves" a man. Her father, Saul, plans her to be a "snare" for David, but that plan does not work out, and Michal, from being in charge of such a powerful verb as love, moves to the passive state of being *given* to David as wife (1 Sam 18:27). In counterpoint, however, the text reiterates that she loves David.

1 Samuel 18:28–29

28 Saul saw and knew
that Adonai was with David.
And Michal, Saul's daughter, loved him.
29 Saul increasingly feared David,
and Saul became David's enemy all the time.

Here, Michal's restated love is caught between Saul's *seeing* and *knowing* about David's status in the eyes of God and his daughter

63. David J. A. Clines, "The Story of Michal, Wife of David, in Its Sequential Unfolding," in *Telling Queen Michal's Story: An Experiment in Comparative Interpretation*, ed. David J. A. Clines and Tamara C. Eskenazi (Sheffield: Sheffield Academic, 1991), 129.

64. Robert Ehle, "The Grace of God," in *Telling Queen Michal's Story: An Experiment in Comparative Interpretation*, ed. David J. A. Clines and Tamara C. Eskenazi (Sheffield: Sheffield Academic, 1991), 150.

and his *fear* and *animosity.* There are three references to David and four to Saul in this segment, with Michal, as she often is, called "Saul's daughter." She is caught between father and husband—not a good place for a daughter and wife to be.

Soon, we meet her in an active role as she counsels David to get away from the murderous intentions of her father or he will be dead in the morning. She speaks for the first time in 1 Samuel 19:11. Her tone is blunt and straightforward, ending with the word "dead." It is interesting that no reply from David is recorded, and he becomes the object of her actions when she "lets him down through the window." In addition, she concocts a ruse to delay her father's henchmen. Actually, it's a double ruse, because she declares David "sick" when they come to get him, so the household gods she has put in the bed do not come into play until her father orders David brought to him bed and all and the messengers discover the deception: "Look, the household gods in the bed and a braid of goat hair at the head" (1 Sam 19:16). It's not such a good thing for a wife to have lifeless figures in her bed where a warm, loving husband should be. When Saul reproaches his daughter, she speaks in this part of the story one more time: "He said to me: Let me go, why should I kill you?" (1 Sam 19:17). She makes her father believe that David wanted to go and threatened her to make her help him. We know that this is not how it went, because the storyteller informs us otherwise, but her words ring ominously, as they are bound to feed her father's suspicion and rage against David. In this section of the text, she is not called Saul's daughter but David's wife, or else by her own name. She is a determined woman who does not mince words, who is able to think of a ruse in a tight spot, who lies to her father. Still, the two times she has spoken, she mentions death.

The next glimpses of her are fleeting—once when Saul "gives" her to another husband (1 Sam 25:44) and once when she is the object of verbs once again. David orders Abner to *bring him* Michal, Saul's daughter, and Ishboshet to *give* him *his wife Michal*; and Ishboshet *sent* and *took her* (2 Sam 3:13–15). We see her husband following her weeping but hear nothing about Michal or from Michal. At this point in the story, David has gathered a large family, and we assume that she simply becomes a part of his household. Was she safer under his eye than outside of his control? Did he need her as an adjunct to his rising star? Was he worried about her brewing a rebellion? We can only guess from silence in the text that her return was not so important to David on an emotional level that it needed comment. Or perhaps it was obvious that getting Michal back was "a political move to reinforce his claims to the kingship."[65] We do know that Michal comes back to David a bereaved woman. Her father and brothers are dead, her second husband is left behind weeping at her departure. Not only does he weep, but he follows her, so there must have been great depth of feeling, at least on his part.

When we see her looking from her window at David carrying on in front of everybody, she becomes the subject again.

2 Samuel 6:16

When the Ark of God came to the city of David,
Michal, the daughter of Saul,
looked out from the window,
and she saw King David leaping
and dancing before Adonai,
and she despised him in her heart.

Earlier, we considered the verb for Michal's looking out of her window (see pp. 246–47 above). Both Genesis 26:8 and Proverbs 7:6–7 use identical expressions in which a person *looks* out from a *window* and *sees* something that reveals the truth about someone. In Genesis, Abimelech discovers that Rebekah is Isaac's wife, and in Proverbs the onlooker finds out what befalls the naïve young man who follows the woman entrapping him in illicit intercourse. In Judges 5:28, Sisera's mother *looks out* from her *window* and laments the delay of her son Sisera's homecoming; she does not (yet) see what has taken place. In each case, the truth is something other than what is expected or hoped for, and you could say that the ones looking

65. So Clines, "The Story of Michal," 136.

out get an eye-opener. Michal *looked out* and *saw* and *despised*. The verb "despise" (*bazah*) elsewhere means especially to "consider of no account," as Esau of his birthright (Gen 25:34), the people who reject Saul at first (1 Sam 10:27), or Goliath of David because he is a "good-looking lad" (1 Sam 17:42). Is it reading too much into the text to conclude that she looks out and sees something she does not expect and that at that moment David loses the place he may have still had in her heart?

From her words, we conclude that Michal despises David because he "exposed" himself, in particular in front of the women servants.[66] Is her emotion one of sexual jealousy, as some have it?[67] While this feeling is likely a factor in her reaction, her state of mind may be more complex. Once, she had high hopes for the young man she loved; she helped him survive by abetting his escape from her enraged father, and she has watched him rise to his potential. It may very well appear to her the utmost in unseemly behavior for a king to flaunt himself before the populace the way David has. Perhaps she is sensitive about her own background as the granddaughter of a farmer and the wife of a farmer's son? It is difficult to know how class was experienced in ancient Israel, but clearly Michal refers to women of a lower class than herself as the ones to whom David *exposed* himself.

If the statement about Michal is unique regarding her love for David, it is also unheard of for a woman to accost a man the way Michal does. Women in the Historical Books may speak in request or complaint mode, but the biting sarcasm that comes David's way from Michal stands out as the sole example of this type of speech from a female to a male character, a wife to a husband. First, she *goes out*, a verb not often used with women as subject, and in other cases involving sexual intercourse (e.g., Leah and Dinah in Gen 30:16 and 34:1) or with an invitation to the possibility of such an

66. The word *amah* used in v. 20 is sometimes rendered "slave girls," and most likely class enters into the description, but it is not clear that the word in Hebrew means "slave." The emphasis here is more likely on gender than class.

67. Clines, "The Story of Michal," 139.

encounter on the woman's initiative (e.g., Yael in Judg 4:18, 22). Michal takes initiative, as we know from the earlier narrative comment, not for a positive purpose. Then, she gives David a piece of her mind: in Clines' words, "her showdown and shootout with David, out in the street, for all to see and hear."[68] Michal is not a woman who is portrayed as fearful or lacking initiative. The narrator's final comment about her relates to her lack of children but does not ascribe this to a divine punishment. If her childlessness is the result of an absence of sexual contact between the two, we are still left to wonder who took the initiative for this lack. I agree with the suggestion made by Clines and others that a woman who so despises a man might not be eager to have children with him.[69] Childlessness in the world of ancient Israel indeed put a woman in a precarious social and economic position, but such would not be the case for Michal, and her situation raises the question whether there were also women in ancient Israel for whom offspring was not the most important thing in the world.

Finally, the narrator allows Michal words that have bearing on more than the immediate situation and future, with double-voiced references to "glory" and "exile." David's reply to her sounds almost childish in comparison: "Well, I do it all for God, who after all chose me over your father, and I will do even worse things than this if I have a mind to! So there!" Perhaps there were worse fates than having no future intimate relations with David for Queen Michal, who stepped out of her place to speak honestly and prophetically and to put her husband in his place.[70]

68. Clines, "The Story of Michal," 137.

69. Clines, "The Story of Michal," 139. See also Danna Nolan Fewell and David M. Gunn, *Gender, Power, and Promise: The Subject of the Bible's First Story* (Nashville: Abingdon, 1993), 155.

70. Jenni Williams, *God Remembered Rachel: Women's Stories in the Old Testament and Why They Matter* (London: SPCK, 2014), 78: "She could have been politic, played politics, and lived to be an honoured queen; instead she chooses to be honest about her feelings." See also Benjamin Morse, "The Defence of Michal: Pre-Raphaelite Persuasion in 2 Samuel 6," *BibInt* 21 (2013): 19–32.

Act II, Scene 3: A King at Rest (2 Samuel 7)[71]

David did not build a temple because he had no need to do so.[72]

2 SAMUEL 7:1–3

1 When the king sat in his house,
Adonai gave him rest
all around from all his enemies.
2 The king said to Nathan the prophet:
See now, I sit in a house of cedar,
and the Ark of God sits in tent fabric.[73]
3 Nathan said to the king:
All that is in your heart, go and do,
for Adonai is with you.

The final words of David in the previous chapter sound as if he foresees no checks on his freedom and power. Such notions are put to rest among others in an account of plans and notions thwarted and redirected by God through the word of a prophet. Besides Samuel himself, prophets have made only rare appearances in the Historical Books so far, popping up here and there, named or un-

71. The perceived importance of this chapter as it relates to core theological issues of ancient Israel and Christianity has resulted in a flood of material on both its possible redaction and synchronic readings. In this discussion, I focus on the received text and its significance within the context of the David narratives as they were finalized in the early postexilic period. For detailed analyses of its literary structure, see Fokkelman, *Throne and City*, 207–254. For a reading that understands 2 Samuel 7 as especially significant in terms of the Deuteronomistic History, see Polzin, *David and the Deuteronomist*, 71–87. Campbell (*2 Samuel*, 70–79) provides a nuanced interpretation while at the same time recognizing different layers in the chapter, including Deuteronomistic editing and early core and prophetic layers.

72. Baden, *The Historical David*, 177.

73. The word is "curtains," which, as Alter (*The David Story*, 231n2) notes, is an "obvious synecdoche" for tent (cf. 6:17). I think the reference to fabric is important to maintain, as it forms the counterpoint to "cedar."

named, appearing and disappearing almost as quickly as they make their entrance.[74] In the introduction to this scene (1–3), "Nathan the prophet" is addressed by the king as if he is a familiar character (2). Although prophets will remain only occasional visitors in the text of 2 Samuel, the presence of Nathan marks a point of departure. Until now, the text has usually described David in direct communication with God without mentioning the means of consultation, recording simply the phrase "and David asked Adonai" (cf. 1 Sam 23:2; 30:8; 2 Sam 2:1; 5:19, 23). In the future, contact with God will come to King David via the prophet. The declaration "so says Adonai" issues from Nathan's lips to David both here (5, 8) and in 12:11, an expression specifically at home in prophetic literature.[75] Prophets in preexilic Israel are thus coming to the fore as critics of the monarchy in David's time, and they will remain on the scene in this capacity until the Babylonian exile and beyond.[76]

It does not look at first as if Nathan will offer a contrasting view to that of the king, who compares his own housing to that of the Ark, cedar to tent fabric. Nathan counsels him to go and do "all that is in your heart" (3). It is also not clear that the king is asking for advice, since he merely makes an observation (2), but Nathan clearly takes the statement as a question and offers counsel. It turns out that he is wrong and needs to redirect his king. Most of the chapter consists of two long speeches, one by God and one by David. The first is divine

74. In Judg 6:8–10, there is one mention of an unnamed prophet. Groups of prophets make an appearance in 1 Sam 10:5, 10; 19:20, especially in connection with Saul. Prophets are part of Saul's efforts to consult the Deity in 1 Sam 28:6. The term "man of God" (*ish elohim*) likely points to the same position in 1 Sam 2:27 and is used alternatively for the prophets Elijah and Elisha in 1–2 Kings (1 Kgs 17:18, 24; 2 Kgs 1:9, 10, 12, 13; 4:7, 9, 16, for example). The prophet Gad appears in 1 Sam 22:5 and is called the "seer of David" in 2 Sam 24:11. Samuel is identified as a prophet in 1 Sam 3:20 and 9:9, but he combines in his person also the offices of judge and priest.

75. Of the 291 times the phrase occurs in the Hebrew Bible, about two-thirds may be found in the Prophets, especially Isa and Jer. In 1–2 Kgs, it occurs frequently, whenever a prophet is on the scene.

76. Samuel fulfilled this role vis-à-vis Saul, but his office is less clearly defined in this respect than is the case for those who follow him.

instruction to Nathan directed to David (4–16), the second a prayer by King David (18–29). The linking verses are the only narrative portions in the chapter; they constitute context, time and/or place. David sits in "his house" (1) and moves to "sit" in the presence of God (18). Nathan receives "the word of Adonai" from God in "the same night" (4), upon which he reveals to David "all these words and this vision" (17). Moreover, David sits in a place of "rest" granted to him by God without "enemies" plaguing him (1). Everything here takes place inside, in contrast to the chapters immediately preceding and the one following. *Place* and *sitting* or *dwelling* will continue to be unfolded in the divine speech for God, for David, and for God's people. *Words* from God to David through the prophet find a response in the *words* David speaks to God.

Adonai refers to David, up till now called "the king," as "my servant," a title in the Historical Books reserved exclusively for David, Moses, and Joshua (Josh 1:2, 7; 24:29; 2 Kgs 21:8).[77] The speech circles around two rhetorical questions concerning a house of God (5, 7): Is David the one to build such a thing and has God ever asked for it? Words for house, building, and sitting tumble over one another like an avalanche aimed at making clear that David is not the one and Adonai never wanted one.

2 SAMUEL 7:6–7A

6 For I have not stayed[78] in a house
from the day I brought the Israelites up from Egypt until today;
but I was the one going about[79] in a tent and dwelling
7 in all my going about with all the Israelites.

A significant statement about the preference of Israel's God, who from the days of Israel's liberation on was not stationary, is sur-

77. In 1–2 Kgs, David will consistently be referred to as God's servant. See 2 Sam 3:18; 1 Kgs 11:13, 32, 34, 36, 38; 14:8; 2 Kgs 19:34; 20:6.

78. The verb here translated "stayed" is the same as "to sit" or "to dwell."

79. The construction of this phrase is complex, beginning with "I was" and continuing with a form of the verb *halakh*, literally meaning "to walk." The intention here appears to be, "I was in the business of walking around."

rounded by the questions of verses 5 and 7. The third line begins with the word *va'ehyeh*, strongly reminiscent of the self-revelation of God in Exodus 3:14, where God promises presence to Moses in the way God will decide: *ehyeh asher ehyeh*—"I will be who I will be" or "I will be there as I will be there."

Verse 8 resumes the instruction ("Say this to my servant, to David"), moving to the theme of God's assured presence for David, beginning with past action: "I myself took you," with expression of the personal pronoun (*ani*) in the Hebrew sentence unnecessary. *We'ehyeh* sounds again in verse 9 ("I was with you") before the speech moves to the future: "I will make for you a great name." From this statement to David, the promise continues to unfold in terms of God's people, who will receive a place and rest just as David has (10):

2 Samuel 7:10

I will establish a place for my people Israel,
and I will plant it and it will dwell on its own,
and no longer will it tremble,
and worthless people will no more afflict it as in earlier days.

Since the years of the early Israelite invasion and settlement of the land, *rest* from enemies has been an important marker of divine approval and blessing (Josh 21:44; 22:4; 23:1; cf. Josh 11:23; 14:15; Judg 3:11, 30; 5:31; 8:28). This reassurance toward Israel is put in the midst of the guarantees provided for David regarding a name and "rest from all enemies." David's *rest* from his enemies, reiterated in verse 11, encompasses rest for God's people. It is not God who needs a house but rather it is David who is in need of a house provided by God as a guarantee of rest and stability not only for the monarchy but also for the people.

The last segment (11b–16) continues to round out this notion of the lasting nature of David's monarchy. A "firmly founded kingship," which might have been Saul's but was withheld from him (1 Sam 13:13), will be David's and his offspring's. This is first stated in verse 12 and reiterated in 13 and 16. David's kingship will now be firmly founded through God's support of David's offspring. David's house will be a house "for the ages" (16). The promise of a house for David (11, 16) surrounds the announcement that David's offspring will be the one to build a house for God's "name"—an announcement in one line occurring almost as an afterthought (13). There is a strong emphasis on divine approval for one of David's line to be his successor, going into detail in verses 14 and 15. For the last time, the *ehyeh* sounds ("It is I who will be for him"), making the rare parental comparison "father" in the Hebrew text. Punishment may come his way, but God's loyalty to David's house will last.[80]

David's response in prayer takes place "in the presence of Adonai" (18–29). It stands out for David's expressions of humility. He refers to God as "my lord Adonai" seven times and to himself as "your servant" ten times. The opening lines speak only of the greatness of Adonai, who has done all these things for him, David, and besides whom there is no other deity (19–22). From the praise of God, David segues into the praise of God's people, picking up on the themes of the divine speech: Israel is Adonai's people "for the ages" (24). This expression (*ad olam*) is reiterated in subsequent lines of David's prayer and applied to the house God promised him and then to God's name (26). It is repeated twice in his closing words, in which he begs a blessing for his house "for the ages" (29). We note that in this prayer, there is no mention of building a house for God. A different David than the exuberant monarch and sharp-tongued husband of the previous chapter comes into view. Here,

80. The strong emphasis on the Davidic dynasty with the subtext of divine approval for his son Solomon as his successor causes one to suspect a layer of pro-Solomonic advocacy in this chapter. Such a layer is strongly argued by Tryggve Mettinger in his essay "Cui Bono? The Prophecy of Nathan (2 Sam 7) as a Piece of Political Rhetoric," *SEÅ* 70 (2005): 193–214. The chapter would then originally have been a prophetic defense of Solomon's reign, possibly by the prophet Nathan or someone from his circle, composed during Solomon's kingship with later Deuteronomistic redaction. It is an attractive proposal, although suffering from the usual circular reasoning in which a text becomes both the testing ground and the proof of a theory. Mettinger's recognition of this problem (209–210) does not quite put it to rest.

human and divine discourse is filled with rich theological thoughts and humble acknowledgment of human insignificance in the face of God's greatness. This is a David we will not meet again in what follows. He "sits" positioned between the agitated movement of the beginning years of his kingship and his continuation as a conquering monarch and an inadequate head of his family and his people. The chapter is like a banner stretched over events that exhibit all too human interchange and dysfunction. If the vision of the land partook of Utopian aspects—a land grander, more beautiful, more fruitful than the reality—the vision of the ideal monarch may share some of these features: a king as God's servant, humble, and eager to magnify the Holy Name.

Perhaps the perspective on God shares in this. For what are we to make of the declaration that Israel's God is not one for sitting but for moving about with the people and not one in need of a house? Is this also the ideal view of God, not stationary but on the move, not caught in one name but *ehyeh*—"I will be"? Perhaps the editors intended the expression that the house will be for "my name" in verse 13 as a compromise or accommodation on God's part.[81] Once, the people desired a king and the divine response was one of dismay that they had rejected their God (1 Sam 8:7–9), yet God did not deny them their wish. There is an accommodation to human need taking place in the reflection on kingship in 1 Samuel 8 and here in the contemplation of a sanctuary for God. Like the monarchy, a sanctuary corresponds to a human rather than a divine need.[82]

81. The expression is specific to the Deuteronomistic literature (Deut 12:11, 21; 14:23, 24; 16:2, 11; 26:2).

82. Kenneth Craig ("The Character[ization] of God in 2 Samuel 7:1–17," *Semeia* 63 [1993]: 174) argues that the issue about a temple for God was the person who should build it not whether it should be built or not: "The initiative for building the temple and the choice of that builder shall come from God and not from the individual king." While there may be something to this insight, the theological issue of tension between God's freedom and placing the presence of God in a sanctuary is present also in other texts in the Hebrew Bible, even voiced by Solomon himself at the dedication of the temple in 1 Kgs 8:27.

Act II, Scene 4: A King at War (2 Samuel 8)

Victorious warriors win first and then go to war.[83]

David is pictured to be coldly more arbitrary, claiming for himself the power of life and death.[84]

After the heights of piety and divine promises of chapter 7, the survey of David's conquests in chapter 8 comes as a shocking about-face (1–14). The temporal modifier "afterward" opening the chapter is immediately followed by the verb "struck down" with David as the subject, an action that will be repeated five more times. In order, David "strikes down" Philistia, Moab, Aram, Ammon, and Edom. Although no separate campaign against Amalek is mentioned, booty from this people is included in verse 12, perhaps referring to the earlier occasion on which David gathered plunder from this group (1 Sam 30:18–19). David places garrisons in several locations, and two peoples are said to be "subservient" to David: Moab and Edom. All the campaigns here listed are aggressive rather than defensive, some involving such extreme cruelty as the measuring of victims with a rope, killing two lengths and leaving one length alive, a custom unknown elsewhere in the ancient context. Moab, the place to which David is linked by ancestry and where he once brought his family for shelter (1 Sam 22:3–4), is the recipient of this particular kind of treatment. The excessively harsh practice of hamstringing horses is mentioned in the Historical Books only here and in Joshua 11:6, 9 and also stands out as harm of a particularly vicious type, both disabling and intolerably painful.

The list of campaigns taking up fourteen verses is most likely reflective of those David waged during the time of his entire reign, here presented in capsule form. The detailed notation of the plunder he brings to Jerusalem in the center of the chapter (7–12)—gold, bronze and silver, saved for the treasury used by Solomon for the Temple (1 Kgs 7:51)—may be part of the reason the list is inserted here follow-

83. Sun Tzu, *The Art of War*.

84. Susan Niditch, *War in the Hebrew Bible*, 130.

ing the consideration of temple building. By its nature, this overview fits more adequately with the final four chapters of 2 Samuel, in which we find lists of heroes and famous fighters of David's day. No doubt, a desire to exhibit David's success and greatness, going everywhere with the support of Adonai, makes it a somewhat logical follow-up to chapter 7. The account paints a rosy picture, implying complete conquests, far more complete than was probably the case. On the west coast of ancient Israel, the "land of the Philistines" still exists in Solomon's day (1 Kgs 5:1[4:21]), and Hezekiah is reported to have conquered them in the last quarter of the eighth century (2 Kgs 18:8). With Moab we are familiar from Judges; they will be a significant force at the time of King Omri in the ninth century. The Arameans were to constitute a formidable power in the northwest, becoming dominant a century and a half after David. The struggle with Ammon is to continue in subsequent chapters and represents an effort to expand to the east that may have been successful. Edomite territory was at the time located in the southern Negev, and it seems likely David at least gained a foothold there and placed garrisons, as the text states (14).[85]

We note too that the list of conquered peoples is a standard one, including most of ancient Israel's traditional foes: Philistia, Moab, Aram, Ammon, Edom, and Amalek. A similar list is mentioned relative to Saul's campaigns with the notation that wherever he went, Saul inflicted damage (1 Sam 14:47). Different from the descriptions of Saul's activities is the affirmation of Adonai's support for David's conquests in this chapter (6, 14). Exaggerated descriptions of victories, combined with divine support, are a hallmark of war reports of the context and period. It is, of course, not impossible that David indeed waged military campaigns and put to rest aggressive assaults on his people, be they from inside or outside the country. For the rest, we should likely concur with Baden that "Israel under David remained what it had always been: a minor state, largely confined to the central hill country of Judah and Israel."[86]

85. Miller and Hayes, *A History of Ancient Israel and Judah*, 144–88; Megan Bishop Moore and Brad E. Kelle, *Biblical History and Israel's Past* (Grand Rapids: Eerdmans, 2001), 232–34, 310–13.

86. Baden, *The Historical David*, 186. Cf. Miller and Hayes (*A History*

The chapter concludes with a short list of David's administrators and religious officials (15–18), with David's own sons among the priests (18). Even though there is no direct statement about his appointing them, it is clear that he keeps a degree of control over the worship apparatus. The mention of his sons as priests is a faint, uncomfortable echo of Samuel, who appointed his own sons as "judges," a matter that did not turn out well because they were precisely those who perverted justice (1 Sam 8:1–3). The list is preceded by the statement that David administered "justice and righteousness for all his people" (15). There is little sign of the perverted "justice" (*mishpat*) spoken of by Samuel on an earlier day, when he warned about the abusive practices of the king the people wished for (1 Sam 8:9–18). So far, David has only "taken" from non-Israelite peoples. The two qualities that characterize his reign powerfully reinforce the notion that in David the people indeed have the one they wanted: a military leader who brings peace and prosperity to the people. The theme of the just and righteous king, who vanquishes enemies, under whose rule and with God's support the people thrive, is eloquently expressed in Psalm 72, a prayer dedicated to Solomon.[87]

We may still wonder why the editor-collectors who put their final stamp on this material inserted the chapter just here, even if there is enough linkage with its immediate context. It has been my argument that the David who arises from torturing human beings

of Ancient Israel and Judah, 180): "The core of David's direct rule would have been Jerusalem and the central hill country. Beyond that he apparently exercised some degree of authority over the Jezreel Valley, Galilee and Northern Transjordan. But nothing suggests that his realm included Philistia, and it is unlikely that he ever controlled any of the Transjordan south of the Arnon River."

87. Ps 72:1–3:

To Solomon.
O God, your justice give to the king
And your righteousness to offspring of the king.
May he judge your people righteously
And your wretched with justice.
May the peaks bear peace to the people
And the hills in righteousness.

and animals is not the same person who rose to kingship and certainly not the same one who bowed in humility before his God in prayer and gratitude.[88] While this chapter is a fitting conclusion to the cycle I've entitled "Ascent to Kingship," it also prepares in its own way for the negative depiction that is to follow. In the course of events just around the corner, we may well wonder whether this king indeed "did justice and righteousness" on behalf of his people.[89]

88. I observe that the David we meet in 2 Sam 8 "has indeed stepped onto fundamentally different ground, from which he emerges a different person," and I suggest that it may be "no coincidence" that the more negative picture of David follows immediately on the military forays of David in ch. 8 (van Wijk-Bos, *Reading Samuel*, 184).

89. Richard Smith (*The Fate of Justice and Righteousness During David's Reign: Narrative Ethics and Rereading the Court History According to 2 Samuel 8:15–20:26*, LHBOTS 508 [New York; London: T&T Clark, 2009], 42–64) takes 2 Samuel 8:15 as the beginning of the Court History and argues that these two qualities are the test by which to judge the David in 2 Sam 9–20 and 1 Kgs 1–2. One can, however, use the concepts, which are indeed central to the understanding of kingship not only in Israel but beyond its borders, as touchstones without changing the perimeters of the Court History. This narrative judgment about David can function as a touchstone for what follows whether it originally belonged to the Court History or not.

Cycle IV: A King and His People (2 Samuel 9–20)

Written by a great artist who was presenting life in its multifaceted complexity.[1]

The end of the road to kingship comprises sixteen chapters. Twelve of these (9–20) follow a continuous timeline, while four others (21–24) veer in a new direction to conclude Samuel with reports on various events during David's rule. Although the first two chapters of 1 Kings, with their close focus on David and his family, are often considered to be part of the twelve in this cycle—together entitled either the Court History of David or the Succession Narrative—we will reflect on that material in the context of the beginning of Solomon's kingship.[2]

1. James S. Ackerman, "Knowing Good and Evil: A Literary Analysis of the Court History in 2 Samuel 9–20 and 1 Kings 1–2," *JBL* 109 (1990): 59.

2. The identification "Succession Narrative" goes back to Leonhard Rost, who argued for such a continuous narrative ending in 1 Kings 1–2 in his work *Die Überlieferung von der Thronnachfolge Davids* (Stuttgart: Kohlhammer, 1926). This book was more recently translated and edited by Michael D. Rutter and David M. Gunn in the series Historic Texts and Interpreters in Biblical Scholarship as *The Succession to the Throne of David*, with a foreword by Edward Ball (Sheffield: Almond, 1982). Rost's thesis was later supplemented by many scholars, such as G. von Rad and R. H. Whybray, with numerous modifications. It should be noted that Rost did not simply identify 2 Sam 9–20 and 1 Kgs 1–2 as the Succession Narrative. He begins the story in 2 Sam 6:16, 20–23, continues in 7:11b, 16, and on with many sections omitted in the following chapters, leading to the usual splintering of the narrative in the fashion of early source critics, constructing a theory about text units and using the text to prove the theory.

Second Samuel 9–20 is marked by a distinct style and a rich portrayal of characters in the setting of family relations. David is present in every chapter. Divine intervention occurs especially at moments of crisis, but the easy David-God discourse of previous chapters is absent. Human counsel takes the place of direct divine guidance of human affairs. The stories are told with deftness and verve, drawing the reader/listener directly into what transpires, revealing motivation and inclination while holding back other elements to enhance the sphere of intrigue and the mystery of human behavior. We know, for example, that Absalom hated his brother Amnon for having violated his sister, Tamar (2 Sam 13:22) but not if that is the main reason for the murder of his brother (2 Sam 13:28–29). Amnon may have provided the pretext for Absalom to do away with a rival for the throne. As Ackerman, borrowing from Meir Sternberg, notes, "The art of biblical narrative challenges us with what we are not told but must attempt to discern."[3] The tales thus fascinate both because of the information they provide and what they leave out, what the characters know and do not know, and what the listener/reader may discern within the gaps.

In the review of the material that follows, I have opted for the identification Court History rather than Succession Narrative, understanding the theme to be deteriorating family relations in David's house with serious repercussions in the political realm.[4] On the whole, David is depicted in less than admirable ways; he is deceptive and cruel, passive when he should be active, weak when he should be strong. I have entitled the cycle "A King and His People" because there is more going on than simply a description of a king and his court, and the issue of how people around David relate to him and view him is of great interest in the story.

3. Ackerman, "Knowing Good and Evil," 41.

4. The collection appears to be from one hand and was evidently important enough for the postexilic compilers/editors to keep intact. We note that the account is entirely missing in Chronicles (1 Chr 20:1–29:25) and that Chronicles refers to other "records" which contain "accounts" of David's rule (1 Chr 29:29–30).

We begin the story with chapter 9 because it starts a new time-flow and together with chapter 10 establishes the theme of "loyalty" or "kindness" (*hesed*), an important aspect of the "justice and righteousness" assigned to David in 8:15 (see pp. 208, 256–57n90 above). Chapter 10 introduces the war with Ammon and together with 12:26–31 sets a frame around the David-Bathsheba-Uriah episodes.

Act I of the cycle (2 Sam 9–12), "The Justice of the King," concerns itself with matters both inside and outside the borders of David's rule. David attempts "kindness" (*hesed*) toward a descendant of Saul's house and toward a foreign ruler (2 Sam 9; 10). While the first succeeds to a degree, the second misfires spectacularly and sets in motion a protracted battle with Ammon. At the time of this military adventure, David engages in rape and murder in his own house, actions that earn him divine disapproval and consequences for the future of his house. From then on, it is as if each new episode begets another disaster.

Act II (2 Sam 13–14), "A House Divided," opens with the rape of one of David's daughters, Tamar, by her brother Amnon and continues with the slaughter of Amnon by his brother Absalom, which results in Absalom's banishment. Cordial relations between father and son are restored through the mediation of Joab. In acts I and II, David is forced to face reality through the lens of a story, one presented on God's instruction by the prophet Nathan and the other on Joab's instruction by an unnamed "wise" woman.

Act III (2 Sam 15:1–19:9), "Absalom's Rebellion," tells of a palace coup engineered by David's son Absalom, David's flight from Jerusalem, and Joab's eventual victory over the rebellious forces, which includes the death of Absalom.

In Act IV (2 Sam 19:10–20:26), "The King Returns," David comes back to Jerusalem, but fractures, always on the horizon, between Judah and the rest of the tribes occur, and he is faced with another rebellion in chapter 20. After the successful putting down of the insurgency by Joab with the help of a woman, the thread of the narrative with its spotlight on David is cut.

Act I: The Justice of the King (2 Samuel 9–12)

How does David fare?[5]

Two initial chapters (2 Sam 9–10) divide into separate occasions on which David becomes involved with very different individuals, one a descendant of Saul's house and one the heir to the throne of Ammon. We shall see how he and others fare in both circumstances and whether his efforts to show "kindness" have satisfactory results. These episodes are followed by a concentration on David in his own house and what transpires when he takes some time off from the battlefield (2 Sam 11–12). While chapter 11 details the underhanded dealings of the king with two of his subjects, ending in the death of one of them, the consequences of his activities unfold in chapter 12. After the prophet Nathan, sent by Adonai, faces David with his misdeeds, the child born of adultery and rape dies. Each of the chapters thus centers on the death of an individual in the wake of David's miscarriage of justice and righteousness. *Hesed* in these chapters is turned on its head, and the king has done what "is evil in the eyes of Adonai" (11:27).

Act I, Scene 1: A Man from Nowhere (2 Samuel 9)

There is an opaqueness that garbs the characters, giving even the minor ones both humanity and mystery.[6]

The opening unit (1–5) begins abruptly with the words "David said." This type of start we have met only once before, when David decided that Saul would never give up coming after him (1 Sam 27:1). At that time, when he spoke only to himself ("in his heart"), the narrative took a turn in a different direction. Chapter 10 also turns the attention from a general overview of David's actions to precise

5. Ackerman, "Knowing Good and Evil," 42.
6. Ackerman, "Knowing Good and Evil," 43.

engagements with specific individuals. David wonders if "there is anyone left of the house of Saul." The purpose of his question is to "show loyalty [*hesed*] on account of Jonathan." We assume that he is speaking aloud to an unspecified audience of retainers, since in the next breath a certain Tsiva, in the text identified as "a servant of the house of Saul," appears before David. David reiterates the question about a survivor of Saul's house, adding that he will show him "the loyalty of God."

We met *hesed* in the narratives of Joshua.[7] It is the quality that goes above and beyond what is strictly required, shown by individuals to one another and by Adonai to God's people. It can be translated as "loyalty," "kindness," or "devotion." The "loyalty of Adonai" is what Jonathan once asked David to swear to him and his house in the field outside his father's palace (1 Sam 20:14–15) and what David swears to Saul and his house (1 Sam 24:23[22]). It may seem a bit late in the day for David to remember his promises, but it shows an effort at least.

Tsiva informs David that there is indeed one left, a son of Jonathan who is crippled in both feet; this character was first introduced in 4:4 as a seemingly unrelated bit of information in the story of Ishboshet's assassination. Tsiva does not mention his name, and David does not ask it, inquiring only of his whereabouts. Tsiva places him with one Machir in Lodevar. Lodevar may indeed have been a town of uncertain location near Mahanaim on the other side of the Jordan just north of the Jabbok River. Wherever the precise locality may have been, the name itself arouses interest. Lodevar occurs again in 2 Samuel 17:27, together with Machir, with a slightly different spelling. In Amos, either the place or the expression is cited by the prophet. However it is spelled, Lodevar sounds like a combination of two words, together meaning "nothing," "nobody," or "nowhere."[8] Mephiboshet is crippled and a man from nowhere, a nobody, according to his servant not worth mentioning by name, identified only as "a son of Jonathan, crippled" (3). His disabled state is clearly of interest in this text since it is mentioned both in the opening section and

7. See van Wijk-Bos, *The End of the Beginning*, 67n10, 70, 107.

8. "Nothing" is how the Septuagint and the Vulgate render the word in Amos 6:13: "You who are glad about nothing. . .!"

again in the final phrase (13). In addition, while David may not know the man's name, the reader/listener has already been informed of it.

Mephiboshet, the son of Jonathan, the son of Saul, is the only character in the Hebrew narratives with a disability. We know very little about the way people with visible deformities were treated in the biblical world. Legal material in the Torah bars those with physical deformities from serving at the altar (Lev 21:18–23). On the other hand, Leviticus 19, the chapter reviewing humane treatment of the poor, outsiders, and strangers to an extreme extent, includes the "deaf and the blind" specifically in an exhortation not to add difficulties to their lives.[9] Job, in speaking of his virtues in days past, mentions that he provided "sight for the blind and a foot for the lame" (Job 29:15–16).[10] The "blind and the lame" occur as a group in chapter 5 on the occasion of David's conquest of Jerusalem, and some scholars deduce from this episode that David had a hatred of people with disabilities.[11] The text in 2 Samuel 5 is notoriously difficult, and it is not clear that it assigns emotions of distaste or hatred to David.[12] Be that as it may, the servant

9. Lev 19:14:

You shall not declare accursed a deaf person,
and in front of the blind you shall not put an obstacle.
The laborer's wages shall not spend the night with you until morning.

For a discussion of this chapter and its central function in a Torah ethic regarding the stranger and the outcast, see Johanna W. H. van Wijk-Bos, *Making Wise the Simple: The Torah in Christian Faith and Practice* (Grand Rapids: Eerdmans, 2005), 192–93.

10. As in Lev, Job's statement is made in a general context of care for the poor and wretched.

11. So, for example, Schmuel Vargon ("The Blind and the Lame," *VT* 46 [1996]: 499, 507), who assumes that 2 Sam 5:8 should be translated "the lame and the blind who are hateful to David." Vargon understands the story in ch. 9 as a test for David, which he passes in this episode but subsequently undermines in 2 Sam 16:1–4 and 19:25–31[24 –30].

12. I translate the relevant phrase in 2 Sam 5:8 as follows: "Should blind and lame be hated by David's soul?/ Therefore it is said: The blind and the lame say: He shall not enter the house." In this, I follow Buber (Martin Buber and Franz Rosenzweig, *Bücher der Geschichte* [Cologne: Jakob Hegner, 1965], 260): "Sollen blinkende, sollen Blinde/ Dawid's Seele verhasst sein? Daher heists:/ ein Blinder und ein Hinkender sprechen:/ Der kommt uns nicht ins Haus!"

Tsiva certainly underlines his master's helpless state, and one might wonder what if anything David will do in this case and how else the disabled feet of Mephiboshet will have significance in the story.[13]

When Mephiboshet appears before David (6–8), he makes full prostration, a customary posture when facing a monarch but a feat difficult to execute for a person with both legs disabled. One assumes that some sort of method was devised to carry him from place to place, perhaps in a chair, so he would have to fall out of it in order to make the gesture of obeisance. David paid the same homage to Saul (1 Sam 24:9[8]), and Abigail prostrated herself before she addressed David during her diplomatic mission (1 Sam 25:23).[14] It is possible that Mephiboshet is afraid, since David's first words to him are to not fear (7). The implication may be that stories had gone around about David's complicity in the murders of Saul's associates.[15] Or this story may originally have been connected to David's execution of Saul's sons, told in 2 Samuel 21:7–9, which for Mephiboshet could have created the anticipation of a death sentence. David, however, assures Mephiboshet that he is intent on showing *loyalty* (*hesed*) for the sake of Jonathan and promises him that he will have him cared for in his household: "You will eat food at my table always." Mephiboshet renews his gesture of homage, comparing himself to "a dead dog" (2 Sam 9:8; cf. 1 Sam 24:15[14]).

To make the arrangements permanent, David commissions Tsiva, clearly a man of some standing, with fifteen sons and twenty

13. Ackerman ("Knowing Good and Evil," 43) points out that the name Lodevar can also be read as "he has a word/thing," which could be interpreted as "he has something up his sleeve."

14. Polzin (*David and the Deuteronomist,* vol. 3 of *A Literary Study of the Deuteronomic History* [Bloomington: Indiana University Press, 1993], 97) views this action as "not as ideologically innocent as it might at first appear to be. . . . The History makes it crystal clear that this submissive practice—of bowing down before one's fellow human being—is one of those unseemly actions belonging to the royal baggage that weighed Israel down during the monarchic period."

15. Thus Alter (*The David Story: A Translation with Commentary of 1 and 2 Samuel* [New York: Norton, 1999], 241n6), who considers Mephiboshet to have been "terrified that the king may have summoned him in order to put him to death."

servants of his own, to work the land originally belonging to Saul after he grants it to Mephiboshet (9–13). The food that Mephiboshet will eat at David's table will thus be provided for by Mephiboshet himself. This is a deed of loyalty/kindness, but also one that has advantages for David, keeping Mephiboshet and no doubt his family (note the mention of Mephiboshet's son Mica in v. 12) under his eye without having to cough up any finances for his upkeep.[16] We witness in this story a disabled member of the house of Saul—in fact one who has difficulty moving around—eating "always at the king's table," a phrase repeated with some variation four times (7, 10, 11, 13). This particular phrase occurs only here and in 2 Kings 25:29, where king Jehoiachin eats at the table of the Babylonian monarch.[17] The emphatic statements about Mephiboshet's condition may anticipate the status of the last king of Judah and the conditions of the Babylonian exile.

Act I, Scene 2: The King Who Refused Comfort (2 Samuel 10)

David was perhaps naïve about how the Ammonites might perceive things.[18]

The Ammonites, familiar from the time of the judges and from Saul's adventures early in his kingship (1 Sam 11:1–11) appear, and once again David sets out to show *loyalty*, an attempt that lands him and

16. Although David's action here may have been both self-serving and loyal, it is not necessary to ascribe to him nefarious motives in appointing Tsiva, as Richard Smith (*The Fate of Justice and Righteousness During David's Reign: Narrative Ethics and Rereading the Court History According to 2 Samuel 8:15–20:26*, LHBOTS 508 [New York; London: T&T Clark, 2009], 110) deduces: "The magnanimous gesture toward one man has brought about the unjust enslavement of another." Tsiva appears to have enough support to have the land worked for him; the expression "you shall work the land for him" need not be taken so literally that we have to envision Tsiva himself toiling in the fields.

17. Polzin, *David and the Deuteronomist*, 103 argues that such details, particular to the house of Saul and the house of David, are "ideological carriers and reciprocal models for each other."

18. Smith, *The Fate of Justice and Righteousness*, 118.

his people in a war. The content of this chapter fills in the details sketched in 8:5–11, clarifying the role of the Arameans in the war with Ammon. In contrast to the previous chapter, where everything took place at David's residence, the scene widens into the battlefield east of the Jordan, and we get more of a closeup view of the military engagements than is often the case in the biblical narratives. First (1–4), David sends a delegation to the new king of Ammon, Hanun, after the death of Nahash "to comfort him over his father." The Ammonite king, rather than receiving the comfort in peace, stirred up by his counselors, understands David's overture to be made with hostile intent and sends David's servants back in shame, cutting off half their beards and half their clothes. David comforts his deeply embarrassed commissioners, while Ammon hires Arameans to reinforce their troops as they get wind of David's state of mind.[19] On hearing of this, David "sent Joab" with the army, noticeably staying home himself.

We view Joab and his brother Abishai in close cooperation as they divide forces, face the Arameans, and draw out the Ammonites from the city (8–14). We hear Joab's voice as he speaks movingly and with eloquence to Abishai.

2 SAMUEL 10:11–12

11 Joab said: If Aram is too strong for me,
you will become my rescue;
and if the Ammonites are too strong for you,
I will come to your rescue.
12 Now be strong and let us be strengthened
for our people and the cities of our God;
and Adonai will do as is good in his eyes.[20]

19. Literally, the text states that the Ammonites "saw they had become stinking to David" (10:6).

20. In Hebrew, the lines reveal strong sound-rhyme:
Hazaq we nithazaq be'ad ammenu
uve'ad arey elohenu;
w['adonai] ya'aseh hattov be'enayw.

Encouragement to be strong takes central place, on behalf not of David the king but of "our people and the cities of our God," and in the end it will be Adonai who will decide the battle. All they can do is have each other's back in the fight and be of good courage. The tactic works in the sense that the Arameans are overwhelmed by Joab's forces and flee, which causes the Ammonites to withdraw to their city. This is not the end of the war with Ammon, only the beginning of the first stage, with Aram back in Rabbah and Joab with his cohorts back in Jerusalem.

The chapter concludes by describing a defeat of the Arameans under David's leadership (15–19). Aram reassembles after its defeat by Joab, which provokes a successful counterattack from David. At the end, their commander, Shobach, is killed by David. Aram knows when to call for a truce and refrains from further supporting Ammon (19). The defeat of Aram leaves the struggle with the Ammonites unresolved.

We have no reason to doubt David's good intentions in regard to Ammon, but on the other hand, the action of sending a delegation might fulfill a dual purpose, if not to "spy out the city" as Hanun's counselors charge, then to review the situation at Hanun's court while at the same time assuring him of the goodwill of a neighbor. It backfires spectacularly, but even that result may not have been such a surprise to David. He is in this episode clearly concerned with his people, who have been shamed, and waits for Aram to make the first move of aggression. The episodes are constructed around references to *sending*, in verses 2–7 occurring in every verse, an action that will take on great force in the next chapter. David is especially the subject of sending, first comforters (his servants), then people to reassure the shamed delegation, and finally Joab to the battlefield. Hanun also sends: the servants of David in their humiliated condition and then to the Arameans for help. Together with this action, words for noticing or hearing prevail after the first segment—the "Ammonites *saw*," "they *told* David," "David *heard*," "Joab *saw*," "Aram *saw*," and in the end, "all the kings *saw*." If David has so far, on the surface at least, upheld the quality of *hesed* ("loyalty"), it is not much in evidence in the aftermath of David's victory over Aram.

Act I, Scene 3: War Within, War Without (2 Samuel 11)

Serious trouble for the house of David.[21]

The first verse of chapter 11 joins easily with the last verses of chapter 12 to complete a story of victory over Ammon and its capital, Rabbah. The as-yet unresolved conflict with Ammon thus envelops the story of David's interactions at home, depicting private conflict inseparable from conflicts in the larger world. In Fokkelman's words, "The war and the affair at the court are interwoven and attuned to each other."[22] The episode opens with Joab laying siege to Rabbah and concludes with David's capture of the city and his return to Jerusalem. In between these activities, David commits adultery and murder and suffers the death of a child in the aftermath. I divide the scene in two parts.

Scene 3, Part 1: The King Who Needed a Break (11:1–13)

It can be expected that a man who stands on the roof in the beginning of a story will lie in the dust before it ends.[23]

It is springtime, war time, the time when men go out to fight, but David stays home and sends his general Joab instead to besiege Ammon's capital city. The tale is filled with sending, especially on David's part. He sends and sends and sends, beginning with the moment after the siesta on his rooftop where we view him in the opening unit (1–5). It is not in his initial lying down that David commits trespass but once he gets into action that he gets into trouble. In a few verses, he is in charge of seven action verbs: he "walked

21. Tod Linafelt, "Taking Women in Samuel: Readers/Responses/Responsibility," in *Reading Between Texts: Intertextuality and the Hebrew Bible*, ed. Danna Nolan Fewell (Louisville: Westminster John Knox, 1992), 104.

22. J. P. Fokkelman, *King David*, vol. 1 of *Narrative Art and Poetry in the Books of Samuel* (Assen: Van Gorcum, 1982), 41.

23. Greger Andersson, *Untamable Texts: Literary Studies and Narrative Theory in the Books of Samuel* (London: T&T Clark, 2009), 92.

back and forth," "saw," "sent" (2×), "took," "entered," and "lay" with her. What he saw he wanted and took. It is sordid, against the ethics and laws of his people, but it looks as if with the first action verb in which Bathsheba is in charge, "she returned," all reverts to normal. Except that it does not, for the story has hardly begun.

The opening line has put David in contrast to what men, especially "kings," usually do. He is staying in Jerusalem while his soldiers are out on the battlefield. The spring of the year, so the story goes, is "when kings go forth to battle." The word "kings" read in this way by the transmitters of the biblical text also sounds and can be read as the word "messengers," and instead of choosing between them, we shall keep the ambiguity intact, because the actions of both kings and messengers are crucial to the unfolding of events. In the end, it is a message from God that will open the eyes of the king to his wayward behavior.[24] Polzin writes, "The verse doubles back on itself in a marvelous display of narrative virtuosity: at a time when kings go forth, David did not, making a time, therefore, when messengers must go forth; at a time when messengers go forth, David, remaining in Jerusalem, sent Joab, his servants and all Israel to ravage Ammon."[25] While staying away from the battlefield, David does some "ravaging" of his own.

2 Samuel 11:2–5

2 At eventide, David arose from his couch
and walked back and forth on the roof of the palace.
And he saw a woman washing herself from the roof,
and the woman was very beautiful.
3 David sent to inquire about the woman
and they said: Is this not Bathsheba,

24. With others Alter (*The David Story*, 236n1) opts for "kings" as the most likely reading but suggests that "the ghost of 'messengers' shows through the letters of the text." Polzin (*David and the Deuteronomist*, 109–15), in an extensive discussion of both meanings, states that "one does not have to choose between kings and messengers, because both meanings hover over the verse from the start."

25. Polzin, *David and the Deuteronomist*, 111.

the daughter of Eliam,
wife of Uriah the Hittite?
4 So David sent messengers, and he took her,
and he entered her[26] and lay with her.
When she was ritually clean of her impurity,
she returned to her house.
5 Then the woman was pregnant,
and she sent and told David, and she said:
I am pregnant!

The activities are described with the greatest economy of words and thus leave a number of questions. Beginning with what we know: We are with David on the rooftop looking at a woman bathing. The fact that she is washing herself does not necessarily mean she is naked, although famous artists have painted her that way.[27] She is identified as "very beautiful," literally in Hebrew "very good of appearance" (2).[28] When David asks about her, the reply comes back in rhetorical question form ("Is this not . . . ?"), perhaps indicating that he should have known her. She is given her patronymic and marital status: daughter of Eliam and wife of Uriah, the Hittite. Both men are listed among the "heroes of David" in 2 Samuel 23:34, 39. In fact, Bathsheba is the granddaughter of Ahitophel, whom we

26. I read with the Septuagint, "he entered her," as "she came to him" is illogical in the string of verbs with a third singular masculine subject and the verb "to enter" is often used of sexual intercourse. Also, from a text-critical point of view, it is easier to understand the change from the third masculine to the third feminine than vice versa, because in the transmission a tendency to ascribe some agency to Bathsheba is more likely than a change in which the seriousness of David's actions is aggravated.

27. For an analysis of visual arts and the Bathsheba story, see J. Cheryl Exum, *Plotted, Shot, and Painted: Cultural Representations of Biblical Women* (Sheffield: Sheffield Academic, 1996), 19–53.

28. Rebekah is identified the same way in Gen 24:16 and 26:7. David himself is characterized as "ruddy with beautiful eyes and good-looking" (1 Sam 16:12). Sometimes the expression is *tov mar'eh* and sometimes *yefat mar'eh.* Later in the David narratives, his daughter Tamar will be described as "beautiful" (*yafah*), and Absalom's daughter, another Tamar, is also identified as *yefat mar'eh.*

meet later in the story. Perhaps David has been away from home too much to pay close attention to his neighbors.

The sequel to the statement about her identity is jarring, because David engages in illicit actions indicated with the piling up of three verbs: "he took her," "he entered her," and "he lay with her." This is not the way a king should treat someone's wife, least of all the wife of a trusted soldier. Where now is David's vaunted "justice and righteousness" and his desire to "show loyalty/*hesed*"? Once, David bragged to Queen Michal that he would do whatever he liked, before both God and the maids. And so he has. Once, Samuel warned the people that a king's most obvious characteristic would be *taking*, and so David has done, in a worse way than predicted by Samuel.

We note that the short segment includes a note about Bathsheba being in a state of ritual purity before she returns home in verse 4. By common consent of most interpreters, this comment refers back to her washing herself in verse 2 and relates to her menstrual period. More recent explorations of this assumption reveal that washing following menstruation is not required in biblical law, a state of impurity which is regular and "time-linked."[29] If it is intended to refer to the earlier occasion of Bathsheba's bath, the phrase is in any case oddly placed. As Frymer-Kensky points out, washing can be a part of the "impurity that comes with all sexual relations,

29. Tikva Frymer-Kensky (*Reading the Women of the Bible* [New York: Schocken, 2002], 147–48) argues the point extensively. A related but differently slanted argument is made in an article by J. D'Ror Chankin-Gould et al., "The Sanctified 'Adulteress' and Her Circumstantial Clause: Bathsheba and Self-Consecration," *JSOT* 32 (2008): 339–52. In this essay, Chankin-Gould, Derek Hutchinson, David Hilton Jackson, Tyler Mayfield, Leah Rediger Schulte, Tammi Schneider, and E. Winkelman make similar observations as Frymer-Kensky but ignore her explanation for the term. To their view, the earlier mention of "washing" may point to Bathsheba's non-Israelite origin, as the two other women who "wash" in the Bible are Pharaoh's daughter (Exod 2:5) and Ruth (3:3). Their conclusion that washing as a proactive deed is therefore only carried out by non-Israelite women seems a bit of a stretch. The point is well taken that a bath, at times, may just be a bath and in the Bible is not related to menstruation.

even licit ones."[30] Bathsheba's is thus a postcoital purification, after which she returns home.[31] Some time must go by before she sends the message about her pregnancy to David. Again Frymer-Kensky: "The mention of Bathsheba's purification, like the verbs that precede it, underline [*sic*] the unhurried, nonsecretive nature of this affair. There is no rush here. . . . Their affair is deliberate, measured, slow and obvious."[32]

As Frymer-Kensky points out, "Pregnancy changes everything."[33] Because her husband is away on the battlefield, it will expose Bathsheba as an adulteress, an offense deserving of the death penalty in the biblical text. It forces Bathsheba to do a *sending* of her own. The stakes may not be as high for David, who has set himself above the common folk with his actions, but the announcement causes him to have Uriah sent to him, upon which he goes to great lengths to make sure Uriah sleeps with his wife. But the stubborn and obviously pious Hittite refuses to do so (6–13). At Uriah's first appearance, David bombards him with three general questions about the well-being of Joab, the people, and the war. It is all shalom, shalom, shalom, while of course shalom is far to seek. When David finds out that Uriah has not followed through on his invitation to take time off with his wife at his house, he asks for the reason, and Uriah replies:

2 SAMUEL 11:11

Uriah said to David:
The Ark and Israel and Judah
are sitting in tents,

30. Frymer-Kensky, *Reading the Women of the Bible*, 147.

31. Wilda Gafney (*Womanist Midrash: A Reintroduction of Women of the Torah and of the Throne* [Louisville: Westminster John Knox, 2017], 215) also emphasizes the need of Bathsheba "to purify herself as a Torah-observant woman because of the sexual encounter, whether consensual or not." In addition, Gafney suggests, "It is also possible that she washes herself after the violation like many raped women, to cleanse herself from the touch of her violator."

32. Frymer-Kensky, *Reading the Women*, 147–48.

33. Frymer-Kensky, *Reading the Women*, 148.

and my lord Joab and my lord's servants
are encamped in the open field.
And I? Should I go into my house
to eat and drink and lie with my wife?
By your life and the life of your soul,
I would not do this thing!

The reply is telling and not telling, for we do not know what Uriah knows or what he wants. Some things are clear. The Ark is apparently out in the field with the army, and Uriah refers to Joab as his lord two times but withholds this title from David. Striking is the verb "sitting," which Uriah uses for the first three subjects. While the *sitting* of David in the opening verse of the chapter is put in direct contrast to the activity of his troops, the troops are here depicted as *sitting* on the verge of facing grave danger in contrast to the king safely ensconced in his palace.[34] Under these circumstances he will not go home to have a good time with his wife and have sexual intercourse. It is David who *lay* with Bathsheba; Uriah swears by the life and soul of David that he will not do "this thing."

David is not so quickly dissuaded and once more prevails on Uriah to stay around for at least another day, using the verbal root for *sitting* or *staying*, and Uriah *stayed* in Jerusalem in an echo of the king's lack of activity in verse 1 (12–13). He actually stays for two days, engaging in eating and drinking, proof that he has no objection to eating and drinking—only to eating and drinking with his wife. Although David manages to make him drunk, he still *lies* with the servants on his "sleeping-place," the same word for lying down used for King David before he arose and saw a beautiful woman washing herself in verse 2.[35] At the very end of the description of Uriah's activities, the narrator states emphatically, "And to his house he did not go down" (13).

34. The Hebrew *yashav* is one of the words with multiple meanings employed in the take according to Gale Yee, "Fraught with Background: Ambiguity in II Samuel 11," *Int* 42 (1988): 246.

35. The noun "sleeping place" uses the same verbal root as the verb for the lying David did with Bathsheba and Uriah refused to do.

Scene 3, Part 2: The King Who Exacted a Price (11:14–22)

There are not many places in the Bible where a character's reputation is so suddenly and effectively demolished as in 2 Samuel 11.[36]

The picture of David gets even more negative when he *sends* a letter to Joab ordering him to place Uriah at a spot in the battle where he is sure to be killed and has his victim carry the message himself (15–17). Joab does not exactly follow David's orders but in his own way sees to it that Uriah indeed dies, together with other soldiers in David's army. In this unit, verbs for death prevail, "he may be struck down," "die," "fell," "died." The first death of the story has transpired.

The report of Joab to David is told in great detail, both as Joab hypothesizes David's reaction and as the messenger actually tells it. In Joab's instructions, the messenger is to report "all the matters" of the battle and then proceed on presumed anger of the king (because some of his soldiers had died?). Joab draws on the story of Abimelek and his death at Tebes (Judg 9:53–54) in constructing the hypothetical angry reply of the king. According to that story, a woman threw down a millstone from the wall, a potential death that Abimelek considered too shameful to be remembered by. Of course, it is just such events that go down in history. Joab's series of questions can be distilled as follows: "Why did you come so close? Did you not know? Who struck down Abimelek? Was it not a woman? Why did you come so close?" The "coming too close" frames all the other questions, in the middle of which stands the death of Abimelek by the hand of a woman. It is pretty clear what Joab is aiming at. No human interaction in the episode has been particularly secret. In fact, everyone knows what went on between David and Bathsheba, including Uriah and Joab. With his questions, Joab hints at the fact that it may be dangerous to come too close to the hand from which the deathblow may arrive. *Did you not know?* It is of course Uriah who has received that blow, so there may be an embedded reproach in the speech Joab assigns to David.

36. Polzin, *David and the Deuteronomist*, 112.

It is in the end a speech that remains in the hypothetical realm (22–25). When the text observes that the messenger "came and told to David all that Joab sent him for," we hear nothing about any anger on David's side, and the messenger matter-of-factly announces Uriah's death at the end of a general report on the heavy fighting the men endured at the wall of Rabbah. David takes it laconically, telling the man to counsel Joab not to take "this thing" to heart, for in battle men die, "now this one, then that one" (25). In the words of a current U.S. politician attempting to console a woman after the death of her son in a military engagement abroad: "He knew what he signed up for."

As laconically as the story describes the encounter between David and Bathsheba, so brief is the final note in which a span of months goes by (26–27). Bathsheba, still called Uriah's wife, hears about the death of "her husband," and after the appropriate mourning period has passed, David does his final *sending* and "gathered her to his house." She is added to the harem and, as one of David's wives, in due time bears him a son. Only now the bell tolls of divine displeasure: "And evil was the thing that David had done/ in the eyes of Adonai."

David and Bathsheba

Pregnancy changes everything.[37]

So much telling, so much left unsaid. A sexual affair starts with a glance from a rooftop without a word about what either party is feeling. David is not said to be moved, or to love, and neither is Bathsheba. The only person in the story to mention feelings is Joab, but the emotions he assigns to the king are only hypothetical. Uriah, who must know what is going on and who deliberately avoids going to his wife's house, thwarting David's will, may speak sarcastically or simply be too good to be true. We do not know, for we cannot tell tone from the story. When Bathsheba sends David the message

37. Frymer-Kensky, *Reading the Women of the Bible*, 148.

of her pregnancy, for example, we can only guess at her intentions. Does she mean to say, "I am pregnant, my darling," or, "I am pregnant, you bastard"?[38] Her words, "I am pregnant" (*harah anokhi*) are spoken by only one other woman in the Bible. Tamar utters them, in a reversed order, to her father-in-law Judah who impregnated her (Gen 38:25). There are other links with the Tamar-Judah story to which we will return.

I have assigned the "entering" to David in verse 4, but it is possible that the original reading is that "she came to him," as the Masoretic Text has it, which assigns her at least one active verb in a context where she can have little say in what happens to her. The power differential between David and Bathsheba is simply too great to assign her blame.[39] Frymer-Kensky writes, "To say that Bathsheba set out to entice the king is to say that violated women were 'asking for it' because they smiled, wore tight clothes or went to a club." Alexander Abasili argues that we cannot assign the category "rape" to David's act—although he judges David to bear the "lion's share of the consequences of the sexual transgression" and exonerates Bathsheba from any complicity—because there is too great a distance between the "biblical concept of rape and the contemporary notion." I understand his argument to assert that the biblical

38. Antony F. Campbell, S.J., *2 Samuel*, FOTL 8 (Grand Rapids: Eerdmans, 2005), 115. For an overview of the multiple questions raised by the story, see Campbell, 113–17.

39. This fact has not prevented commentators from drawing the inference, particularly based on this one verb, that Bathsheba was a "willing and equal partner to the events which transpire" (Randall C. Bailey, *David in Love and War: The Pursuit of Power in 2 Samuel 10–12* [Sheffield: Sheffield Academic, 2009], 88). Alter (*The David Story*, 251n4) is of the opinion that Bathsheba's later behavior in regard to the succession to David's throne shows someone "who has her eye on the main chance, and it is possible that opportunism, not merely passive submission, explains her behavior here as well." Lillian Klein ("Bathsheba Revealed," in *Samuel and Kings*, ed. Athalya Brenner, *A Feminist Companion to the Bible*, Second Series [Sheffield: Sheffield Academic, 2000], 49) argues, "The use of 'come,' with its connotations of sexuality, insinuates Bathsheba's complicity in sexual adventure." Klein assigns to Bathsheba the desire to bear sons, which drives her to bathe within sight of the king "with the hope of seducing King David into 'seducing' her" (53).

writers did not consider the occasion rape because they used none of the vocabulary and verbal categories that would identify it as such.[40] Argument from absence of terms is, however, tenuous, and it is by no means clear in what light the biblical storytellers and collectors viewed the position of Bathsheba. Moreover, as interpreters who have a stake in this text as more than simply ancient literature, we are required to evaluate characters and their behavior. Antony Campbell argues, "Bathsheba is not reported as consenting; she is innocent until alleged in the narrative to have consented [cf. 1 Sam 25:41–42]. . . . Fidelity to the text suggests the charge should be rape."[41] Wil Gafney writes, "He sees her, he sends for her, and has sex with her without her consent. He rapes her."[42] Moreover, her becoming pregnant by a man other than her husband is a capital offense and could cost her life. In hindsight, then, Uriah, who is not willing to play the part of husband and father-to-be of his wife's child, is perhaps also less than admirable in his refusal to go home, if he knows of the situation. As Frymer-Kensky points out, it is precisely from her husband that Bathsheba is in danger. "Uriah is a man of piety. And a man with a strict sense of justice. . . . Such a man can be dangerous."[43]

Compared to Bathsheba, David's actions are without doubt wicked. His steep decline from at least the semblance of rectitude to depravity, whether judged by ancient or modern standards, is hard to fathom, especially for one who is said to uphold "justice and righteousness" and is eager to practice "loyalty." First, Bathsheba's identity is known to him, which is somewhat unusual for a woman in the Bible, provided with both her husband's name and her father's. Uriah is listed in chapter 23 as one of David's companions, as is Bathsheba's father Eliam, who is the son of Ahitophel (2 Sam 23:34, 39). Her link with these three men provides her with stand-

40. Alexander Izuchukwu Abasili, "Was It Rape? The David and Bathsheba Pericope Re-examined," *VT* 61 (2011): 14.

41. Campbell, *2 Samuel*, 104. Campbell decides in the end that "Bathsheba's person, or her relationship to Uriah, and in light of the text probably both, were violated."

42. Gafney, *Womanist Midrash*, 215.

43. Frymer-Kensky, *Reading the Women of the Bible*, 149, 151.

ing in the community. If there is some question about whether her origin is Israelite or Hittite like her husband's, there is no question that she lives in adherence to Israel's customs and laws, as is clear from her action of "cleansing herself" (11:4). Both her husband and father are among David's heroes—that is to say, his companions from the early days. Her grandfather Ahitophel is one of the most trusted royal counselors of the time. Uriah is a member of an indigenous Canaanite group according to the Bible, among the list of inhabitants proscribed by the Deuteronomic text (Deut 7:1; 20:17; cf. Exod 23:28). Uriah is always listed as "the Hittite" and thus lives in Israel as a *stranger*, one who derives his ancestry from elsewhere and lives as a member of the community, and to go by his speech, he is a faithful member. The category of *stranger* in the Bible is a particularly protected one (see p. 218n8 above), and the underhanded and vicious way in which David orchestrates his death, scandalous under any circumstances, becomes especially odious in light of Uriah's status.

Uriah refuses David's invitation to go home to his wife, saying he will not do "this thing" (11:11); David counsels Joab not to let "this thing [i.e., the death of Uriah, a man with whom Joab also must be acquainted] be evil in his eyes," for that is just the way it goes in war. When all is said and done, however, "this thing" is indeed evil in the eyes of someone. It has caused displeasure in the eyes of Adonai. We will encounter more references to "this thing" in what follows. Has God chosen a new king Bramble, whose presence provides no shelter but rather harm and devastation? (cf. Judg 9:7–21).

Act I, Scene 4: Death of a Son I (2 Samuel 12)

Who is this man before and who is he afterwards?[44]

The fallout from the mischief perpetrated in the matter of Bathsheba and Uriah develops in three stages. First, the prophet Nathan is

44. Goldingay, *Men Behaving Badly*, 94.

sent by God with a story, which has the effect of David condemning himself (1–7). Next, the prophet launches into a speech condemning David in God's name for his transgressions and announcing future consequences (8–14). Third, Bathsheba and David's child falls ill and dies, followed by the birth of another son (15–25). A final section describes the capture of Rabbah, initiated by Joab and completed under David's leadership (26–31)

Scene 4, Part 1: A Rich Man and a Lamb (2 Samuel 12:1–15)

David leaps into the gap between the rich man and the poor man in the story.[45]

The ending of the David-Bathsheba-Uriah affair sets up expectations that more is to follow, so the sending that takes place on God's behalf comes as no surprise. The person sent is Nathan, who appears throughout the scene by his name only, except for the final verse, where the reference is "Nathan the prophet" (25). Nathan arrives at the palace with a story.

2 SAMUEL 12:1–4

1 Adonai sent Nathan to David,
and he came to him and said to him:
Two men were in a certain city,
one rich and one poor.
2 The rich one had flocks, and cattle very many.
3 And the poor one had nothing
but one small ewe lamb he had bought.
He kept it alive, and it grew up with him
together with his children.
From his bite it ate,
from his cup it drank,

45. Jonathan Kruschwitz, "2 Samuel 12:1–15: How (Not) to Read a Parable," *RevExp* 109 (2012): 253–59.

in his lap it lay down;
it was to him like a daughter.

4 Then came a wanderer to the rich man,
and he thought it a pity to take from his flock and cattle
to prepare a meal for the one who came to him.
He took the ewe lamb of the poor man
and prepared it for the traveler who came to him.[46]

A short story, artfully told, paints a vivid scene of vast differences between rich and poor: "flocks, much cattle" versus "nothing." Yet the poor man has *something*, albeit something insignificant, small and female. All the same, it is treasured and cherished "like a daughter." The rich man, greedy after the manner of the rich everywhere, "took" precisely that small treasure and "prepared it." In between the rich man and the poor one is a wanderer, identified also as a *traveler*.[47]

Campbell points to the discrepancy between the events that have transpired and the homespun nature of the story: "David is guilty of sex with a married woman and of having her husband

46. I understand Nathan's story to be a parable, a short story reflecting a recognizable human social context which demands a judgment from the listener. It is true that the presence of the ewe lamb could draw the tale closer to the category of a fable, yet there is nothing of the "fabulous" in the story, no speaking plants or animals as there are in Jotham's fable for example (Judg 9:8–15; see van Wijk-Bos, *The End of the Beginning*, 246–48). The story unfolds as it *could* have happened in a human context. A parable contains an implied or explicit question. It is possible that in the case of Nathan and David, David's judgment interrupts the posing of a direct question.

47. As Polzin (*David and the Deuteronomist*, 121) points out, "All the players in the parable, rich man, poor man, wayfarer, and lamb, are designated by words that are rarely used in the History: ewe lamb . . . occurs only here, the words for the traveler (two different ones in Hebrew) are rare in form, and the words for 'rich' and 'poor' are rare in the History." See also Jeremy Schipper, "Did David Overinterpret Nathan's Parable in 2 Samuel 12:1–6?" *JBL* 126 (2007): 383–407, esp. 385.

murdered. Nathan's parable is about sheep stealing in a particularly obnoxious set of circumstances."[48] Of course, that may just be the reason David falls for it and roundly condemns the rich man's actions, for as soon as Nathan is finished (or perhaps even before he is finished), David declares the perpetrator of the theft "a child of death" because "he did *this thing* and had no pity!" (5).[49]

The ploy used by Nathan, or God, is easy to follow, and quite expectedly David falls for it, whether he heard the tale as a parable that demanded a judgment or indeed as a case in which he was expected to pronounce judgment.[50] David is the one who has done the *taking*; he is the rich man. David has pronounced the death penalty and restitution, and "this thing" finally comes to rest at David's door when Nathan utters the words "you are the man" (7). Did David identify the guilty party in the story as a specific person, for example Joab, the one who was indirectly responsible for Uriah's murder? Or did he hear the story as unconnected to his own situation? Is he thinking that Nathan's story is asking for a solution as to the identity of the rich man? If he understood the culprit to be Joab, and understood the story to be about recent events, did he suppose himself to be the traveler? Just an innocent bystander as he has declared himself to be

48. Campbell, *2 Samuel*, 116.

49. The verb here is *hamal*, literally "to spare," a verb that resonates in the story of Saul as something he did against the will of Adonai in the victory over Amalek (1 Sam 15:3, 9, 15). There, Saul is guilty of "sparing," which he was commanded not to do, while here David has not spared the ones he ought to have protected.

50. Jeremy Schipper ("Did David Overinterpret?" 387–88; *Parables and Conflict in the Hebrew Bible* [Cambridge: Cambridge University Press, 2009], 41–56) makes a strong case for David recognizing the story as a parable and reacting to it because he identifies himself with the traveler and Joab, the immediate cause of Uriah's death, with the rich man. I disagree with Fokkelman (*Throne and City*, vol. 3 of *Narrative Art and Poetry in the Books of Samuel* [Assen: Van Gorcum, 1990], 79) who judges the David who pronounces judgment to be "congenial": "David is a good listener who puts his heart into the matter, gets very involved and feels pity." Any perpetrator of injustice may find it quite easy to pronounce negative judgment on another person who commits a trespass.

on previous occasions when he could be implicated?[51] Who is the lamb? The word "daughter" (*bat*) leads one to think of Bathsheba; but it was not Bathsheba who was killed. Was Uriah the lamb, who *ate* and *drank* and *lay down* in *the lap* of Bathsheba? Bathsheba was not killed, but her life was turned upside down, her previous identity ruined, and her husband killed. If we consider the story from the point of view of who benefits the most, the traveler is implicated also. Rich man or traveler, David is the man. As Schipper points out: "Nathan does not focus on one act over the other. Rather, his accusation focuses on how David destroyed Uriah and Bathsheba's family unit."[52]

In his prophetic speech, beginning with "so says Adonai," it is precisely the destruction of a house for which David is taken to task (7–14). Both the *striking down* of Uriah and the *taking* of his wife for himself constitute evil in the eyes of Adonai. This evil will beget evil for the *house* of David. The second half of Nathan's speech (11–14) announces the unraveling of David's house to come. *This thing* that David has done secretly, thinking no one would find out—*taking* and *murdering*—will be done to him openly. When he confesses his sin, the word is that God has "caused his sin to pass"—that is to say, it will *pass him by.* Instead, others in David's house will bear the repercussions of what he has done: the wives God *gave* in David's lap will be *taken* by another (8–12). The child of David and Bathsheba, here still called "the wife of Uriah" (15), will be the *child of death,* a sentence pronounced by David himself. Unsaid, but surely implied, is the fall of the houses of Israel and Judah.

Scene 4, Part 2: A Child of Death (2 Samuel 12:16–31)

By parable and act, God and Nathan have taught David about the limitation of the right of kings.[53]

51. We can think, for example, about David distancing himself from Abner and Ishboshet's murders (2 Sam 3:32–39; 4:10–12).

52. Schipper, *Parables and Conflict*, 52.

53. Frymer-Kensky, *Reading the Women of the Bible*, 156.

David struck innocent Uriah, and God strikes the child (15). One may wonder who is better off between the two, the father or the child. The illness and death of the infant follow in some detail, partly viewed from the perspective of the servants (15–23). David engages in prayer, a rare occurrence in the Court History. No eating and drinking or *lying down* with his wife for this husband and father, but fasting, and spending the night *lying* on the ground (16). When the servants fear to tell him the child has died, he surmises the truth, which they verify on his inquiry. Two verses, 18 and 19, sound the death knell: "the child died," "the child was dead," "the boy is dead," "is the boy dead," "dead." Upon hearing the news, David resumes his normal activities, which stuns the servants and causes them to question him, raising once again the issue of *this thing* in the narrative: "What is this thing you have done?" (12:21). His matter-of-fact reply is that there was still a chance to save the life of the child while it lived, but there is no longer need for prayer now that this fragile possibility is gone.

2 Samuel 12:22–23

22 He said: As long as the child was alive,
I fasted and wept,
for I thought: Who knows,
Adonai may repent,
and the child will live.
23 Now that he is dead,
why should I fast?
Can I bring him back again?
I am going to him,
and he will not come back to me.

The child's life and his death are clamped between David's fasting and weeping on the chance of God repenting and David's stark acknowledgment of his death. There is no reason to believe that David felt no sorrow just because it is not mentioned. David's words after his child dies are much like those of Achilles in Homer's *Iliad* when he counsels Priam not to grieve his son overmuch because he will not raise him from the dead; David's reflection may thus be part of a generally shared perspective on death in the ancient world.[54] The story is everywhere, in Gale Yee's terms, a "stripped down narrative" in which the "psychological motivations of the characters" are not discussed. It is this very ambiguity which draws the reader into its "fictive world."[55] A recognition that David is not the only parent deprived of a child is provided with the note that David "comforted Bathsheba," now referred to as "his wife" (24). There is also no reason to doubt David's remorse, nor his prayer, which counts on the possibility of God's repentance (cf. Joel 2:14; Jonah 1:6; 3:9). This is the last occasion in the Court History when David is said to pray, and although he will make reference to Adonai, there is no evidence in this material of the earlier easy-sounding discourse between the two (cf. 1 Sam 23:2; 30:8; 2 Sam 2:1; 5:19, 23).[56]

After the birth of a new son, one beloved by Adonai—Solomon—the text returns to the capture of Rabbah, which is still to be completed (26–31). The events at Rabbah are best understood as a literary frame around David's personal life rather than taking place in chronological time, so that the war without and the war within are interwoven in the story. Capture of the city is left to David, who has to be called by Joab to take care of it so it will be done in his lord's name rather than his own (28). One last *sending* of messengers takes place, and the entire episode ends on a positive note: a new child born and the enemy city captured, its inhabitants put to hard labor. We do not miss the point that a report of David's destruction of a family, constituting its own kind of *plunder*, ends in his *plundering* a city. "And the plunder he brought out from the city was very great" (30).

54. "For nothing will you achieve by grieving for your son, nor will you raise him up; fresh woes will find you soon enough" (*Iliad*, 24.550–51, translation mine). We note that in the same section of the *Iliad*, Achilles sheds bitter tears over Patroklos' death. In regard to David's reactions to the child's death, there is no reason to assume David is "cool and calculating," as suggested by Ackerman ("Knowing Good and Evil," 45), even if he broke behavioral norms.

55. Gale A. Yee, "Fraught with Background," 246, 252. Alter (*The David Story*, 262n23) remarks on the "stark simplicity" of David's words, which reveal a "vulnerable David."

56. Although the exclamation in 2 Sam 15:31 is identified by many scholars as prayer, I do not characterize it as such. See p. 312 below.

Act II: A House Divided (2 Samuel 13–14)

One of the major themes in the stories of David and his family is precisely the unavoidable link between public and private life within a ruling family.[57]

The mayhem about to overcome David´s house has only just begun. Chapter 13 tells of the violation of David´s daughter Tamar by her half-brother Amnon, her brother Absalom's subsequent hatred of Amnon, and the resulting murder. This complex tale begins the story of Absalom's alienation not only from his brother but also from his father. It takes a double intervention, engineered by Joab in chapter 14, to bring the two together in a seeming reconciliation. In both chapters, women take a leading role, albeit in very different ways.

Act II, Scene 1: Brother against Sister (2 Samuel 13:1–22)[58]

Rescue me from those who do evil and from men of blood save me. (Ps 59:3[2])[59]

Who will protect sister wisdom from the loose man, symbolized not by a foreigner but by her very own brother?[60]

As much as emotions were left out of the previous episode, they are emphatically present in the story of Tamar's rape by her brother

57. Jo Ann Hackett, *1 and 2 Samuel*, The Women's Bible Commentary Expanded Edition, edited by Carol A. Newsome and Sharon H. Ringe (Louisville: Westminster John Knox, 1998), 101.

58. For detailed analyses of this story, see Shimon Bar-Efrat, *Narrative Art in the Bible* (Sheffield: Almond, 1989), 239–81; Frymer-Kensky, *Reading the Women of the Bible*, 157–69; van Wijk-Bos, *Reading Samuel*, 201–6.

59. Translation by Elana Keppel Levy, "Impact" (senior sermon preached February 2, 2014, at Louisville Presbyterian Theological Seminary's Caldwell Chapel). Used with permission.

60. Phyllis Trible, *Texts of Terror: Literary Feminist Readings of Biblical Narratives* (Philadelphia: Fortress, 1984), 57.

Amnon. The entire account begins with the statement that Amnon "loved" his sister Tamar and continues with expressions that emphasize distress on account of this love.

2 SAMUEL 13:1–2

1 It happened after this—
Absalom, David's son, had a beautiful sister.
Her name was Tamar,
and Amnon, David's son, loved her.
2 Amnon was so distressed
that he became ill on account of Tamar his sister,
for she was a virgin,
and it seemed impossible in the eyes of Amnon
to do something to her.

It does not sound like such a bad beginning. Between Absalom and Amnon there is a beautiful sister sharing a mother with Absalom and only a father with Amnon. Lovesickness is possible for anyone, and love between a brother and a half-sister, though by Levitical law not permissible (Lev 18:9, 11), may be allowed by royal fiat according to Tamar (13). The Song of Solomon, a poem that celebrates love between a woman and a man, speaks of love and of its sickness (Song 2:5; 5:8). In fact, the vocabulary of the Song has seeped into the Tamar and Amnon story in other places. *Sister* or *my sister* is part of the Song's love language (Song 4:9, 10, 12; 5:1, 2; 8:8), and out of the ten times this word appears in the books of Samuel, nine are in this chapter. Food as comfort for lovesickness is appealed to in Song of Solomon 2:5. The "heart-cakes" Tamar prepares for Amnon (*levivot*) are reminiscent of the phrase "you have ravished my *heart,* my sister bride" (*libbavtini ahoti kallah*) in Song of Solomon 4:9. But all celebration of love, all comfort of love, all its glorious song is turned into cries and ashes of mourning in the tale of Tamar and Amnon.

Nothing goes as might be expected in a love story. Tamar is caught between powerful men: the cousin who plots how to lure her to Amnon's side (3–5), the father who acts as her procurer

(6–7), the brother who rapes her (14), and the other brother who silences her (20). Tamar is a young woman who visits a friend, a relative, with a plateful of food because he is not feeling well, then gets violated for her efforts and thrown off the premises because her rapist loathes her as much as he first lusted for her. Of all the sad stories in the Historical Books, this is one of the saddest; of the stories about outrageous violence against women, one of the most outrageous. Echoes are here of the Joseph narratives—"Come lie with me" (11; cf. Gen 39:7), the "ornamented tunic" (18, 19; cf. Gen 37:3)—and of the Dinah account—"he abused her" (14; cf. Gen 34:2). There are echoes of those who called "outrage/disgrace" (*nevalah*)—Dinah and the violated concubine in Judges (Gen 34:7; Judg 19:23, 24; 1 Sam 25:25)—in the text's "Do not commit this disgrace!" (12). There are echoes, finally, of all who have cried out under crushing, shameful, unbearable violence against body and mind (19; cf. Exod 2:23). Tamar is not a silent victim. She protests Amnon's invitation to "lie down" with him, emphatically refusing ("No . . . do not . . . such is not done . . . do not do," 12), and then once again stammering, "Do not. . ." when he orders her to leave (16). Even in her distress, her language is reasonable, calling what he proposes a disgrace which "is not done in Israel" (12), arguing that she would have nowhere to go with her shame and urging him to speak to the king, whose decision could decide things in their favor (13). In the end, when she is forced to leave, she does not go in silence.

2 Samuel 13:18–19

18 She wore an ornamented tunic,
for the virgin daughters of the king
were dressed in such robes.
His attendant led her outside
and closed the door behind her.
19 Tamar put ashes on her head,
and the ornamented tunic that she wore, she tore.
Then she put her hand on her head,
and went about crying aloud.

Only Joseph and Tamar are said to wear the type of garment mentioned here, a *ketonet passim.* As Alter observes, "Tamar's tunic may well be blood stained too," like Joseph's (Gen 37:31–33).[61] Her crying is like the ones who cry out to God under their burden, like the people of Israel in Egypt and under their oppressors in the time of the judges, who expect God to hear them (Exod 2:23; Judg 3:9, 15; 6:6, 7; 10:10). Frymer-Kensky points to the necessity of her crying out. "Tamar needs the world to know that she is a victim. . . . A girl who cries out when she is attacked is considered innocent of sexual wrongdoing (Deut 22:24)." She may have cried "rape!" or "woe" or "somebody do something!"[62]

And then there is someone who turns up just at the right moment, who does hear her and immediately discerns what has gone wrong. Her brother Absalom, the first person who appeared on the stage in this scene, asks, "Has your brother Amnon been with you?" That he has this information testifies to the fact that Amnon's besotted state was known in the palace and that no one has done anything to protect Tamar from her fate. Her crying out is the last we hear from her, for Absalom does what those in the circle of a raped woman do best, be they friend or family: He shushes her. What was the rest of her life like? The text states that she "stayed and was desolate in the house of Absalom her brother" (20).

Sexual violence from a friend, an acquaintance, a lover is as common today as it was in the past. One person who experienced it in our world describes the aftermath like this:

> For me, to be raped was to be powerless, helpless and to be made to feel utterly alone. Well-intentioned friends weren't equipped to be supportive for as long as I needed them. People didn't know what to say so they said nothing at all; they avoided me, perhaps for fear of saying the wrong thing. . . . Their silence echoed in my mind. I felt that I didn't fit in the world that I knew anymore. I could never again be the person that I was before—the person who had never been raped, the

61. Alter, *The David Story*, 270n18.

62. Frymer-Kensky, *Reading the Women of the Bible*, 165–66.

> person who had held an unknown innocence and lightness. My rapists made themselves powerful and I thought that they stole my name, my very self, my ability to be whole.[63]

This or something like this is what Tamar may have felt about "this thing," which her brother Absalom tells her "not to take to heart" (20) and about which David is incensed but refuses to do anything. A final note remarks on the hatred of Absalom against Amnon because he raped his sister. The violation of Tamar has become something to fight about between men.

Act II, Scene 2: Death of a Son II (2 Samuel 13:23–39)

When Absalom finally takes matters into his own hands two years later, it is not because he was impatient with the slow turning of the wheels of his father's justice but rather with the fact that the wheels of his father's justice were not turning at all.[64]

This scene begins and ends with a time marker, two years and three years, a typical feature in the account leading up to Absalom's rebellion (cf. 14:28). Absalom waits two years, perhaps for his father to do something, perhaps to work on a perfect plan, and evidently does a slow burn, for his hatred of Amnon has not gone away. The plan he comes up with does not seem very clever or foolproof, but it works. First, he plans a sheep-shearing event, a festive occasion to which he invites his father (23–25). When the king declines, Absalom urges him to let family accompany him. Apparently, such an affair needs the king's permission, perhaps a sign that David is keeping a tight(er) rein on his sons. In this case, Absalom asks for his brother, Amnon, which puzzles the king ("Why should he go with you?" 26), but in the end he sends both Amnon and "all the sons of the king." The

63. Elana Keppel Levy, "Impact" (senior sermon preached February 2, 2014, at Louisville Presbyterian Theological Seminary's Caldwell Chapel). Quoted with the author's permission.

64. Smith, *The Fate of Justice and Righteousness*, 154.

phrase "all the sons of the king" will occur like a refrain throughout the chapter (27, 29, 30, 33).

Once at the feast, Absalom, apparently not much of a soldier himself, orders his servants to assassinate Amnon while he is in his cups (28). Although not a commander, Absalom orders like a commander in the field (cf. Josh 10:25; 1 Sam 4:9; 2 Sam 10:12), encouraging his servants to "be strong and valiant," using almost the exact words his father once employed with his subjects-to-be in Jabesh Gilead (2 Sam 2:7). Once the deed is done, "all the sons of the king" flee the scene of slaughter (29). In the meantime, David has not yet seen any of his sons come back and receives a report that Absalom has struck down "all the sons of the king," news that sends him and his servants into immediate mourning.

Once again, David's nephew Jonadab pops up, this time with the "good" news that only Amnon is dead (32–33). The unit resounds with the word "dead," as it once did when the child of David and Bathsheba died: "they put to death," "dead," "dead," "dead." Counting Uriah, three deaths have been the consequence of adultery and rape. Even when the "sons of the king" get to their father, there is copious weeping. The entire episode, with Absalom having safely fled to his mother's home country, Geshur, ends with the word "dead." David is in mourning, grieving the death of Amnon, perhaps angry with Absalom but also mourning his absence, for he has in fact lost two of his sons.[65] The passive role of David throughout is remarkable. He has taken no action in the matter of Amnon raping his sister and takes no action against Absalom. He mostly sits and waits.

65. Enigmatic Hebrew in the last lines of the chapter does not make it entirely clear for whom David mourns or if he intends to retrieve Absalom or hunt him down. Scholars disagree on how to translate 13:37–38. Patricia Willey ("The Importunate Woman of Tekoa and How She Got Her Way," in *Reading Between Texts: Intertextuality and the Hebrew Bible*, ed. Danna Nolan Fewell [Louisville: Westminster John Knox, 1992], 117) observes that the words here are multivalent and that perhaps even the king was not sure whom he mourned.

Act II, Scene 3: A Woman from Tekoa and Her Story (2 Samuel 14:1–20)

Unlike Nathan, the woman has to coax a balky customer.[66]

Just as the violence involving David, Bathsheba, and Uriah elicited a story, so the violence of the rape of Tamar and murder of Amnon brings a story in its wake. Chapter 14 consists for the most part of discourse, set in motion not by God but by David's general, Joab. Where Nathan's motives as God's spokesperson were clear, however, motivations behind words and actions in this chapter are murkier. It all begins with the statement that "Joab, the son of Tseruyah, knew that the heart of the king was upon Absalom" (1).[67] What exactly does Joab know? The sentence about the "heart of the king" lacks a verb, and the preposition "upon" (*al*) is ambiguous, open to both positive and negative interpretations. Is Joab afraid that his lord will go after Absalom and lose another of his sons? Is he aware that the king longs for the presence of his son? In the next lines, he reportedly sends a woman from Tekoa to David with specific instructions about her dress—like someone "mourning for many days over a dead one," mentioning the word for mourning three times—and gives her words to tell, but we do not know what they are (2–3). Joab may have given her broad outlines for her presentation, but it is unlikely that he could foresee all the king's replies, so the woman must have been able to improvise.

The woman is called "wise," one of two women to be given this adjective in the Samuel texts, both appearing in connection with Joab (see 20:16). "Wise" and "wisdom" are complex concepts in the ancient world, and in the Bible deal with the art of living together with the related ideas "understanding" and "insight." True wisdom

66. Willey, "The Importunate Woman of Tekoa," 123.

67. The Hebrew word *al*, a preposition that will recur with regularity and at key moments in the chapter, lends itself to ambiguity. In vv. 1, 8 and 13 it is not clear if the word means "concerning" or "against." See Polzin, *David and the Deuteronomist*, 139.

helps one to get along, to avoid major pitfalls or follies in life and human interactions, and to be successful. It comes about through close observation of what transpires in human relationships, conversation, and so on, as well as in nature. Joab may have viewed David's concerns with Absalom, whatever their precise nature, as an unhealthy obsession, and the Tekoite becomes the medium to restore family relations so that the king can once again become an effective ruler. Women may have been special transmitters of the type of wisdom needed in this case.[68]

The woman of Tekoa goes unnamed in the story but has a great deal to say, and so becomes one of the "transition-makers and connectors," in the terms used by Susan Niditch (see p. 12n11 above).[69] She poses as a widow and may well be one, but her antecedents are not given, and she thus stands alone, without a patronymic and with only the reference to a location, like the shaman of Endor. In her story, she is a victim of violence, but the fact that Joab thinks she is the right person to send to the king suggests she is someone of standing in her community. In any case, she is portrayed as having enough status to approach the king on her own, with Joab staying in the shadows.

The story she brings to David is a family story of violence and alienation, one in which a widow loses a son to another—she mentions "dead" and "death" three times in her opening lines—and in which more violence threatens around the corner (5–7). Her concerns are that her remaining son will be killed, the inheritance may go to other members of the clan, and "the name" of her husband will be blotted out.[70] There are at least three potential victims in the case

68. Claudia Camp ("The Wise Women of 2 Samuel: A Role Model for Women in Early Israel?" *CBQ* 43 [1981]: 14) argues that together with the woman of Abel Beth-Ma'acah in 2 Sam 20:16–22, the wise woman of Tekoa represents a "significant political role available to women" in this period of ancient Israel's history.

69. Niditch, *War in the Hebrew Bible: A Study in the Ethics of Violence* (Oxford: Oxford University Press, 1993), 135.

70. I agree that her mention of a "divine inheritance" (14:16) refers to alienation of the ancestral heritage, even if the Hebrew word *elohim* is translated as usual. Theodore J. Lewis ("The Ancestral Estate [*nahalat elohim*] in

she presents: her remaining son, her dead husband, and of course herself. A widow without sons and without resources might as well be dead. David responds obligingly but vaguely, and she goes on to speak at greater length (9–11). The ideal king provides "justice" for the unfortunate and saves "the needy" (Ps 72:4). Standing before David is a widow, one who from her deprived position appeals to him for help. So, she keeps pushing the king to make a stronger commitment, as he finally does, promising that her surviving son will not die (11). Before he pledges that "not a hair of your son's head will fall to the ground" (11), the woman makes sure he invokes the name of Adonai—in other words, that he takes an oath on the matter.[71] Now is the moment for the woman to approach the issue at hand. The king has taken an oath that no harm will come to the surviving son, but what has happened to his own son who committed fratricide? The lines in the Hebrew original are particularly difficult in this section, perhaps a testimony to the woman's hesitancy in speaking of the king's guilt.

2 Samuel 14:16," *JBL* 110 [1991]: 597–612) argues for the translation of *elohim* as ancestors. This reference to a divine estate is noteworthy, because David, when he is outside Israel, is in his own words "driven out from the inheritance of Adonai" (1 Sam 26:19). The designation of the people as the "inheritance of Adonai" occurs also in the anointing of Saul (1 Sam 10:1). In Deuteronomic usage, the word *nahalah* ("inheritance") can refer to the entire land or a part thereof, a share, or to the people so granted or designated by Adonai. See, for example, Deut 4:20, 21; 9:26, 29; 10:9. In Joshua, the reference is usually to land, either as a whole or a specific assigned part (Josh 11:23; 13:6, 7, 8, 14, 23, 28, 33). See, van Wijk-Bos, *The End of the Beginning*, pp. 144, 312. *Nahalah* occurs in Samuel only six times, always with the connection to Adonai (here "God"), apart from one instance with a connection to David (2 Sam 20:1; cf. 1 Kgs 12:16).

71. Jacob Hoftijzer ("David and the Tekoite Woman," *VT* 20 [1970]: 428) argues that an oath such as the king takes for a case which may be fictitious would be binding for what set the story in motion, i.e., Absalom's exile. Because David's initial responses are vague, the woman induces him "to confirm the last one on oath" (14:11). Hoftijzer judges the tale far from being about "a talkative and rambling woman to whom the king shows extraordinary leniency"; rather, it shows her capable of building her case step by step (444).

2 SAMUEL 14:13–14

13 The woman said:
Why have you devised in this against the people of God?
For in speaking this thing, the king is like a guilty one
in that the king has not brought back his banished one.[72]
14 For we will surely die like water poured on the ground,
which will not be gathered up,
and God will not restore life.[73]
And he will devise a plan so as not to banish from him a banished one.[74]

Her language is bold and accusatory. She accuses the king of guilt against God's people—that is, of harming the entire body politic by his refusal to "bring back" the "banished one"—making reference to banishment three times in two sentences.[75] She also accuses the

72. Alter (*The David Story*, 278n13) suggests and I agree that the awkwardness of the language is a sign of the woman's inability to declare the king guilty outright. Compare Nathan's "You are the man."

73. Literally, the phrase is, "God does not lift (a) life." Scholars are divided on its meaning. The most sensible solution seems to me the one offered by Richard Smith (*The Fate of Justice and Righteousness*, 172) who argues that the phrase expresses the same thought as the one of the proverb, i.e., that God does not restore life. The last two lines of v. 14 would thus express the thought that "God does not bring back the dead, but he does bring back exiles."

74. With this translation, I take the line about God not restoring life to be the end of the phrase beginning with "we will surely die." But see Hoftijzer ("David and the Tekoite Woman," 437) who understands the line as a rhetorical question, rendering the translation, "Will not God dedicate himself to seeing that a banished one does not remain exiled from him?"

75. There are two verbs used (one extremely rare, only occurring elsewhere in Jer 23:12) for the word here translated "banished." In Jer 23, it refers to the people who are about to be "driven out." The other root is more frequent, used also in the prophetic context for the people who are to "be scattered/become outcast." Absalom was not exactly driven out by David but had caused his own banishment, becoming an outcast. The verbs are interesting in that they do not point to the usual root for "exile" (*galah*) but to the action of God against God's people on account of their wrongdoing. Jeremiah, for example

king of going "against the people of God" in this matter. What she says next is difficult to decipher, not so much in the meaning of the words as in their intention. Hoftijzer understands the opening lines of verse 14 as a statement about the result of the king's refusal to recall Absalom rather than as a proverb. In other words, the king's action or inaction vis-à-vis Absalom has repercussions beyond the family. If the king does not let Absalom return, he will be guilty, but punishment will likely fall on the people, who may be targets of death, something that will be final since God does not bring the dead back to life.[76] If it is a proverb, it could be to state that indeed everyone dies, but God would surely not let someone die in exile.[77] Even though the lines are, in Alter's words, "knotty and oblique,"[78] the triple reference to "the banished one" probably alerts king David to the real subject of the case. We note that the Tekoite has set the king's *devising* in opposition to God's *devising.* In the face of the king's silence following her accusation (there is no "I have sinned against Adonai" here), the Tekoite is forced to push on. She shifts her recital to raising the motivation for her approach to the king, mentioning that in this case she would also have been victimized and that the king is the right person to "rescue" her. She refers to herself twice as "your maid" (15–16), putting herself in the company

---

speaks for the most part to the "scattering" or "driving away" of the people by God (Jer 8:3; 16:15; 23:3, 8; 27:10; 29:14).

76. Hoftijzer, *David and the Tekoite,* 432–33. Hoftijzer argues that in the expression *mot namut,* "we will surely die," the infinitive absolute of "die" followed by a verbal form of the same root, the issue is virtually always untimely death and in most cases a punishment for the sins of others. The people will thus have to die "an untimely death because they will be punished for the king's sin."

77. The use of a proverb regarding death, far from being a trite or obvious truth, underscores her authority according to Camp ("The Wise Women," 19–20): "A saying . . . is employed by a wise person for a particular purpose, possibly to educate another (which always involves some implicit directing as to what is 'right' or 'wrong'), or, as in this case, to exert influence over another's action in a way that carries some authority." Camp identifies the saying by the wise woman of Tekoa as a "shining example of a proverb 'in action.'"

78. Alter, *The David Story,* 278n14.

of Hannah, Abigail, and the wise woman of Abel (1 Sam 1:11, 16; 25:24, 25, 28, 31, 41; 2 Sam 20:17).[79]

The king does not address the issue of the woman's welfare but turns unexpectedly to the question whether Joab is behind all this (18–20). The very abrupt nature of the turnaround on David's part most likely arises because he has been ruminating on Absalom's situation and Joab's likely interference for a while. He may have been well aware of Joab's disapproval of his treatment of Absalom. When the Tekoite allows that indeed Joab is the one who "did this thing" in order to "turn the thing around" (20), she finishes her discourse with a final flourish of flattery to the king, complimenting him especially on his wisdom.

A number of questions remain: What does the story imply by Joab's need to send someone rather than approaching the king directly? Is there some alienation between the two? If so, what is the issue about which they disagree? Is it David's inaction in response to the rape of his daughter—his neglect in calling Amnon to account? Is it David's ignoring the tension between Amnon and Absalom? Is Joab siding with Absalom? Or does Joab think Absalom is dangerous and so better to have close by? Is Joab seeking reconciliation with the king while also lobbying for Absalom's return? What were Joab's instructions to the woman?

The story told by the Tekoite is often called a parable, but it sounds more like a petition, what Schipper calls a "petitionary narrative, presenting a difficult case rather than the straightforward one we encountered in Nathan's story."[80] The case involves family conflict, customs of revenge, and the threatened impoverishment and further bereavement of a widow, and David has a difficult time

79. Another striking resemblance between the Tekoite and Abigail is the phrase "upon me, my lord, be the responsibility" (v. 9; 1 Sam 25:24) with only a slight variation in phrasing. I agree with Hoftijzer ("David and the Tekoite," 427) that this expression is not meant to express guilt but is used as a special pleading for mercy and that they hope the formula will "further the chance that their request will be granted."

80. Schipper, *Parables and Conflict*, 61. Schipper borrows the term from Simon Parker, *Stories in Scripture and Inscriptions: Comparative Studies on Narratives in Northwest Semitic Inscriptions and the Hebrew Bible* (Oxford: Oxford University Press, 1997), 18–34.

coming to a decision about it because he has not exactly proven himself to be someone who deals well in this area. Does David understand all along that something else is going on than what appears to be the case in the story of the wise woman? Conflict in the family of the woman is about to tear apart not only her individual situation but the harmony in the clan. Family conflict spills over into the wider community in her case. The problems in David's family, also involving violence among siblings, including murder, have the more serious potential of affecting the entire body politic. Joab may hope that the recall of Absalom will be a way to solve this very issue. In any event, Absalom's return will only bring danger closer, but neither the king nor Joab has as yet truly taken the measure of Absalom.

Act II, Scene 4: The Return of a Son (2 Samuel 14:21–33)

Absalom comes home. Except that he does not exactly come home.[81]

2 Samuel 14:21–24

21 The king said to Joab:
See now, I have done this thing,
go and bring back the lad, Absalom.
22 Joab fell on his face to the ground
and bowed down and blessed the king.
Joab said: Today your servant knows
that I have found favor in your eyes, my lord King,
for the king has done the thing your servant asked.
23 Then Joab arose and went to Geshur,
and he brought Absalom to Jerusalem.
24 The king said: Let him turn round to his house,
and my face he shall not see!
Absalom turned round to his house,
and the face of the king he did not see.

81. John Goldingay, *Men Behaving Badly* (Exeter, UK: Paternoster, 2000), 277.

Joab appears at David's side without any transition, and the king announces bluntly that he has taken care of the matter, so Joab can go and fetch his wayward son. Literally, the king says that he has done "this thing." The woman referred to "this thing" in her accusation and further explanation (14, 15, 20). It was the *thing* in which the king was guilty, about which she came to speak to him, the one Joab intended to turn around. In stating the matter as a fait accompli, the king allows that he made the decision for Absalom's recall when he swore the oath in regard to the woman's son. Joab, like the Tekoite (cf. 4), makes full prostration and also refers to "the thing," identifying it as his request for the return of Absalom. Joab fulfills his task, but the king's goodwill goes no further, for once back home, Absalom is not allowed to "see the face of the king." The interweaving of words in verse 24 shows the dilemma that is now created: Absalom returned to his house (twice) without seeing the face of the king (twice); home and yet not home! Barring the son from seeing his father's face is serious indeed. It makes of Absalom an unworthy individual. On the other hand, it would put David in a bad light to welcome the fratricidal son back at the court. As Smith points out, the king is "determined to maintain an uneasy equilibrium by keeping Absalom in Jerusalem under house arrest."[82] The homecoming of Absalom has resolved one tension but created another.

The text makes a brief detour at this point to speak of Absalom's beauty, his hair, and his offspring (25–27). Comments of this nature strike an unusual note in narratives that rarely describe appearance. Where physical features are noted, they rarely go beyond "good-looking," "very beautiful" or something equally vague. Verse 25 not only speaks of his beauty but also of the admiration it elicits; there was no blemish in him "from the sole of his foot to the crown of his head." The last phrase occurs elsewhere in Deuteronomy, Job, and Isaiah to indicate a plague of welts and boils as a punishment, or in Job's case a test (Deut 28:35; Job 2:7; Isa 1:6). In contrast to such disfigurement, here is a man without blemish on his entire body. His hair is so luxuriant that he has to shave it every year, at which time he weighs it. It is perhaps not the abundance of hair that stands

82. Smith, *The Fate of Justice and Righteousness*, 177.

out so much as this last piece of information. One gets the sense that admiring bystanders witness the shaving and the weighing, so its weight becomes known throughout the town and perhaps even the land. The elaborate emphasis on the head and hair of Absalom casts a shadow forward toward his eventual fate. In addition, a final comment recalls the past by referencing three unnamed sons and a daughter. The daughter is the only one named, Tamar, like her aunt. Of her too it is said that she is beautiful to look at (27). While Absalom, together with his family no doubt, is not allowed to *appear* before the king, his and his daughter's *appearance* is highlighted, which draws attention at the same time to her father's sister, also reportedly beautiful, and her fate, something that is perhaps never far from Absalom's mind.

The situation of being kept at arm's length by the king becomes too much for Absalom, and he forces Joab's hand (28–33). When Joab refuses twice to accede to his demand for access to the king, Absalom sets fire to a parcel of Joab's land, forcing Joab to give in. We are reminded of Samson, not only because of the emphasis on Absalom's hair but because of the ungovernable side of his nature. His setting fire to a parcel of land recalls Samson's vengeance on the Philistines (Judg 15:4–6). When Absalom visits the king, he is the third person to make full prostration (33)—the third act of obeisance in a chapter in which David is referred to only by his title. It remains to be seen if the title and all the bowing and scraping are enough to keep David safe on his throne. It all ends with a kiss from the king, but there is no mention of a true reconciliation.

Act III: Absalom's Rebellion (2 Samuel 15:1–19:9)

Righteous indignation, long-term resentment, and natural vanity are an explosive combination.[83]

The act presents a coherent narrative with a consistent time sequence, beginning with four scenes that focus on Absalom's rebel-

83. Smith, *The Fate of Justice and Righteousness*, 178.

lion and his eventual death (15–18) Each chapter flows naturally into the next creating a story filled with complex characters, both in terms of the main protagonists, Absalom and David, and a large group of adjacent named individuals, all of whom play a role in the larger drama. In addition, anonymous groups appear, milling around the central persons—runners, tribes, all Israel, troops, servants, mercenaries—adding a layered background for the main story. Key terminology, such as the verb "to cross," the nouns "head" and "heart," and the frequently repeated "look!" provides the material with strong linkage and depth on the verbal level. An interweaving of divine and human purpose in these episodes, fueled by narrative comment, characterizes the material throughout.

In chapter 15, we read of Absalom's preparation for the rebellion against his father and its execution (15:1–12), causing the hasty flight of David and his entourage from Jerusalem. David's trek outward is interrupted by numerous encounters and conversations, and at the end of the scene, he is still no further than the Mount of Olives (15:13–37). In the next chapter, David's party comes to a halt, probably at the Jordan (16:14), and at that point the scene switches to Jerusalem, where Absalom is able to make use of two counselors, one friendly to him and his cause, Ahitophel, and one loyal to David, Hushai (16:15–23). These two are on stage in full display with their advice to Absalom, the one urging speed, the other delay for thorough preparations (17:1–14). Upon receipt of reports delivered by spies, David and the people with him cross the Jordan and begin to move north until they arrive at Mahanaim, directly south of the Jabbok river, about fifteen miles to the east and twenty miles north of Jerusalem (17:15–29). It is there, in a forested region, that the battle takes place between the two parties, Absalom and his army against David and those loyal to him, ending in defeat and death for Absalom (18:1–18). This scene ends with David receiving the news of the battle and mourning his son's death (18:19–32) followed by Joab's rebuke of David for bringing shame on his servants (19:1–9 [18:33–19:8]).

Act III, Scene 1: His Father's Son (2 Samuel 15)

Avshalom is many things, but none so much as his father's son, with his good looks, worldly wisdom, and charisma.[84]

In the lead-up to a full-fledged rebellion, we watch Absalom gradually increasing his status and influence until he has himself declared "king in Hebron" (1–12). The details of his preparation take four years, evidence of the leisurely and thorough manner with which he goes about laying the foundations. The main concern with which Absalom occupies himself is the matter of *justice*. He places himself at a strategic place—the city gate, the primary location of "civic and judicial activity"[85]—early in the morning so he will be able to catch those who come to plead their case at the palace. The introduction of a chariot and horses accompanied by a bodyguard in the first verse is most likely part of the legal proceedings, pointing to Absalom's assigning himself this crucial part of the monarchial role.[86] The description highlights the importance both the narrative and Absalom assign to the issue of justice. "In vv. 1–6, Absalom is portrayed as

84. Everett Fox, *Give Us a King! Samuel, Saul, and David* (New York: Schocken, 1999), 211.

85. Stephen C. Russell, *The King and the Land: A Geography of Royal Power in the Biblical World* (Oxford: Oxford University Press, 2017), 73. See pp. 78–79 for a close description of the city gate in the ancient world. The gate of the town highlighted the importance of the town as a political unity and thus was the "location of civic and judicial activity" (80).

86. In this regard, Meir Malul ("Absalom's Chariot and Fifty Runners [II Sam 15,1] and Hittite Laws: Legal Proceedings in the Ancient Near East," *ZAW* 122 [2010]: 50) is convincing when he argues that the introduction of the chariot, horses, and runners is not a separate issue in the text. Based on a comparison with Hittite literature, Malul argues that "the king's chariot or cart is the central place within the legal proceedings presided over by the king" and that such proceedings took place at the city gate with the petitioner being called "to the wheel." At the same time, of course, the presence of the chariot, horses, and runners plays with the words of warning issued by Samuel on precisely such accoutrements to indicate the monarchial perversion of justice (1 Sam 8:11).

attempting to take over the primary *function* of kingship: promoting social justice."[87] From his initial introduction in the text (13:20–22) throughout the story until this point, it is clear that he believes his "justice," including the murder of his brother, to be more adequate than his father's. King David committed rape and had one of his faithful soldiers killed in a cowardly fashion; he abetted the rape of his own daughter, and though reportedly very angry at Amnon did nothing to face the culprit with consequences. Although he has recalled Absalom and formalized his presence at the palace with a kiss, there is no mention of further dealings between father and son.

The style of encountering plaintiffs and lodging critique of the king's way of dealing with cases ("you will get no hearing from the king," 3) plays on the tension between the political autonomy of towns and the sovereignty of the centralized power (cf. 1 Sam 8:11–18).[88] I agree with Stephen Russell that Absalom here paints the king's justice as inaccessible and himself as someone who will be a "just king, one who will not be isolated in a palace, but 'in the land' (v. 4), i.e., present and accessible in the territory of Israel."[89] He shows himself approachable, embracing the litigants (5). In this way Absalom "stole the heart of the men of Israel" (6), that is to say of the corporate body. Here the narrative manages both to disparage Absalom by referring to him as a thief and to embed a critique of David's reign.[90]

After four years, Absalom requests the king's permission to go to Hebron to fulfill a vow made while still on the run from the king's wrath, a vow made to Adonai in case God allowed him to return to Jerusalem (7–8). The status of Hebron is well established (see

87. Smith, *The Fate of Justice and Righteousness*, 182.

88. For more on this issue in the ancient Near East, specifically as it relates to the groundwork for Absalom's rebellion, see Russell, *The King and the Land*, 68–83.

89. Russell, *The King and the Land*, 82.

90. Russell, *The King and the Land*, 83: "The allegiances embraced by Absalom and the plaintiff, town and tribe, were based on distributed, collective power and were inadequately addressed by the current king." Joel Baden, *The Historical David: The Real Life of an Invented Hero* (New York: HarperCollins, 2013), 201: "What Absalom promised was a return to the 'good old days.'"

pp. 228, 239–40 above); Absalom succeeds in sounding pious and humble, referring to the name of God three times and to himself as intending to "serve." The king wishes him well, and he goes on his way. "Go in peace" will be the last words David speaks to a son whose name combines the words "father" and "peace" but whose designs are far from peaceful toward his father. Does David suspect nothing? Years have gone by with Absalom publicly wooing his subjects and he has received no "report"? Once, he had no trouble finding out his pursuer's designs and whereabouts, and here he lets his most dangerous son, whom he knows to be capable of great violence, head out to Hebron, a city where he himself was first declared king (2 Sam 2:4)! Is the portrayal of David here of one so secure in his power that he suspects nothing, or is it of one letting it all go on and biding his time? We have no information about David's inner life until he is fleeing Jerusalem on the run from his son (30).

On his way to Hebron, Absalom makes two important moves: He sends agents or spies throughout the land to bring the news that he "is king in Hebron," and he acquires as counselor one of David's most important advisors, Ahitophel (10–12).[91] There is no mention of a declaration of his kingship in Hebron or of any anointing. Absalom, like Napoleon in the modern era, crowns himself king. The narrative heightens tension by noting the strength of the conspiracy and the multitude of people following Absalom.

When David finally gets a "report" about the state of affairs, he immediately heads out of the city with his servants and bodyguard. The rest of the chapter is devoted to his journey on foot in the direction of the Jordan, which he does not reach until well into the next chapter. In counterpoint to the great haste with which David and his retinue flee the city, the description of the journey takes place in slow motion, filled with details of many encounters and discussions between David and individuals. The phrasing of the report to David about the rebellion makes clear that the king's son has a large group of followers. Where we heard earlier that Absalom "stole the heart of

91. The news is to be proclaimed "at the sound of the shofar," in the Samuel texts most often used in the context of battle (cf. 1 Sam 13:3; 2 Sam 2:28; 18:16; 20:1, 22).

the men of Israel," here the news goes, "The heart of the men of Israel has gone after Absalom." Such a statement is of course far more fear-inducing than the mere information about Absalom declaring himself king, because it uncovers not only what Absalom is up to but also that he has been successful. It could thus be that David has watched his son all along and is well aware of his ambitions but has considered them ineffective and is only now becoming aware of the extent of Absalom's reach for power. In any case, he judges Jerusalem not to be a safe place, because although it is difficult to capture, it will also be difficult to escape from once it is besieged. The latter is David's judgment as he packs up and leaves "with all his house on foot" (16). He "left ten concubines" behind "to guard the house." The word used in the Hebrew sentence for "left" also carries the connotation of "abandon." The women were left not just to safeguard the palace, but they were the guardians of David's rule in Jerusalem.[92] We will see how effective their guardianship will turn out, both for themselves and "the house."[93]

At the outskirts of the town, David's Philistine palace guard files by (cf. 2 Sam 8:18), and David has his first conversation (18–22). In this section, the verb "to cross/pass by" (*'avar*) becomes central. All the servants *cross* and the bodyguard *crosses* "before the king." Eventually David commands Ittai to *cross*, and he does so. The first encounter, then, is with not an Israelite but a Gittite, a Philistine from Gath, "a foreigner and an exile," as David points out (19).[94] It

92. Ilse Müllner, "Books of Samuel: Women at the Center of Israel's History," in *Feminist Biblical Interpretation: A Compendium of Critical Commentary on the Books of the Bible and Related Literature*, ed. Luise Schottroff and Marie-Theres Wacher, trans. Lisa E. Dahill et al. (Grand Rapids: Eerdmans, 2012), 151: "These women represent in this moment the (in)stability of the Davidic dynasty. Leaving them behind also means positioning them as a point of attack."

93. The sentence construction in 15:16–17 serves to highlight David's action of leaving the women behind by framing it with the act of the king's departure: "with all his house on foot" (15:16) // "with all the people on foot" (15:17).

94. Properly, Ittai should be designated a *ger*, a resident alien, but the two words used by David in the text, a "foreigner" (*nokhri*) and an "exile" (*goleh*), point to a greater vulnerability, thereby highlighting Ittai's loyalty.

only takes this encouragement from David to return to his hometown with all his household to make Ittai, a name that connotes the word "with," avow that he really is "with" the king, now and forever. In verse 23, the outcasts have only reached the Kidron creek, just at the foot of the slope descending eastward from the city. Once again, a group and individuals from the group come to the center, with the priest Zadok and the Levites carrying the "Ark of the Covenant of God," which they have apparently managed to cart away from the city. Once again, "all the people" are "crossing." This time the king is adamant in his directive to take the Ark back to the city. It is, after all, up to God if he will return safely to the city, but the Ark must be there when he does so. As he expresses his pious sentiment, he is also shrewd enough to seize an opportunity to plant a few spies on location who can bring him news of what goes on in the city. Zadok and Abiatar turn back, together with their sons, who will serve as spies, and return the Ark to Jerusalem (27–29).

Two narrative notes precede a final move on David's part that will stand him in good stead. The first describes the weeping and mourning of David and the crowd that accompanies him and the second another report to which David has a strong reaction.

2 Samuel 15:30–31

30 Now David was going up the Mount of Olives,
going up and weeping, his head covered,
and he was going barefoot.
And all the people that were with him,
everyone with their heads covered,
went up all along weeping.

31 And David was told the report:
Ahitophel is with the conspirators with Absalom.
David said: confound, please, the counsel of Ahitophel, Adonai.

The verb translated here "confound" literally means "to make foolish." Samuel accuses Saul of having "acted foolishly" toward God (1 Sam 13:13) and Saul confesses the same toward David (1 Sam

26:21). The verb occurs especially in Ecclesiastes when Qohelet speaks of "fools" and "foolishness" (Eccl 2:19; 7:17; 10:13 3×; 10:6, 14). David's words, often identified by commentators as "prayer," sound more like a pious wish or exclamation than a prayer. The pitiful scene of everyone going along weeping creates an overwhelming picture of grief on David's part and that of his retinue. David's feelings have finally come to the surface.

A pious wish gives rise to a smart action (32–37). The next person to encounter David is his friend Hushai from Arkai, who was apparently not with David in Jerusalem.[95] This is the very person David sends back to Jerusalem in order to "break" the counsel of Ahitophel, using a strong verb often employed for the breaking of an oath or a covenant (34). To bolster Hushai's courage, David mentions the support he already has in the city, Zadok and Abiatar and their two sons who can deliver news about all that goes on. We hear only from David in this encounter, but that Hushai complies is clear from verse 37, in which he enters Jerusalem at the very moment that Absalom arrives in the city. Hushai's appearance before David on the heels of his expressed wish for the undoing of the counsel of Ahitophel is part of the narrative's implication that God's hand is moving events even as human beings are seemingly in control. Such occasional narrative comments will point to the purpose of God in the story. In the meantime, the human actors still have to step up to the plate to fulfill their destiny, for good or ill. We note that David does not seek divine counsel for his actions and movements in these episodes. He may speak *of* God and God's purpose, but he does not speak *to* God.

95. Hushai is referred to three times as "David's friend" (15:32, 37; 16:17), the only person so designated in these episodes. He is evidently also an advisor or counselor, for it is in this capacity that David sends him to Jerusalem and in which he functions for Absalom. It is precisely about the quality of his friendship for David that Absalom questions him on their first encounter (16:17).

Act III, Scene 2: Close Encounters (2 Samuel 16)

For with good advice you wage war, and there is help in a multitude of counselors. (Prov 24:6)

In the first part of this chapter, we follow David on his flight to the wilderness, where he meets two more individuals (1–14). The first is Mephiboshet's servant Tsiva, who brings provender and a tale of disloyalty (1–4). David, not distracted by the provisions that accompany Tsiva, demands to know the whereabouts of Mephiboshet and is told that he stayed behind out of disloyalty and hopes for the restoration of Saul's house. David does not question Tsiva's veracity but leaves him all Mephiboshet's property. Clearly, he has heard only one side of the story, and the moment does not seem to be a good one for making rash decisions, but his trust in the loyalty of Saul's descendants toward him may not be strong.

Tsiva and Mephiboshet have brought to mind King Saul, and the next character to cross David's path continues this thread of the narrative (5–13). One Shimei from Saul's clan comes out to curse David, throwing stones at him and his retinue. Shimei, a man of some courage as he faces the armed soldiers surrounding David, hisses his words, "Get out, get out!" (*tse, tse*), while calling David "a man of blood" twice and a "worthless fellow" (*ish beliya'al*). Abishai is all for taking care of this "dead dog," but David resigns himself to being cursed all along the way, as he professes there is nothing so odd in a Benjaminite coming after him compared to the treachery of his own son.[96] His statement ("My son who came from my loins is seeking my life," 11) makes clear that David has no illusions about what Absalom is really after. In his response to Abishai David refers

96. Polzin (*David and the Deuteronomist*, 163–67) judges the cursing of Shimei to reveal the connection between curses and kings. The story of Absalom's revolt is "a complex and nuanced story of the doomed struggles of those whose lives are touched by the cursed sphere of kings." This understanding follows Polzin's understanding of the mostly negative view of kingship that is woven throughout the Historical Books.

twice to Shimei acting on divine instruction, once as a possibility and once as a certainty.

2 Samuel 16:10–12

10 The king said: What do we have in common, sons of Tseruyah?
Let him curse. For if Adonai said to him: Curse David!
Who shall say: Why are you doing this?
. . .
11b Let him curse, for Adonai has spoken to him.
12 Perhaps Adonai will see my punishment[97]
and bring back to me good in place of his curses this day.

The exchange with Abishai presents a David who is willing to accept what comes from the hand of God in view of his wrongdoing, or at least one who appears to do so. It could also be that the moment for tangling with an opponent, even one who could be dispatched fairly easily, is at this point judged to be inopportune. Besides, who knows how many more Benjaminites are on Shimei's side, some of whom may be lying in ambush. One impulsive killing may cost him more in the long run, or even immediately, than he can afford to lose. Both faith and canniness may play a role in the picture we get of David.

The final verse of the section records an arrival of the "king and all his people" (14). Although it is not clear where they have arrived, the place is apparently at a safe enough distance from Jerusalem that they can catch their breath in an exhausted state, just at the time when Absalom and his followers, including Ahitophel, reach the city.

Absalom does not have a "multitude" of counselors, or if he does, it is not recorded, for there are only two that count: Ahitophel and Hushai (15–23). Hushai has to make his presence credible to Absalom and does so with an eloquent statement, much of which can be interpreted in more than one way. When he preempts Absalom's questions by declaring, "Long live the king! Long live the king!" the absence of a name leaves it open as to whom he has in mind. The same is true for his declaration that he will be loyal to the one chosen

97. Reading *avoni* as written in the Masoretic Text.

by Adonai (18). He has on the face of it just betrayed the father but promises to "serve" the son just as he did his father (19).

For the time being Hushai's words apparently satisfy Absalom, but he turns first to Ahitophel for counsel and follows through on Ahitophel's advice to extend his reach to his father's concubines by having intercourse with them in public. On the political level, the "possession" of these women by Absalom cements his power in Jerusalem insofar as these "guardians" of David's house and his representatives in that city will be forced into acceptance of a new ruler. Ilse Müllner writes, "If Absalom can take possession of them he will force his way, over the bodies of women, into his father's sphere of power."[98] On a moral and ethical level, it spells a low point in the story of Absalom, as David's concubines join the violated concubine of the Levite in the days of the judges (Judg 19:22–27) and Tamar the king's daughter in her father's house (13:1–20), suffering the exercise of barbarous power and violence. Absalom has made himself odious not only in the eyes of his father (21) but in the eyes and ears of all who read and hear the story. David has indeed "abandoned" the women to the tender care of Absalom (see p. 310 above).

The text closes the episode by observing that the "counsel of Ahitophel" in those days was like "a word from God for David as well as Absalom" (23). As Alter observes, there is "a sour irony in likening the sordid, if pragmatic, counsel to have sex with the king's concubines to a divine oracle."[99] We remember that Ahitophel is Bathsheba's grandfather, and in comparing the two men, father David and son Absalom, he may well find the former, his erstwhile employer, wanting in comparison. As counselor, Ahitophel may have been privy to much of the machinations engaged in by David in regard to his granddaughter and his relative by marriage, her husband. "Absalom, faithful champion of his sister, appears incomparably more reliable."[100] Ahitophel could have been on site when Nathan

98. Müllner, "Books of Samuel," 151.

99. Alter, *The David Story*, 295n23.

100. David Daube, "Absalom and the Ideal King," *VT* 48 (1998): 322. Daube discusses extensively the possible motivations of Ahitophel in joining the rebel Absalom (320–22).

prophesied to David that God would take his wives "from before your eyes and give them to your neighbor,/ and he will lie with your wives/ in the eyes of this sun" (12:11). To Ahitophel's eyes, the time must appear right to fulfill the prophecy. The concluding note, with its comparison of Ahitophel's counsel to God's word, also highlights the omission of anyone seeking divine advice during these events.

Act III, Scene 3: The Thwarting of Counsel (2 Samuel 17)

Establish plans by counsel, and with shrewd guidance make war. (Prov 20:18)

In the usual tale of sons challenging aging fathers, the sons win out. This will not be the case for Absalom, although so far his road to an overthrow of the old regime has been smooth. The encounter with his father's concubines may have been a new low, even for Absalom, but at the same time it cements the break between him and his father and counts as another victorious move. Ahitophel is ready with advice for the next step and counsels a quick chase to dispatch the exhausted king (1–4). It is prudent advice, not only in terms of getting David out of the way but also in avoiding kin-strife and bloodshed: "For it is the one man you seek, and all the people will be at peace" (3).[101] The counselor refers to David initially by his first name, then as "the king," and finally as the one Absalom is really after, creating distance between the son and the father.

It sounds good to Absalom, but he has another counselor available, and following the guideline of "the more advice the better," he proposes to ask Hushai also (5–6).[102] Revealing to Hushai the content of Ahitophel's advice appears to be his first wrong step, because this information gives Hushai an advantage. Bluntly, he declares the counsel of Ahitophel "not good" (7). The

101. With this translation, I follow Alter (*The David Story*, 297), who bases it partly on Bar-Efrat's (*Narrative Art in the Bible*, 296) reading.

102. For a close analysis of Hushai's speech, see Bar-Efrat, *Narrative Art in the Bible*, 223–37; Fokkelman, *King David*, 215–20.

Hebrew sentence is constructed carefully, with the declaration "not good" in first place, adding the qualification "this time" at the end. A literal translation of Hushai's words reads: "Not good is the counsel that Ahitophel counseled this time" (7).[103] One can almost hear the pause before he pronounces the final two words. Hushai's opening salvo constitutes a bold move. It is guaranteed to make his audience sit up and take notice, but it runs the risk of everyone shutting him down right away. Bar-Efrat suggests that there is a pause between this beginning and the continuing words of advice: "Hushai waits a while to see how his audience reacts, as can be learned from the seemingly superfluous repetition of the words 'Hushai said.' It would appear that the audience is stunned into silence."[104]

Hushai's counsel (8–13) stands out for its length compared to Ahitophel's and provides an example of the eloquent use of convincing language, illustrating, as Song-Mi Suzie Park points out, "wise" guidance not only in *what* it says or *how* it is said but in terms of how it is linked to theological issues. Park writes, "Hushai, by speaking in this high, eloquent manner made his advice sound more poetic and spiritual, and thus more akin to divine speech."[105] First, Hushai's focus is on David, whom he consistently refers to as "your father," emphasizing the connection between son and parent, while he underlines at the same time David's prowess as a fighter among fighters ("man of war," 8; "warrior," 10; cf. 1 Sam 16:18). The people with him—"his men"—are called "warriors" and "bitter in spirit" (8; cf. the men who first gathered around David when he fled from Saul, 1 Sam 22:2), and "valiant men" (10). He compares David and his men to "a mother bear" looking for her cubs and refers to the fear such men would engender in even those with "the heart of a lion" (10), drawing on metaphors for ferocity and strength (cf. David in his speech to Saul on the verge of his face-off with Goliath,

103. Most translations put the words "not good" toward the end or at the very end of the sentence, which reduces the force of Hushai's words.

104. Bar-Efrat, *Narrative Art in the Bible*, 225.

105. Song-Mi Suzie Park, "The Frustration of Wisdom: Wisdom, Counsel and Divine Will in 2 Samuel 17:1–23," *JBL* 128 (2009): 455, 463.

1 Sam 17:34–36).[106] These are things Hushai allows that Absalom already knows: "You yourself know" (8) and "all Israel knows" (10). It's stating the obvious, what you know and everybody knows: Such an opponent of legendary strength surrounded by battle-hardened troops cannot be faced without preparation.

Preparation is the issue to which Hushai turns in the second half of his guidance (11–13). Everything he has said so far only lays the groundwork for his counsel. In the face of such an adversary, there is need to muster more troops, "like the sand of the sea in multitude," who will march under the banner of Absalom: "Your presence will walk with them" (11). Then when they locate David, they can kill not only him but everyone. Even if he takes refuge in a city, "all Israel" will destroy the city. Unlike Ahitophel, Hushai makes the adventure a grand one: Not only David but also the entire ragtag rabble with him will go down, all due to the might of Absalom and his army. They will fall on them as "dew falls on the ground," a poetic image that points not so much to strength as to an inexorable event. The dew falls everywhere, and no one can stop it from falling. They will drag them off even if they hide in a fortified town.

To those privy to David's anguish and exhaustion, as portrayed earlier in the text, it is easy to see that Ahitophel's advice is right, but to Absalom and everyone else around, Hushai's counsel sounds better. A narrative comment closes the episode by pointing out that it is all in God's plan (14). "In one fell swoop, the statement pushes God, a character who until this point remained passively in the background, to the forefront as the ultimate director of the drama."[107] This statement raises the issue of the interaction between divine plans and human volition. It may of course be that human hearts and hands can make divine intentions go awry, as they will in the biblical text.

106. See Bar-Efrat (*Narrative Art in the Bible*, 231–32) for references in the first part of Hushai's speech that recall phrases used in connection with David elsewhere, especially in 1 Sam. Bar-Efrat also points out how many of Hushai's phrases occur elsewhere in the Bible, so that he creates the impression of relating "widely-known and acknowledged facts" (234).

107. Park, "The Frustration of Wisdom," 465.

In contrast to all the speechifying that precedes it, the next section is filled with action as Zadok and Abiatar and their sons, the spies planted by David, come into play (15–20). The narrative leaves unclear whether Absalom's preference for Hushai's counsel is known to anyone outside his immediate circle, even to Hushai. Hushai reports both his and his counterpart's advice to the priests without mention of the preferred option; they in their turn pass it on to their sons Jonathan and Ahimaaz nearby in a place aptly named either Scout's or Spy's Well (*eyn rogel*). In a tense interlude (17–20), these two have to find another hiding place, as their whereabouts are in danger of being revealed, but with the help of a woman they are able to hide in a well while she sends pursuers in the wrong direction.[108] The false lead gives the two men the opportunity to reach David and advise him to get across the Jordan post haste. They report only the counsel of Ahitophel, another piece of evidence that they are unaware of Absalom's choice. In view of Ahitophel's reputation, they may be convinced his counsel will be Absalom's choice, or else they decide to only provide the advice that will spur David on to get away as fast as possible. In any case, their report is effective, and in the next sentence, David and all with him are east of the Jordan.

The episode of the dueling counselors ends with the account of Ahitophel's suicide after he finds out that his counsel has not been followed. No doubt Ahitophel sees the writing on the wall for Absalom and is not willing to wait to be executed as a traitor. His death is told in some detail, making clear that he is able to settle his affairs in his own city and house, where he hangs himself, and that he is buried in the grave of his ancestors (23).

A brief note on the movements of troops with both David and Absalom follows (24–29). David is able to reach Mahanaim, located about twenty miles north of Jerusalem on the east side of the Jordan just south of the Jabbok. He gets there ahead of Absalom, who must have followed Hushai's counsel. David receives support from

108. The protection by a woman who hides the two in a well while spreading out grain over its covering and sending off would-be pursuers clearly plays on the same motifs as the story of Rahab (Josh 2:5–7). It is perhaps a common motif in "spy" stories.

another quarter: Three allies arrive with more supplies (27–29), and it looks as if David at least has gained some advantage. The allies come from different directions, not all of them known to us today but most likely familiar to the ancient reader, indicating that David is receiving more widespread support—an additional advantage of the time he has gained—so he is able to provide sustenance for his tired troops.

Act III, Scene 4: Death of a Son (2 Samuel 18:1–19:9)[109]

David is caught in the narrative's web, flying in the face of what his own troops avow and what Ahitophel advised.[110]

Mahanaim was the place where Abner installed Ishboshet as Saul's successor in the early days of David's kingship at Hebron. Once again, there are two kings in the land, and this time the issue will be decided by armed conflict. Actually, the text reveals very little about the battle itself; after a short review of preparations (18:1–5), there are three sentences in reference to armed struggle (18:6–8) without providing strategy or detail, and from then on the focus is on Absalom, his death, the sending of messengers, and the reception of the news by his father (18:9–31). We hear that David divides the army into three groups under three commanders—Joab and Abishai, the sons of Tseruyah, and Ittai from Gath—but nothing of the purpose of this three-pronged movement. There is dialogue, but with the troops rather than their commanders, and the conversation refers to Absalom, who in this way becomes the focus almost immediately. The king states explicitly that he will go with the army, but the people dissuade him. The narrator makes clear that a public conversation takes

109. I am following the chapter divisions of the Masoretic Text of the Hebrew Bible, in which the verse that appears as 18:33 in the NRSV and other English translations appears as 19:1. In ch. 19, subsequent verses are one number higher compared to their counterparts in English translation.

110. Campbell, 2 *Samuel*, 157.

place in which "all the people/troops" participate or overhear that David *commanded* Joab, Abishai and Ittai to be "easy on the lad, Absalom" (18:5).

The army is presented in "hundreds and thousands," numbers we may understand to reflect the usual exaggeration when the text deals with armed struggle. The impression is nevertheless important that here is a significant force assembled in support of David. From Absalom's side, it has been reported only that "all the men of Israel" were with him (17:24) without mention of specific numbers. The reference to "Israel" or "all Israel" in the chapters about Absalom's rebellion is most likely not intended to indicate the northern tribes only, since Absalom clearly has adherents in Jerusalem, but it does herald the division always latent to an extent among the tribes that will one day come to full flowering. It is likely that most of David's followers, besides the palace guard, include a good part of his own tribe. The terminology "Israel," eventually reserved for the Northern Kingdom, clearly bleeds into the record here. When the two armies engage, the battle takes place between "the army of Israel" and "the servants of David" (18:6–7).

Apparently, it all takes place in a forest, which seems an odd place for a battle, but it may have worked to David's advantage, as the forest is said to have "devoured more of the people than the sword devoured" (18:8). Absalom is not "devoured" but is riding on a mule as befits his status and gets caught in a tree.

2 Samuel 18:9

Absalom happened to be in front of David's servants;
now Absalom was riding on the mule,
and when the mule entered under the branches of the great
oak,
his head caught in the oak,
so he dangled[111] between heaven and earth.
And the mule that was under him passed on.

111. Reading, with Alter (*The David Story*, 304), the Aramaic, Syriac, Greek and Latin, as well as Qumran: "dangled" (*wytl*).

Absalom is portrayed riding (perhaps fleeing?) rather than fighting, and the verb "to be strong," used often in the context of battle in the Samuel texts, is here used ironically of his head being "grabbed," so he dangles between earth and heaven while his mule wanders on. The identification of the tree as "the great oak" hints at a once well-known site, a significance which eludes us today. Oaks in the Hebrew Bible often have cultic significance, and by this image the text may imply that Absalom becomes a sacrifice to his own nefarious plans.[112] The mule, a mount reserved for royalty, "passes on," the same verb used as the key term for David's flight from the city. Alter writes, "Absalom losing his mule from under him is an image of his losing his royal seat."[113] His long hair may not be an advantage in this situation. Nature and animal conspire against him, soon to be joined by a human foe.

First a soldier finds him. He reports the dangling Absalom to Joab, and when Joab reproaches him for not having dispatched the prince, the text once again makes clear that everyone heard the king regarding Absalom. What the soldier heard was that Absalom should be protected, and the soldier is not ready to risk his life by killing the son of the king (18:10–13). Joab impatiently silences him and takes the matter in hand. He strikes Absalom out of the tree but then orders his weapon-bearers, ten of them, to dispatch him: "And they put him to death" (18:14–15). Absalom is buried in a great pit, but there is also a monument to him in "king's valley," one put up by Absalom himself, apparently before he had offspring (18:17–18). Absalom leaves two memorials, one a pit with stones heaped on it in the forest, the other a testimony to self-promotion.[114] Absalom,

112. For "oak" as a symbol for Israel's idolatry, see, for example, Hos 4:13; Ezek 6:13. The word, *elah*, sounds uncomfortably close to a noun meaning "curse" (*alah*; see Deut 29:19; Isa 24:6; Ezek 16:59; Prov 29:24, 2 Chr 34:24, for example).

113. Alter, *The David Story*, 305n9.

114. The note on his lack of children in verse 18 is not necessarily in contradiction to the note in 14:27 if Absalom, who does not seem to have suffered from an abundance of modesty, erected a monument before he became a parent. This solution is proposed by Randy McCracken ("How Many Sons Did Absalom Have? Intentional Ambiguity as Literary Art," *BSac* 172 [2015]: 298), who suggests that the issue is the "time frame" in which the different

hung in a tree that in the prophetic books is condemned as a symbol of idolatry (Hos 4:13; Ezek 6:13), is buried like the transgressor Achan under a heap of stones (Josh 7:26), while for himself he had erected a pillar for which the narrative uses a term that becomes virtually synonymous with the abandonment of the worship of Adonai in the Book of Kings (1 Kgs 14:23; 2 Kgs 3:2; 10:26; 17:10; see Hos 10:2; Mic 5:12[13]).[115] The heap of stones over a pit and the memorial stone, though contrasting images, each provide a similar testimony.

Renewed tension arises in the story when Ahimaaz, Zadok's son, one of the spies for David at Absalom's court (15:27, 36; 17:17, 20), offers to bring the "good news" to the king ("Let me bring good news," 18:19), but Joab, who knows his lord well, tries to dissuade him: "You will not bring good news . . . bring good news another day . . . you will not bring good news" (18:20). The lines ring with the verb for bringing good tidings.[116] Joab chooses another candidate, a non-Israelite, but Ahimaaz still insists, and soon two messengers are on the way.[117]

---

statements occur: "The author has simply pulled a statement from Absalom's past that *precedes* the assertion of 14:27."

115. The word for "pillar," here *matsevet,* is clearly a variant for *matsevah,* a votive stone, which in the Torah can be a neutral term (cf. Gen 28:18–23; 31:13; 35:14; Exod 24:4) but is also symbolic of idolatry (Exod 23:24; 34:13; Lev 26:1; Deut 7:5; 12:3; 16:22; cf. 1 Kgs 14:23; 2 Kgs 3:2; Jer 43:13).

116. Translations are divided as to the rendering of the Hebrew verb here. In my judgment, it is most often used in the Bible for a positive announcement, consistently translated by the Septuagint with the Greek word *euangelizo,* "to bring good news" (cf. 1 Sam 31:9; 2 Sam 4:10; Isa 52:7; 61:1; Jer 20:15; Ps 68:12[11]). For an extensive discussion of the verb and its meaning see Smith, *The Fate of Justice and Righteousness,* 194n129.

117. The messenger sent by Joab, in Hebrew a *Cushite,* is either Nubian or Ethiopian and is the third outsider messenger in the David story. The two others were the Egyptian who informed David of the Amalekite raiding party (1 Sam 30:11–16) and the Amalekite who informed David of Saul's death (2 Sam 1:2–15). Ethiopians, renowned in the modern world for their running talent, may have had the same reputation in the ancient world. On the other hand, we are not sure exactly what ethnic grouping the word intends to identify, and perhaps Joab simply picked a non-Israelite for the task. See Charles Patrick Conroy, M.S.C., *Absalom, Absalom!: Narrative and Language in 2 Sam 13–20* (Rome: Biblical Institute Press, 1978), 69.

The narrative conveys that Joab believes the king will not receive the news of Absalom's death well, as he clearly states. What else he fears is not spelled out—most likely some type of mistreatment of a man who had risked his life for David earlier. David had messengers executed on other occasions (2 Sam 1:15; 4:12), and who knows what a man driven to madness by betrayal and bereavement may do. We cannot be sure. Joab clearly considered Absalom alive a permanent threat, but he also understands the depth of David's feelings.

A switch of perspective has the reader waiting anxiously with David at the city gate with a lookout stationed above him on the roof. Actually, as Absalom is *hanging between* heaven and earth, David is *sitting between* two gates, their literal position pointing to their precarious situation.[118] As we view events from the perspective of the two stationary men, we see two figures *running* toward them. The intricate structuring of dialogue between the lookout and David while the runners, first one then a second, speed toward them has the effect of drawing the reader as closely as possible into the scene (18:24–27). Before Ahimaaz, who has managed to outrun the other messenger, gets near, the king states three times that there will be good news in response to the lookout's report. Illogically and testifying to David's anxiety, he equates a "good man" with "good news" (18:27).[119]

2 Samuel 18:28–29

28 Ahimaaz called and said to the king:
It is well!
And he bowed down to the king,

118. "Between the gates," an unusual expression, occurs only here, clearly referring to the in-between situation of father and son. Literally, the plurality points to the presence of an outer and an inner wall. Alter (*The David Story*, 308n24) surmises there were actually two gates. Fox (*The Early Prophets*, 515) translates "two gateways."

119. In vv. 25 and 27, it is especially clear that David speaks of "good news." Declaring that a runner, obviously a messenger, would be coming with "news" (so NRSV and TNK) would be stating the obvious to a ridiculous degree. In the last verse, the text adds the word "good" to the noun "good news": This good man is coming with *really* good news.

his brow to the ground; he said:
Blessed be Adonai your God,
who has delivered up the men
who lifted their hand against my lord, the king.
29 The king said: Is it well with the lad,
with Absalom?
Ahimaaz said: I saw a great tumult
when Joab sent the servant of the king;
and your servant and I did not know what.

Ahimaaz, whose arrival is not stated, calls out his first word while perhaps within shouting distance: "Shalom!" After he pays his respect to king and God, in the text causing a delay before he can utter more detail, he simply declares victory.[120] We note that he refrains from speaking of David's enemies and uses a circumlocution to refer to them. David has heard *shalom* but wants to know about the *shalom* of one person mainly, that of Absalom. Ahimaaz, earlier so eager to bring the "good" news to the king, fails gloriously in the accuracy of his report at this point; in fact, he fails to make sense at all. He stammers about a great tumult—a *hamon*—around Joab, and then . . . and then . . . and then. . .[121]

The king has to wait for the Cushite to give him the information he really wants (18:31–32). The second runner too begins his announcement with the good news of the victory over those "who rose up against you," and when the king repeats his inquiry regarding

120. The verb used here for the defeat of David's enemies (*sagar*) is used with this sense in the *Piel* elsewhere only of the defeat of an opponent of David in 1 Sam 17:46 (Goliath) and of David's encounters with Saul in 1 Sam 24:19[18] and 26:8. The verb literally means "to close" or "to shut off" and is used in this sense in 1 Sam 1:5, 6.

121. With others, I understand the Hebrew of the second half of v. 28 to be deliberately contorted, mirroring "the speaker's unease" according to Conroy (*Absalom, Absalom!*, 73). Alter (*The David Story*, 309n29) writes, "Ahimaaz has been posed a question he does not dare to answer and so he begins to talk nervously and incoherently." We note the use of the word tumult (*hamon*), recalling the aftermath of battle and news brought to the home front when Eli too sat near the gate waiting to hear in 1 Sam 4:14.

Absalom, he makes clear what happened to him, albeit still in an indirect way. Rather than giving a plain statement of Absalom's death, the messenger wishes the fate of David's enemies to be the same as that of Absalom: "May they become like the lad/ the enemies. . ./ who rose up against you for evil" (18:32). The messenger avoids the word "death," but his last word is "evil" (*ra'ah*), an apt word with which to draw the curtain on the enterprising Absalom, a man of beauty and no doubt great promise who came to such an ignominious end.

David's extravagant reaction to this news is well known.

2 Samuel 19:1–5

1 Then the king shook
and went up to the upper room of the gate.
He wept and spoke thus as he went:
My son, Absalom!
My son, my son Absalom!
Would that I had died in your place!
Absalom, my son, my son!

2 They reported to Joab:
Look, the king is weeping and mourning over Absalom.
3 On that day deliverance became mourning for all the people,
for the people heard on that day:
The king is sorely pained on account of his son.
4 And the people stole away on that day
to come into the city,
as people steal away ashamed when they flee in battle.

5 Now the king had covered his face,
and the king cried in a loud voice:
My son Absalom!
Absalom, my son, my son!

Logic dictates, of course, that Absalom alive would continue to pose a threat to the kingdom and to David himself. Far from regretting his actions, Absalom was clear that the purpose of the chase was mainly to capture and kill David, and he accepted the advice he thought would most adequately accomplish this. Even David earlier admitted his son's intentions (16:11). But David, who throughout this section is referred to as "the king," responds only as a father. There is no logic or reason behind his stutter of grief, repeating the name Absalom and the words "my son," a keening wail in Hebrew with its alternating *o* and *i* sounds. When he expresses his wish to have died in his son's place, he literally says, "Who will grant my dying, I in your place?"

It has become increasingly fashionable to view David entirely in a cynical light. The question for the reader/listener is, however, not whether David's grief is genuine but whether the narrative wants us to understand his tears as reflecting a father's sorrow or as "crocodile tears."[122] In preceding events, David has been shown to be capable of grieving over the death of opponents: Upon their deaths, both Saul and Abner received words of lament. Absalom is portrayed in the text as a person of violence and charm, someone willing to wipe his own father off the map for his advancement. The text has been ambiguous about David's feelings toward Absalom except for the fact that David did not call him to account for the murder of his brother. With his extravagant mourning, there seems little doubt that the narrative portrays a "king" who has momentarily lost his capacity to react as a ruler by rejoicing in the victory and congrat-

122. Thus Pamela Tamarkin Reis, "Killing the Messenger: David's Policy or Politics?" JSOT 31 (2006): 185. For Reis, David's ascent to an upper room in the gate means that the narrator aims to convey a high place from which David can "broadcast his propaganda." In contrast to David's "nadir" this is his "apogee." "Not only is he physically high, he is mentally high" (188). Baden (*The Historical David*, 210), who attempts to reconstruct a picture of the historical David, believes that the text deliberately obfuscates the truth, that David ordered his son to be killed and that the description of his grief is a part of the "pro-David apology." One of the problems with this type of reconstruction, creating a historical figure of out-and-out villainy, is that it results in a flat rather than a complex character, where the text allows for a more layered approach. In Conroy's (*Absalom, Absalom!*, 112) words: "The narrator's presentation of David . . . is sympathetic but not uncritical. . . . If one takes into account the artistic complexity of this presentation, one will be less inclined to affirm a straight-forward pro-Davidic or anti-Davidic bias in the story."

ulating the soldiers who supported him, instead responding only in his role of parent.

Of course, in the real world such a separation of roles is not possible, especially not under the circumstances. The soldiers who had refused to have their hearts *stolen* by Absalom (cf. 15:6), *steal away* in shame because they feel they have contributed to the grief of the king. Joab, who has clearly understood both that the death of Absalom was necessary and that it would not be good news for David, steps in when he hears of the situation (19:6–9). He goes to the king in private and gives him a serious tongue lashing. Caught as he is in his own emotional turmoil, he is nevertheless clear-eyed about the present danger and becomes eloquent in his rage against what he sees as unreasonable and dangerous behavior on David's part.[123] This time, there is no prostration, no bowing and scraping, but a sharp attack. The king has piled shame on his "servants," who saved not only David's life but that of the rest of his family, and if he is not able to set grief aside and "speak to the heart" of his servants, he will lose everybody. Joab does not plead; he bluntly commands: "Arise, go out, and speak" (19:8). The king is silent in response but does as his general commands and sits "in the gate," the place where a ruler dispenses "justice and righteousness." The news causes "the people" to appear before the king, with the last line repeating the information that "Israel had fled, each man to this tent" (19:9b; cf. 18:17).

Act IV: Return of the King (2 Samuel 19:10–20:26)

David would return to his throne in Jerusalem, but his reign would never be quite the same.[124]

Two chapters round off the aftermath of Absalom's rebellion. After Joab has shaken David out of his grief-stricken posture, squabbles

123. Conroy (*Absalom, Absalom!* 77) ranks Joab's speech with those of the wise woman of Tekoa and Hushai "as one of the rhetorical highlights" of the material. For Conroy's close reading of Joab's speech, see *Absalom, Absalom!*, 77–80.

124. Baden, *The Historical David*, 210.

break out among the tribes, framing the return of David and the meetings he has on the way (19:10–16[9–15]; 19:41–44[40–43]). Before he is safely back in Jerusalem, a new rebellion breaks out, which is put down by Joab. Everything points in the direction of more turmoil to come, anticipating the eventual breakup of the tribes into two kingdoms.

Act IV, Scene 1: Who Shall Bring Back the King? (2 Samuel 19:10–44)[125]

Absalom's death has deprived the rebellion of its leader; apparently, it has not deprived the rebellion of potential energy.[126]

Although the king is back in the gate, things are still hanging by a thread, and some clever tactics have to be put in place before David can actually return to his city and his throne. The argument that arises in the next section (10–16) is not between two leaders or between people and their leaders but among the people themselves. Resentments with a long history bubble up between Judah and the rest of the tribes. Noteworthy is the reference to the "anointing" of the now dead Absalom by the squabblers, something so far not mentioned in the text (11; cf. 15:11). There must have been at least two factions, one of which is questioned by the others about "sitting idly by" in terms of "bringing back the king" (11).[127] In the meantime, David is negotiating with his own tribe, Judah, to help him get back home. He handles the negotiations through Zadok and Abiatar, the priests he had sent back to Jerusalem on his flight out of the city, who presumably remain in Jerusalem. They are to address the elders of Judah, calling them his kinsmen, his "bone and flesh," asking them

125. As noted above, I am following the chapter divisions of the Masoretic Text of the Hebrew Bible, in which the verse that appears as 18:33 in the NRSV and other English translations appears as 19:1. In ch. 19, subsequent verses are one number higher compared to their counterparts in English translation.

126. Campbell, *2 Samuel*, 160.

127. The text of v. 11 literally says, "Why are you silent about bringing back the king?"

why they should be "the last to bring back the king" (12).[128] The argument both among the Israelites and from David to his kinsmen centers on the root of the verb "return," both in its plain form and in the form meaning "to bring back," occurring in every verse in the unit except one (vv. 11, 12, 13, 15, 16).

The verse that interrupts the central concern reports the appointment of Amasa, who was introduced as commander on Absalom's side in the lead-up to the battle at Mahanaim (17:25). David calls Amasa also his "bone and flesh" and puts him in charge of the army in "place of Joab" (14). Amasa turns out to be a key person, for he "inclined the heart of all the men of Judah like one man" (15). Judah's loyalty is of course a crucial issue to David's success in regaining his throne; without its support, he may as well stay east of the Jordan. He needs to hear from his own kinsmen that they want him to come back. On their word, "return," the king "returned," and each party sets out in the direction of the Jordan (16).

While David's focus on his own tribe is logical, because his own people are divided in their loyalty toward him, it comes at the cost of a lack of attention to the rest of the tribes and increases the rift between north and south. Since David is working through negotiators (he does not himself speak "to the heart" of the people as Joab had commanded him to do), he could have used the same mode of communication with the rest of Israel to calm down the agitated emotions. Negotiating with only one side will not stand him in good stead in the long run, and his omission can be seen as a sign that he is still operating under a cloud of grief. Joab has been set aside without any notice, perhaps without being informed, another step that will have repercussions. For the time being, however, David is able to face former opponents and supporters who come his way, delaying his crossing of the Jordan in the same way as happened on his flight out of the city.

Three characters come to meet David: Shimei, who cursed him, Mephiboshet who was said to have betrayed him, and Barzillai from

128. Each group is thus being asked about bringing back their ruler. The question to Judah is clever because it presumes that the other tribes will get there *first.* No one wants to be last!

the Transjordan, who supported him (17–40).[129] Shimei, together with Mephiboshet's servant Tsiva and a large group of Benjaminites—without doubt an armed escort—reaches the king first, filled with remorse and begging forgiveness (17–24). Abishai, usually the one ready to silence an opponent for good, wants to kill him once again (cf. 16:9), and David once again creates distance between himself and "the sons of Tseruyah."[130] David's retort echoes with the word "today" (3×), ending in the rhetorical question regarding his kingship in Israel: "Do I not know that *today* it is I who is king over Israel?" (23). Shimei can leave unmolested, protected by an oath from the king. Mephiboshet, who arrives next, has a tricky case, because there is only the word of one against the word of the other (25–31). He approaches in a disheveled state, noted by the narrator as a permanent condition since the day the king left, a narrative comment that seems to lend trustworthiness to his statements. He declares that it was his intention to go after the king but that his servant Tsiva betrayed him. David solves the issue by dividing the property which he earlier granted to Tsiva between the two, and Mephiboshet, perhaps all too glad to get away with his life, protests that Tsiva can have it all, perhaps a polite way of saying "thank you" (31). Echoing the wise woman of Tekoa, Mephiboshet calls David "a messenger of God" (28). Barzillai from Gilead, the last with whom David has an exchange (32–39), is invited by the king to *cross* the

129. The flight from Jerusalem and the return have a certain symmetry in terms of encounters, in reverse order. See, for example, David Gunn's observations in "From Jerusalem to the Jordan and Back: Symmetry in 2 Samuel XV-XX," *VT* 30.1 (1980): 109–113. Gunn views the elegance of the description to provide both aesthetic satisfaction and contribute to the meaning in the sense that he discerns "an undertone of deterioration." While the symmetric arrangements lead one to expect "a movement from a low point back to a high one," there is a "falling tone which counterpoints it. David's return is far from triumphal" (113).

130. As he did earlier, David asks what he has in common with these men, the "sons of Tseruyah" (cf. 16:10). Verse 22[21] contains interesting echoes of statements regarding "Adonai's anointed" made by David himself (cf. 1 Sam 24:7[6], 11[10]; 26:16; 2 Sam 1:14, 16). David also spoke of the difference between himself and "the sons of Tseruyah" after the killing of Abner.

Jordan with him, but Barzillai demurs.[131] He is too old to spend time at a court with food, drink and entertainment.[132]

When the king finally crosses the Jordan to Gilgal, it is with "all the people of Judah and also half of the people of Israel." All is, however, not well in David's kingdom, as renewed quarreling breaks out between Judah and the rest of the tribes (41–44). The "men of Israel" accuse Judah of "stealing" the king (42), and the Judahites retort that they have escorted the king because he is their close relation, not because they got anything material out of it. It has become a matter of who was first, and David, who does not speak in this debate, is apparently not able to calm the furor. Campbell writes, "The drift of the passage is clear: Israel and Judah disputed their support for the king and Judah prevailed. . . . The details escape us."[133]

Act IV, Scene 2: A Fragile Union (2 Samuel 20)

Perhaps, some of the women were glad never to see the king again.[134]

All having a husband earns you is the likelihood of being burned, raped, chopped up or given away. We free women just get to earn our own living.[135]

131. The comment in v. 32 that Barzillai "had crossed the Jordan with the king" is presumptive on v. 37, in which Barzillai promises to go a little way across the Jordan, and v. 40, in which the king is said to cross and then kiss Barzillai and bless him.

132. In verse 36, Barzillai speaks of "male and female singers." Such a combination of participial forms referring to singers at court occurs in the text only here and in two other places (Ecc 2:8; 2 Chr 35:25). As Campbell (*2 Samuel*, 164) points out, these verses testify to the presence of male and female storytellers in ancient Israel.

133. Campbell, *2 Samuel*, 164.

134. Danna Nolan Fewell and David M. Gunn, *Gender, Power, and Promise: The Subject of the Bible's First Story* (Nashville: Abingdon, 1993), 143.

135. Fay Weldon, "Samson and His Women," in *Out of the Garden: Women Writers on the Bible*, ed. Christina Büchmann and Celina Spiegel (New York: Fawcett Columbine, 1995), 81.

Even before David's arrival in Jerusalem, renewed unrest breaks out in the form of a new rebellion led by one Sheba from the tribe of Benjamin. The phrases in the opening sentences call forth declarations to be made at the eventual breakup of the people following the death of King Solomon (1; cf. 1 Kgs 12:16): "No share in David,/ no inheritance in the son of Jesse,/ each to his tent, O Israel!" Unlike at that future date, there is still a loyal commander on hand to squash the uproar, but it takes a while for him to surface. David's first act is in any case not to deal with the new revolt but to take care of his concubines.

2 SAMUEL 20:3

David came to his house in Jerusalem,
and the king took the ten women,
the concubines whom he let stay to guard the house,
and he placed them in a house under guard;
he supported them but did not have intercourse with them.
They were shut up until the day of their death,
living as widows.

As the women have become taboo for David, they are taboo for anyone and remain sequestered until their death, widows while not widowed, reminiscent of Tamar, who lived desolate in her brother's house (13:20). The word "shut up," from the Hebrew root *tsarar* ("to wrap" or "to tie up") mostly has a negative connotation. It is applied to Saul and David on different occasions when they feel trapped and are in distress (1 Sam 28:15; 30:6). The women who were abandoned by David to "guard the house" are now "in a house under guard," *trapped* in their enclosure. Once, Abigail prophesied that David's life would be "bound" (*tsarar)* into the bundle of the living (1 Sam 25:29); of course, there was no telling what David's life or that of his house would be like. According to Polzin, as foretold by Abigail, the punishment "of David's house . . . is its prolonged existence in a reduced state, full of torment and distress such as the living widowhood of David's concubines . . . an image of perpetual domestic powerlessness." Polzin believes that the narrative thus casts a negative light on not just David's rule but on the rule of dynastic monarchy. "Protecting David's house placed Israel in the prison house of history."[136]

Continuing the theme of murder and mayhem that prevails in the cycle, when David sends Amasa to muster troops against Sheba (4–6), Amasa is tardy, and "Joab's men" march out under Abishai. When Amasa turns up, Joab is ready and skewers him through the belly (7–10). The location at which this takes place is Gibeon, and many features in this episode remind of the encounter between Joab and Abner's troops in 2 Samuel 2:12–32. There, as here, a commander in David's army is struck in the belly by an opponent (10; cf. 2 Sam 2:23). There, as here, the body of the victim becomes an obstacle for the troops in pursuit of the enemy (11–13; cf. 2 Sam 2:23).[137] Amasa, first introduced as Absalom's commander in 17:25, is related to Joab by blood.[138] Joab is clearly not ready to lay down his command and once again gets rid of a rival. He may have also been distrustful of Amasa's loyalty in view of his past allegiance to Absalom. The narrative, silent about emotions or motives as it often is, may intend to imply both.

Joab sets out for Abel Beth-Ma'acah—a town in the far north, a few miles across from Laish—where Sheba and his followers are holed up, and begins a siege against it (14–15). It is here that Joab has a conversation with a "wise woman," who calls out to him so that he approaches the wall, where she commands him to listen (16–22). *Speaking* and *listening* are emphatically used in the initial exchange. The woman repeats a call to Joab to *listen* (16 2×) and for him to approach so she may *speak* to him.[139] Once she is sure of his

136. Polzin, *David and the Deuteronomist*, 198, 199. Polzin thus views the three major events or focal points of ch. 20—the seclusion of the concubines, the murder of Amasa by Joab, and the liberation of Abel Beth-Ma'acah—as metaphors for "the institution of kingship as a major cause of fratricide on the tribal and national level" (201). Abel escapes the fate of destruction by severing the "head" of their would-be ruler and casting it away.

137. For other similarities between the two episodes, see Polzin, *David and the Deuteronomist*, 199.

138. The parentage of Amasa is listed differently in 2 Sam 17:25 than 1 Chr 2:17, but in either case he would be Joab's cousin, as their mothers are listed as sisters.

139. Coming "close to the wall" is reminiscent of both Abimelek at Tebes

identity, she once again admonishes him to *listen*, upon which he assures her, "I am *listening*" (17). Listening—in English translations often erroneously translated with "obey"—is in the Hebrew Bible not the equivalent of simply hearing without obligation and is often best rendered with "heed" or "hearken"—that is to say, listening with close attention and the intent of active engagement following.[140] When young Samuel hears a voice speaking to him in the night, he says, as Eli instructed him, "Speak, for your servant is listening" (1 Sam 3:10). The invitation to speak, followed by the assurance of listening, puts the speaker into the position of authority and the listener into a potentially subordinate one. Coming close to the city wall has put Joab in a vulnerable position, and he now establishes himself as the inferior to the "wise woman" who wants to speak to him. She launches into a short, powerful speech.

2 Samuel 20:18–19

18 She said, saying:
In the old days they spoke, yes spoke, saying:
Let them ask, yes, ask in Abel,
and that was the end of it.
19 I am one of the peaceful faithful ones of Israel,
and you are seeking to kill a town, a mother in Israel;
why would you devour the inheritance of Adonai?

In her short speech, she manages to identify her town, her own place in the town, and its place in the nation. With her proverb about the town of Abel she establishes its authority and subsequently her

(Judg 9:52) and of Joab's own words, hypothetically ascribed to David during the siege at Rabbah: "Why did you come so close to the wall?" (2 Sam 11:20). Camp ("The Wise Women of 2 Samuel," 22) compares the wise woman's address to Joab to the confrontation with the Chief of the Assyrian army in 2 Kgs 18:17–36 as well as to the encounter between Abner and Joab in 2 Sam 2:24–28.

140. For a discussion of translating the Hebrew verb *shama* without resorting to "obey," see van Wijk-Bos, *Making Wise the Simple*, 18, 18n8–9. It is especially in *not listening* to the word of Adonai that people and individuals fall short of their tasks; this was a special failing of Saul (see pp. 111, 113, 120 above).

own authority within it.[141] Abel is the town where, of old, resolutions to baffling questions were found, and she positions herself in this place as one of those who is peace/wholeness-loving and trustworthy in Israel, a *prima inter pares*. This is the city Joab is seeking to destroy, a "mother in Israel"; by killing it he would "devour" the inheritance granted by God to the people.[142] The word "devour" is used elsewhere of the ground "devouring" those who rebelled in the wilderness (Num 16:30, 32, 34; Deut 11:6) and a similar image occurs when Abner questions Joab about a situation in which the sword will "devour" forever (2 Sam 2:26). The expression "mother in Israel" we find elsewhere in reference to the judge and prophet Deborah (Judg 5:7), and rather than pointing to nurture, it refers to authority, guidance, protection, and governance.[143]

That the woman has great authority not only vis-à-vis Joab but in her town becomes clear when she convinces her townspeople to hand the head of Sheba to Joab.[144] "She came to all the people in her wisdom" (22), and no more needs to be said. Camp writes, "Her authority is without question, both in her commanding stance before Joab and in her obvious influence among her people. We can, in fact, probably interpret her 'going to all the people in her wisdom' as an

141. On the significance of the use of a proverb, see Camp, "The Wise Women of 2 Samuel," 19–21; also see pp. 300–301 above.

142. The words "heritage of Adonai" remind of the words from the Tekoite to David in 2 Sam 14:16, where the term is "divine inheritance."

143. For an extensive discussion of the power of the mother image, see Camp, "The Wise Women of 2 Samuel," 24–26. Adele Reinhartz ("Anonymity and Character in the Books of Samuel," *Semeia* 53 [1993]: 137), while referring to the nurturing role of the wise woman of Abel, also recognizes her as one of three women, together with the shaman of Endor and the Tekoite, who "focus our attention as readers . . . on their autonomy and independence from the king or his general and on their unstereotypical actions as women."

144. A haunting review of the use of texts like these, in view of the sacrifice of one man to save the entire town, and the selection process during the time of the persecution and shoah of the Nazi era, may be found in Aaron Rakeffet-Rothkoff's "Surrendering Jews to the Nazis in the Light of the Halakhah," *Tradition: A Journal of Orthodox Thought* 25 (1991): 35–45: "Even in the 'Valley of the Shadow of Death,' Jews committed to Torah continued to seek Halakhah guidance."

act of counsel similar to that which a court advisor may give a king."[145] Joab blows the shofar as a sign that the battle is over before it began, and all go their way—Joab back to Jerusalem, "to the king" (22).

In a direct connection with verse 22, the list following, concluding the chapter (23–26), begins with Joab as the commander of "the entire army of Israel." Other commanders and administrators at the court are mentioned. Together with the list in 2 Sam 8:16–18, this serves to bookend the narratives of David's rule in Jerusalem, with their straightforward timeline and their close focus on King David and his people.[146]

Who Wrote This Story?

Expanded knowledge about the lives of Israelite women . . . helps us to confront the problematic stereotype projected onto the biblical past in popular culture and biblical scholarship, both of which follow the long tradition of reading later ideas about women into Israelite contexts.[147]

Even more than a hundred years later, many scholars would still agree with the statement made by Henry Preserved Smith that 2 Samuel 9–20 is a "homogeneous and continuous narrative of David's experiences from the time when he was firmly settled on the throne until near the close of his life. . . . The unity and integrity of the section, except some minor interpolations, is generally conceded."[148] Smith also assumes that a male author wrote at a time close to the era of King David. Not everyone agrees that the story begins at chapter 9 and ends at 1 Kings 1–2, but no matter where one puts the boundaries of the narrative, the core of it is by most considered to be a literary work of art. Antony Campbell suggests that

145. Camp, "The Wise Women of 2 Samuel," 18.

146. Alter, *The David Story*, 328n23.

147. Carol Meyers, *Rediscovering Eve: Ancient Israelite Women in Context* (Oxford: Oxford University Press, 2006), 201.

148. Henry Preserved Smith, *A Critical and Exegetical Commentary on the Books of Samuel* (Edinburgh: T&T Clark, 1899), 310.

the characteristic qualities of this material may be "its capacity to create space for so many questions and to answer so few."[149] He decides that it "would be the height of temerity to determine a setting for such elusive texts" and then suggests that a "serious contender is the late tenth-century court of Jeroboam."[150] Where the temerity is so high and the field so wide open, it may be possible to argue an unorthodox point of view.

First, Smith's opinion that the author was "not very remote from the events" has much merit. The liveliness of the tale, the eye for detail, and the complexity of the characters speak in favor of someone who witnessed at least some of these events or was close to them. The perspective on characters, especially David, is multifaceted, although with much negative coloring. A gifted politician, David is caught in the web of his personal failings and the schemes of his family and advisors. At the height of his power, as a ruler with many wives as well as a harem at his disposal, he embarks on a path that leads from sexual transgression to the murder of one of his longtime trusted companions. He can be humble, is willing to listen to advice from a local woman, and understands what path to take in order to overcome a rebellion. At the same time, like many parents, he has no insight into his children or what they are up to and dotes on the one who does him the most harm.

Some scholars have suggested the prophet Nathan or Gad as a possible source.[151] If we assume it to be in origin a *written* story of high literary quality, composed during or shortly after the time of King David, the writer most likely belonged to a class of people trained in this skill. Such training may have been the prerogative of

149. Campbell, *2 Samuel*, 99. Campbell, together with others, assumes the story to begin at ch. 11 and argues against understanding it as a *succession narrative* and connecting it with 1 Kgs 1–2. He reviews questions that find no answer in 2 Samuel 11–20 on pp. 99–100 of his work. The discussion on pp. 97–110 also reviews the most important current theories regarding the stories.

150. Campbell, *2 Samuel*, 107–108.

151. In considering possible authorship, Fokkelman (*King David*, 11), who judges 2 Samuel 9–20 together with 1 Kings 1–2 to be one *Scene*, observes that "he was a writer who possessed a high degree of autonomy" without assigning a specific time period to him.

elite youth, especially those associated with the court.[152] Although prophets like Nathan and Gad, both associated with David in significant ways, could be candidates, it is just as possible that the story originated with one of David's children, who evidently did not all put their father on a pedestal. We must ask if it is a given in that case that the writer was male.

Women in the ancient world, though in many ways part of a society with patriarchal features (see van Wijk-Bos, *The End of the Beginning*, 19, 21–22; also pp. 12, 23, 42–43 above), were able to hold a great variety of positions according to the biblical record, including the texts here under review. In her book *Rediscovering Eve*, biblical scholar Carol Meyers lists food processing, textile work, trading in commodities, healthcare, cultic activities, prophecy, and musical composition and performance as well as "herald" among professions open to women in the biblical world.[153] Clearly, the skill of musical creation included the composition of text. Although literacy beyond alphabet recognition, required to create a literary work, was most likely restricted to a limited class of people, there is no evidence that it was confined to males only. Wilda Gafney has convincingly argued for female scribal guilds, both in the larger ancient Mediterranean world and in Israel.[154] There are several texts in the Hebrew Bible that could be traced to female composition, among them the story of Tamar and Judah in Genesis 38.[155] That tale is one of a Tamar who,

152. Scholars suggest that court and temple provided training for elite youth also in reading and writing and in other particular tasks. The sayings collected in the book of Proverbs may have once belonged to instructional material from this educational environment. For an extensive discussion of literacy and scribal activity and groups, see Eric A. Seibert, *Subversive Scribes and the Solomonic Narrative: A Rereading of 1 Kings 1–11* (London: T&T Clark, 2006).

153. Meyers, *Rediscovering Eve*, 171–79.

154. Wilda C. Gafney, *Daughters of Miriam: Women Prophets in Ancient Israel* (Minneapolis: Fortress, 2008), 123–30.

155. Similarly, Ruth and Ecclesiastes most likely originated with women. In her book *In the Wake of the Goddesses: Women, Culture and the Biblical Transformation of Pagan Myth* (New York: Macmillan, 1992), Tikva Frymer-Kensky cites a Sumerian female poet from the end of the third millennium

deprived of her rights by her father-in-law, Judah, takes control of her destiny and tricks him into sexual intercourse and eventually into confessing to having caused her pregnancy. The theme is the establishment of the line of Judah, but it is Tamar who moves to the center of the action in Genesis 38. We observed earlier that the unusual phrase "I am pregnant" occurs only in 2 Samuel 11:5 and Genesis 38:25. There is, in addition, the similar illicit nature of the sexual encounter between family members. Although Judah in the Genesis account is not held answerable for his intimacy with his daughter-in-law, such unions are declared forbidden and deserving of the death penalty in the Torah (Lev 20:12), as is the one between brother and sister (Lev 20:17). Furthermore, only in Genesis 38 and 2 Samuel 12 is God said to be the direct cause of the death of a central character's male offspring (Gen 38:7, 10; 2 Sam 12:15). I suggest that the Genesis account, possibly originating in women's storytelling circles, was well known at the time of King David, himself a descendant of the line established by Tamar and Judah.

We came across at least three women who speak in the story with eloquence and conviction: Tamar and the "wise women" of Tekoa and Abel. Tamar, by the biblical account, stayed and was "desolate" in the house of Absalom her brother. The root "desolate" (*shamam*) is used only a handful of times and occurs elsewhere for destroyed and deserted land (Isa 1:7; Ezek 23:33; 35:7; Joel 2:20; Zeph 2:9). We may thus assume that she never married, never had a household to manage or children to rear and teach. But it is not impossible that she was a literate woman. Living in the house of her brother did not mean she was imprisoned, and there were other clever women at court with whom she may have spoken and from

BCE, Enheduanna, who composed major poems. Frymer-Kensky writes, "There is really no reason to assume that anonymous compositions of this period were written by men" (42). Although Frymer-Kensky does not pursue this line of thinking in her discussion of biblical compositions, one could argue the same for texts of the Bible. Qohelet (Ecc 1:1), for example, is clearly a female name (feminine participle of the root *qahal*). Qohelet writes under a pseudonym as "king in Jerusalem"—a pseudonym she uses only twice (1:1, 12), each time accompanied by the feminine participle. The rest of the book is written in the gender-neutral first person.

whom she may have learned—her own mother Ma'acah, Abigail, and Bathsheba among them. From them she may have heard stories, including the story of her father's ancestry and therefore of her namesake. As a king's daughter, she had access to much information and would be able to observe what transpired in the court of her father. Tamar, granddaughter and daughter of kings, wrote it all down, including the story of Bathsheba and Uriah and the story of her own rape and humiliation, drawing on material she knew about from earlier traditions.[156] One of the devastating blows in the aftermath of rape is the inability of the world to listen, the silencing of the victim's voice. Tamar's voice of protest and woe is silenced by her brother Absalom. As readers, we can resist the silencing of Tamar's voice by assigning to her the creation of the work of art that became the Court History of David. Her father at least colluded in the violence done to her and did nothing to punish the culprit. In the end, both father and rapist brother come face to face with the result of their shortcomings, their weakness and vanity.

156. Tamar would then belong to a class of "untethered scribes"—that is, scribes who were not under close supervision. See Seibert, *Subversive Scribes*, 53. Seibert also assumes that all scribes, regardless of the class to which they belonged, were male.

Cycle V: Hazards, Heroes, and Poetry (2 Samuel 21–24)

Like the end of Deuteronomy, the book of Samuel . . . moves toward its conclusion on a note of heightened rhetoric.[1]

Far from presenting a random mishmash of information, three concentric rings form an elegant structure in the final chapters of 2 Samuel. The outer ring of two narratives describes events at an indeterminate time during the reign of David (21:1–14; 24:1–25); the second ring presents heroic deeds of David's men and lists of the heroes themselves (21:15–22; 23:8–39); the central portion contains two poems of uneven length, both ascribed to David: one a prayer of praise to Adonai and one identified as David's last words (22:1–51; 23:1–7). The narrative sections deal with national crises during King David's rule, the first a famine, the second a plague, and the efforts of David to assuage the wrath of Adonai. The lists of heroic exploits and their perpetrators set David in the midst of others, men of renown, as a fighter among other elite fighters in the context of ongoing wars. The central sections, with their orientation to Adonai and themes of praise, assign the same warlike action to the Holy One of Israel as mirrored by David and his men on the human level. The poems in some ways echo Hannah's prayer in ascribing to Adonai the role of strengthening the warrior's might and glorying in the defeat of the enemy. The glue that holds the material together is the portrayal of royal power as overshadowed by divine authority and

1. Everett Fox, *Give Us a King! Samuel, Saul, and David* (New York: Schocken, 1999), 263.

grandeur in times of national distress, the subject of both the outer and the central rings.[2]

God acts in unpredictable ways in the narratives, and a confounded David has to find a way on behalf of his people to come to terms with ungovernable divine control. As Brueggemann puts it, "The king and his learned, legitimated advisers may want to reduce all of life to their plans, but there is more on the loose than they can manage."[3] Divine power is lauded in the poetic sections as the force that enhances military prowess and brings deliverance but also as the power that founded David's house as a lasting one, and both prayers testify to a deep abiding trust in God.[4] On the human level, the lists of the second ring depict a David who takes a backseat to others as a warrior, surrounded as he is by mighty heroes whose successes may outshine his own. Throughout the chapters, there is thus a reflection on royal authority and skill checked by both human and divine presence. The land, in the narrative sections as well as the lists, is portrayed as endangered by various calamities. Whether the danger is drought or infectious disease or the ever-looming presence of powerful enemies, royal power, even if divinely protected, will not save it from being overcome by famine or plague or hostile

2. I disagree with Antony Campbell (*2 Samuel*, FOTL 8 [Grand Rapids: Eerdmans, 2005], 185), who discerns no "thematic unity" in the chapters. Polzin (*David and the Deuteronomist*, vol. 3 of *A Literary Study of the Deuteronomic History* [Bloomington: Indiana University Press, 1993], 213), on the other hand, finds both thematic and literary unity in the chapters, especially in the narrative framework with its reflections on God's anger against the nation—an anger that "endures well beyond the life and death of David—indeed, until the very end of the History."

3. Walter Brueggemann, "2 Samuel 21–24: An Appendix of Deconstruction," *CBQ* 50 (1988): 392.

4. The poetry of chs. 22 and 23 is notoriously difficult, as is the language of the list in ch. 23. Alter (*The David Story: A Translation with Commentary of 1 and 2 Samuel* [New York: Norton, 1999], 348n8) calls them "fragmentary recollections of particular heroic exploits" which "do not sound like the invention of a later writer, but . . . like memories of remarkable martial acts familiar to an audience." He considers ch. 23 "the strongest candidate of any passage in the Book of Samuel to be considered a text actually written in David's lifetime."

powers, and it may easily become victimized in the wake of royal transgression. The sword that will not depart from David's house forever (2 Sam 12:10) cuts a wide swath after all and affects not only the royal house but the entire people.

Ring I: A Land at Risk (2 Samuel 21:1–14; 24:1–25)

In both narratives, the land suffers on account of a king's failure. In the first, the failure appears to be Saul's, but the reek of human sacrifice clings to David, and it is only upon his reaction to the brave and loyal act of a woman that the famine devastating the land comes to an end. In the second story, the anger of Adonai on account of a census initiated by David results in a plague killing thousands of people. It is halted eventually by a propitiatory sacrifice brought by the king.

Ring I, Scene 1: David and the Gibeonites (2 Samuel 21:1–9)

Saul is guilty of violating a treaty that should not have been made.[5]

The story seems quite straightforward: The land is struck by famine for three years at an unspecified period during David's rule. To underline the severity of the situation, the text reiterates "year after year." The first verse announces the national calamity and makes a pronouncement about Saul's bloodguilt by divine oracle, including a statement about Saul having "killed the Gibeonites." Nothing is mentioned elsewhere of this attack, but the narrative of the subsequent verse verifies at least an *attempt* of Saul to "strike them down" (2). The Gibeonites are native inhabitants of the land who tricked Joshua into making a covenant with them (Josh 9:3–27)[6] and continued to live among Israelites. David asks them what he can do to make things right, and the Gibeonites demand seven of Saul's offspring as

5. J. Cheryl Exum, "Rizpah," *Word and World* 27 (1997): 261.
6. See van Wijk-Bos, *The End of the Beginning*, 114–19.

a sacrifice "so we may execute them to Adonai" (6).[7] David agrees to hand them over, sparing Jonathan's son Mephiboshet, and two sons of Saul and five of his grandsons are delivered to the Gibeonites.

2 SAMUEL 21:8–9

8 Then the king took two sons of Rizpah,
the daughter of Ayah, whom she bore Saul,
Armoni and Mephiboshet,
and five sons of Merab,[8] the daughter of Saul,
whom she bore Adriel,
the son of Barzillai from Meholah.
9 He gave them over in the hand of the Gibeonites,
and they executed them on the hill before Adonai,
and the seven fell together;
they were killed in the days of the harvest, at the start,
the beginning of the barley harvest.

All the sons are listed together with mother as well as father, with the mother in first place. "The seven fell together" and "were killed" at the time of the harvest, with the emphasis on the word "harvest" and the fact that it is the initial period. While this period ordinarily would herald a phase of abundance, there is likely very little to harvest during a famine. The time of the year is spring, and the ground that should produce bounty instead generates the shocking harvest of seven human beings, offspring of the house of Saul killed "before Adonai."

So far, the story has been of a problem on a national scale and the search for a solution. We note that at the end of the episode, however, there is no abatement of the famine; it appears, therefore,

7. The mode of execution is uncertain, and there are a number of gruesome possibilities, such as impaling, dismemberment, exposure, and so on. Because the text notes that "the seven fell together; they were killed . . . " it is my assumption that of the possibilities, a violent quick method is the most likely.

8. The Masoretic Text lists Michal, but I here read "Merab" with the Septuagint and other translations.

that the sacrifice of human beings has not done the job. Much depends on the interpretation of the chapter's first verse, which introduces the famine and both the king's and God's reaction. There was a famine, and David "sought the presence of Adonai" (1). Entering into a consultation with God is not usually expressed with the verb "to seek." This verb occurs earlier in the David stories when David beseeches God on behalf of his ill child (12:16). In that case, however, the usage is appropriate and clear. On other occasions when David needs divine advice, the text uses direct address: "David said to Adonai" or the verb "to ask" (*sha'al*) with explicit mention of the question's content (1 Sam 23:2, 10–11; 30:8; 2 Sam 2:1; 5:19, 23). The Hebrew verb for "seek" (*biqqesh*) certainly carries a note of urgency, often employed in 1 Samuel of Saul's *search* for David in order to kill him (1 Sam 19:10; 23:10, 14, 15, 25; 24:3[2]; 27:1). Here, the purpose of David's search remains unstated; and it does not become evident from God's response.[9] Did David want to know the cause of the national disaster? Did he ask *how* it could be brought to a halt? *When* it would end?

9. God's reply, often translated in ways that make it sound clear, is oddly formulated in Hebrew. Literally, the text reads, "Adonai said to Saul and the house of blood because he killed the Gibeonites." The Hebrew preposition *'el* is directional, and even if read as *al*, the phrase needs a verb somewhere. Hence the NRSV translation: "There is bloodguilt on Saul and on his house because he put the Gibeonites to death." We might try reading with the Geneva version ("It is for Saul and for his bloodie house because he slew the Gibeonites"), in which "for" means "on account of," but the preposition *el* cannot be read that way. In sentences where *vayyomer* is followed by *el*, the translation would be "he said to" followed by what was said, which is not possible in the context of 2 Sam 21:1. Exum ("Rizpah," 265), who appears to read *al*, translates, "Against Saul and against his house there is bloodguilt because he sought to kill the Gibeonites." Apart from adopting the Septuagint, as others do also in reading "his house," Exum's translation blurs the distinction between the divine statement in v. 1 and that of the narrative in v. 2 regarding Saul's actions. Most translations assume that David asked the *reason* for the famine. The best we can do with the Hebrew line is to read the preposition as *el* and translate "regarding": "Adonai said [spoke?] regarding Saul and the house of blood because he killed the Gibeonites." *El* is used in this way in 2 Sam 1:24: "Weep over Saul." All the same, it does not result in a smooth or a clear sentence in English.

The reply points to Saul and bloodguilt on account of his killing of the Gibeonites, a possible cause for the famine. What it does not reveal is the means to end it. There is also no reference to anger on God's side, an anger which would need appeasement in order for the famine to end.[10] Events in the human world, especially natural disasters that befall the land, are in the Bible often understood to derive from divine interference in response to human transgressions (Deut 28:24). Indeed, the end of the story is that "God was moved on behalf of the land," implying that God caused the famine in the first place. Yet it is not God's anger but Saul's trespass against Gibeon and the resulting Gibeonite anger and desire for vengeance that are pointed to as the cause. If that is the case, however, Gibeon's attempt to appease God by human sacrifice should produce the desired results, but it meets with no response.

There are other unresolved issues. Taking the story at face value, there is a matter of "bloodguilt" which needs to be atoned, but David does not follow through with a request about the sort of atonement he should provide. Instead, he invites the Gibeonites and asks them what *they* want from him as atonement (3). There is no divine demand of any kind laid on David, and certainly not a demand for human sacrifice. In this brief account told so summarily that one does not even know how the victims are executed, seemingly superfluous detail stands out. The Gibeonites get five lines of explanation as to their status in Israel. First, they are described as non-Israelites ("They were not from the children of Israel," 2), and the text clarifies that the "Israelites were sworn to them." In other words, they are outsiders to whom Israel has an obligation of protection established by oath. The non-Israelite origin of Gibeon can hardly have been forgotten, so spelling it out serves to highlight the matter. Saul, the narrative says, "sought to strike them down/ in his zeal for the Isra-

10. In his discussion of the episode, Fokkelman (*Throne and City*, vol. 3 of *Narrative Art and Poetry in the Books of Samuel* [Assen: Van Gorcum, 1990], 271–76) refers throughout to Adonai's "wrath." It is, however, worth noting that there is no mention of God's anger, unlike in ch. 24, and it is not clear we are to assume it. The word "anger" does not occur in the story, although we may infer from the speech of the Gibeonites that *they* are indeed angry.

elites and for Judah" (2), an elaboration on the word from God that Saul "killed" them. According to the narrative, he only *tried* to do so, and he did it out of passion for his own people.

When the Gibeonites explain that they have nothing and no one available to bring about atonement—"no man in Israel," as they point out, "to kill"—David amends his earlier question to a promise.[11] "What shall I do for you?" turns into, "Whatever you say, I shall do for you," notably following on the heels of the information about the absence of a human victim. The Gibeonites then state their requirement after elaborately describing the destruction Saul wrought on them. They clearly intend their vengeance to be a sacrifice, as they specify they want to execute Saul's offspring "to Adonai" (6). The idea of sacrificing human beings to appease God, who has presumably caused the famine, thus comes from a group emphatically designated as non-Israelite. David's flawed behavior consists in his collaboration with this group.

Another unexpected expansion occurs with the list of names and parents in verse 8, especially with its inclusion of the mothers' names. Even if it could be argued that they are named on account of their relationship to Saul, such specificity is not necessary unless the text intends to draw attention to their presence. The first name is Rizpah's, the secondary wife of Saul, a woman who became a cause of contention between Abner and Ishboshet (3:7–8). Rizpah's name means "glowing coal" or "ember"; her father is Ayah, "falcon." She is named together with her father throughout the second half of the story of the human sacrifice. We note once again that the execution of her two sons and five of Merab's sons does not occasion an abating of the famine.

11. The Gibeonites in Josh 9 are clever with their words, and it appears they have not changed their ways. Just as they drew the Israelites and Joshua into a commitment of which they could not foresee the extent, they get David to promise something of which he does not yet know the nature. See Johanna W. H. van Wijk-Bos, *Reading Samuel: A Literary and Theological Commentary* (Macon, GA: Smyth and Helwys, 2011), 137. It is noticeable that they work slowly up to stating their demand in v. 5, beginning with the words "the man who finished us off" and adding a detailed rationale before they state their requirement of "seven of his sons."

The story remains odd, and because of its opaque nature, it is open to a suspicious reading. Saul's action against Gibeon comes out of the blue, and only David would have heard of it since the information is based on a divine oracle. If David indeed somehow, whether through Gibeonites or other outsiders, had Saul's male offspring killed, it would be convenient to construct a rationale for this by blaming Saul. Brueggemann writes, "Read suspiciously, the narrative presents David as a political killer, who hides his actions in religious justification."[12] The sacrifice of human beings, in this case perhaps also including children, has a deeply disquieting effect similar to the one elicited by the story of Jefta's daughter.[13] The storyteller cannot bring her/himself to clarify that such was indeed a divine command and ascribes it to those originally not "from the Israelites." The advantage of assigning the responsibility for human sacrifice at least partly to outsiders is to put David once again at one remove from the decimation of Saul's line. Like the story of Jefta's daughter, however, it may also herald a trajectory in which Israel's adventure with kingship is "spiraling downward," carrying in its very establishment the seeds of the nation's eventual demise.

Ring I, Scene 2: Rizpah, Daughter of Ayah (2 Samuel 21:10–14)

David and the Gibeonites offer a sacrifice of atonement, aimed at cleansing the land of evil. . . . Rizpah prevents a horrible sacrilege.[14]

2 Samuel 21:10–11

10 And Rizpah, the daughter of Ayah,
took sackcloth and stretched it for herself to the rock[15]

12. Walter Brueggemann, "2 Samuel 21–24: An Appendix of Deconstruction," *CBQ* 50 (1988): 383–397, here 386.

13. See the discussion of Judg 11:29–40 in van Wijk-Bos, *The End of the Beginning*, 259–67.

14. Exum, "Rizpah," 267.

15. Most translations read "on the rock," taking the directional Hebrew preposition *el*, meaning "toward," to be a variant for *al*, meaning "over, upon."

from the beginning of the harvest
until water poured on them from the sky.
She did not let the birds of the sky rest on them by day,
nor the wild animals of the field by night.
11 It was reported to David what Rizpah did,
the daughter of Ayah, Saul's concubine.[16]

Rizpah moves out of her static position as past wife of Saul and mother of two sons in verse 8 into the center of the action. It may not sound like much, but what she does testifies to extraordinary bravery and endurance. Leaving dead bodies unburied was sacrilege. She frames the short unit in such a way that it is her *action* ("what Rizpah did") that comes to David's ears, and she takes her place with the bodies of her own sons and those of her fellow clan member Merab to ward off further desecration by wildlife.[17] When David hears the report, he has the bones of Saul and Jonathan retrieved from Jabesh Gilead and buried in the grave of Kish, Saul's father (12–14). Rizpah's long steady vigil, from spring until fall, sitting like the "glowing coal" evoked by her name among the ashes of death without speech or indications of her grief except the sackcloth, results in royal action that *does* bring an end to the calamity of the famine; or, at least, so we presume on the basis of the statement in verse 14 that "God was moved on behalf of the land after that"—that is to say after the burials of the bones of Saul and Jonathan and (one hopes) the victims of the sacrifice (13). While the action of the Gibeonites is thus unsuccessful, Rizpah's long, faithful watch meets ultimately with success.

The effect of the story is that David's power to restore the land to health is constrained, first by a group of outsiders and subsequently

I maintain the more literal translation and assume she secured the cloth on the rock, stretching out the cloth as a makeshift tent. See Stanley Walters, "To the Rock" (2 Samuel 21:10), *CBQ* 70 (2008): 461.

16. "Concubine" is an approximate translation of the Hebrew word *pilegesh*, which indicates a secondary wife. See van Wijk-Bos, *The End of the Beginning*, 256, 277, 311–21.

17. As Exum ("Rizpah," 265) points out, "David's actions are determined by others." First, he responds to the request of the Gibeonites, and subsequently to what Rizpah "did."

by the persistent presence of a woman at the scene of execution. It is difficult to deny the impression that the tale intends to put David once again at a remove from the extinction of Saul's line. Baden calls the story "fiction built upon fiction" and believes the historical David to be responsible for the murder of Saul's family.[18] In any case, the episode serves to distance David from such a crime by assigning it to non-Israelites, who would not know any better than that deities require human sacrifice. At the same time, assigning the execution of the human victims to Gibeonites, who turn it into a sacred event, creates distance between the God of Israel and the gods of the nations who require this kind of devotion. Thus, no matter what the historical truth underlying the events, David's authority is checked by both the divine and the human context. Ironically, it is a woman's action that elicits a response leading to the restoration of the land.

A Difficult Story

As Stanley Walters asks, "How could this story . . . ever have been deemed appropriate for the long narrative sequence known as the 'Former Prophets'? It is not just one word or one-letter features of the text . . . that are difficult. The whole story is difficult."[19] Not only are there complications concerning David's consultation and the divine response, the absence of any reference elsewhere to Saul assaulting Gibeon, and the unclear method of executing the descendants of Saul, but there is also the issue of human sacrifice as such and the punishment for a misdeed of one generation descending on the next—both of which are practices that Torah and Prophets argue against.[20] While the narrative lacks the emotional detail of

18. Joel Baden, *The Historical David: The Real Life of an Invented Hero* (New York: HarperCollins, 2013), 147–48. Baden argues that most likely David had Saul's descendants killed early in his reign and got Gibeon to take the blame, "probably in exchange for a peace treaty" (148).

19. Walters, "To the Rock," 463.

20. For the prohibition of human sacrifice, see Lev 18:21; 20:3; Deut 12:30–31; 18:10. For the issue of children suffering for the iniquity of the father, see Deut 24:16; Jer 31:29–30; Ezek 18:1–4.

the sacrifice of Jefta's daughter, it is even less explicable; and the view of Rizpah keeping watch over the decomposing bodies of her children does nothing to ameliorate the gruesome nature of the events. Is it possible for the story to have another purpose beyond showing David in an ambiguous light, his power diminished by God and people—a light in which at worst "David killed Saul's family but provided a rationale by blaming Saul" and in which at best the "king is portrayed as a modest agent who functions as a priest implementing rites, but without power beyond these conventional religious perimeters"?[21]

One royal house decimated and the other portrayed in a less than glorious light is perhaps a useful picture for the postexilic community, for whom the monarchy had brought no escape from destruction and exile, to contemplate. Walters suggests looking also in the direction of the portrayal of Rizpah both as a figure for the land as a bereaved widow and as one awaiting a new beginning. The curious expression in verse 10 that she stretched sackcloth *to the rock* leads him to consider the few places where this exact expression occurs in the context of the threat of national destruction and the dawning of hope.[22] Following an announcement of disaster, Isaiah 30:29 promises joy like that of those who go to the "mountain of Adonai, *to the Rock* of Israel," while in Isaiah 51:1, the community in exile is encouraged to "look *to the rock* from which you were cut," to their father Abraham and to Sarah who gave them birth. The word "rock" by itself, although possibly a reference to a literal part of the landscape, occurs in a great number of instances as a metaphor for God in the biblical text. Notably, we find it as such multiple times in the poetic sections of these final chapters of 2 Samuel.[23] Based on these and other possible echoes of 2 Samuel 21:1–14 in the Isaiah passages, Walters argues for a "figural understanding" of Rizpah already at the time that this "block of text became part of the Former

21. Brueggemann, "2 Samuel 21–24," 386.

22. Walters, "To the Rock," 458. The threefold occurrence is noted in the margins of the Hebrew text as Isa 30:29 and 51:1, besides 2 Sam 21:10.

23. 2 Sam 22:3, 32, 47 2×; 23:3. This usage is especially prevalent in the Psalms.

Prophets."[24] Rizpah, as a powerful, faithful woman, thus closes texts that opened with the figure of Hannah, a woman who breathed trust and hope for the future. Rizpah, in her present state of bereavement, also looks to a future of hope. Most of all, this perspective on Rizpah "relativizes the story's violence and transcends its dissonance with the law and the prophets."[25] It is an attractive proposal shedding additional light on the possible function of this particular story in its current place.

Ring I, Scene 3: Pestilence and Affliction (2 Samuel 24)

The narrative logic of 2 Sam 24 is . . . driven by the conceptual connections between census, pestilence and expiation.[26]

Another disturbing story closes the narrative ring and the books of Samuel. God is angry with Israel and incites David to take a census, which David does against the protests of his commander Joab (1–9). Upon its completion, David is contrite and confesses his sin, after which God gives him a choice of punishments via the prophet Gad (10–15). Then God is sorry about all the destruction brought about by the plague and stops the messenger of destruction at the threshing floor of one Arauna, a Jebusite. David then pleads with God to spare the people further harm (17). A final section tells in detail of David's purchase of the threshing floor of Arauna, where he builds an altar and makes sacrifice, after which God grants David's plea (18–25).

Apart from the objectionable element that God is said to *incite* David to do the thing for which the *people* then are punished,[27]

24. Walters, "To the Rock," 463. A strong argument for this reading is the use of the rock imagery together with the preposition "to" in front of it, which appears out of place here and connects directly to the Isaianic material. In addition, Walters argues that the word *shivatayim* ("sevenfold") should be maintained in v. 9. This term occurs only seven times in the Hebrew Bible and also links to Isa 30 (v. 26).

25. Walters, "To the Rock," 464.

26. Russell, *The King and the Land*, 23.

27. The version of this event in 1 Chronicles changes the author of the

almost everything is told in reversed order. God is angry *before* the census, David is contrite *before* the punishment, the plague stops *before* David's plea and sacrifice and then is said to stop again. As we pick through the different elements of the story, a few issues rise to the surface: First, a census of military men was not a good idea;[28] furthermore, the God-David relationship is awry, with the notion that God incited David to do the wrong thing, reminiscent of the bad spirit of God that overcame Saul; perhaps most significant is the idea that a monarch's trespass affects the entire people. When David does wrong, the results are not limited to his house—or perhaps do not even affect his house—but they redound on his subjects. Taking all the elements of the story into account reveals David's power as seriously limited by divine control and interference.

A last issue, and also one that reflects on the boundaries of David's authority, is the purchase of Arauna's threshing floor. The purpose of the elaboration on this detail may have been allusion to the eventual construction of the temple at this location. Although there is no explicit mention of the temple, the knowledge of its original location could hardly have been forgotten. Stephen Russell has argued that the acquisition of the land by David is an integral part of the plot of the story, in which each element, *census*, *pestilence*, and *land* purchase, does not stand on its own but together with the others forms a coherent whole. "The chapter is constructed around a shared conception of cause and effect as it relates to census, pestilence, and expiatory sacrifice."[29] The purchase of the land in order

inciting to Satan: "Then stood up Satan against Israel and incited David to count Israel" (1 Chr 21:1).

28. The reading in 24:4 is that Joab went out "to muster the people," but as is often the case, we need to understand "people" here as troops, in view of both the verb "muster" and the reading in v. 9 that the census concerned "mighty men of valor," a common expression for warriors.

29. Russell, *The King and the Land*, 19. Russell also argues the connection between census, plague, and expiation, made clear in the biblical text in Exod 30:12: "When you take registration of the Israelites by mustering, each person shall give a ransom for his life to Adonai, when mustered, so there will be no affliction for them when they are mustered." The word for "affliction" (*negef*)

to bring the appropriate sacrifice is, according to Russell, related to the "nature of royal power over land in the biblical world." To Russell's insights, David has no automatic legal right to Arauna's property and wishes to establish such rights through purchase. By building an altar and bringing sacrifice, David achieves also that this particular site is dedicated to God.[30] While these actions have the effect of shedding a more positive light on David, portraying him as a legitimate ruler in his context, they also clarify the extent to which royalty does not have natural rights to land even when it belongs to an original inhabitant of Canaan.

Ring II: There Was War Again (2 Samuel 21:15–22; 23:8–39)

We consider the lists together that frame the two poems, with the first one reviewing encounters with giants at the time of the Philistine wars, in which heroes among David's servants accomplish heroic deeds. The list in chapter 23 continues with the same theme, reflecting early stages in David's career and crediting individuals other than David with military victories against the Philistines.

Ring II, Scene 1: The Lamp of Israel among the Heroes (2 Samuel 21:15–22)

[David's] only achievement in the text is to grow weary.[31]

Everything in the first listing of valiant men takes place in a context of war. Four units (15–17, 18, 19, 20–21) begin with the phrase "there

---

in Exod is an alternative noun in Hebrew from the same root as the word in 2 Sam 24:25 (*maggefah*).

30. Russell (*The King and the Land*, 38–39) sets the acquisition of the threshing floor in the context of the larger ancient Near Eastern world. The chapter thus becomes a portrayal of David as an "ideal ancient Near Eastern king": "David . . . personally secures land, protects it from legal claims, and sets it aside for direct cultic use."

31. Campbell, *2 Samuel*, 194.

was war again" with small variations. Introductions of a Philistine champion and the defending Israelite hero follow this opening line. The outer units (15–17 and 20–21) list the Philistine fighter first, together with features of armament or physical attributes, while the inner two are shorter and name the Israelite fighter first followed by the defeated Philistine. Four Philistine champions are descended from the Raphah, faced by four heroes of David's servants, each said to "strike down" his opponent. Each encounter, except the first one, takes place at a defined location, Gov and Gath. Alter calls the tightly structured section a "formulaic epic catalogue."[32] It ends with the announcement of the birth and the death of the Philistine descendants of the Raphah.[33]

2 SAMUEL 21:22

These four were born to the Raphah in Gath,
and they fell by the hand of David
and the hand of his servants.

David actually takes very little part in the action. He only participates in the first encounter and almost right away "grew faint."[34] The first giant may have taken David captive, but whatever the exact circumstances, he threatens to kill David and Abishai comes to his aid. This incident causes David's men to plead with him not to go into battle with them, because he might "extinguish the lamp of Israel." While the metaphor of the lamp for a human being is unique,

32. Alter, *The David Story*, 335n22.

33. The Raphah is presumably the ancestor of a legendary race of giants among the peoples, called the Refa'im, who were in the land before the Israelite entry (Gen 14:5; 15:20; Deut 3:11; Josh 12:4; 13:12). In Job, these are presumably the shades of the deceased (Job 26:5). The Septuagint translates everywhere "giants." Alter (*The David Story*, 333n16) suggests that the name Raphah may allude to a female progenitor.

34. Growing faint or weary in the context of battle occurs outside of this chapter in 1 Sam 14:31 and of David and the people with David in 2 Sam 16:14; 17:29. The expression is also used of the land in Ps 63:2[1] and of a person's being/soul (*nefesh*) in Ps 143:6.

the request itself is reminiscent of the plea by David's troops at the battle of Mahanaim (18:3). It shows the deep loyalty and regard of David's men for their leader but has the effect of taking David out of the action, even though the final lines assign the death of the champions to *David and* his servants (22).

The third Philistine champion is Goliath, whose slayer is here listed as Elhanan. Most likely the heroic deed belonged to Elhanan in the original telling and later clung to David as such stories will to popular heroes. As Fokkelman observes, "Upon the appearance of a great man in history the normal procedure in the history of the reception of his greatness is to extract some triumph or another from a contemporary in the background and award it to the national hero."[35] The remarkable feature is that the collectors maintained the tradition of Elhanan as the hero at all. The mocking of Israel, in 1 Samuel 17 ascribed to Goliath, here is assigned to an unnamed giant with unusual physical features besides his gigantic size. Presumably, the larger size of his hands, six fingers on each, enables him to grasp a larger weapon, although one wonders about the advantage of having six toes on each foot.

Ring II, Scene 2: The Three and the Thirty (2 Samuel 23:8–39)

Water and bread, both in reality and in a work of art, usually signify more than matter.[36]

The list of David's heroes in this chapter includes references to "the Three" and "the Thirty" in the first section (8–23), a hierarchical division among David's troops not mentioned elsewhere in the David narratives which must have had significance for the ancient listener. In any case, the divisions show an organized war band. The text is difficult in many places, and according to Alter is "perhaps the strongest candidate of any passage in the Book of Samuel to be considered a text actually written in David's lifetime." It sounds like "memories

35. Fokkelman, *Throne and City*, 296.
36. Fokkelman, *Throne and City*, 304.

of remarkable martial acts familiar to the audience, requiring only the recital of epic listing."[37] The last section consists of names only and is remarkable for its cadence and melodious repetition of sound in Hebrew.

The opening units list Adino, El'azar, and Shammah as the Three. Each performs a heroic deed, defeating Philistine enemies, which in two places is in addition credited to Adonai (10, 12). A short anecdote about David's thirst and his men breaking through enemy lines to get it for him draws David into the limelight, but merely as the passive recipient of a gift of water, no doubt significant both as simple refreshment and a symbol of life (14–17).[38] David is said to have had a "craving" and asks who will give him "water to drink from the well at Bethlehem at the gate" (15). It may have been more idle speculation than a serious question for water from his hometown, but his men take it seriously. Bethlehem is apparently in enemy territory, and they have to "break through" the enemy lines to get to the town and the gate in order to bring David the water (16). Once David realizes what he has made his soldiers do, he pours the water out as a libation to God, claiming that he would not drink what amounts to "the blood of the men." The word "craving" occurs in many places in the Bible of an unreasonable greedy desire (cf. Num 11:4, 34; Deut 5:21; Jer 2:24; Prov 13:4; 21:10, 26; 23:3). David wants water in a bad way, and especially the water he remembers from his growing up in Bethlehem. The picture of his men is that they will go to any lengths to please their leader. A contrite David becomes aware at the end that in his circumstances, idle wishes are best kept unexpressed.

Abishai appears as one of the fighters, as does Benayah (18–23), but Joab is absent, perhaps another indication that these lists go back to David's early days as a guerilla fighter, when Joab was not on the scene. The last section (24–39) lists thirty-seven names by its own accounting (39). Lists are not favorite material for contemporary readers of the Bible, but they testify to the importance of

37. Alter, *The David Story*, 348n8.

38. There are references to "the three" in this episode (23:13, 16, 17), but it is not clear if the same heroes are intended as the ones already described in 23:8–12. Perhaps this is a different contingent, since they go unnamed.

keeping ancestral names in the memory, which in certain cultures of today's world is still significant. Furthermore, a defeated and demoralized people may be sustained by memories that recall the old glory days at the dawn of a nation's existence. In Hebrew, the list is noteworthy for the beauty of its rhythm and sound, cast as it is in poetic form, with many alternations of short and long *a* varying with *o* and *i*, especially at the end of the lines.[39] The heroes are listed with their place names, towns, and villages of origin, so that the list not only brings to life the men of valor but the places they hail from, many of which no longer existed at the time the collection was finalized. We find Eliam here, the son of Ahitophel and the father of Bathsheba, and the list ends with Uriah the Hittite, a non-Israelite and a man who died on David's orders. Even glorious memories have their somber, realistic annotations.

Ring III: The Darling of Israel's Songs (2 Samuel 22:1–51; 23:1–7)

Two poetic sections make up the inner rings of the four chapters. Together with Hannah's prayer in 1 Samuel 2, these poems bracket the tale of the road to kingship in ancient Israel. In addition, David's own poetry (here and in 1:19–27) frames the sections of text that focus on his rise to the throne. The second poem is cast as David's last words, headed by a relatively long introduction of self-identification. Both poems speak to the king's trust in God and divine promises to his house while at the same time relativizing royal power as under God's control.

Ring III, Scene 1: Praise after Rescue (2 Samuel 22)

The king achieves nothing, deserves nothing, guarantees nothing.[40]

39. Many lines end with a sequence of *a*'s plus one *o* and an *i* (In Hebrew, *a* as in father, *o* as in mode, and *i* as in feet). There are few *u* sounds (as in smooth). Alternating *o* and *u* sounds are more at home in lament.

40. Brueggemann, "2 Samuel 21–24," 189.

A long poem, set during David's flight from Saul's persecution, presents David in a mode of praise for God, who rescues him, who liberates him from his enemies, and who has exalted him. Due to God's delivering power, David strides the earth as a vanquishing foe stomping down his adversaries, as the poem moves from exaltation of Adonai to reveling in the glory of God's king and the nature of his enduring house.

Although the language is not always easy to decipher, the poem is clear enough in theme and content.[41] The personal prayer, using the first person for the poet throughout, shows a clear progression from personal trust in God because of God's rescuing action (2–7) to an elaborate section on God's powerful and triumphant appearance (8–16) to a return of praise for God's deliverance of the poet and reward for the poet's righteousness (17–25). In most of this section, God is spoken of in the third person. The second half opens with the second-person address and a general statement about God's loyalty and greatness (26–32) to continue with the personal benefits derived from God's support by the poet in his victorious engagement with the enemy (33–43). The final stanzas elaborate on both the stature of the poet as "head of the nations" and God's greatness (47–49) to end with another expression of praise (50–51). Many stanzas alternate between descriptive third-person references to God and the second-person address, which lends a more intimate tone to the poem wherever it appears.

Hebrew poetry relies for its dramatic effect on repetition and intensification, which can be done in various ways.[42] Here, the opening lines are noteworthy for their piling up of nouns to describe God in relation to the poet.

41. The poem is virtually identical to Ps 18, and both poems are considered by many scholars to be among the most ancient poetic material in the Bible. Alter (*The David Story,* 336–44) considers the version in 2 Sam 22 the more likely to be the more original. For a more technical analysis of the poetry, see Alter, *The Art of Biblical Narrative* (New York: Basic Books, 1985), 29–37.

42. For a helpful understanding of the way Hebrew poetry works, see "The Dynamics of Biblical Parallelism," ch. 1 of Robert Alter, *The Art of Biblical Poetry* (New York: Basic Books, 1985), 3–26.

2 Samuel 22:1–3

1 Then David spoke to Adonai the words of this song,
on the day that Adonai rescued him
from the hand of all his enemies and from the hand of Saul.
He said:

2 Adonai, my crag,
my stronghold, my deliverer;
3 my God, my rock where I will shelter;
my shield and horn of my salvation,
my haven and my refuge,
my savior, from violence you will save me.

I take the lines as address rather than description, working up to the declaration "you will save me." The images are standard metaphors for God available in the poetry of the Psalms. What makes them stand out here is their accumulation. The static nature of the string of nouns is alleviated by the use of active participles, with "crag" and "stronghold" ending in "deliverer" (a participial noun in Hebrew), "shield," "horn," "haven," and "refuge" in "savior" (another participial noun), and finally the verb "you will save me." Everything together works up to the last line of the stanza, which reveals the context as one of "violence," the basis for the metaphors for God that point to safety and strength. While rocks and crags might not come to our mind as appropriate for providing such conditions, in an arid land these offer needed shade and in the wilderness a hiding place. We remember that David fled to the "stronghold" when on the run from Saul (1 Sam 22:5; 24:23[22]). The saving element of the relationship of Adonai with the poet is strongly emphasized in this opening and picked up right away in what follows.

Standard images of water that threatens to engulf the believer occur in the next stanza (4–6) with the metaphor of "breakers" and "torrents," opening up into the constriction of "cords" and "snares" that accompanies the death imagery. Everything in this section is in the first person, highlighting the personal relationship of the poet to God, who is not just a rock and a bulwark, but "my crag," "my fortress," and so on. In Hebrew, the *i* ("ee") sounds associated with the first person predominate. Taken all together, these signal the distress from which rises praise, "ee-ee-ee," like a cheeping bird. The conviction that the poet's cry has reached God's ears flows into an elaborate section on God's appearance.

The coming of God in the theophanic section (8–16) is a violent affair, accompanied by nature's uproar, earthquakes and thunder, storm and lightning. Upheaval and tumult arrive with God's presence, which here serves to draw the beleaguered poet out of the waters of hostility and victimization into a "wide open place," a noun used in verse 20 that is found only in a poetic context, connoting the place where a person can draw a breath. In Psalm 118:5, for example, the believer calls from a place of constriction or distress (*tsar*, as here in 2 Sam 22:7), and in response God leads her into an open space. From this place, the poet reflects on the grounds for God's benevolent action toward him, listed as "righteousness," "purity of the hands," refraining from "evil," following God's statutes, and keeping the self from "sin" (21–25). This does not sound like the penitent David who was aware of his trespass with Bathsheba and Uriah or the humbled David who leaves it up to God to do to him as is good in God's eyes if God takes delight in him. This is a self-confident recipient of God's benevolence.

After a reflection on God's nature of purity, loyalty, and protection (26–33), the poem moves into the arena of a Deity who strengthens the warrior (34–43). In graphic images, the poem describes the power God lends to the hero: swift feet, a sturdy and stable tread, robust hands, and ability with weaponry so that the enemy is destroyed. Then follows a series of verbs of action against the enemy: I "pursued," "destroyed," "finished them off," "battered," "smashed," "annihilated," "crushed," "pulverized," "stomped." Nine verbs of extravagant violence are paired with the enemy's falling, being bowed down, on the run. Even foreigners come to bow down before this mighty warrior king. The entire poem ends with more praise for Adonai, who is called "blessed," resuming the image of rock (47 2×). It is God who brings all this about, exacting vengeance and obtaining release from hostile forces (47–49). The final two verses begin with the resumption of praise for God and end in a third-person reference to God's king, who is also called "his anointed" and "David and his seed." While the poem in the context of the last chapters of 2 Samuel is assigned to David, the speaker could be anyone who composed a praise song on behalf of David. Like Hannah's poem, the prayer ends with a reference to "God's anointed," but in other ways it forms a counterpoint to Hannah's praise. There, God is the one who reverses the fate of the poor, bereft, and lowly, while here God is on the side of the warrior vanquishing the foe.

A Difficult Poem

While it may be solace for a defeated people to look back on the glory days when God supported the strong warrior king, such material has difficulty finding resonance with modern believers. A God who helps God's chosen monarch to stomp on the enemy and pulverize them may not be what we are looking for, or if we are, we most likely shy away from such desires as soon as they raise their head. Indeed, religion that relishes the defeat of those who are on another side than ours is something we need to turn our back on. It may help to remember that the words composed here are assigned to David when he was not exactly on top of things and was sorely in need of support. Brueggemann, who discusses such material in his book *Praying the Psalms*, suggests that for those of us who are "troubled about the psalms of vengeance, there is a way beyond them." But he cautions that this is not an "easy" or "natural way." Rather, we can get beyond them in going through them, in "accepting the rage and grief and terror of evil in ourselves in order to be liberated for compassion toward others."[43] Erich Zenger in his treatment of psalms of violence, vengeance, and enemies, puts forward that those who pray psalms of enmity are "inevitably faced with the question of their own complicity in the web of violence." Furthermore, "what does it mean to speak of enemies, if not to speak of our own fears?"[44]

43. Walter Brueggemann, *Praying the Psalms: Engaging Scripture and the Life of the Spirit* (Eugene, OR: Cascade Books, 2007), 80.

44. Erich Zenger, *A God of Vengeance? Understanding the Psalms of Divine Wrath* (Louisville: Westminster John Knox, 1994), 76–77.

I return to the sermon by the student who preached in the context of her own experience of rape (see pp. 291, 294–95 above). In unfolding the text of Psalm 59, she compared the enemies, for whose defeat and humiliation the psalmist prays, to her fears. She said:

> These fears, these new names, these daily injustices make a claim on you. They know your name—they whisper it in the endless stretches of dark night. They scream it during an otherwise pleasant dinner with a friend. They cultivate nervousness, distrust, anger, and hate where there was none before. To heal, to move forward, we have to open up again—even if it's just for a moment, even though it feels like the scariest thing in the world. We have to trust someone just a little—to take the risk that things can be good, that people can be kind. As we practice reconnecting with the world around us, we stumble, we retreat, we succeed, and sometimes we laugh. Reaching out, we can hear our God, Author of Life, creator of all that lives and moves and breathes speaking a message to us.[45]

Here was a young person who knew that the way out of a prayer that glories in the defeat of the enemy is not around it but *through* it.

Ring III, Scene 2: The Last Words of David (2 Samuel 23:1–7)

. . . as morning light at sunrise. (2 Sam 23:4)

A short poem consisting of four stanzas and cast as an oracle ends the poetic section. The text is filled with difficult and archaic words, of which the central section regarding a just ruler stands out for its powerful imagery. I render the poem in its entirety.

45. Elana Keppel Levy, unpublished Senior Sermon "Impact." Cited with author's permission.

2 Samuel 23:1–7

1 These are the last words of David:
An oracle of David son of Jesse,
oracle of the strong one raised up high,
anointed of the God of Jacob,
darling of the songs of Israel.
2 Spirit of Adonai speaks in me,
His utterance on my tongue.

3 The God of Israel has said:
For me—so speaks the Rock of Israel—
a righteous ruler of humanity
is a ruler in awe of God;
4 as morning light at sunrise,
a morning without clouds from its shining,
as from rain grass comes from earth.

5 But not thus my house with God.
For an enduring covenant he set up for me,
arranged in everything and guarded.
For all my deliverance and desire he will make sprout.[46]

6 The worthless man like thorns,
blown away all of them;
for no hand can pick them up.
7 Should a man touch them
he must get himself iron,
the shaft of a spear.
With fire they burn,
yes, burn where they settled.

46. The Hebrew words “for not” at the beginning of this line cause most translations to read the phrase as a question: “will he not cause . . . to sprout?” I consider them an inadvertent repetition, a so-called haplography, resulting from the identical words at the beginning of the verse—thus I do not translate “not.”

David is identified elaborately as "the son of Jesse," a "strong man"—that is to say a warrior who is raised up from being merely the son of a farmer, even though a strong one. The term "anointed" points to his royal status, and the identification as the "darling of the songs of Israel" highlights the quality of David as well-spoken, a man of eloquence with a gifted tongue, as he is first introduced by Saul's servants and as he demonstrates in his long speech to Goliath and in the poetic utterance assigned to him after the death of Saul and Jonathan. Rather than the overpowering warrior, it is the talented speaker, the gifted musician, who comes to the fore. While the first lines speak of "an oracle of David," I understand this to refer to a prophetic utterance *about* David rather than *by* David. The oracle concerns David as the kind of king desired by God, and is uttered through the divine spirit. In verse 3, God speaks about a righteous ruler in God's estimation. Righteousness and awe of the Holy One of Israel are key qualities of this ideal leader, producing fruit through his rule as naturally as the sun rising and rain falling causing grass to sprout.[47]

In what follows, David points out that his house is not like the natural rising of the sun or the falling rain, productive just because it is there. His house is established because of God's lasting covenant, even if he is not a righteous ruler. The lasting nature of the Davidic house is here due to the beneficence of God, not to the inclinations or the orientation of the ruler toward God.[48] An altogether different point is made here than the one in the previous poem, where the speaker establishes his purity and righteousness (22:21–25) and God's treatment as a reward for a blameless life. To forestall the thought that the ruler of David's house is therefore free to act like worthless people, the last stanza pursues the consideration of hu-

47. Following Buber's translation, I do not understand these words to be from David about himself but as a divine utterance about the righteous king. Verse 5 is thus the response from David. The Hebrew word *ne'um* is not ordinarily used with a human subject (but there are exceptions: Num 24:3–4; 15–16; Prov 31:1).

48. Most translations understand v. 5 to be a rhetorical question: "Is not thus my house with God?" The Hebrew text, however, makes a statement rather than posing a rhetorical question: "It is not like that with my house!"

man behavior in pointing out that the worthless person is also a useless one, scattered on the ground, good only for burning.

In this arrangement, the first and the last stanza form a contrasting frame. David is the man who is raised by God from a low status to a high one, imbued by God's spirit as he was said to be in 1 Samuel 16:13, the one who gives voice to eloquent words in song. The worthless person in the final stanza is the lowest of the low of natural growth, good only to be burned, low on the ground and unable to be even picked up without a tool. The middle stanzas speak to the issue of the ruler and his house. A righteous ruler in awe of God will automatically produce good results as sun and rain cause the fields to produce. David's house, even if not righteous, is upheld by a divine covenant. Unlike the sun and the rain which come at set times, it is God who upholds it and makes it productive. Nothing is here in David's power, not his kingship, not the lasting nature of his house, not even the results of his rule, which are all due to God's arrangement and guardianship.

A Shaky Throne

The texts of Samuel are at an end, although the story of David will be continued in the opening chapters of 1 Kings. That material will focus on King David's last days and the issue of the succession to the throne that begins the narratives about King Solomon. So far, David has appeared before us multifaceted: the radiant youth facing the overwhelming gigantic opponent, outdoing Saul in all his military ventures, charming everyone around him with his charisma, becoming the friend and lover of Jonathan and Michal. At the same time, he becomes the usurper who threatens Saul and spends years on the run from his former employer until the erstwhile chosen of God dies on the battlefield. Even then, he holds his throne in a tenuous grasp as the land divides in its loyalties, and he may have done whatever it took to become Israel's ruler in fact. Once he is settled on his throne, the close view of this king and his court depicts a flawed human being, engaging in immoral activity toward both his subjects and his household. In the end, he has to ward off two rebellions, one instigated by his own son and another by a fellow clan member of Saul. The power of the king in David's day was still shaky, circumscribed by tribe and ancestral tradition as well as divine authority. We will see how closely the role of the monarch in the land will align with the negative picture provided by the prophet Samuel in 1 Samuel 8 and what will be the outcome of such a relationship of king, people, and land.

Appendix: Hebrew Words in This Volume

Throughout this book, Hebrew words are transliterated in italics. When reading these words, observe the following:

a is always as in father, not as in dad.

e generally as in met, sometimes a light sound as in about, rendered by ’.

i generally as in fleet, sometimes as i in kiss.

o is always as in bone, not as in got.

u is always as in ruler, not as in run.

ey as in pray.

g is always hard as in gold.

Hebrew has no syllables that contain two vowels. If an *a* word is spelled with two consecutive vowels, it is pronounced with two syllables: Baal = bah-al.

Each word below is followed by a phonetic pronunciation to provide further help articulating the Hebrew words. Stressed syllables are underlined. They occur generally at the end of the word, but not always. Pronunciation of /*ch*/ or /*kh*/ is always as in Bach; Hebrew has no /*ch*/ as in cheese.

Abbreviations

adj. = adjective

adv. = adverb

conj. = conjunction

n. = noun

pr. = pronoun

prep. = preposition

v. = verb

adam (ah-dahm) n.—human being, 191
ad olam (ad oh-lahm) prep + n.—for the ages, always, 258
Adonai (ah-doh-nai) n.—name of God, throughout
aharey (ah-cha-ray) prep.—after, behind, 114n32
ahoti (ah-choh-tee) n.—my sister, 292
al (ahl) prep.—on, upon, above, against, to, over, concerning, 26n19, 297, 346n9, 349n15
amah (ah-mah) n.—female servant, 252n56
ani (ah-nee) / or *anokhi* (ah-noh-chee) pr.—257, 282
appayim (ah-pah-yeem) n.—noses, face, 18n8
aron (ah-rohn) n.—chest, box, Ark, 58
avar (ah-var) v.—cross, 310
avon (ah-von) n.—sin, guilt, punishment, 202
avoni (ah-vo-nee) n.—my guilt, punishment, 314n97

Baal (bah-al) n.— Baal, master, 216n3, 237n40
baalat ov (bah-ah-lat ohv) n.—mistress of the pit, 201
baaley (bah-ah-lay) n.—masters of, 243n54
baaley Yehudah (bah-ah-lay Y'-hoo-dah) n.—the masters of Judah, 243n54
bahar (bah-char) v.—choose, 158
baharu (bah-chah-ru) v.—choose!, 131n60
bamah (bah-mah) n.—height, 78n105
basar (bah-sahr) v.—bring (good) news, 223n18
bat (baht) n.—daughter, 39, 288
bazah (bah-zah) v.—despise, 45n52, 252
ben (ben) n.—son, child, 173
ben beliya'al (ben b'-lee-yah-al) n.— scoundrel, worthless man, 188
beney (b'-nay) n.—sons, children, 39
beney beliya'al (b'-nay b'-lee-yah-al) n.—scoundrels, worthless men, 39, 71, 87
beney yemini (b'-nay y'-mee-nee) n.—Benjaminites, lit. children of the right hand
beneyhem (b'-nay-hem) n.—their sons/children, 63
beni (b'-nee) n.—my son, 173
ben yishai (ben yee-shai) n.—son of Jesse, 173
biqqesh (bik-kaysh) v.—seek, 346
bo (boh) v.—enter, come, 168n97, 192

daqar (dah-kahr) v.—run through, pierce, 210
derekh (deh-rech) n.—way, road, conduct, 77

ehyeh asher ehyeh (eh-yeh ah-sher eh-yeh) v.—I will be who I will be, 257
el (el) prep.—to(ward), 346n9, 344n15

elohim (eh-loh-heem) n.—gods, or God (i.e., the God of Israel); also used as adjective: mighty, 203n15, 255n74, 298n70
erets (eh-rets) n.— land, 223n16
eyn (ayn) n.—spring, well, eye, 201
eyn dor (ayn dohr) n.—well of generation, Endor, 201
eyn rogel (ayn ro-gel) n.—well of the scout/spy, 319

galah (gah-lah) v.—uncover, expose, take into exile, 248, 300n75
galut (gah-loot) n.—exile, 248
gam (gahm) adv.—also, even, 200
ger (gayr) n.—stranger, 310n94
goleh (goh-leh) n.—(person in) exile, 310n94

halakh (hah-lach) v.—walk, go, 256n79
hamal (chah-mal) v.—to spare, 287n49
hammelukhah (ham-m'-loo-chah) n.—the kingship, 87
hamon (hah-mohn) n.—tumult, 325
harah (cha-rah) adj.—pregnant, 282
hemdah (chem-dah) n.—desire, desired thing, 80n107
herem (cheh-rem) n.—consecration, total destruction, 100, 108, 112, 175
hesed (cheh-sed) n.—kindness, loyalty, devotion, 110, 228, 266–68, 270, 273, 277
higgalot niglot (hig-gah-loht nig-loht) n.—shameless exposure, 248
hil (cheel) v.—writhe, tremble, 210n163

ish (eesh) n.—man, 216n3, 255n74, 313
ish beliya'al (eesh b'-lee-yah-al) n.—scoundrel, worthless man, 313
ish elohim (eesh eh-loh-heem) n.—man of God, 255n75

ka'as (kah-as) v.—torment, 19
kallah (kal-lah) n.—bride, 292
kavad (kah-vahd) v.—be heavy, 63n86
kaved (kah-vayd) adj.—heavy, 55
kavod (kah-vohd) n.—honor, glory, 55
ketonet (k'-toh-net) n.—garment, tunic, 294
ketonet passim (k'-toh-net pas-seem) n.—colored/ornamented tunic, 294
ki (kee) conj.—because, for, 18n8

lakhad (lah-khad) v.—catch, take, 86n117, 97
levivot (l'-vee-voht) n.—cakes shaped like hearts, 292

ma'as (mah-as) v.—reject, 119n41
magen (mah-gayn) n.—shield, 224
maggefah (mah-gay-fah) n.—affliction, 354n29
malakh (mahl-ach) n.—messenger, 181

matsevah (mah-tsay-vah) n.—pillar, votive stone, 323n115
matsevet (mah-tseh-vet) n.—memorial stone, 323n115
me'aharey (may-ah-chah-ray) prep.— from after, from behind, 114n32
meh (meh) pr.—what?, 153
meh asiti (meh ah-see-tee) v.—what have I done?, 153
me'il (m'-eel) n.—garment, cloak, 41
melekh (meh-lech) n.—king, 85, 181
melukhah (m'-loo-chah) n.—kingship, 87
me'od (m'-ohd) adv.—very, 150
meshiakh (m'-shee-ach) v.—anointed, 38n40
meshuggah (m'-shoo-gah) adj.—insane, 168n97
mishpat (meesh-pat) n.—justice, 39, 72n98, 87, 262
mishpat hammelukhah (meesh-pat ham-m'-loo-chah) n.—the justice of kingship, 87
mot (moht) v.—die, 301n76
mot namut (moht nah-moot) v.—we will die, (yes) die; we will surely die, 301n76

na'ar (nah-ar) n.—young boy, lad, 32
nagid (nah-geed) n.—leader, 85, 190
nahalah (nah-chah-lah) n.—inheritance, 298n70
navi (nah-vee) v.—we bring, 77
navi (nah-vee) n.—prophet, 77
nazir (nah-zeer) n.—Nazir(ite), 27
nefesh (neh-fesh) n.—throat, soul, being, 356n34
negef (neh-gef) n.—affliction, 359n29
ne'um Adonai (n'-oom ah-doh-nai) n.—oracle of Adonai, 46
nevalah (n'-vah-lah) n.—outrage, disgrace, wanton folly, 293
nokhri (noch-ree) n.—foreigner, 310n94

ov (ohv) n.—groove, pit, 201, 202

pilegesh (pee-leh-gesh) n.—concubine, secondary wife, 350n16

qarni (kar-nee) n.—my horn, 36n34
qinah (kee-nah) n.—dirge, a type of poetic meter found in laments, 223
qum (koom) v.—stand up, arise, 111n25

ra'ah (rah-ah) n.—evil, 326
rahamim (rah-chah-meem) n.—compassion
rahum (rah-choom) adj.—compassionate
ramah qarni (rah-mah kar-nee) v. + n.—lifted (is) my horn, 30n34
rehem (reh-chem) n.—womb
req (rayk) adj.—empty, 248n61

rum (room) v.—lift up, raise, 36

sagar (sah-gahr) v.—close, shut, 180n119, 325
sahaq (sah-chak) v.—make music, 244nn55–56
samat (sah-mat) v.—to drop, 169
sar (sahr) n.—leader, officer, 169
sarey (sah-ray) n.—leaders, officers, 208n162
savav (sah-vahv) v.—encircle, turn, 170n108
sha'al (shah-ahl) v.—ask, 25, 29
sha'alti (shah-ahl-tee) v.—I asked, 29
shagah (shah-gah) v.—rave, 168n97
shakhal (shah-chal) v.—miscarry, be bereft of children, 114n33
shama (shah-mah) v.—listen, heed, 44n48, 113n29, 335n140
shamam (shah-mam) v.—be desolate, 340
sha'ul (shah-ool) v.—(the one) asked for, Saul, 25
shem (shaym) n.—name, 29
shemo (sh'-moh) n.—his name, 29
Shemu'el (sh'-moo-ayl) n.—Samuel, 29
sheol (sh'-ohl) n.—Sheol, 37
shivatayim (sheev-ah-tah-yeem) adv.—sevenfold, 353n24
shuv (shoov) v.—turn, return, 114n32
simlah (sim-lah) n.—cloak, 41n45

tardemah (tar-day-mah) n.—deep sleep, 195
terafim (t'-rah-feem) n.—Terafim, household gods, 151
tov (tohv) adj.—good, 276n28
tov mar'eh (tohv mar-eh) adj.—good-looking, 276n28
tsar (tsahr) n.—distress, 362
tsarar (tsah-rahr) v.—wrap/tie up, 333
tsava (tsah-vah) n.—service, 42n46
tse, tse (tseh tseh) v.—get out! get out!, 313
tseva'ot (ts'-vah-oht) n.—hosts, armies, 42n47
tsevi (ts'-vee) n.—ornament, gazelle, 223

va'ehyeh (vah-eh-yeh) v.—I was, 257
vattiqrah (vah-teek-rah) v.—she called, 29
vayyomer (vah-yoh-mer) v.—and he said, 346n9

yafah (yah-fah) adj.—beautiful, 276n28
yashav (yah-shahv) v.—sit, dwell, stay, 279n34
yefat mar'eh (y'-fat mar-eh) adj. + n.—of beautiful appearance, 276n28
yishay (yee-shai) n.—Jesse, 173

zavakh (zah-vach) v.—slaughter, 205

Bibliography

Books

Aharoni, Yohanan. *The Land of the Bible: A Historical Geography.* Translated by A. F. Rainey. Philadelphia: Westminster, 1979.

Ahn, John J., and Stephen L. Cook, eds. *Thus Says the Lord: Essays on the Former and Latter Prophets in Honor of Robert R. Wilson.* New York; London: T&T Clark, 2009.

Alter, Robert. *Ancient Israel: The Former Prophets: Joshua, Judges, Samuel and Kings.* New York: Norton, 2013.

____. *The Art of Biblical Narrative.* New York: Basic Books, 1981.

____. *The Art of Biblical Poetry.* New York: Basic Books, 1985.

____. *The David Story: A Translation with Commentary of 1 and 2 Samuel.* New York: Norton, 1999.

Amit, Yairah. *Hidden Polemics in Biblical Narrative.* BibInt 25. Leiden: Brill, 2000.

____. *History and Ideology: An Introduction to Historiography in the Hebrew Bible.* Sheffield: Sheffield Academic, 1999.

Auld, A. Graeme, and Erik Eynikel, eds. *For and Against David: Story and History in the Books of Samuel.* Leuven: Peters, 2010.

Bach, Alice, ed. *Women in the Hebrew Bible.* New York; London: Routledge, 1999.

Baden, Joel. *The Historical David: The Real Life of an Invented Hero.* New York: HarperCollins, 2013.

Bar-Efrat, Shimon. *Narrative Art in the Bible.* Sheffield: Almond, 1989.

Berquist, Jon, and Claudia V. Camp, eds. *Construction of Space II: The Biblical City and Other Imagined Spaces.* New York; London: T&T Clark, 2008.

Borowski, Obed. *Daily Life in Biblical Times.* Atlanta: Society of Biblical Literature, 2003.

Botterweck, G. Johannes, and Helmer Ringgren, eds. *Theological Dictionary of the Old Testament.* 16 vols. Grand Rapids: Eerdmans, 2001–2018.

Brenner, Athalya, ed. *A Feminist Companion to Samuel and Kings*. Sheffield: Sheffield Academic, 1994.

_____. *Samuel and Kings*. A Feminist Companion to the Bible, Second Series. Sheffield: Sheffield Academic, 2000.

Bronner, Leila Leah. *From Eve to Esther: Rabbinic Reconstructions of Biblical Women*. Louisville: Westminster John Knox, 1994.

Brueggemann, Walter. *First and Second Samuel*. IBC. Louisville: Westminster John Knox, 1990.

_____. *Ichabod Toward Home: The Journey of God's Glory*. Grand Rapids: Eerdmans, 2002.

Buber, Martin. *The Prophetic Faith*. New York: Harper Torch, 1960.

Buber, Martin, and Franz Rosenzweig. *Bücher der Geschichte: Verdeutscht von Martin Buber gemeinsam mit Franz Rosenzweig*. Cologne: Jakob Hegner, 1965.

Buck, Christopher. *God and Apple Pie: Religious Myths and Visions of America*. Kingston, NY: Educator's International, 2015.

Campbell, Antony F., S.J. *1 Samuel*. FOTL 7. Grand Rapids: Eerdmans, 2003.

_____. *2 Samuel*. FOTL 8. Grand Rapids: Eerdmans, 2005.

Caquot, André, and Philippe de Robert. *Les Livres de Samuel*. Geneva: Labor et Fides, 1994.

Carr, E. H. *What Is History?* 40th ann. ed. Basingstoke, UK: Palgrave, 2001.

Clines, David J. A. *Interested Parties: The Ideology of Writers and Readers of the Hebrew Bible*. Sheffield: Sheffield Phoenix, 2009.

Clines, David J. A., and Tamara C. Eshkenazi, eds. *Telling Queen Michal's Story: An Experiment in Comparative Interpretation*. Sheffield: Sheffield Academic, 1991.

Collins, John, ed. *Worship, Women and War: Essays in Honor of Susan Niditch*. Providence: Brown University Press, 2015.

Conroy, Charles Patrick, M.S.C. *Absalom, Absalom!: Narrative and Language in 2 Sam 13–20*. Rome: Biblical Institute Press, 1978.

Coogan, Michael, ed. *The Oxford History of the Biblical World*. New York: Oxford University Press, 1998.

Cook, Joan E. *Hannah's Desire, God's Design: Early Interpretations of the Story of Hannah*. JSOTSup 282. Sheffield: Sheffield Academic, 1999.

Exum, J. Cheryl. *Plotted, Shot, and Painted: Cultural Representations of Biblical Women*. Sheffield: Sheffield Academic, 1996.

_____. *Tragedy and Biblical Narrative: Arrows of the Almighty*. Cambridge: Cambridge University Press, 1992.

Fewell, Danna Nolan, ed. *Reading Between Texts: Intertextuality and the Hebrew Bible*. Louisville: Westminster John Knox, 1992.

Fewell, Danna Nolan, and David M. Gunn. *Gender, Power, and Promise: The Subject of the Bible's First Story.* Nashville: Abingdon, 1993.

Fishbane, Michael, Emanuel Tov, and Weston W. Fields, eds. *Sha'arei Talmon: Studies in the Bible, Qumran, and the Ancient Near East Presented to Shemaryahu Talmon.* Winona Lake, IN: Eisenbrauns, 1992.

Fokkelman, J. P. *King David.* Vol. 1 of *Narrative Art and Poetry in the Books of Samuel.* Assen: Van Gorcum, 1981.

____. *The Crossing Fates.* Vol. 2 of *Narrative Art and Poetry in the Books of Samuel.* Assen: Van Gorcum, 1986.

____. *Throne and City.* Vol. 3 of *Narrative Art and Poetry in the Books of Samuel.* Assen: Van Gorcum, 1990.

____. *Vow and Desire.* Vol. 4 of *Narrative Art and Poetry in the Books of Samuel.* Assen: Van Gorcum, 1993.

Fox, Everett. *The Early Prophets.* New York: Schocken, 2014.

____. *The Five Books of Moses: A New Translation with Introductions, Commentary, and Notes.* New York: Schocken, 1995.

____. *Give Us a King!* New York: Schocken, 1999.

Frymer-Kensky, Tikva. *In the Wake of the Goddesses: Women, Culture and the Biblical Transformation of Pagan Myth.* New York: Macmillan, 1992.

____. *Reading the Women of the Bible:* New York: Schocken, 2002.

Gafney, Wilda C. *Daughters of Miriam: Women Prophets in Ancient Israel.* Minneapolis: Fortress, 2008.

____. *Womanist Midrash: A Reintroduction to the Women of the Torah and the Throne.* Louisville: Westminster John Knox, 2017.

Garsiel, Moshe. *The First Book of Samuel: A Literary Study of Comparative Structures, Analogies and Parallels.* Ramat-Gan, Israel: Revivim Publishing, 1985.

Gilmour, Rachelle. *Representing the Past: A Literary Analysis of Narrative Historiography in the Book of Samuel.* VTSup 143. Leiden: Brill, 2011.

Goldingay, John. *1 and 2 Samuel for Everyone.* Louisville: Westminster John Knox, 2011.

____. *Men Behaving Badly.* Exeter, UK: Paternoster, 2000.

Good, Edwin M. *Irony in the Old Testament.* Philadelphia: Westminster, 1965. Repr., Sheffield: Almond, 1981.

Gordon, Robert P. *I & II Samuel: A Commentary.* Grand Rapids: Zondervan, 1986.

Gravett, Sandra L., Karla Bohmbach, F. V. Greifenhagen, and Donald C. Polaski, eds. *An Introduction to the Hebrew Bible: A Thematic Approach.* Louisville: Westminster John Knox, 2008.

Guest, Deryn. *When Deborah Met Jael: Lesbian Biblical Hermeneutics.* London: SCM Press, 2005.

Gunn, David M. *The Fate of King Saul: An Interpretation of a Biblical Story.* Sheffield: JSOT Press, 1980.

Gunn, David M., and Danna Nolan Fewell. *Narrative in the Hebrew Bible.* Oxford; New York: Oxford University Press, 1993.

Habel, Norman C. *The Land Is Mine: Six Biblical Land Ideologies.* Minneapolis: Augsburg, 1995.

Halpern, Baruch. *David's Secret Demons: Messiah, Murderer, Traitor, King.* Grand Rapids: Eerdmans, 2001.

Hertzberg, Hans Wilhelm. *I and II Samuel: A Commentary.* Translated by J. S. Bowden. Philadelphia: Westminster, 1964. Translation of *Die Samuelbücher.* ATD 10. Göttingen: Vandenhoeck & Ruprecht, 1960.

Hester, David C. *First and Second Samuel.* Louisville: Geneva Press, 2000.

Hornsby, Teresa J., and Ken Stone, eds. *Bible Trouble: Queer Reading at the Boundaries of Biblical Scholarship.* Atlanta: Society of Biblical Literature, 2011.

Isserlin, B. S. J. *The Israelites.* Minneapolis: Fortress, 2001.

Jobling, David. *1 Samuel.* Berit Olam. Collegeville, MN: Liturgical Press, 1998.

Klein, Lillian. *From Deborah to Esther: Sexual Politics in the Hebrew Bible.* Minneapolis: Fortress, 2003.

Knoppers, Gary N., and J. Gordon McConville, eds. *Reconsidering Israel and Judah: Recent Studies on the Deuteronomistic History.* Winona Lake, IN: Eisenbrauns, 2000.

Lapsley, Jacqueline E. *Whispering the Word: Hearing Women's Stories in the Old Testament.* Louisville: Westminster John Knox, 2005.

Leuchter, Mark. *Samuel and the Shaping of Tradition.* Oxford: Oxford University Press, 2013.

Linafelt, Tod, Claudia V. Camp, and Timothy Beal, eds. *The Fate of King David: The Past and Present of a Biblical Icon.* New York; London: T&T Clark, 2010.

Lozovyy, Joseph. *Saul, Doeg, Nabal and the "Son of Jesse": Readings in 1 Samuel 16–25.* New York; London: T&T Clark, 2009.

Mann, Steven T. *Run, David, Run! An Investigation of the Theological Speech Acts of David's Departure and Return (2 Samuel 14–20).* Winona Lake, IN: Eisenbrauns, 2013.

Mann, Thomas W. *The Book of the Former Prophets.* Eugene, OR: Wipf and Stock, 2011.

March, W. Eugene. *Israel and the Politics of Land.* Louisville: Westminster John Knox, 1994.

McCarter, Kyle, Jr. *1 Samuel: A New Translation with Introduction and Commentary.* AB 8. New York: Doubleday, 1980.

____. *2 Samuel: A New Translation with Introduction and Commentary*. AB 9. New York: Doubleday, 1984.

McKenzie, Stephen L., and Stephen R. Haynes, eds. *To Each Its Own Meaning*. Louisville: Westminster, 1999.

Meyers, Carol. *Discovering Eve: Ancient Israelite Women in Context*. Oxford: Oxford University Press, 1988.

____. *Rediscovering Eve: Ancient Israelite Women in Context*. Oxford: Oxford University Press, 2011.

Miller, J. Maxwell, and John H. Hayes. *A History of Israel and Judah*. 2nd ed. Louisville: Westminster John Knox, 2006.

Miscall, Peter D. *1 Samuel: A Literary Reading*. Bloomington, IN: Indiana University Press, 1986.

Moore, Megan Bishop, and Brad E. Kelle. *Biblical History and Israel's Past: The Changing Study of the Bible and History*. Grand Rapids: Eerdmans, 2011.

Nicholson, Sarah. *Three Faces of Saul: An Intertextual Approach to Biblical Tragedy*. Sheffield: Sheffield Academic, 2002.

Niditch, Susan. *War in the Hebrew Bible: A Study in the Ethics of Violence*. Oxford: Oxford University Press, 1993.

Polzin, Robert. *David and the Deuteronomist*. Vol. 3 of *A Literary Study of the Deuteronomic History*. Bloomington, IN: Indiana University Press, 1993.

____. *Samuel and the Deuteronomist*. Vol. 2 of *A Literary Study of the Deuteronomic History*. Bloomington, IN: Indiana University Press, 1989.

Rosenblatt, Jason P., and Joseph C. Sitterson Jr., eds. *"Not in Heaven": Coherence and Complexity in Biblical Narrative*. Bloomington and Indianapolis, IN: Indiana University Press, 1991.

Russell, Stephen. *The King and the Land: A Geography of Royal Power in the Biblical World*. Oxford: Oxford University Press, 2017.

Schipper, Jeremy. *Parables and Conflict in the Hebrew Bible*. Cambridge: Cambridge University Press, 2009.

Scholz, Susanne. *Sacred Witness: Rape in the Hebrew Bible*. Minneapolis: Fortress, 2010.

Schottroff, Luise, and Marie-Theres Wacher, eds. *Feminist Biblical Interpretation: A Compendium of Critical Commentary on the Books of the Bible and Related Literature*. Translated by Lisa E. Dahill. Grand Rapids: Eerdmans, 2012. Translation of *Kompendium Feministische Bibelauslegung*. Gütersloh: Gütersloher Verlagungshaus, 1999.

Schulz, Kathryn. *Being Wrong: Adventures in the Margin of Error*. New York: Harper Collins, 2010.

Schwartz, Regina M. *The Curse of Cain: The Violent Legacy of Monotheism*. Chicago: University of Chicago Press, 1997.

Smith, Henry Preserved. *A Critical and Exegetical Commentary on the Books of Samuel*. Edinburgh: T&T Clark, 1899.

Smith, Richard G. *The Fate of Justice and Righteousness During David's Reign: Narrative Ethics and Rereading the Court History According to 2 Samuel 8:15–20:26*. New York; London: T&T Clark, 2009.

Stone, Ken, ed. *Queer Commentary and the Hebrew Bible*. LHBOTS 334. Sheffield: Sheffield Academic, 2001.

Trible, Phyllis. *God and the Rhetoric of Sexuality*. Philadelphia: Fortress, 1978.

_____. *Texts of Terror: Literary-Feminist Readings of Biblical Narratives*. Philadelphia: Fortress, 1984.

Tsumura, David Toshio. *The First Book of Samuel*. NICOT. Grand Rapids: Eerdmans, 2007.

Vikander Edelman, Diana. *King Saul in the Historiography of Judah*. Sheffield: Sheffield Academic, 1991.

Wijk-Bos, Johanna W. H. van. *The End of the Beginning: Joshua and Judges*. A People and a Land 1. Grand Rapids: Eerdmans, 2019.

_____. *The Land and Its Kings: 1–2 Kings*. A People and a Land 3. Grand Rapids: Eerdmans, forthcoming 2020.

_____. *Making Wise the Simple: The Torah in Christian Faith and Practice*. Grand Rapids: Eerdmans, 2005.

_____. *Reading Samuel: A Literary and Theological Commentary*. Macon, GA: Smyth and Helwys, 2011.

Williams, Jenni. *God Remembered Rachel: Women's Stories in the Old Testament and Why They Matter*. London: SPCK, 2014.

Zenger, Erich. *A God of Vengeance? Understanding the Psalms of Divine Wrath*. Translated by Linda M. Maloney. Louisville: Westminster John Knox, 1996. Translation of *Ein Gott der Rache: Feindpsalmen Verstehen*. Freiburg im Breisgau: Herder, 1994.

Articles and Chapters

Abasili, Alexander Izuchukwu. "Was it Rape? The David and Bathsheba Pericope Re-examined." *VT* 61 (2011): 1–15.

Ackerman, James S. "Knowing Good and Evil: A Literary Analysis of the Court History in 2 Samuel 9–20 and 1 Kings 1–2." *JBL* 109 (1990): 41–64.

Amit, Yairah. "'Am I Not More Devoted to You than Ten Sons?' (1 Samuel 1:8): Male and Female Interpretations." Pages 68–76 in *A Feminist Companion to Samuel and Kings*. Edited by Athalya Brenner. Sheffield: Sheffield Academic, 1994.

Arabi, Ionel. "Quand les Intrigues S'Entrelacent: Une Etude de l'organisation de 2 S 11–12." *Ephemerides Theologicae Lovanienses* 87 (2011): 35–56.

Bailey, Randall C. "Reading Backwards: A Narrative Technique for the Queering of David, Saul, and Samuel." Pages 66–81 in *The Fate of King David: The Past and Present of a Biblical Icon*. Edited by Tod Linafelt, Claudia V. Camp, and Timothy Beal. New York; London: T&T Clark, 2010.

Batten, Loring W. "Helkath Hazzurim, 2 Samuel 2, 12–16." *ZAW* 26 (1906): 90–94.

Bellefontaine, Elizabeth. "Customary Law and Chieftainship: Judicial Aspects of 2 Samuel 14:4–21." *JSOT* 38 (1987): 47–72.

Brueggemann, Walter. "2 Samuel 21–24: An Appendix of Deconstruction." *CBQ* 50 (1988): 383–97.

Buber, Martin. "Die Erzählung von Sauls Königswahl." *VT* 6 (1956): 113–73.

Burnside, Jonathan. "Flight of the Fugitives: Rethinking the Relationship between Biblical Law (Exodus 21:12–14) and the Davidic Succession Narrative (1 Kings 1–2)." *JBL* 129 (2010): 418–31.

Camp, Claudia V. "The Wise Women of 2 Samuel: A Role Model for Women in Early Israel?" *CBQ* 43 (1981): 14–29.

Camp, Claudia V., and Carole F. Fontaine. "The Words of the Wise and Their Riddles." Pages 127–49 in *Text and Tradition: The Hebrew Bible and Folklore*. Edited by Susan Niditch. Atlanta: Scholars Press, 1990.

Chankin-Gould, J. D'Ror, Derek Hutchinson, David Hilton Jackson, Tyler D. Mayfield, Leah Rediger Schulte, Tammi J. Schneider, and E. Winkelman. "The Sanctified 'Adulteress' and Her Circumstantial Clause: Bathsheba and Self-Consecration." *JSOT* 32 (2008): 339–52.

Clines, David A. J. "Psalm 23 and Method: Reading a David Psalm." Pages 175–84 in *The Fate of King David: The Past and Present of a Biblical Icon*. Edited by Tod Linafelt, Claudia V. Camp, and Timothy Beal. New York; London: T&T Clark, 2010.

____. "The Story of Michal, Wife of David, in Its Sequential Unfolding." Pages 129–41 in *Telling Queen Michal's Story: An Experiment in Comparative Interpretation*. Edited by David J. A. Clines and Tamara C. Eskenazi. Sheffield: Sheffield Academic, 1991.

Craig, Kenneth M., Jr. "The Characterization of God in 2 Samuel 7:1–17." *Semeia* 63 (1993): 159–76.

____. "Rhetorical Aspects of Questions Answered with Silence in 1 Samuel 14:37 and 28:6." *CBQ* 56 (1994): 221–39.

Daube, David. "Absalom and the Ideal King." *VT* 48 (1998): 315–25.

Davis, Ellen F. "Losing a Friend: The Loss of the Old Testament to the Church." Pages 83–94 in *Jews, Christians and the Theology of the Hebrew Scrip-*

tures. Edited by Alice Ogden Bellis and Joel Kaminsky. Atlanta: Scholars Press, 2000.

Deem, Ariella. "And the Stone Sank into His Forehead: A Note on 1 Samuel XVII 49." *VT* 27 (1978): 349–51.

Eissfeldt, Otto. "Ein gescheiterter Versuch der Wiedervereinigung Israels." *La Nouvelle Clio* 3 (1951): 110–27; *La Nouvelle Clio* 4 (1952): 55–59.

Exum, J. Cheryl. "Rizpah." *WW* 17 (1997): 260–68.

Fewell, Danna Nolan. "A Broken Hallelujah." Pages 101–122 in *The Fate of King David: The Past and Present of a Biblical Icon*. Edited by Tod Linafelt, Claudia V. Camp, and Timothy Beal. New York; London: T&T Clark, 2010.

_____. "Feminist Criticism." Pages 268–82 in *To Each His Own Meaning*. Edited by Steven L. McKenzie and Stephen R. Haynes. Louisville: Westminster John Knox, 1999.

Flanagan, James W. "Court History or Succession Document: A Study of 2 Samuel 9–20 and 1 Kings 1–2." *JBL* 91 (1972): 172–81.

Fokkelman, J. P. "Algemene Inleiding: Oog in Oog Met De Tekst Zelf." Pages 7–32 in *De Bijbel Literair: Opbouw en Gedachtegang van de Bijbelse Geschriften en hun Onderlinge Relaties*. Edited by J. Fokkelman and W. Weren. Zoetermeer: Meinema, 2003.

Fontaine, Carol R. "The Sharper Harper (1 Samuel 16:14–23): Iconographic Reflections on David's Rise to Power." Pages 135–52 in *The Fate of King David: The Past and Present of a Biblical Icon*. Edited by Tod Linafelt, Claudia V. Camp, and Timothy Beal. New York; London: T&T Clark, 2010.

Galpaz-Feller, Pnina. "David and the Messenger: Different Ends, Similar Means in 2 Samuel 1." *VT* 59 (2009): 199–210.

Green, Barbara. "Enacting Imaginatively the Unthinkable: 1 Sam. 25 and the Story of Saul." *BibInt* 11 (2003): 1–23.

Grossman, Yonatan. "The Design of the 'Dual Causality' Principle in the Narrative of Absalom's Rebellion." *Bib* 88 (2007): 558–66.

Guest, Deryn. "Looking Lesbian at the Bathing Bathsheba." *BibInt* 16 (2008): 227–62.

Gunn, David M. "From Jerusalem to the Jordan and Back: Symmetry in 2 Samuel XV–XX." *VT* 30 (1980): 109–113.

Hentrich, Thomas. "Being Disabled in the Ancient Near East: A Brief Compilation from Mesopotamia to Qumran." Self-published.

_____. "Disability in Ancient Israel: The 'Lame' (נכה/פסח *nkh/psḥ* in 2 Samuel." Self-published.

Hill, Andrew E. "On David's 'Taking' and 'Leaving' Concubines (2 Samuel 5:13; 15:16)." *JBL* 125 (2006): 129–39.

Hoftijzer, Jacob. "David and the Tekoite Woman." *VT* 20 (1970): 419–44.

Jacobs, Jonathan. "The Role of the Secondary Characters in the Story of the Anointing of Saul." *VT* 58 (2008): 495–509.

Jobling, David, and Catherine Rose. "Reading as a Philistine: The Ancient and Modern History of a Cultural Slur." Pages 381–417 in *Ethnicity and the Bible*. Edited by Mark Brett. Leiden: Brill, 1996.

Klein, Lillian R. "Bathsheba Revealed." Pages 47–64 in *Samuel and Kings*. Edited by Athalya Brenner. A Feminist Companion to the Bible, Second Series. Sheffield: Sheffield Academic, 2000.

____. "Hannah: Marginalized Victim and Social Redeemer." Pages 77–92 in *A Feminist Companion to Samuel and Kings*. Edited by Athalya Brenner. Sheffield: Sheffield Academic, 1994.

Kleven, Terence. "Rhetoric and Narrative Depiction in 2 Sam. 1:1–16." *Proceedings of Eastern Great Lakes and Midwest Biblical Studies* 9 (1989): 59–93.

Kruschwitz, Jonathan. "2 Samuel 12:1–15: How (Not) to Read a Parable." *RevExp* 109 (2012): 253–59.

Lemos, Tracy M. "Were Israelite Women Chattel? Shedding Light on an Old Question." Pages 227–43 in *Worship, Women and War: Essays in Honor of Susan Niditch*. Edited by John J. Collins, T. M. Lemos, and Saul M. Olyan. Providence, RI: Brown University Press, 2015.

Levenson, Jon. "1 Samuel 25 as Literature and as History." *CBQ* 40 (1978): 11–28.

Levenson, Jon, and Baruch Halpern. "The Political Import of David's Marriages." *JBL* 99 (1980): 507–18.

Lewis, Theodore J. "The Ancestral Estate (נחלת אלהים) in 2 Samuel 14:16." *JBL* 11 (1991): 597–612.

Linafelt, Tod. "Private Poetry and Public Eloquence in 2 Samuel 1:17–27: Hearing and Overhearing David's Lament for Jonathan and Saul." *JR* 88 (2008): 497–526.

____. "Taking Women in Samuel: Readers/Responses/Responsibility." Pages 99–113 in *Reading Between Texts: Intertextuality and the Hebrew Bible*. Edited by Danna Nolan Fewell. Louisville: Westminster John Knox, 1992.

Malul, Meir. "Absalom's Chariot and Fifty Runners (II Sam 15:1) and Hittite Laws (par. 198): Legal Proceedings in the Ancient Near East." *ZAW* 122 (2010): 44–52.

Marx, Dalia. "Women and Priests: Encounters and Dangers as Reflected in 1 Sam. 2:22." *Lectio Difficilior* 1 (2011): http://lectio.unibe.ch/11_1/marx_dalia_2011.1.html.

McCracken, Randy. "How Many Sons Did Absalom Have? Intentional Ambiguity as Literary Art." *BSac* 172 (2015): 286–98.

Mettinger, Tryggve N. D. "Cui Bono? The Prophecy of Nathan (2 Sam 7) as a Piece of Political Rhetoric." *SEÅ* 70 (2005): 193–214.

Meyers, Carol. "Hannah and Her Sacrifice: Reclaiming Female Agency." Pages 93–104 in *A Feminist Companion to Samuel and Kings*. Edited by Athalya Brenner. Sheffield: Sheffield Academic, 1994.

Michael, Matthew. "The Prophet, the Witch and the Ghost: Understanding the Parody of Saul as a 'Prophet' and the Purpose of Endor in the Deuteronomistic History." *JSOT* 58 (2014): 315–46.

Morse, Benjamin. "The Defence of Michal: Pre-Raphaelitie Persuasion in 2 Samuel 6." *BibInt* 21 (2013): 19–32.

Müllner, Isle. "Books of Samuel: Women at the Center of Israel's History." Pages 140–58 in *Feminist Biblical Interpretation: A Compendium of Critical Commentary on the Books of the Bible and Related Literature*. Edited by Luise Schottroff and Marie-Theres Wacher. Translated by Lisa E. Dahill. Grand Rapids: Eerdmans, 2012. Translation of *Kompendium Feministische Bibelauslegung*. Gütersloh: Gütersloher Verlagungshaus, 1999.

Na'aman, Nadav. "David's Sojourn in Keilah in Light of the Amarna Letters." *VT* 60 (2010): 87–97.

Nihan, Christophe, and Dany Noquet. "1–2 Samuel." Pages 358–83 in *Introduction à l'Ancien Testament*. Edited by Thomas Römer, Jean-Daniel Macchi, and Christophe Nihan. Geneva: Labor et Fides, 2009.

O'Connor, Michael Patrick. "The Biblical Notion of the City." Pages 18–39 in *Construction of Space II: The Biblical City and Other Imagined Spaces*. Edited by Jon Berquist and Claudia V. Camp. New York; London: T&T Clark, 2008.

Park, Song-Mi Suzie. "The Frustration of Wisdom: Wisdom, Counsel, and Divine Will in 2 Samuel 17:1–23." *JBL* 128 (2009): 453–67.

Perdue, Leo G. "'Is There Anyone Left of the House of Saul. . . ?' Ambiguity and the Characterization of David in the Succession Narrative." *JSOT* 30 (1984): 67–84.

Pigott, Susan M. "1 Samuel 28: Saul and the *Not* so Wicked Witch of Endor." *RevExp* 95 (1998): 435–44.

Rakeffet-Rothkoff, Aaron. "Surrendering Jews to the Nazis in the Light of the Halakhah." *Tradition: A Journal of Orthodox Thought* 25 (1991): 35–45.

Reinhartz, Adele. "Anonymity and Character in the Books of Samuel." *Semeia* 53 (1993): 117–41.

Reis, Pamela Tamarkin. "Eating the Blood: Saul and the Witch of Endor." *JSOT* 72 (1997): 3–23.

_____. "Killing the Messenger: David's Policy or Politics?" *JSOT* 31 (2006): 167–91.

Rezetko, Robert. "David over Saul in MT 2 Samuel 6:1-5: An Exercise in Textual and Literary Criticism." Pages 255–73 in *For and Against David: Story and History in the Books of Samuel*. Edited by A. Graeme Auld and Erik Eynikel. Leuven: Peeters, 2010.

Rudman, D. "The Commissioning Stories of Saul and David as Theological Allegory." *VT* 50 (2000): 519–30.

Rudnig, Thilo Alexander. "König ohne Tempel: 2 Samuel 7 in Tradition und Redaktion." *VT* 61 (2011): 426–46.

Schipper, Jeremy. "Did David Overinterpret Nathan's Parable in 2 Samuel 12:1–6?" *JSOT* 126 (2007): 383–407.

Schneider, Laurel C. "Yahwist Desires: Imagining Divinity Queerly." Pages 210–27 in *Queer Commentary and the Hebrew Bible*. Edited by Ken Stone. JSOTSup 334. Sheffield: Sheffield Academic, 2001.

Schroer, Sylvia, and Thomas Staubli. "Saul, David, and Jonathan: The Story of a Triangle? A Contribution to the Issue of Homosexuality in the First Testament." Pages 22–36 in *Samuel and Kings*. Edited by Athalya Brenner. A Feminist Companion to the Bible, Second Series. Sheffield: Sheffield Academic, 2000.

Schwartz, Regina M. "The Histories of David: Biblical Scholarship and Biblical Stories." Pages 192–210 in *"Not in Heaven": Coherence and Complexity in Biblical Narrative*. Edited by Jason P. Rosenblatt and Joseph C. Sitterson Jr. Bloomington and Indianapolis, IN: Indiana University Press, 1991.

Sergi, Omer. "The Composition of Nathan's Oracle to David (2 Samuel 7:1–17) as a Reflection of Royal Judahite Ideology." *JBL* 129 (2010): 261–79.

Shalom-Guy, Hava. "Three-Way Intertextuality: Some Reflections of Abimelech's Death at Thebez in Biblical Narrative." *JSOT* 34 (2010): 419–32.

Spijkerboer, Anne Marijke. "Geheimzinnigheid en Geheimenis in 1 Samuel 9–10." Pages 35–41 in *Amsterdamse Cahiers voor Exegese en Bijbelse Theologie*. Edited by K. A. Deurloo, B. P. M. Hemelsoet, F. J. Hoogewoud, K. A. D. Smelik, and R. Zuurmond. Vol. 11. Kampen: H. J. Kok, 1992.

Spina, Frank Anthony. "A Prophet's 'Pregnant Pause': Samuel's Silence in the Ark Narrative (1 Sam. 4:1–7:2)." *HBT* 13 (1991): 55–73.

Toorn, Karel van der. "David and the Ark." *JBL* (1994): 209–31.

Tsevat, Matitiahu. "Was Samuel a Nazirite?" Pages 199–204 in *Sha'arei Talmon: Studies in the Bible, Qumran, and the Ancient Near East Presented to Shemaryahu Talmon*. Edited by Michael Fishbane, Emmanuel Tov, and Weston W. Fields. Winona Lake, IN: Eisenbrauns, 1992.

Vanderhooft, David. "Dwelling Beneath the Sacred Place: A Proposal for Reading 2 Samuel 7:10." *JBL* 118 (1999): 625–33.

VanderKam, James C. "Davidic Complicity in the Deaths of Abner and Eshbaal: A Historical and Redactional Study." *JBL* 99 (1980): 521–39.

Vargon, Schmuel. "The Blind and the Lame." *VT* 46 (1996): 498–514.

Walters, Stanley. "'To the Rock' (2 Samuel 21:10)." *CBQ* 70 (2008): 453–64.

Wijk-Bos, Johanna W. H. van. "Writing on the Water: The Ineffable Name of God." Pages 45–59 in *Jews, Christians, and the Theology of the Hebrew Scriptures*. Edited by Alice Ogden Bellis and Joel Kaminsky. Atlanta: Society of Biblical Literature, 2000.

Willey, Patricia K. "The Importunate Woman of Tekoa and How She Got Her Way." Pages 115–31 in *Reading Between Texts: Intertextuality and the Hebrew Bible*. Edited by Danna Nolan Fewell. Louisville: Westminster John Knox, 1992.

Wolde, Ellen van. "A Leader Led by a Lady: David and Abigail in 1 Samuel 25." *ZAW* 114 (2002): 355–75.

Wright, David F. "Music and Dance in 2 Samuel 6." *JBL* 121 (2002): 201–225.

Yee, Gale A. "Fraught with Background: Ambiguity in II Samuel 11." *Int* 42 (1988): 240–53.

Author Index

Subject Index

Scripture Index